Exposing U.S. Government Policies on Extraterrestrial Life:

The Challenge of Exopolitics

Exposing U.S. Government Policies on Extraterrestrial Life:

The Challenge of Exopolitics

Michael E. Salla, M.A., Ph.D.

www.ExopoliticsInstitute.org
Kealakekua, Hawaii, USA

Exposing U.S. Government Policies on Extraterrestrial Life: The Challenge of Exopolitics

Published by the Exopolitics Institute
PO Box 2199
Kealakekua, HI 96750
USA

ISBN-13: 978-0-9822902-0-0
ISBN-10: 0-9822902-0-9

Library of Congress Control Number: 2008943848

Printed in the USA

Cover Design, Angelika S. Whitecliff

Author's Website: www.Exopolitics.Org

Publisher's Website: www.ExopoliticsInstitute.Org

Contents

Tables & Illustrations

Endorsements

"In this book, Dr. Michael Salla addresses the core challenge of exopolitics - preparing the general public for the exposure of secret governmental policy on extraterrestrials. We the public are fortunate, for Dr. Salla has written a monumental, evidence-based work, firmly establishing exopolitics as the new political science of outer space, mapping relations between our human civilization and other intelligent civilizations in the Universe. His documentation of U.S. Government secret human-ET liaison programs and of Manhattan Project II - a CIA black budget funding of a advanced ET-based New Energy technology and genetic farming programs – is a profound public service. Dr. Salla's analysis of the flaws inherent in the Rockefeller-Kissinger power politics approach to extraterrestrial society makes the military-industrial complex transparent. Dr. Salla rightfully distinguishes between ethical and unethical extraterrestrials and concludes it is the very secrecy of Treaty agreements with unethical Extraterrestrials that threatens our constitutional order and human sovereignty. Dr. Salla supports a ban on the weaponization of space, and concludes that disclosure and not space weapons are the exopolitical solution to a future healthy relationship with extraterrestrial civilizations. This comprehensive book provides a first history of the development of exopolitics, and of its significant contributors. Dr. Salla sets out the possible paths of First Contact – from the "Evil ET" False Flag operation, to a genuine upper-dimensional federated galactic intervention on Earth. This book will be a standard reference in exopolitics for many decades to come."

Alfred Lambremont Webre, J.D., M.Ed., author of *Exopolitics: Politics, Government and Law in the Universe*.

"Any public official or private citizen who wants to 'open the books' on UFO/Extraterrestrial evidence should open Dr. Salla's book first. He creates an essential historical perspective on both the challenges and need for disclosure. Most important, he highlights the basic requirement of engaging, and not ignoring, the public in this paradigm-shifting process."

Jeff Peckman, Director, Extraterrestrial Affairs Commission Campaign, www.extracampaign.org

"Dr. Michael Salla has written a definitive and groundbreaking expose on the historical reality of extraterrestrial diplomacy. He traces the deep penetration of extraterrestrials into government, military, corporations, and society.The reader discovers that initial core questions of diplomacy—who are our neighbors and how do we live together—have been answered. According to Salla, protocols were developed, professionals trained, budgets approved and national security breached through hidden channels. This book is a clarion call for the electorate to acknowledge this history in order to exercise their constitutional, inalienable human rights."

Rebecca Hardcastle, Ph.D., author of *Exoconsciousness: Your 21st Century Mind*

There are two places one can learn about the Truth Embargo with regard to extra terrestrials and their interaction with this planet; the first being the Military Industrial Complex; (if one can get in) the second is by reading "Challenge of Exopolitics" by Dr Michael Salla. This book is a revelation of cosmic proportion illustrating 60 years of secrecy by the Military Intelligence Services. These include agreements with ETs without congressional oversight, the squandering of Tax revenues on Black operations and a truth embargo which prevents the media reporting high profile cases of UFO sightings or ET human contact. Consequently planet Earth has been deprived of a planetary voice; divided and ruled over by the Elites. Dr Salla's book contains testimonies by whistleblowers, all with first hand knowledge of the shocking truth. This book is powerful, a superb achievement –and finally, the truth is out."

Neil Gould – Founder of Exopolitics Hong Kong

"Michael Salla continues to expand the political and social consciousness of a planet of beings in desperate need of a vision. His portrayal of our current reality and his vision of the future will become an historical masterpiece and an awakening for our species. Michael tells a profound story about us and weaves a tapestry of things to come with those who live beyond the stars. Dare to read it and ponder."

Victor Viggiani, M.Ed., Director of Exopolitics Toronto

"Dr. Michael Salla says in this new book that the main challenge for exopolitics practitioners is to expose the truth of extraterrestrial life and associated secret public policies to a largely unprepared general public. With his detailed analysis of evidence of secret treaties that were signed with certain ETs, it becomes clear that legitimate constitutional government has been subverted in America, and that this culture of secret governance is continuing to damage our fundamental rights and spread like a cancer. Dr. Salla also offers us solutions to this problem through education and a proposed "truth and reconciliation" process. This new book is another step forward for exopolitics research and practical application."

Thomas Hansen, Ph.D., Founder and former President of the Peace Exchange Foundation

Meticulously documented, profoundly researched and intensely interesting, *Exposing U.S. Government Policies on Extraterrestrial Life* written by Dr. Michael Salla reveals a historical piece of evidence outlining how the U.S. has been secretly implementing and creating policy concerning the Extraterrestrial presence without the awareness of Congress, the general public and the National Security System. It goes beyond the study of UFOS to credibly demonstrate that someone is preparing or has prepared for Contact. This book becomes the ultimate support for the discipline of Exopolitics and a major contribution to the field.

Paola Harris, M.Ed., Photojournalist/Reseacher.
Author Exopolitics: How does one speak to a ball of light?

"Michael Salla's new book raises probably the most important issue and yet also the most ignored and misunderstood one among those confronting mankind today. He analyzes systematically, on the basis of a number of official documents and personal testimonies from witnesses, the systems and methods devised by some major powers under the leadership of the United States, to deal with and respond to the revelation of a massive, technologically advanced Extraterrestrial presence since the Second World War.

In doing so, the author incidentally exposes some of the major but hidden factors for the Cold War, the seemingly unjustifiable growth of the military-industrial complex in the US and lately the major economic crisis now befalling America and the world. It appears, in the light of Salla's research, that more than one trillion Dollars a year has been covertly diverted from the US economy by the CIA and the Pentagon, over and above the official defense budgets, partly in order to finance an extremely complex and ambitious program, in the likeness of the Manhattan project, for reverse engineering of ET technology and for building a planetary defense system. This has been done by an unacknowledged, unelected, unsurpervised secret or "deep" government which has mostly operated outside the law and the framework of the Constitution on an international level,sponsoring a very large number of "black" projects, otherwise known as Special Access or Controlled Access Programs, without any regard for budgetary stability or the welfare of the civilian economy which seems to have thereby been hallowed out over the years.

The thesis laid out by Salla provides convincing reasons to believe in the existence of this long-suspected secret government, which has been accused of carrying out a number of far-reaching actions abroad and on the home soil, such as the JFK and RFK assassinations and the 911 "false flag" attacks in New York and Washington. The author cites and discusses a number of testimonies alleging that the US secret government has made agreements with certain Extraterrestrial visitors who have gained pervasive and probably undue influence over it. He proposes an alternative policy of disclosure, openness, public debate and scrutiny to deal with the Extraterrestrial challenge in a global cooperative manner, as opposed to the secretive, arbitrary and illegal methods used so far. This book does not just show us a time bomb ticking away under our current civilization. It also gives us a sensible method to disarm that bomb."

Come Carpentier de Gourdon, Convener of the Editorial Board, *World Affairs Journal*.

Dr. Michael Salla's latest book *Exposing U.S. Government Policies on Extraterrestrial Life* is a powerful revelation about America's darkest secrets interlocked with identifiable extraterrestrial civilizations and their impact on our culture and our freedom. Americans have been technologically assisted; while spiritually and intellectually deterred by the unconstitutional compromises negotiated between our government and the aliens.

A courageous pioneer, Dr. Salla is a learned scholar who is dedicated to uncovering the truth in his quest to uphold the Constitution of the United States and its spirit of freedom and equality.

Dr. Salla identifies some of the nation's foremost agencies, including the CIA, DoD, NSA, Presidential Administrations, the military services, private corporations and Special Access Programs as complicit in this well-funded, unlawful cover-up. The governmental, corporate and military leaders, who are aware of these programs, maintain a level of secrecy, coercion and compartmentalization that defies detection.

With a well formulated, clearly presented analysis and his educated commentaries, Dr. Salla provides reliable, factual data proving that billions of dollars in tax-payers' money and resources, have been funneled into these secret projects for more than 60 years. There is the strong possibility that indefensible human abuses have occurred and been condoned in military-E.T. laboratory facilities underground in America and elsewhere. Dr. Salla brings us the truth of these inhuman practices with well-documented and historical references.

Giving hope and understanding to his readers, he explores positive conclusions regarding our responsibility as Earth's citizens to educate ourselves in preparation for First Contact with humanitarian extraterrestrial civilizations who genuinely wish to assist the people of Earth. These extraterrestrials who have not participated in secret treaties with the governments of the world are the galactic civilizations who are devoted to upholding the welfare of humanity. These are the ones we welcome as we begin a new accountable era of honest communications with integrity on Earth.

This is a magnificently documented and meticulously indexed book. A reference book for many of the strange and secretive cases we have studied and sought to comprehend. Dr. Salla wisely and fascinatingly takes us through the eventual visitations with humanitarian extraterrestrials and the subsequent world implications of our mutual friendship.

Joan Ocean, MS, Executive Director,
Dolphin Connection International, USA

Dedication

For Angelika,
I live each day in gratitude for the friendship, love, wisdom, and wonderful spirit of adventure you bring to my life.

Other Books by Michael E. Salla, Ph.D

Exopolitics: Political Implications of the Extraterrestrial Presence (Dandelion Books, 2004)

The Hero's Journey Toward a Second American Century (Greenwood Press, 2002)

Co-Editor, *Essays on Peace* (Central Queensland University Press, 1995)

Co-Editor, *Why the Cold War Ended* (Greenwood Press, 1995)

Islamic Radicalism, Muslim Nations and the West (Indian Ocean Center for Peace Studies, 1993)

Acknowledgements

It has been five years since the publication of my last book, *Exopolitics: Political Implications of the Extraterrestrial Presence* (2004), which presented my initial research on evidence of extraterrestrial life, and helped introduce the new field of exopolitics. For those familiar with my exopolitics website and articles, they will recognize that this book offers a more nuanced set of analyses than offered in the earlier book. This has been made possible by the many courageous whistleblowers that have come forward to give their testimonies and/or provide evidence of U.S. government policies on extraterrestrial life. To all, I and the world owe a profound debt of gratitude.

In some cases, I have been fortunate to be able to directly interview these individuals. This helped me more accurately evaluate the importance of their testimonies. I am especially grateful to Paola Harris, M.Ed., who maintains one of the world's most extensive personal networks of whistleblowers and witnesses of the extraterrestrial phenomenon, for introducing me to many of these courageous individuals, and/or sharing their insights. I am also very thankful to Dr Steven Greer, Bill Ryan and Kerry Cassidy for their pioneering work in bringing many whistleblower testimonies to the general public. Collectively these testimonies from an invaluable research tool for all interested in probing the depths of U.S. government policies concerning extraterrestrial life.

I am very grateful to the many whistleblowers, researchers, 'experiencers' and colleagues from around the world that have shared with me their own testimonies, insights and/or the fruits of their own research. In particular, I wish to thank (all U.S. based unless otherwise indicated): Haktan Akdogan (Turkey); Maurizio Baiata (Italy): Stephen Bassett; Wesley Bateman; Al Bielek; Mike Bird (Canada); Dan Burisch; Art Campbell; Grant Cameron (Canada); James Courant; Alex Collier; David Coote; Philip Corso (Jr.); Paul Davids; Robert Dean (C.S.M. U.S. Army, ret.); Richard Dolan, M.A.; Robert Fleischer (Germany); Neil Freer, Neil Gould (Hong Kong); James Gilliland; Come Carpentier de Gourdon (India); Charles Hall, William Hamilton, III; Dr Thomas Hansen; Dr Rebecca Hardcastle; Paul Hellyer; Richard C. Hoagland; J. Antonio

Huneeus (Chile); Dr Lynne D. Kitei; Ed Komarek; Dr Scott Jones (Commander, USN ret.); Eric Julien; John Kuhles (Netherlands); Manuel Lamiroy, Lic. Juris. (South Africa); John Lear; Melinda Leslie; Dr Joe Lewels; Antonello Lupino, Laurea (Italy); Jim Marrs; Joan Ocean, M.Sc.; Luis Fernando Mostajo Maertens (Bolivia); Jaime Maussan (Mexico); Shirley MacLaine; Steve Moreno; Steve Natale; Jeff Peckman; Hector Palacios (Mexico); Clay and Shawn Pickering, Mary Rodwell (Australia); Robert Salas (Capt., USAF, ret.); Dr Richard Sauder; Luca Scantamburlo (Italy); Clifford Stone (ret. U.S. Army), Wendelle Stevens (Lt. Col., USAF ret.), Victor Viggiani, M.Ed.; Dr Thomas Valone; Donald Ware (Lt. Col., USAF, ret.); Alfred Webre, J.D.; Dr Robert Wood (McDonnell Douglas); Ryan Wood; and also those who have chosen to remain anonymous.

As far as the production of this book is concerned, I am grateful to Jack Davis (dec.), Mike Schaefer and Dana Tomasina for identifying errors and/or proof reading earlier versions of individual chapters of this book. I am also grateful for Joan Ocean's help in removing a number of errors in the final version. Special thanks to Jeff Peckman who laboriously went through the entire manuscript and weeded out many errors, and made many helpful substantive suggestions for improvement. My heartfelt thanks go to Hugh Matlock who in addition to helping proof read, generously provided the hospitality, intellectual stimulation, editorial suggestions and research environment for completing several chapters of this book.

My most heartfelt thanks go to Angelika S. Whitecliff without whom this book would not have been possible. She assisted with the editing of several chapters, created the cover design, and assisted at critical times in the production process. Much more importantly, over the five year period that this book has been in the making, she tirelessly supported my research with great intelligence, love and inspired advice.

Introduction

On July 8, 1947, the Roswell Army Air Field (AAF) issued a Press Release that a flying saucer had crashed near the town of Roswell, New Mexico. This generated instant media interest around the world. As the media interest began to build, another press release was quickly issued, this time by more senior U.S. military authorities, claiming the initial release was mistaken. It was only a weather balloon and not a flying saucer. Sixty years later, a posthumous affidavit by Walter Haut, the Public Information Officer responsible for the initial Press Release, disclosed the truth about the alleged crash of an extraterrestrial vehicle at Roswell.[1] Haut says that he was personally taken to one of the Roswell hangars by the base commander, Colonel William Blanchard, where he saw part of the wreckage of an extraterrestrial vehicle and the bodies of two extraterrestrial entities.

Concerning the conflicting press releases, Haut revealed that a staff meeting occurred on the morning of July 8 where senior military commanders from both Roswell AAF and nearby Carswell AAF, Fort Worth, Texas, discussed how to deal with growing public and press interest in the wreckage found at TWO crash sites. Haut reveals that General Roger Ramey devised a strategy for throwing the public and press off track about the two crash sites. Ramey approved a press release pointing to the more remote and less important site, and later retracting this announcement with the weather balloon story that appeared in the news later on July 8 and the morning of July 9. This strategy succeeded in taking the flying saucer story off the news headlines, and confusing members of the public and press that had witnessed or were investigating events.

Haut's affidavit is startling evidence that senior U.S. military officials had in their possession physical evidence of extraterrestrial life and technology, and had approved a policy of keeping this secret from the public. His testimony of events at Roswell reveals that U.S. national security officials had secretly approved a range of government policies on extraterrestrial life that would have the highest security classification. More than sixty years after the initial press release disclosing the truth about a flying saucer crash at Roswell, U.S. government policies concerning extraterrestrial life continue to remain highly classified, and veiled by a contrived cloud of controversy and disinformation.

Haut's testimony is an eyewitness account of events that occurred at Roswell. Most significant is his revelation that physical evidence of extraterrestrial life is hidden from the public on national security grounds. In considering Haut's and other eyewitness accounts of similar events concerning extraterrestrial life, I therefore ask the reader to pause and consider the following question. Would you accept the eyewitness accounts of credible individuals if there was no conclusive physical evidence or documentation to support their claims? The answer to this question often determines the jury verdict in courts of law. It will also determine this book's usefulness to you. Much of the evidence I present comprises eyewitness testimonies by individuals I believe to be very credible. Eyewitness testimony is the most persuasive category of evidence available to a sub-field of political science I helped create called exopolitics.[2]

Exopolitics is the study of the political actors, institutions and processes associated with extraterrestrial life. While exobiology studies the biology of extraterrestrial life found on Earth or elsewhere in the universe, exopolitics studies the politics concerning extraterrestrial life either found on or visiting Earth, or existing elsewhere in the universe. The institutional processes, policies and decisions taken to deal with extraterrestrial life have occurred mostly in secretly appointed committees and governmental agencies. Allegedly 'the best minds' have discussed problems supposedly too complex and disturbing for the general public.

The main justification for non-disclosure of evidence confirming the existence of extraterrestrial life is that U.S. policy makers believe that the general public is simply not ready. The first officer in charge of Project Blue Book, a US Air Force Investigation into UFOs, Captain Edward Ruppelt, explained why the USAF decided not to release the conclusion of a 1948 official report that UFOs were likely extraterrestrial in origin.[3] According to General Hoyt Vandenberg, former Chief of Staff of the USAF, disclosing the truth about extraterrestrial life "would cause a stampede."[4] This view was echoed in a 1961 Brookings Institute study commissioned by NASA on behalf of the U.S. Congress. The "Brookings Report" described the devastating societal impact of any announcement confirming the existence of extraterrestrial life: "of all groups, scientists and engineers might be the most devastated by the discovery of relatively superior creatures."[5] This view is also shared by policy makers from other nations as illustrated in comments by Margaret Thatcher, former Prime Minister of Britain, in 1997. In response to a question about UFOs and extraterrestrial technology Thatcher privately told a respected British researcher: "You must have the facts and you can't tell the people."[6]

The primary challenge confronting exopolitics is to prepare the general public for the exposure of secret U.S. government policies concerning extraterrestrial life. This requires disclosure of evidence confirming the reality of extraterrestrial life so the public can participate in an informed way in future debates over appropriate government policy. Another aspect of this challenge is to persuade policy makers that extraterrestrial disclosure is the most sensible policy to take despite the risks it poses in terms of a loss in public trust and confidence in government institutions.

Disclosing the truth about extraterrestrial life must deal with the public's capacity to integrate the more disturbing aspects of evidence concerning an extraterrestrial presence and associated governmental policy. This requires exposing the actions and policies of 'shadow governmental' entities secretly managing extraterrestrial affairs. Furthermore, 'shadow governmental' authorities must acknowledge their failures in managing extraterrestrial affairs, and accept the associated risks of a substantial loss in public trust and confidence. These difficulties in exposing the existence of extraterrestrial life and associated government policy make up what I call the "challenge of exopolitics".

The challenge confronting exopolitics in exposing government policies on extraterrestrial life cannot be underestimated. Exopolitics is a relatively new discipline dedicated to studying the political implications of extraterrestrial life and presenting this information to the general public so that it spurs informed and 'democratic' decision making. This requires that relevant information on extraterrestrial life enters the public arena so it can be discussed in a dispassionate and objective way to fully inform public debate. Such debate will lead to responsible and informed policy decisions about human response to an undisclosed extraterrestrial presence. The general public must be prepared for the truth concerning an extraterrestrial presence, and public policies secretly developed to respond to this presence, no matter how disturbing or complex the truth is. Disseminating the truth about secret government policies associated with extraterrestrial life requires faith in the democratic process, and in the capacity for ordinary citizens to handle this complex reality hidden from them for decades.

Full disclosure of extraterrestrial life visiting earth will shatter the illusions many Americans and citizens of other nations have created concerning the nature of their governments, their socio-economic systems, religions, human history, and life in the universe. Full disclosure will force many to rethink their fundamental values, and the roles of their political elites in 'protecting society' in an uncertain future involving extraterrestrial beings with technologies and abilities far beyond that of Earth humans. The likely loss of public trust and confidence in governmental institutions is undoubtedly a major risk for those appointed to secretly develop national security policies concerning extraterrestrial life.

Full disclosure of extraterrestrial life will not be easy. Exopolitics advocates need to reveal the overwhelming evidence of a secret extraterrestrial presence that has fundamentally affected life on this planet. Most citizens, elected political representatives and even senior military leaders have been denied "need to know" access to relevant information. They have consequently been kept out of the decision making process. Finally, secretly appointed committees need to be persuaded that extraterrestrial disclosure presents long term advantages that outweigh its short term losses.

This book is dedicated to the main challenge of exopolitics - exposing the truth of extraterrestrial life and associated secret public policies to a largely unprepared general public. It is hoped that the determination to expose this information will persuade secretly appointed policy makers that full disclosure of extraterrestrial life has significant strategic advantages from the perspective of national and economic security. Full disclosure of extraterrestrial life must become a viable public process that promotes global peace and harmony. The general public needs to play a constructive role in decision making towards suitable public policies concerning extraterrestrial life.

This book successively deals with a number of U.S. government policies secretly implemented to deal with extraterrestrial life. The book is divided into four parts. Part A presents evidence concerning secret agreements between extraterrestrial civilizations and U.S. shadow government authorities. It outlines the full extent of the disturbing activities and information that make up the primary challenge for exopolitics. Part B outlines critical responses to shadow government policies that contribute to the challenge of exopolitics. The goal is to outline specific policy changes that need to be made in how governments respond to extraterrestrial life. Part C introduces the concept of exopolitics and how it has developed as a systematic way of examining public policies concerning extraterrestrial life. The goal here is to equip the public with the conceptual tools so they can contribute to the policy making process regarding extraterrestrial life. Part D outlines the significance of public perception concerning extraterrestrial life, and how important public attitudes are in overcoming the challenge of exopolitics. The goal is to encourage the development of an empowered and informed citizenry that can constructively deal with an undeclared extraterrestrial presence.

The material in this book will come as a profound shock to many. That will be especially so for public policy professionals who have mistakenly believed that seniority, responsibility and merit determine access to a country's most deeply hidden national security secrets. The main goal is to prepare the general public for the truth about extraterrestrial life, and how select government agencies in the U.S. and elsewhere have secretly implemented public policy over six decades. The hope is that exposing such information will inspire the general public to seek to participate in an informed way in future public debate over appropriate public policy on extraterrestrial life. Furthermore, shadow government agencies need to be persuaded of the strategic failure of their current policies which require drastic overall and greater public participation. It is for those prepared to meet the challenges confronting exopolitics that this book is intended. You are the key to exposing secret U.S. government policies concerning extraterrestrial life and the transformation of our planet.

Michael E. Salla, M.A., Ph.D
January 5, 2009
Kona, Hawaii, USA

ENDNOTES - INTRODUCTION

[1] The affidavit by Lieutenant Walter Haut is the final chapter of Tom Carey and Donald Schmitt, *Witness to Roswell: Unmasking the 60-Year Cover-Up* (New Page Books, 2007). Also available online at: http://roswellproof.homestead.com/haut.html#anchor_8 .

[2] I first argued that eyewitness or 'whistleblower' testimonies comprised the most persuasive category of evidence concerning extraterrestrial life in an online 2003 paper that was later revised and included in my book, *Exopolitics: Political Implications of the Extraterrestrial Presence* (Dandelion Books, 2004) 7-9. The paper is still available online at: http://exopolitics.org/Study-Paper1.htm . I discuss the historical evolution of the exopolitics concept in chapter nine.

[3] For discussion of the report called "Estimate of the Situation", see Michael D. Swords, "Project Sign and the Estimate of the Situation," *Journal of UFO Studies* 7 (2000): 27-64.

[4] Donald Keyhoe, *Aliens from Space: The Real Story of Unidentified Objects* (New American Library) 14.

[5] "Proposed Studies on the Implications of Peaceful Space Activities for Human Affairs." *The Brookings Institute* (1961): 225. Elsewhere, the Brookings Report discusses the possible collapse of western civilization as a result of such announcements. For an overview of the Brookings Report, go to: http://www.enterprisemission.com/brooking.html .

[6] Georgina Bruni, *You Can't Tell the People: The Cover Up of Britain's Roswell* (Pan Books, 2001) 3.

Part A –Foundations of U.S. Government Policies on Extraterrestrial Life

The history of secret U.S. government policies concerning extraterrestrial life in terms of their scope, how they were implemented, and government agencies involved, all need to be exposed. This will encourage the public to participate in an informed way in future debates over appropriate government policy. However, some of the policies concerning extraterrestrial life are very disturbing, and need to be carefully considered in efforts to publicly expose such policies. Preparation of the general public by revealing the historical foundations of contemporary government policy on extraterrestrial life is a reliable way to start the exposure process. There is much evidence that confirms the historical reality of extraterrestrial life and associated secret government policies.

The four chapters in Part A present evidence of the historical foundations of U.S. government policies on extraterrestrial life. While there is striking historical evidence that extraterrestrial civilizations have interacted with humanity for millennia, I concentrate on the post-Second World War era. This era is the most documented and supported by witness testimony and physical evidence. Significantly, the internet has allowed the wide distribution of such testimonies making it possible for interested persons to read these testimonies or watch interviews of witnesses. The available evidence helps greatly in developing an accurate understanding of the history of secret government policies on extraterrestrial life.

The first chapter presents evidence of a number of historic meetings and agreements between representatives of the U.S. government and extraterrestrial civilizations. It outlines the scope and nature of these agreements, and subsequent implementation by the U.S. government and its international allies. Chapter two discusses evidence of joint government extraterrestrial bases and focuses on an alleged base at Dulce, New Mexico. The Black Budget used to fund such bases and associated classified extraterrestrial related projects is discussed in Chapter three. The fourth and final chapter in Part A gives an overview of how personnel have been historically recruited and managed for extraterrestrial related projects. At the end of Part A, the reader should have a solid grasp of how government policies on extraterrestrial life have historically been developed and implemented.

Chapter One

The Scope and Nature of Secret U.S. Government Agreements with Extraterrestrial Life

A number of credible witnesses have come forward to reveal experiences and evidence of secret agreements involving extraterrestrial life. The testimonies of these witnesses point to quasi-governmental entities drawn from government, military and corporate sectors that have implemented various aspects of such agreements. It appears that human and earth resources, sensitive information and/or advanced technology are exchanged through these agreements which in some cases have 'treaty' status. If accurate, the witness testimonies suggest that quasi-governmental entities have kept secret the signing and implementation of agreements or 'treaties' with extraterrestrials. These agreements flagrantly violate constitutional principles and processes. In the U. S., for example, only the Senate has the power to ratify treaties which is a power granted to the legislative branch of government. Yet it appears that secret treaties or 'agreements' have been signed by senior national security officials and implemented through Presidential executive orders without any effort to have the U.S. Senate learn about, discuss or ratify these 'treaties'.

What follows is evidence in the form of first hand testimonies of those claiming to have witnessed events or documents concerning secret agreements with extraterrestrial life. These agreements involve entities drawn from government agencies, military departments and corporations, with representatives of advanced extraterrestrial life. Evidence reveals that such agreements have been in place since at least the 1950s in the U.S. Other countries do not appear to have been signatories, but have provided different levels of support to the implementation of agreements signed by U.S. authorities.

The witnesses offering testimonial evidence can be divided into three categories. The first is Whistleblowers. This comprises individuals with military, government or corporate backgrounds, who have held various security classifications for whom public documentation is available to confirm their credentials. Public documentation supports their claims of being at classified facilities where events or documents suggesting secret agreements may have been witnessed as they claim. Importantly, while documentation supports their credibility as witnesses, no documentation exists to support their specific claims of directly witnessing extraterrestrial life or related official documents. Whistleblowers are among the most credible and reliable witnesses substantiating the existence of secret agreements with extraterrestrials since they often run the risk of severe career or financial penalties for making their disclosures. Consequently, their testimony deserves special scrutiny in understanding the scope and nature of secret agreements.

The second category of witnesses are civilians. This comprises individuals with civilian backgrounds who did not have any government, military or corporate position, nor did they have any security classification for the event or document which they witnessed. In some cases, they were hired as private consultants for a limited period to a national security related project. Public documentation is available to confirm their professional credentials which helps make them credible witnesses of the events or documents they claim to have observed. Again, while documentation supports their credibility as witnesses, no documentation exists to support their specific claims of directly witnessing extraterrestrial life or related official documents..

Unconfirmed witnesses make up the third category. This comprises witnesses for whom no reliable public documentation is available to confirm their credentials. This does not, however, dismiss the testimony of those whose credentials have not been publicly confirmed. The witnesses typically appear sincere, are not motivated by financial gain, and sometimes suffer career/job or personal relationship setbacks due to their testimonies. There is a reason to believe that in some cases documentation may have been expunged from public records as a security precaution for those employed in highly classified projects involving extraterrestrial life.[7] Importantly, their testimonies remain unchanged after several years of publicly revealing their stories. This contributes to their credibility as witnesses despite the lack of documentation for their credentials.

In sum, witnesses with 'confirmed' credentials are generally accepted as the most credible sources for confirming the existence of secret agreements concerning or with extraterrestrial life. This is especially the case for those claiming to have worked on classified military or corporate projects, and possessed security classifications giving them access to sensitive information. What follows are all based on first hand testimonies that could be admitted into a court of law and/or legislative investigation of extraterrestrial life. To help distinguish between each category of witness and degree of reliability, I will use the following abbreviations after their names:

> [W] Whistleblower in relation to the events and/or processes described.
> [C] Civilian witness in relation to the events and/or processes described.
> [U] Unconfirmed witness in relation to the events and/or processes described.

The background and testimony of each witness is presented the first time a reference is made to any of their statements. This will be done to get an idea of their level of credibility in terms of available background documentation. When I subsequently refer to these witnesses I will use the above abbreviations after their name so the reader can quickly determine the level of credibility each witness brings to the event or process being described.

The implications of what each witness revealed is discussed in terms of five key events or processes related to secret agreements with extraterrestrials. The ultimate goal is to develop an idea of the scope and nature of the secret agreements that have been in place since at least the 1950s. Witness testimonies will be discussed in relation to the following events or processes.

1. Meeting between President Eisenhower and extraterrestrial visitors.
2. Official agreements with extraterrestrials.
3. Sightings of extraterrestrials at classified facilities or operations.
4. Official communications with extraterrestrials.
5. Extraterrestrials living and/or working among us with official approval.

1. Meetings between President Eisenhower with extraterrestrial visitors

The most discussed incident concerning a meeting between political/military leaders with extraterrestrials dates back to the evening of February 20, 1954. President Eisenhower was secretly whisked away to Edwards Air Force Base to meet with extraterrestrials. There have been a number of witnesses who have provided testimony concerning this incident in terms of witnessing official films, documents, or even being physically present.[8] I begin with testimonies from those who claimed to see a film of the alleged meeting.

Don Phillips was a former U.S. Air Force and aerospace engineer with Lockheed Martin. He directly worked on advanced aerospace projects, and witnessed events and documents confirming that some of these projects were based on extraterrestrial technologies. His military and corporate credentials have been confirmed so he can be viewed as a whistleblower [W].[9] In the following passage Phillips refers to secret documents and a film that describe a meeting between President Eisenhower and extraterrestrials:

> We have records from 1954 that [there] were meetings between our own leaders of this country and ET's here in California. And, as I understand it from the written documentation, we were asked if we would allow them to be here and do research. I have read that our reply was well, how can we stop you? You are so advanced. And I will say by this camera and this sound, that it was President Eisenhower that had this meeting. And it was on film, sort of like what we are doing now.[10]

Phillips' testimony is significant since it claims that a film was taken of Eisenhower's meeting with extraterrestrials, and that negotiations took place. Phillips alludes to a situation wherein the extraterrestrials exploited their negotiation strength with the Eisenhower administration that felt it had no way of preventing the extraterrestrials from doing what they wanted. The following testimony gives an account of what happened at the claimed meeting between President Eisenhower and extraterrestrials.

More testimony concerning a film of Eisenhower secretly meeting with extraterrestrials comes from an anonymous Jesuit priest working within a Vatican intelligence organization, the Servizio Informazione del Vaticano (S.I.V.).[11] The Jesuit met with Cristoforo Barbato, an Italian researcher, and showed his credentials to Barbato who was subsequently convinced of the Jesuit's bona fides. The Jesuit chose to speak anonymously and no public documentation has been released to corroborate his background, making him an unconfirmed witness [U]. In 2001, he confirmed that President Eisenhower met with extraterrestrials at Edwards (Muroc) AFB in 1954. Another Italian researcher, Luca Scantamburlo, found circumstantial evidence supporting the existence of the top secret Vatican organization S.I.V. and the 'Omega' security classification the Jesuit claimed to possess. He interviewed Barbato and discovered more details about the filming of the alleged 1954 meeting:

> The Jesuit member of the S.I.V. told Barbato that on occasion of the secret meeting at Muroc Air Field Base, in 1954, military cameramen filmed the outstanding event "with three movie cameras (16 millimeters), detached in different places, loaded with color film and working by spring engines; this last rather unconformable [sic] resolution, because it compelled every cameraman to change reel every 3 minutes, it was necessary since in the presence of the Aliens and of their spacecrafts, the electrical engines of the biggest movie cameras did not work.[12]

Barbato's disclosure is revealing since it is consistent with the testimonies of witnesses claiming to have been in the presence of extraterrestrial craft, that electrically powered devices simply do not work. So a hand powered spring camera would have seemed the logical solution. The Jesuit furthermore claims that a senior catholic bishop, Francis MacIntyre, subsequently flew to Rome to brief Pope Pius XII and that the S.I.V. was created as a consequence of Eisenhower's meeting. Barbato writes:

> According to this person the reason to establish [sic] the S.I.V. was the meeting with an Alien delegation at Muroc

> Air Field Base in February 1954 in [the] presence of President Dwight Eisenhower and James Francis McIntyre, bishop of Los Angeles. After that incredible event McIntyre flew to Rome to refer everything to Pope Pius XII who decided to found the S.I.V with the aim to get every possible information [sic] about Aliens and how they interacted with the American Government.[13]

While the anonymous Jesuit's testimony is helpful insofar as it reveals information about the Vatican's alleged role in the Eisenhower extraterrestrial meeting. The Jesuit's identity has not been publicly revealed and thus he is an unconfirmed witness [U].

The next three testimonies come from those who claimed to have been physically present at the meeting and/or witnessing the extraterrestrial craft that landed at Edwards Air Force Base (Muroc). I begin with Charles Suggs, Sr., who was a former Commander in the U.S. Navy. His son, Charles Suggs, Jr., relates what his father told him about an incident involving President Eisenhower in 1954. Commander Suggs was allegedly physically present at the meeting which according to Don Phillips (see above) was visually taped:

> Charlie's father, Navy Commander Charles Suggs, accompanied Pres. Ike along with others on Feb. 20th. They met and spoke with 2 white-haired Nordics [Scandanavian looking extraterrestrials] that had pale blue eyes and colorless lips. The spokesman stood a number of feet away from Ike and would not let him approach any closer. A second Nordic stood on the extended ramp of a bi-convex saucer that stood on tripod landing gear on the landing strip. According to Charlie, there were B-58 Hustlers on the field even though the first one did not fly officially till 1956. These visitors said they came from another solar system. They posed detailed questions about our nuclear testing.[14]

Suggs testimony, though relayed through his son, gives further support for the claimed Eisenhower meeting with extraterrestrials on February 20, 1954. His military background and available public documentation allow him to be categorized as a whistleblower

[W]. [15] Furthermore, Suggs has many similarities with the independent testimony of another witness.

Another alleged eyewitness of the secret meeting between President Eisenhower and extraterrestrials is a former U.S. Air Force test pilot and Colonel. He chose to remain anonymous due to a secrecy oath and possible repercussions. The anonymous Colonel [U] revealed his experiences to a member of the British aristocracy, Lord Clancarty or Brinsley Le Poer Trench, who was best known as an authority on UFOs in Britain as well as being a member of the House of Lords. In 1979 he had introduced a motion calling for the government to end its cover-up of UFO evidence. While the motion was defeated, it generated much interest in the UFO phenomenon among other members of the House of Lords and in the British public. [16] Lord Clancarty's long public life gives a degree of confidence that he was well placed to judge the credibility of his anonymous source. What follows are the details of what the USAF Colonel told him:

> The pilot says he was one of six people at the meeting… Five alien craft landed at the base. Two were cigar-shaped and three were saucer-shaped. The aliens looked humanlike, but not exactly…. The aliens spoke English, and supposedly informed the President that they wanted to start an "educational program" for the people of Earth… [17]

Unfortunately, there is no way to identify the anonymous Colonel nor is there any public documentation available making him an unconfirmed witness [U]. Yet the Colonel's description is very consistent with what other sources have claimed about Eisenhower's meeting with extraterrestrials.

Another anonymous military eyewitness, a U.S. Air Force officer, revealed to former Royal Air Force pilot Desmond Leslie, that a flying saucer had landed at Edwards AFB, and President Eisenhower was taken to it:

> … a disc, estimated to be 100 feet in diameter, had landed on the runway on a certain day. Men returning from leave were suddenly not allowed back on the base. The disc was

> allegedly housed under guard in Hangar 27, and Eisenhower was taken to see it.[18]

An important point to note for later discussion is that the anonymous USAF officer referred to the base being closed to returning personnel. If confirmed, that would be important circumstantial evidence for highly classified activities occurring at Edwards AFB over the period in question. The anonymity of the USAF officer and lack of any public documentation available makes him an unconfirmed witness [U]. In his most recent book, *Need to Know*, British researcher Timothy Good refers to another three eyewitness accounts of flying saucers seen near and/or landing at Edwards AFB on February 20, 1954.[19]

William Cooper was a member of the US Naval Intelligence Briefing Team for the Commander of the Pacific Fleet, with the rank of Petty Officer. In performing his intelligence briefing functions he claims he witnessed naval documents describing the recent history of extraterrestrial life on Earth, and how extraterrestrials have interacted with various government and corporate entities.[20] He was honorably discharged in December 1975, and has provided documentation verifying his military service making him a confirmed whistleblower [W].[21] On May 23, 1989 Cooper gave his first public lecture revealing the contents of the documents he witnessed, and his subsequent research into secret communications and negotiations with extraterrestrial life. Included among his many startling revelations was reference to a meeting between President Eisenhower and extraterrestrials:

> A landing at Muroc, now Edwards Air Force Base, took place in 1954. The base was closed for three days and no one was allowed to enter or leave during that time.... On the appointed day the President was spirited to the base. The excuse was given to the press that he was visiting a dentist. Witnesses to the event have stated that three UFOs flew over the base and then landed.... President Eisenhower met with the aliens on February 20, 1954 ...[22]

Cooper's testimony is significant in so far as it supports various elements of what others claimed to have seen by film or personally.

Multiple eyewitness testimonies have been described above concerning several flying saucers being witnessed landing at Edwards [aka Muroc] AFB. Furthermore, other sources have confirmed that Edwards AFB was indeed closed for a period of three days starting from February 20, 1954.[23] According to Lt Col. Wendelle Stevens (ret.), closing an Air Force Base to incoming personnel and sending home others "is a highly unusual practice that is almost never used."[24]

What can be concluded with some confidence is that during secret meeting(s) between President Eisenhower and extraterrestrial visitors negotiations were conducted on a range of issues of mutual interest. There is testimonial evidence that in some cases these negotiations were successful and agreements were subsequently reached with the Eisenhower administration. What follows is testimonial evidence concerning secret agreements having been reached.

2. Official agreements with extraterrestrials

A common theme that emerges in witness testimonies concerning secret agreements or 'treaties' is that the extraterrestrials were able to impose terms that were unfavorable to humanity's long term interests. It appears that extraterrestrials took advantage of government/military perceptions of their bargaining weakness in negotiations. Consequently, agreements or treaties were reached that were unsatisfactory in a number of key regards for humanity as commented upon by the witnesses examined below.

The first is Lt. Col. Philip Corso who was a military intelligence officer, a decorated former battalion commander, and served in the Eisenhower administration as a military liaison. He finished his military career as head of Foreign Technology Desk, for the U.S. Army from 1961-1963 where he claimed he was responsible for seeding extraterrestrial technologies in select corporations for development. Public documentation exists confirming his credentials and whistleblower status [W]. Corso alludes to secret agreements where extraterrestrials exploited military concerns over premature disclosure in the following passage: "We had negotiated a kind of surrender with them [extraterrestrials] as long as we couldn't fight them. They dictated the terms because they knew what we most feared was disclosure."[25]

Corso's testimony is consistent with what was earlier disclosed by Don Phillips in terms of extraterrestrials being in a position to exploit their negotiating position due to the inability of the Eisenhower administration to stop them. Consequently, Corso was very supportive of President Reagan's Star War's initiative since he believed it would help the negotiating position of the U.S. in dealings with extraterrestrial visitors.[26] His comments are testimonial evidence that secret agreements have been reached with extraterrestrials, and that these agreements were resented by military officers familiar with their content.

I again return to the testimony of William Cooper [W] who earlier revealed that Eisenhower had met with extraterrestrials. He believed that this was part of a series of meetings at various Air Force bases that culminated in a treaty being reached between extraterrestrials and the U.S. government. He described the contents of the treaty as follows:

> The treaty stated that the aliens would not interfere in our affairs and we would not interfere in theirs. We would keep their presence on earth a secret. They would furnish us with advanced technology and would help us in our technological development. They would not make any treaty with any other Earth nation. They could abduct humans on a limited and periodic basis for the purpose of medical examination and monitoring of our development, with the stipulation that humans would not be harmed, would be returned to their point of abduction, would have no memory of the event, and that the alien nation would furnish Majesty Twelve with a list of all human contacts and abductees on a regularly scheduled basis.[27]

Cooper's testimony helps reveal that there have been a series of meetings between political/military leaders with extraterrestrial visitors, where negotiations have been conducted, and that agreements have been secretly reached. Importantly, the terms of a treaty concerning extraterrestrials supplying details of abductions has been confirmed by Dan Sherman who worked on a secret NSA communications project. Sherman's testimony will be examined in more detail in chapter four, but confirms that an agreement was reached that contained elements that were very distasteful to whistleblowers who learned about them.

Charles Hall was a former weather observer for the U.S. Air Force from 1963 to 1967. He was stationed at Nellis Air Force Base's Indian Spring facility where he claims he frequently witnessed extraterrestrials called the "Tall Whites" regularly meeting with senior military leaders. He says that a secret underground base was built at Indian Springs to house the extraterrestrials and their advanced interstellar ships. Confirmation has been found for some of Hall's claims concerning anomalous events at the weather ranges, including government funding for a secret underground base at Indian Springs.[28] While Hall did not violate any security oath in coming forward with his testimony, his military background at the time of the events and the official secrecy surrounding them, makes it possible to categorize him as a whistleblower [W].

Hall explained the legalistic way in which agreements with the Tall White extraterrestrials are interpreted in this response to an interview question about why he was chosen to liaise with them:

> … the decision to send me, and no one else, out to the ranges, was made by a committee of individuals that included the Tall Whites as well as high ranking USAF Generals and other high ranking members of the U.S. Government. The Tall Whites are very meticulous about keeping their agreements and expect the U.S. Government to be equally meticulous about keeping its agreements as well. If I were victimized or threatened by anyone, The Tall Whites would interpret that to mean that the U.S. Government could not be trusted to keep its agreements. The consequences would be enormous.[29]

As far as what was received by the extraterrestrials through secret agreements, Hall states:

> The USAF was obviously willing to give them [extraterrestrials] as much of any food item that they requested, no questions asked. The USAF was obviously entirely willing to give them both food and non-animal based

> clothing items (cotton, nylon, etc.) without limit for use as trading materials....The hanger appeared to have been entirely constructed by the USAF for use by the Tall Whites. For example, the inside of the hanger looked just like any other ordinary aircraft hanger.[30]

Hall's testimony is significant since it reveals that extraterrestrials are supplied a number of resources including rights for establishing bases in exchange for technological assistance to the USAF. This has been secretly formalized by officials in the Pentagon and other key government agencies in one or more undisclosed agreements arising out of face to face meetings between national security officials and the Tall Whites.

(Dr) Michael Wolf allegedly worked on an extensive number of secret extraterrestrial related projects. He claims to have worked on a top secret "Alphacom Team" whose responsibility was to acclimate the global public to extraterrestrial life. He claims to have a number of advanced degrees but to date there has not been public confirmation of his alleged credentials or classified activities which has made him both controversial and an unconfirmed whistleblower [U].[31] Yet a number of researchers have privately met him for interviews and find him to be credible.[32] In the following passage, he describes some of the secret agreements reached between elements of the U.S. government and different extraterrestrial civilizations:

> Dr. Wolf states that the most important mission objective of his Alphacom Team was resumption of negotiations with the visiting Star Nations. In the 1950s-1960s, the U.S. Administration entered into agreement discussions with the Zetas (so-called Greys) from the fourth planet of the star system Zeta Reticuli, and other star peoples, but these agreements were never ratified as Constitutionally required. The Zetas shared certain of their technological advances with government scientists, apparently often while prisoner "guests" within secure underground military installations in Nevada and New Mexico.[33]

Curiously, while Wolf contends that agreements were reached, some extraterrestrials were held as 'prisoner' guests. This suggests a high level of distrust and tension between the negotiating parties, and the terms reached in their agreements. More of this distrust and tension emerges in the following testimony.

Paul Bennewitz was an electronic communications specialist who owned his own company, and had a number of U.S. patents. Public documentation is available confirming his credentials thereby making him a credible civilian witness [C]. In 1978 Bennewitz began to monitor electronic communications in conjuction with sightings of UFOs and abduction of civilians in the vicinity of Alburqueque, New Mexico. In 1980 he relayed the results of his electronic intercepts to the Air Force Office of Special Investigations which allegedly attempted to discredit him by compromising his data with misinformation. At the same time, another government agency, the NSA, reportedly provided Bennewitz funding to continue his electronic study. Bennewitz was convinced that he had electronic evidence of aliens residing in an underground facility at Dulce New Mexico that were there as a result of secret agreements. He wrote:

> It is important to note at the outset that the alien is devious, employs deception, and have [sic] no intent of any apparent peace making process and obviously does not adhere to any prior arrangement ... It is not the intent of this report to criticize or point fingers. Obviously who ever made the initial agreement was operating on our basis of logic and not that of the alien and in so doing apparently walked innocently in time into a trap. The alien indicated that the "Greys", apparently the group initially envolved [sic] in the agreement were still upset about the initial capture and subsequent death of the first eight of their -co-fellows.[34]

Bennewitz's testimony is revealing insofar as he refers to a secret agreement being made on terms advantageous to extraterrestrials. His reference to walking "into a trap", echoes the kinds of sentiments expressed by Philip Corso concerning a "negotiated surrender", and to Don Philip's comment that the U.S. did not have the power to stop the extraterrestrials.

(Dr) Dan Burisch allegedly worked on classified microbiology projects at Area 51 and S-4. He began to disclose details of his classified work on extraterrestrial projects while actively working on these. This is unprecedented since it is a clear violation of security procedures for classified projects. In all known previous cases, such violation has led to the termination of the violator's involvement in such projects. Furthermore, there is much controversy over the validity of Dan Burish's credentials such as his Ph.D.[35] Consequently, his background and credentials need to be considered unconfirmed [U]. In the following passage from an interview, he describes his participation in secret negotiations with extraterrestrials which resulted in a treaty signed in New Mexico:

> ... during the course of speaking with extra-terrestrials, and our interactions with them from the 1950s onward, there have been a series of treaties established between we and they... As a consequence of our relationship with them, there have been more than one treaty system in place. During the last one of those treaty negotiation and signing times I had the privilege of being in the presence of the negotiators, at the conference which was held in the state of New Mexico.[36]

More significantly, he refers to the treaties being imposed on government authorities as a result of mismanaging some sensitive technology.

> The treaties were basically inflicted on us by the Orions. As they were enforced upon us by the Orions that we needed to do what we needed to do when they figured out that we weren't able to handle the issue ourselves. They looked at their own history and said, "Huh, look at the cave men and women." OK? After we acted the way that we acted involving the Cube and all of that business. They inflicted the treaty system on us and they said, "You will behave this way."[37]

Burish's view echoes the sentiments of Corso, Phillips and Bennewitz over government authorities not having a strong position in secret negotiations resulting in various agreements.

Finally, Phil Schneider allegedly worked as a civil engineer on the construction of deep underground military bases. He claims to have witnessed documents and personally experienced events proving the existence of extraterrestrials. Schneider began to publicly lecture about his experiences in 1996 showing documents and other material to substantiate his claims.[38] He said that government agencies were attempting to intimidate him into silence and would assassinate him if he didn't comply. In January 1996, he was found dead under very suspicious circumstances. While no public documentation exists to support his background and credentials, the compelling nature of his presentations, people who knew him, and the circumstances of his death make his views well worth considering. Schneider claims that secret agreements were entered into with extraterrestrials by the U.S. government back in 1954:

> Back in 1954, under the Eisenhower administration, the federal government decided to circumvent the Constitution of the United States and form a treaty with alien entities. It was called the 1954 Greada Treaty, which basically made the agreement that the aliens involved could take a few cows and test their implanting techniques on a few human beings, but that they had to give details about the people involved. Slowly, the aliens altered the bargain until they decided they wouldn't abide by it all.[39]

Schneider's testimony is similar to other witnesses who describe a treaty which was very unsatisfactory due to its terms and how the extraterrestrials abided by these terms.

3. Sightings of extraterrestrials at classified facilities or operations

This section examines the testimonies of a number of witnesses who claimed to have seen extraterrestrials at classified facilities, or participating in classified projects. Such sightings are evidence of secret agreements having been implemented between U.S. government authorities and extraterrestrials.

I earlier referred to Charles Hall's [W] testimony concerning secret agreements with a group of extraterrestrials called the Tall Whites. In his memoirs he wrote extensively of viewing the activities of the Tall Whites who were based at the Indian Springs facility at Nellis Air Force Base. Hall observed them and their spacecraft through his theodolite - a type of telescope used for tracking weather balloons. He claimed that they had various sized space vehicles including large interstellar triangular ships several hundred meters in size. He said that the base used by the Tall Whites had been exclusively built for them by the US Air Force. In email correspondence, Hall [C.H. abbreviation] responded to my [M.S. abbreviation] questions over the base as follows:

> M.S. You described the hangar that was used as a base for the larger interstellar spacecraft used by the Tall Whites. Was this built solely by the Tall Whites or did the US military play a role in this?
>
> C.H. The hanger appeared to have been entirely constructed by the USAF for use by the Tall Whites. For example, the inside of the hanger looked just like any other ordinary aircraft hanger. It included ordinary fire extinguishers, arrows marking exits, etc. In addition to writing and signs on the walls in English, it also include hieroglyphics and icons used by the aliens. The alien writing was done in pink paint against a white background.
>
> M.S. When in your view was the hangar supplied by the USAF for the Tall Whites built?
>
> C.H. I have no idea. However, I'm certain that the legends of Range Four Harry go back at least as far as 1954. The hanger construction (i.e. its steel supports, its other materials, it's lighting designs, its concrete doors that raised up in narrow sections by being lifted up from the top, etc) were consistent with the construction techniques used in the late 1940's and early 1950's.

The construction of a large underground hangar facility for interstellar Tall White ships and accommodation for the Tall Whites in a secure mountain location would have required a large outlay of capital. Partial confirmation was found for Hall's claim in a 1951 story by the Las Vegas Review-Journal concerning a classified housing project at Indian Springs in the early 1950s.[40] The story offers documentary evidence that a classified underground project was built at Indian Springs at the enormous cost of 300 million dollars, which converts in 2008 terms to 2.5 billion dollars.[41] Given the lack of surface constructions at Indian Springs that would explain where these 'accommodation' facilities were constructed, it's very likely that these were underground and/or constructed inside the mountains located at Indian Springs as Hall claimed.[42]

Clifford Stone is a retired Staff Sergeant U.S. Army who claims to have secretly worked for 22 years in classified projects aimed at the retrieval of crashed extraterrestrial vehicles. Public documentation has been released confirming his military background and whistleblower status [W]. In the following he describes a meeting with an extraterrestrial at the Pentagon in 1969 after he first began his military service:

> When I got to Fort Meade where he was supposed to be [a friend at the National Security Agency], they said, well, he is going to be tied up ... This person says, by the way, have you ever been to the Pentagon? Well at this time I had never been at the Pentagon.... Why don't we go ahead and give you the twenty-five cent tour. So we went on over.... When we get out there, there are two monorails there. I mean, there are monorails under the Pentagon.... When we got out, he says, well let me show you some interesting sites down this corridor here. So we are going down the corridor and it looked like there was a door at the far end of that corridor.... Well, when you go through the door there is like a field table there. And behind the field table you had this little entity [an extraterrestrial]. The entity was a little bigger than the 3, 3 1/2 foot tall entities that are a lot of times reported. But there were two men on either side of the table slightly behind the creature. When I turned around, I looked right into the eyes of this little creature. And you know, it's like you are seeing it but everything is being pulled from your mind - he was reading my whole life.... I remember going down and grabbing a hold of my head like this and falling to the floor. The next thing I remember I wake up and I am back in my

> friend's office [back at Fort Mead].... I will go this far to state that there is an interaction between entities and certain Government agencies within the U.S. Government.[43]

Stone's testimony reveals that extraterrestrials are physically working with a select group of NSA and Pentagon officials in classified programs as special guests of the U.S. government. The presence of an extraterrestrial at a classified facility, accompanied by two men, suggests that one or more official agreements have been reached with representatives of extraterrestrial civilizations.

Capt. Bill Uhouse is former US Marine Corps, USAF and aerospace engineer. Public documentation is available to confirm his whistleblower status [W].[44] He participated in meetings where an extraterrestrial would enter and give advice on advanced engineering problems:

> We had meetings and I ended up in a meeting with an alien. I called him J-Rod - of course, that's what they called him.... The alien used to come in with [Dr Edward] Teller and some of the other guys, occasionally to handle questions that maybe we'd have. You know? But you have to understand that everything was specific to the group. If it wasn't specific to the group, you couldn't talk about it. It was on need-to-know basis. And [the ET] he'd talk. He would talk, but he'd sound just like as if you spoke - he'd sound just like as if you spoke... The preparation we had before meeting this alien was, basically, going through all of the different nationalities in the world.... So basically, the alien was only giving engineering advice and science advice... Sometimes you'd get into a spot where you [would] try and try and try, and it wouldn't work. And that's where he'd [the alien] come in. They would tell him to look at this and see what we did wrong.[45]

Uhouse's revelation is further testimonial evidence of extraterrestrials being housed in secret military facilities, and giving assistance to military and corporate personnel when required on difficult technological problems. His testimony gives further support to the existence of secret agreements with extraterrestrials.

Significantly, his reference to an extraterrestrial housed at a government facility was also revealed by the following witness.

Richard Doty was a former Special Agent for the U.S. Air Force Office of Special Investigations (AFOSI). He was personally in charge of an AFOSI effort to discredit Paul Bennewitz and derail a forthcoming documentary on extraterrestrial life by Linda Moulton Howe. Public documents have been made available verifying his military background making him a confirmed whistleblower [W]. In 2006, Doty was listed as co-author of a book where he described his own experiences concerning extraterrestrial life and technology, and aspects of his former career in military intelligence.

> There is a closed circuit/videotape interview of an alien (EBE-2 ...) that was an exchanged guest here starting from 1964 until 1984. An AF Colonel did the interview. I attended that interview... From EBE-2 we learned a great deal of information about their race, culture and spacecraft. A third alien, EBE-3 was part of the same exchange program starting in 1979 until 1989.... The extraterrestrials, who are guests of the US government, reside in a number of different quarters around the US.[46]

Doty claims, as did Bill Cooper, that an exchange agreement exists between the U.S. government and extraterrestrial visitors.[47] This was graphically described in the Steven Spielberg movie, *Close Encounters of the Third Kind.* At a June 1982 special screening at the White House, Ronald Reagan confided to Spielberg: "You know, there aren't six people in this room who know how true this really is."[48] A consequence of such an agreement is Doty's claim that some extraterrestrials are guests of the U.S. government. This is consistent with what Charles Hall [W], Michael Wolf [U] Bill Uhouse [W] described earlier, and with what Clifford Stone [W] claims he experienced at the Pentagon.

Steve Wilson claims to have risen to the rank of Lt Colonel in the U.S. Air Force before retiring, and serving on a highly classified crash retrieval team of extraterrestrial vehicles, Project Pounce. He died in 1997 shortly after going public with his remarkable claims and to date no reliable documentation has been found to verify his credentials making him an unconfirmed witness

[U]. In the following incident he described witnessing an 8 foot tall extraterrestrial woman who briefed a room of twenty officers and civilians about the history of both the earth and other planets:

> The woman had finely-chiseled features. Her blonde hair cascaded neatly past her shoulders. Her eyes were the bluest blue I'd ever seen. Somehow she was different. Little did I know then, how different! She sat a large crystal on the table, and without warning, her fingers began to glow as she ran them over this crystal. A 3-D hologram began to form above it! I looked around the room and everyone's mouth was hanging open, and suddenly I noticed mine was, too. Little did I realize that at that moment my life would forever be changed. My past teachings slipped from me as I stared. My whole concept of life did a 180-degree turn, as I watched the Hologram, complete with sound, unfold the mysteries of the past and the present, and of other worlds.[49]

Wilson's testimony is another example of how extraterrestrials are present in secret military facilities providing information to senior military and civilian leaders about extraterrestrial life. His revelation provides further direct support for the existence of secret agreements whereby extraterrestrials can live at secret military facilities, and provide various kinds of assistance when required.

Dan Burisch [U] claims he worked with a sick extraterrestrial biological entity, a 'Gray' he called J-Rod, at the highly secretive S-4 facility which is in the vicinity of Area 51. This J-Rod was contained in a biological 'clean sphere' allegedly to provide the extraterrestrial the optimal environmental conditions given the neural degenerative disease it was experiencing. Burisch was tasked to enter the 'clean sphere' in something similar to an astronaut's spacesuit. The J-Rod essentially performed a 'mind-meld' with him where he downloaded much valuable information on the genesis of life which, according to Burisch, was part of a classified biological project called Lotus.[50] Burisch gave the following account of his encounter with J-Rod in the 'clean sphere' located at S-4:

> I actually came into direct contact with him at the end of 1993, the start of '94... [T]here is something wrong with him.

> During the entirety of my experience around him, he appeared the best that I can describe is "off-shifted." Almost like... I mean, he was physical. I felt him through the glove. There was matter there with me, but almost like he was a ghost with a body.... He did not belong where he was. Yet when he would communicate, when he would do the entrainment... They thump you, and... until they finally come into contact with the brain-level waves where they can begin communicating. And it comes in waves... And then you feel yourself pulled in. As the entrainment is occurring the perception is being pulled in to his eyes. Very unwieldy [chuckle] feeling. But then they entrain, bring you ... bring you down to, you know, relaxed almost to a theta state, like an 8 hertz thing, theta state, where you're very, almost like drowsy and they tell you, you know, they're not going to hurt you. He did that. He actually said that he would not harm me.... I was part of a B-unit team to start with. In fact, that was going to be my actual occupation in there, was assisting the chief scientist and going into the clean sphere, until he identified me as somebody, I guess, special to him... Chi'el'ah [J-Rod]... and he wanted me to be the person to go in there. That's why I was promoted, ultimately, to the working group later in there.[51]

Burisch's testimony is unique insofar as it describes how a sick extraterrestrial would be both treated in classified facilities by medical scientists, and also be part of an ongoing biological project called Lotus.

From 1958-1992, Clark McClelland served as a contractor to NASA on numerous mission projects including Mercury, Apollo, SkyLab, Space Shuttle and International Space Station. Shortly before his dismissal from NASA in 1992 under controversial circumstances, he worked as a SpaceCraft Operator.[52] McClelland has made available public documentation that verify his background and credentials making him a confirmed whistleblower [W].[53] In August 2008, he for the first time publicly announced that during a Space Shuttle mission, he witnessed an extraterrestrial communicating with tethered astronauts:

> I, Clark C. McClelland, former ScO, Space Shuttle Fleet, personally observed an 8 to 9 foot tall ET on his 27 inch video monitors while on duty in the Kennedy Space Center, Launch Control Center (LCC). The ET was standing upright in the Space Shuttle Payload Bay having a discussion with TWO tethered US NASA Astronauts! I also observed on my monitors, the spacecraft of the ET as it was in a stabilized, safe orbit to the rear of the Space Shuttle main engine pods. I observed this incident for about one minute and seven seconds. Plenty of time to memorize all that I was observing. IT WAS AN ET and Alien Star Ship! A friend of mine later contacted me and said that this person had also observed an 8 to 9 foot tall ET INSIDE the SPACE SHUTTLE CREW COMPARTMENT! Yes, inside OUR Shuttle! BOTH missions were DoD (Pentagon) TOP SECRET (TS) encounters![54]

He provided an artist's recreation of the incident which clearly suggests that this is not merely a mysterious third astronaut helping a Space Shuttle mission. The being's height and unconventional space suit strongly points to an extraterrestrial of some kind.[55] The incident is indicative of some kind of official agreement with extraterrestrials where they can secretly assist when needed in space missions.

The above testimonies in this section so far has referred to extraterrestrials being present at classified facilities that have extraordinarily high security in place. As can be expected, this might occasionally lead to difficult circumstances and tension between workers, security personnel and extraterrestrials. According to a number of independent reports, a firefight occurred in at least one joint human extraterrestrial facility. I now examine several testimonies discussing such a firefight.

A witness that lends credence to the possibility that a firefight had occurred between US military forces and extraterrestrials in a secret underground base was (Dr) Michael Wolf. Wolf's book *Catchers of Heaven* described a firefight between extraterrestrials and elite US military forces that had occurred in 1975 at the Groom Lake, Nevada facility that may have been related to what occurred later at the nearby Dulce:

> The Greys shared certain of their technological advances with military/intelligence scientists, apparently often while prisoner "guests" within secure underground military installations in Nevada and New Mexico. The extraterrestrials have given the U.S. government some of their antigravity craft and a huge amount of fuel (element 115). On May 1, 1975 during one such technology exchange in Nevada, a demonstration of a small ET antimatter reactor, the lead Grey asked the Colonel in charge of the Delta Forces guarding the ETs to remove all their rifles and bullets from the room, (so that they would not accidentally discharge during the energy emissions.) The guards refused, and in the ensuing commotion a guard opened fire on the Greys. One alien, two scientists and 41 military personnel were killed. One guard was left alive to attest that the ETs apparently used directed mental energy in self-defense to kill the other attacking Delta Forces. Dr. Wolf states that "this incident ended certain exchanges with (the Greys)." [56]

Documentary confirmation that a firefight occurred can be found in the testimony of controversial whistleblower, Bob Lazar. Lazar worked at Los Alamos National Laboratories as a technician when he claims he met with Dr Edward Teller during a June 27, 1982 lecture. Lazar says Teller was reading a front page story in the Los Alamos Monitor about Lazar's jet propelled car when Lazar walked up and identified himself. Teller was later contacted for a job recommendation. Lazar claims that he was successful in being employed in a secret facility called S-4 that worked on reverse engineering projects. He claimed that the Department of Naval Intelligence was his employer. Some documentation has been found to support Lazar's claims that he worked at Los Alamos, that the Los Alamos Monitor ran a story on his jet propelled car, and that he received at least one payment from the Department of Naval Intelligence in the period he worked at S-4 (1989). Lazar's education and employment record have not been publicly verified making him an unconfirmed witness [U]. The following passage describes Lazar's claims of what he read in a briefing document concerning a firefight between extraterrestrials and military personnel at a secret facility in 1979.

> [T]he most astounding information came from more than two hundred pages of "briefing" documents he [Lazar] was required to read to prepare him for his job.... One intriguing aspect of Lazar's briefing concerned his description of an apparent battle between aliens and humans at a secret based in 1979. He said he read that a human guard tried to take a weapon into the alien's area, which resulted in fatal head wounds to security personnel.[57]

Lazar's description of this incident closely matches with Wolf's account that the firefight was a result of a misunderstanding over the stringent security procedures in place.

Another whistleblower who has emerged to disclose events at an underground facility concerning extraterrestrials is Phil Schneider [U]. Schneider claims that he was directly involved in a firefight with extraterrestrials in 1979 at the Dulce classified facility in New Mexico:

> Back in 1979 ... the fire-fight at Dulce occurred quite by accident. I was involved in building an addition to the deep underground military base at Dulce, which is probably the deepest base. It goes down seven levels and over 2.5 miles deep. At that particular time, we had drilled four distinct holes in the desert, and we were going to link them together and blow out large sections at a time. My job was to go down the holes and check the rock samples, and recommend the explosive to deal with the particular rock. As I was headed down there, we found ourselves amidst a large cavern that was full of outer-space aliens, otherwise known as large Greys. I shot two of them. At that time, there were 30 people down there. About 40 more came down after this started, and all of them got killed. We had surprised a whole underground base of existing aliens.[58]

While Schneider did not speak of the Dulce facility as a joint human extraterrestrial base, it is significant that he was helping build a classified base right over it. This at the very least suggests a secret agreement not to reveal the presence of extraterrestrials at hidden bases on the U.S. mainland. Despite differences between the accounts offered by Wolf, Lazar and Schneider the three accounts agree that a military conflict broke out at a joint human extraterrestrial facility in the 1970s that led to fatalities.

4. Official communications with extraterrestrials

There are a number of witnesses who have come forward to reveal how official governmental communications have occurred with extraterrestrial civilizations. These communications have used innovative technologies and psychic methods. The communications are used to exchange vital information, to arrange extraterrestrial landings at various locations, and to comply with terms of secret agreements. I begin with the testimony of Dan Sherman.

Dan Sherman was a former electronic intelligence expert with U.S. Air Force who worked with the National Security Agency on a highly classified program called Project Preserve Destiny. The Project used "intuitive communications" with a particular group of extraterrestrials.[59] He received specialized training that used innate intuitive or psychic abilities without his normal military superiors being informed. He has provided documentation to confirm his military background and some of the assignments he had as an electronic communications expert. In the following passage he writes about his growing disenchantment with Project Preserve Destiny based on data confirming extraterrestrial abductions that were being relayed by extraterrestrials to governmental authorities:

> The bitterness began a few months after I had started to receive comms from Bones [an extraterrestrial]. It hit a sharp incline when I began to receive the abduction comms and now it hit a crescendo. I was tired of being supposedly so important because of my abilities, yet treated like an underling with no need-to-know.... Why the abduction data? Why had everything been passed in code, mostly, until now? ... I finally came to the conclusion, after reporting over 20 apparent abduction scenarios, that I wanted no part of the program any longer. Although I had no reason to believe anyone was being maliciously harmed, I did get a feeling that the abductions I was reporting were part of some sort of

> higher calling and the feelings of the people involved took a back seat to that calling.[60]

Sherman's testimony reveals that extraterrestrials responsible for abductions are passing on data about their activities to government agencies through a classified project. This indicates the existence of an agreement of some kind where one of the conditions involves extraterrestrials passing on data of their interactions with private citizens. His testimony also helps establish that communication protocols have been reached with one or more extraterrestrial groups.

In his first public lecture in May 1989 William Cooper [W] revealed the extent of secret communications and negotiations with extraterrestrial life:

> In 1953 Astronomers discovered large objects in space which were moving toward the Earth. It was first believed that they were asteroids. Later evidence proved that the objects could only be Spaceships. Project Sigma intercepted alien radio communications. When the objects reached the Earth they took up a very high orbit around the Equator. There were several huge ships, and their actual intent was unknown. Project Sigma, and a new project, Plato, through radio communications using the computer binary language, was able to arrange a landing that resulted in face to face contact with alien beings from another planet. Project Plato was tasked with establishing diplomatic relations with this race of space aliens.... [61]

Cooper's testimony helps reveal that there have been classified communications and meetings between political/military leaders with extraterrestrial visitors, and that agreements have been secretly reached. His testimony is consistent with Sherman's claims concerning secret communications with extraterrestrials.

Another witness to be considered is John Maynard who worked as a military intelligence analyst for the Defense Intelligence Agency. Maynard had a 22 year military career and his whistleblower background has been confirmed.[62] In his testimony, Maynard reveals his discovery of electronic communications from extraterrestrials that were being received by military authorities that were keeping this secret:

> ... we were analyzing traffic patterns [electronic communications] of the Chinese at that particular time. Every once in a while, I would run across an anomaly that wasn't really within the pattern of the type of traffic that would be known within our military network.... I found out that there was more to these communications than was normal, and that they were not basically earthbound [not coming from earth] ... We really didn't have a space program that would be moving that kind of traffic, nor did we have the communications systems and satellites in that particular time that would.... I'm talking about the late 1950s, early 1960s. So as far as the timeframe goes, it had to be something else besides just us.... I think that that was really my downfall – I realized it had to be extraterrestrial – so they found a way to get rid of me and they did it very well. [63]

Maynard's realization was that extraterrestrials were conducting electronic communications with U.S. authorities, and that this was classified information. This leads to the conclusion that electronic communications between extraterrestrials vehicles and government authorities is highly classified information, and military personal discovering this without "need to know" access are quickly reassigned.

Another whistleblower claiming the existence of secret communications with extraterrestrial civilizations is Richard Doty. Doty wrote:

> The National Security Agency has devised a communications system to communicate with the aliens. It's some type of electronic binary pulse. The communications takes place between the Earth and the alien ships. There are reportedly receiving points in Nevada and California. The communications are translated by a computer, which gives the landing coordinates to the National Security Agency, so we know the location of the landing and the purpose, i.e...,

> collect resources for their spacecraft or to have verbal contact.[64]

According to Doty, an electronic communications system has been developed by the NSA to communicate with extraterrestrials. This is consistent with Sherman's testimony regarding the classified communications program he worked on while stationed at the NSA.

5.**Extraterrestrials Among Us**

According to Charles Hall [W], some of the Tall Whites would go to Las Vegas casinos in an effort to blend in with the human population. Apparently, Pentagon officials had implemented a program to assist the Tall Whites in comfortably communicating and working with humans. This was why Hall was tasked with interacting with them so frequently during his military service. He saw one of the Tall Whites at a Las Vegas casino and he described the following conversation with her after she asked him how she was dressed in a telepathic communication:

> "Your dress is perfect," I slowly thought. Then I continued, "Your makeup is perfect. You look just like a young attractive human woman with a very fine eye for detail. I see that you're very good at shopping for clothes and makeup here in Las Vegas." "We learned it from you," she laughed in return. "We learned how to blend in with American society by imitating you. Remember we had to learn how to adjust our electronics properly also, in order to do it. We both laughed. I expected that Las Vegas being what it is, she was probably not alone, so I began looking around to see if I could locate her companion. I found him standing stiffly, off to my right with his back turned mostly toward me. He was wearing an ordinary black suit with a white shirt and tie. He stood about six two. It was easy to tell that under his suit, he was very thin. He was dressed stylishly. I could tell that he also was wearing a wig. This wig covered his head down below the level of his ears and gave him the appearance of being an ordinary businessman.[65]

Hall's testimony reveals that secret agreements have led to some extraterrestrials being allowed to blend in to the human population. Hall's use as a human liaison to the Tall Whites shows how military officials sanctioned his participation in a secret program where extraterrestrials could be assisted in integrating into human society without being exposed. Possible corroboration is found in the following testimony.

Ingo Swann was the first psychic employed in a remote viewing program at the Stanford Research Institute funded by the CIA and the intelligence community that began in 1972: Project Stargate. Public documentation is available verifying Swann's role as a civilian consultant to Project Stargate making him a confirmed civilian witness [C].[66] The success of Swann and Project Star Gate in delivering accurate remote viewing data to the intelligence community quickly led to military intelligence agencies asking Swann to develop the necessary protocol for training military remote viewers. In 1975 he was recruited by a covert government operative, "Mr Axelrod" to spy on extraterrestrials. Swann's involvement with the covert activities of "Mr Axelrod" and his two mysterious companions, Swann called them "the twins", is evidence of agreements concerning extraterrestrials living among us. Swann describes the following incident in a Los Angeles supermarket when he saw a strikingly attractive female who he concluded was an extraterrestrial being followed by Axelrod's two operatives:

> At one of the artichoke tables was standing a ravishing woman... For absolutely no reason at all I experienced an electrifying wave of goosebumps throughout my whole body. The hair on my arms practically stood at attention, and the hair on my neck definitely did. Without rhyme or reason or forethinking or anything at all I suddenly "knew" she was an alien, an extraterrestrial ... Way down the line-up of vegetable cases I recognized, of ALL astounding and possible things, ONE OF THE TWINS [one of Mr Axelrod's operatives]. HE was watching the woman. HE saw that I saw him and there immediately arose in my mind an image of a white card. Please do not speak, and please act normal.... Well, if one of the twins is HERE, of all places, then the other must be, too. And sure enough, the other twin was at

> the opposite end of the vegetable line-up- and he was watching the woman too.... The twins' presence, coupled with my psychic alert, confirmed that the woman WAS an ET. [67]

Swann's testimony shows how some extraterrestrials have been allowed to integrate into the human population. They are monitored by intelligence agencies that go to great lengths to ensure that no members of the public learn the truth about extraterrestrials walking among us.[68] The following testimony concerns what may have been a secret effort to disclose the truth about extraterrestrials among us.

Catherine Austin Fitts is a former Assistant Secretary of the Department of Housing and Urban Development (HUD). She is best known for implementing financial tracking software first at HUD and later her own financial securities company, Hamilton Securities, that exposed financial improprieties at HUD and BCCI; and the Iran-Contra Savings & Loan scandal. Public documents are available to verify her government and corporate background making her a confirmed civilian witness [C]. [69] She claims that in 1998 the Undersecretary of the U.S. Navy had commissioned a "high level strategic plan" to prepare the American public for an official announcement that extraterrestrials exist and live among us.

> In 1998, I was approached by John Peterson, head of the Arlington Institute, a small high quality military think tank in Washington, DC. I had gotten to know John through Global Business Network and had been impressed by his intelligence, effectiveness and compassion. John asked me to help him with a high level strategic plan Arlington was planning to undertake for the Undersecretary of the Navy. At the time I was the target of an intense smear campaign that would lead the normal person to assume that I would be in jail shortly or worse. John explained that the Navy understood that it was all politics ---- they did not care.
>
> I met with a group of high level people in the military in the process --- including the Undersecretary. According to John, the purpose of the plan --- discussed in front of several military or retired military officers and former government officials--- was to help the Navy adjust their operations for a

> world in which it was commonly known that aliens exist and live among us.
> When John explained this purpose to me, I explained that I did not know that aliens existed and lived among us. John asked me if I would like to meet some aliens. For the only time in my life, I declined an opportunity to learn about something important.[70]

I have been able to confirm that Fitts served on the Board of Directors of the Arlington Institute during the period in question, and that extraterrestrial life was discussed at some of its closed door meetings as a hypothetical "wildcard event." However, Fitts specific claim of there being a strategic plan sponsored by the U.S. Navy to prepare the public for disclosure of extraterrestrial life, or of a possible meeting an extraterrestrial, was not supported by other Board members.[71] I contacted Fitts in early 2008 to elaborate or clarify her earlier recollection, but she had nothing to add to what was released to the public.[72] Essentially, she stood by her version of events as reported. Given her former senior position with HUD, and refusal to amend her earlier public statement, a prima facie case can be made for accepting her claims as credible. Her testimony supports the claims made by Hall and Swann that extraterrestrials are living and working among us. Furthermore, official efforts may be secretly underway to prepare the American public for such a reality.

Conclusion

I have summarized in Table 1 witness testimonies concerning the scope and nature of secret agreements with extraterrestrial life. I have arranged each witness in order of available documentation confirming their background credentials, and their credibility as witnesses. The available testimonial evidence cumulatively establishes that secret agreements have been reached with representatives of extraterrestrial civilizations that in some cases have 'treaty' status. Various government, military and corporate entities have been involved in implementing these agreements in a variety of ways that have not been disclosed to the general public.

Considerable resentment has been expressed by a number of witnesses over the scope and nature of the secret agreements. Furthermore, there appears to significant tension among signatories over the content of the agreements and how they are implemented. Exposing secret agreements reached with various extraterrestrial groups will help considerably in promoting transparency and accountability in past and ongoing negotiations. Some of these agreements will be found to be egregious in terms of their content and will need to be immediately terminated. This may be a major factor in why these agreements have remained secret so long. Citizen based efforts have consequently been launched to end all secret agreements with or concerning extraterrestrial life.[73] Most importantly, exposing secret agreements with extraterrestrials will help bring about more responsibility in the way future agreements are negotiated, their contents disseminated for public review, and finally ratified in constitutionally valid ways by elected public officials.

Table 1. Witness Testimony of Secret Agreements with ETs

Events and/or Process Indicating Secret ET Agreements	Witnesses Credentials Confirmed: Whistleblower [W] Civilian [C] Unconfirmed [U]	Scope and Nature of secret agreements with extraterrestrials
Meetings between President Eisenhower and extraterrestrial visitors	Don Phillips [W] William Cooper [W] Charles Suggs [W] Anon. USAF Col [U] Anon. Jesuit [U] Anon USAF Officer [U]	Extraterrestrials have physically met with senior political/military leaders to formally introduce themselves, and discuss confidential issues. Foundation laid for subsequent agreements/treaties.
Agreements with extraterrestrials	Charles Hall [W] Philip Corso [W] William Cooper [W] Phil Schneider [U] Michael Wolf [U] Paul Bennewitz [C] Dan Burisch [U]	Extraterrestrials have reached agreements that have been formally approved and secretly implemented by key national security organizations. Resources and technology have been subsequently exchanged. Some resented the agreements as unfair.
Sightings of extraterrestrials at classified facilities or operations assisting military and/or corporate personnel	Clark McClelland [W] Clifford Stone [W] Charles Hall [W] Bill Uhouse [W] Paul Bennewitz [C] Richard Doty [W] Bob Lazar [U] Dan Burisch [U] Phil Schneider [U] Steve Wilson [U]	Extraterrestrials actively participating in various classified projects with military, governmental and/or corporate entities. Extraterrestrials assist when needed in classified projects involving advanced technologies and/or space operations.
Communications with extraterrestrials with the approval of select government agencies	Dan Sherman [W] William Cooper [W] Richard Doty [W]	Protocols have been established for communicating with ETs. Personnel are secretly trained and/or recruited to participate in these secret communications using state of the art electronic equipment and/or telepathy.
ETs living and/or working among us with the approval of select government agencies	Ingo Swann [C] Catherine Austin Fitts [C] Charles Hall [W]	ETs sighted as living and/or working among us. ETs are monitored by national security agencies. Individuals strongly discouraged from making contact with and/or revealing the existence of ETs among us.

ENDNOTES – CHAPTER ONE

[7] See Michael Salla, "The Covert World of UFO Crash Retrievals - An Overview of Personnel Management in Majestic-12 Group Projects" *Exopolitics Journal* 2:2 (July 2007) 79-96. Available online at: http://exopoliticsjournal.com/vol-2-2.htm

[8] For a detailed discussion of all the evidence concerning the 1954 incident, see Michael Salla, Eisenhower's 1954 Meeting With Extraterrestrials (Feb 12, 2004), published online at: http://exopolitics.org/Study-Paper-8.htm .

[9] Phillips background and credentials were confirmed by Dr Steven Greer and the Disclosure Project, see "Testimony of Don Phillips," in *Disclosure*: *Military and Government Witnesses Reveal The Greatest Secrets in Modern History*, ed., Stephen Greer (Crossing Point, 2001) 375.

[10] "Testimony of Don Phillips," *Disclosure*, ed., Stephen Greer, 379

[11] Discussion of the highly secretive S.I.V. as the Vatican's Espionage network is discussed in Mark Aarons and John Loftus, *Unholy Trinity: The Vatican, The Nazis, and The Swiss Banks* (St. Martin's Griffin, 1998) 18,22-23.

[12] Luca Scantamburlo, "Planet X and the "JESUIT FOOTAGE" Classified "SECRETUM OMEGA." First Indirect Confirmation!" http://www.ufodigest.com/news/1106/jesuitfootage.html .

[13] Christoforo Barbato, "Vatican and UFO: Secretum Omega," http://www.ufodigest.com/secretum.html .

[14] Personal notes from William Hamilton from a 1991 interview with Commander Suggs son, Sgt Charles Suggs, Jr. See also, Bill Hamilton, *Project Aquarius: The Story of An Aquarian Scientist* (Authorhouse, 2005) 85.

[15] Suggs background was investigated by UFO Researcher Bill Hamilton, see *Project Aquarius: The Story of An Aquarian Scientist* (Authorhouse, 2005) 85.

[16] For discussion of Lord Clancarty's motion to the House of Lords, see Timothy Good, *Above Top Secret* (Willaim Morrow, 1988) 73-75.

[17] Cited in Timothy Good, *Alien Contact: Top-Secret UFO Files Revealed* (William Morrow and Co., 1993) 75

[18] Timothy Good, *Need to Know: UFOs, the Military and Intelligence* (Pegasus Books, 2007) 208.

[19] Timothy Good, *Need to Know,* 208.

[20] See William Cooper, *Behold a Pale Horse* (Light Technology Publishing, 1991) 196. Available online as: "Origin, Identity, and Purpose of MJ-12," http://www.geocities.com/Area51/Shadowlands/6583/maji007.html .

[21] Military Record available in *Behold a Pale Horse,* 381-96. See also online at: http://en.wikipedia.org/wiki/Milton_William_Cooper

[22] William Cooper, *Behold a Pale Horse,* 202. Available online as: "Origin, Identity, and Purpose of MJ-12," http://www.geocities.com/Area51/Shadowlands/6583/maji007.html .

[23] Private email correspondence with Lt. Col., Stevens, September 15, 2007.

[24] Personal email correspondence with Lt. Col., Stevens, September 15, 2007.

[25] Philip Corso, *The Day After Roswell* (Pocket Books, 1997) 292

[26] See chapter six. An earlier version printed as Michael Salla, "Using Space Weapons against Extraterrestrial Civilizations," *Nexus Magazine* Vol 13:2 (Feb-March 2006).
[27] Bill Cooper, *Behold a Pale Horse,* 203-204
[28] See Michael Salla, "Further Investigations of Charles Hall and Tall Whites at Nellis Air Force Base: The David Coote Interviews," http://exopolitics.org/Exo-Comment-36.htm .
[29] "Charles Hall and the Tall Whites: Another perception of the extraterrestrial phenomenon and Area 51," http://karmapolis.be/pipeline/interview_hall_uk.htm .
[30] Michael Salla, 'Tall White' Extraterrestrials, Technology Transfer and Resource Extraction from Earth - An Analysis of Correspondence with Charles Hall," http://www.exopolitics.org/Exo-Comment-25.htm .
[31] Critics such as Stanton Friedman, regard Wolf as a fraud. http://www.ufomind.com/misc/1997/jul/d30-004.shtml .
[32] Wolf's major advocates include researchers Poala Harris, M.Ed., Richard Boylan, Ph.D., and airline captain James Courant. For Richard Boylan's response to Stanton Friedman's criticisms of Wolf, go to: http://www.ufomind.com/misc/1998/jan/d29-002.shtml .
[33] "Official Within MJ-12 UFO-Secrecy Management Group Reveals Insider Secrets," http://www.drboylan.com/wolfdoc2.html
[34] Cited in Greg Bishop, *Project Beta* (Pocket Books, 2005) 236-37.
[35] My own thoughts on Burish's credibility are available at: http://www.exopolitics.org/Exo-Comment-37.htm .A supportive case for Dan Burisch's authenticity is found in William Hamilton, *Project Aquarius.*
[36] Out from under Majestic: Dan Burisch uncensored: A video interview with Dan Burisch - Part 1
Las Vegas, July 2006. Available online at: http://projectcamelot.org/dan_burisch_interview_transcript_1.html .
[37] "Dan Burisch: Stargate Secrets – Part 2 Interview transcript," http://projectcamelot.org/dan_burisch_stargate_secrets_interview_transcript_2.html .
[38] His story and lectures are publicly available at: http://www.apfn.org/apfn/phil.htm .
[39] "Mutual UFO Network Conference Presentation, May 1995, available online at: http://users.rcn.com/zap.dnai/schneidr.htm .
[40] For a copy of the story, go to: http://exopolitics.org/IndianSprings-Project.htm .
[41] The American Institute for Economic Research provides an online conversion program at: http://www.aier.org/colcalc.htm .
[42] For more discussion see Michael Salla, "Further Investigations of Charles Hall and Tall Whites at Nellis Air Force Base: The David Coote Interviews," http://exopolitics.org/Exo-Comment-36.htm .
[43] "Testimony of Clifford Stone," in *Disclosure*, ed., Stephen Greer, 332.
[44] A summary of his background is available, see: "Testimony of Captain Bill Uhouse," in *Disclosure*, ed., Stephen Greer, 384.
[45] "Testimony of Captain Bill Uhouse," in *Disclosure*, ed., Stephen Greer, 386-87

[46] Robert Collins with Richard Doy and Timothy Cooper, *Exempt from Disclosure*, 2nd Edition (Peregrine Communications, 2006) 73.
[47] See Bill Cooper, *Behold a Pale Horse,* 204.
[48] "A Young Steven Spielberg Meets the President", available online at: http://www.presidentialufo.com/reagan_spielberg.htm .
[49] Cited in Richard Boylan, "The Man Who "Outed" the U.S. Saucer Program: Colonel Steve Wilson," http://www.drboylan.com/colbirb2.html .
[50] See Michael Salla, "Dr Dan Burisch, Project Lotus and Disclosure of the Extraterrestrial Presence," at http://exopolitics.org/Exo-Comment-12.htm .
[51] Out from under Majestic: Dan Burisch uncensored: A video interview with Dan Burisch - Part 2 Las Vegas, July 2006. Available online at: http://projectcamelot.org/dan_burisch_interview_transcript_2.html .
[52] There is public confirmation that McClelland began his training as a SpaceCraft Operator, and performed SCO duties, but no documentation has been found confirming that he completed his SCO training. See Michael Lindeman, "Ex-NASA Worker Says Space Agency Knows About UFOs," http://www.theforbiddenknowledge.com/hardtruth/nasa_knows_ufos.htm .
[53] Available online at: http://www.stargate-chronicles.com/background.html
[54] Clark McClelland, "A past Space Shuttle ScO, admits ET's are Real. And this ScO has seen them, himself with another witness!" UFODigest (August 7, 2008). Available online at: http://www.stargate-chronicles.com/release_mitchell.html .
[55] For further discussion, see Michael Salla, "Artistic Recreation of Extraterrestrial Visiting Space Shuttle released by former Space Craft Operator," http://exopolitics.org/Exo-Comment-77.htm .
[56] Richard Boylan, "Official Within MJ-12 UFO-Secrecy Management Group Reveals Insider Secrets," http://drboylan.com/wolfdoc2.html
[57] Quote from Jim Marrs, *Alien Agenda* (Harper Paperbacks, 1997) 270-71.
[58] "Mutual UFO Network Conference Presentation, May 1995, available online at: http://users.rcn.com/zap.dnai/schneidr.htm .
[59] He has written a book on his experiences titled, *Above Black: Project Preserve Destiny* (One Team Publishing, 1988).
[60] Dan Sherman, *Above Black: Project Preserve Destiny,* 134, 136.
[61] Cooper, "Origin, Identity, and Purpose of MJ-12," http://www.geocities.com/Area51/Shadowlands/6583/maji007.html .
[62] Maynard was a Disclosure Project witness. See "Testimony of Mr John Maynard (ret.) Defense Intelligence Agency: October 2000," *Disclosure,* ed., Steven Greer, 422.
[63] "Testimony of Mr John Maynard (ret.) Defense Intelligence Agency: October 2000," *Disclosure,* ed., Steven Greer, 422-23.
[64] Robert Collins, et. al., *Exempt from Disclosure*, 75.
[65] Charles Hall, *Millennium Hospitality III: The Road Home*, 196.
[66] Swan's role in Project Stargate is described by Russell Targ & Harold Puthoff, *Mind-Reach: Scientists Look at Psychic Ability* (Dell Publishing Co. Inc., 1977). Information is available online at: http://en.wikipedia.org/wiki/Ingo_Swann .
[67] Ingo Swann, *Penetration*, (Ingo Swann Books, 1998) 73-75.

[68] For further discussion, see: Michael Salla, "Extraterrestrials Among Us," *Exopolitics Journal,* 1:4 (2006): 284-300. Available online at: http://exopoliticsjournal.com/vol-1/1-4-Salla.htm
[69] For biographical information, see: http://en.wikipedia.org/wiki/Catherine_Austin_Fitts .
[70] Catherine Austin Fitts, "What's Up with the Black Budget," *Scoop Magazine*, available online at: http://www.scoop.co.nz/stories/HL0209/S00126.htm
[71] In private email communications with John Petersen, Joe Firmage and a third Board member during March 2008, none confirmed Ms Fitts version of events, or that she was present at meetings when extraterrestrial life was discussed. To varying degrees, they suggested there was no substance to her story. It was suggested that she was untrustworthy and had contrived the story.
[72] Private email received on Thursday, March 27, 2008.
[73] See Galactic Freedom Day Declaration, www.galacticfreedomday.com .

Chapter Two

Human Rights Abuses at U.S. Government-Extraterrestrial Bases

Introduction[74]

I have so far reviewed the testimonies of witnesses who have claimed seeing extraterrestrials at classified facilities. Together with evidence of secret agreements between elements of the U.S. government and extraterrestrials, this raises the possibility of a number of joint bases where extraterrestrials and government/military personnel collaborate on technologically advanced projects. Researchers such as Dr Richard Sauder have done extensive archival research that substantiates the existence of deep underground military bases in the U.S., that are highly classified and estimated to number over 120.[75] Some of these bases are even located under the oceans and this network of underground and underwater bases appear to be connected by a high speed underground MagLev rail networks.[76] In the first chapter, it's worth recalling that Clifford Stone claimed that he was taken from an underground location at the Pentagon by monorail to another military facility where he met a Gray extraterrestrial. Along with Saunder's pioneering research, this raises the possibility that some of these classified underground bases are joint government extraterrestrial bases.

Furthermore, in the first chapter, I examined Charles Hall's claims that he saw senior USAF officers and personnel with Tall White extraterrestrials at a hidden mountain base in the Indian Springs area of Nellis Air Force base. Hall's claim of a secret underground/mountain base at Indian Springs was supported by a 1951 story by the Las Vegas Review-Journal concerning a classified housing project at Indian Springs in the early 1950s.[77] To date no above ground facility exists at Indian Springs that would explain how the vast outlay of expenditure at the time of 300 million dollars (2.5 billion in 2008 terms) was used. This suggests that a large underground facility was secretly built, and may have housed extraterrestrials as Hall claims. This chapter examines evidence of a joint U.S. government and extraterrestrial base where some of the classified projects involve human rights violations. This may have led to an undisclosed firefight between extraterrestrials and human security personnel. I begin with the testimony of Paul Bennewitz concerning the existence of an extraterrestrial base at Dulce, New Mexico.

Paul Bennewitz was an electronics specialist who in 1979 began to film, photograph, and electronically intercept what appeared to be extensive UFO activity and communications over the Manzano mountain range near Albuquerque, New Mexico. He traced this UFO activity to the vicinity of the Archuletta Mesa on Jicarilla Apache Reservation land near the town of Dulce. Bennewitz had earlier researched cattle mutilations in the region and civilians who claimed to have been abducted by extraterrestrials. Based on his film, photographic and electronic evidence, and his field research, Bennewitz concluded that an underground extraterrestrial base existed near Dulce. He believed the base played a role in both cattle mutilations and abduction of civilians.

In 1980, Bennewitz submitted his evidence to nearby Kirtland Air Force base to alert officials of the possibility that extraterrestrials were a threat to the nearby Manzano Nuclear Weapons Storage Area. The Air Force Office of Special Intelligence (AFOSI) quickly became involved in investigating Bennewitz's evidence. This led to what credible sources conclude was a disinformation campaign to discredit Bennewitz. Bennewitz's subsequent electronic evidence and field research alleging that extensive human rights abuses were occurring at the Dulce underground base became associated with the AFOSI disinformation campaign. Most UFO researchers concluded, after Bennewitz had suffered a nervous breakdown in 1987 and the AFOSI disinformation campaign became public knowledge, that Bennewitz had been too influenced by disinformation to be taken seriously.

The strongest support for Bennewitz's claims come from a number of individuals claiming to be 'whistleblowers' who in their capacity as former employees of corporations performing a variety of military contracts worked at or learned of the Dulce base, and subsequently revealed aspects of what had occurred there. A recurring feature of these whistleblower statements is testimony of a violent conflict in 1979 between U.S. military personnel and extraterrestrials at the base that led to a significant number of military fatalities. This seemed to confirm Bennewitz's claim of such a military conflict, and raises the possibility that the conflict's cause was related to his allegations of human rights abuses. Furthermore, Bennewitz's evidence provided an example of how money illegally siphoned from the U.S. economy into 'black budget' programs estimated to be as high as 1.7 trillion dollars annually, related to an extraterrestrial presence.[78]

Was Bennewitz just an overzealous UFO researcher who accidentally tapped into highly classified Air Force research and development projects? Or was he an electronics genius who single handedly uncovered the existence of a joint U.S. government-extraterrestrial underground base where gross human rights violations happened to abducted civilians? Pursuit of clear answers to these questions have spurred a number of books, articles, and Internet websites.[79] The quality of answers has varied greatly since all who have written of Dulce use mixed primary and secondary sources cross-referencing one another without confirming validity and origins. This has led to much confusion and uncertainty for those seeking clear answers to what was occurring under the ground at Dulce. A 2005 book by Greg Bishop analyzing the material on Bennewitz was based on interviews of some key individuals who knew or worked with Bennewitz.[80] While Bishop's book does well in organizing and analyzing the extensive material on Bennewitz, it adopts the unfortunate approach that Bennewitz had been disinformed by an officially sanctioned deception program.[81] Bishop's book ignores objective analysis of whistleblowers and witnesses who supported Bennewitz's claims concerning an extraterrestrial base at Dulce. Bishop concluded that these sources were part of an elaborate disinformation program intended to distract Bennewitz away from highly classified activities at Kirtland Air Force base.

A more objective effort to analyze the primary source material available on Dulce is needed to help answer key questions about the alleged base at Dulce. Most important of these questions is whether human rights violations occurred there as a result of extraterrestrial and U.S. government activities. This chapter helps answer questions arising from primary source material on what has occurred and may still be occurring at Dulce, and elsewhere around the planet at joint government extraterrestrial bases. If Sauder is correct about the number of deep underground classified facilities, the events at Dulce may be the tip of the iceberg of human rights abuses occurring around the planet with government and extraterrestrial complicity.

Paul Bennewitz and Evidence of an Extraterrestrial Base at Dulce

In the mid 1970's, a wave of cattle mutilations began occurring in New Mexico. Paul Bennewitz, a local Albuquerque businessman and electronics specialist, became keenly interested in the phenomenon.[82] In 1979, he took field trips with Gabe Valdez, a well known New Mexico State Trooper to investigate some of these mutilations. They concluded that the mutilations were not caused by anything 'natural'. Bennewitz soon began noticing an unusual amount of UFO activity in the Northern New Mexico area. Using his film and photographic equipment, he began accumulating evidence of what appeared to be UFO's.[83] He then began intercepting radio and video transmissions that he believed were used by different extraterrestrial visitors. He traced these transmissions to a base located under the Archuletta Mesa, near Dulce.

Bennewitz believed he had identified the radio and video frequencies used for communications between the extraterrestrial piloted ships and ground controllers at the underground Dulce base. Bennewitz then created a communication system that he believed enabled him to electronically communicate with what he now was convinced were extraterrestrial piloted ships flying to and from the base. Furthermore, Bennewitz began to track the electronic frequencies extraterrestrials used to control individuals who had been abducted and implanted with miniature electronic devices. Bennewitz tracked down some of these individuals and conducted interviews to detect what they could remember of their extraterrestrial encounters.

Bennewitz eventually issued a report, *Project Beta*, in which he summarized the evidence of his filming, photographing, electronic interception, communications and fieldwork:

> 1. Two years continuous recorded electronic surveillance and tracking with d.F. 24 hr/day data of alien ships plus 6,000 feet motion picture of same.

2. Detection and disassembly of alien communication and video channels - both.
3. Constant reception of video from alien ship and underground base view-screen; typical alien, humanoid and at times apparent homo sapien.
4. A case history of an encounter victim in New Mexico which lead to the communications link and discovery that apparently all encounter victims have deliberate alien implants along with obvious accompanying scars. The victim's catscan. Five other cases were verified.
5. Established constant direct communication with the alien using a computer and a form of hex decimal code communication was instigated apparently.
6. Through the alien communication loop, the true underground base location.[84]

All of the evidence he gathered pointed to the existence of an underground base at Dulce used by different extraterrestrial races. The communications, video images, and the abductee testimonies he found, provided further information that Bennewitz used to understand what was occurring at the base and its national security implications.

Bennewitz arranged for one of the abductees, Myrna Hansen, to be placed under hypnotic regression by Dr Leo Sprinkle from the University of Wyoming.[85] Under hypnosis she claimed to have been abducted in 1980 along with her son, and taken inside an underground extraterrestrial base. She proceeded to describe humans placed in cold storage, and large vats filled with the remains of cattle and human body parts.[86] Hansen also reported that some device was implanted in her "so that the aliens could monitor and control her thoughts."[87] Bennewitz was convinced of Hansen's story when he was able to identify and track the electronic signal emitted from the implant inside Hansen. This became the subject of his initial public letters to other UFO researchers.[88] Bennewitz was able to track the implant signals to Dulce which he was convinced was the underground base where the extraterrestrials had taken Hansen.[89] Hansen's testimony seemed far fetched, but combined with Bennewitz's electronic interceptions, video recordings and communications, it began to appear possible. A researcher using the acronym, Branton, published a book detailing Hansen's and other abductee testimonies concerning abuses at the Dulce base.[90] Bennewitz became convinced that his evidence portrayed an overall pattern of extraterrestrial deception, responsibility for cattle mutilations and massive human rights violations of abducted civilians.[91]

Bennewitz's electronic interceptions and interviews led to him quickly learning much about the activities at the Dulce underground base, the extensive extraterrestrial presence there and the sizable number of civilians abducted and forcibly taken to the base. His electronic intercepts and communications provided him basic information concerning a military conflict having occurred at the Dulce base between extraterrestrials and U.S. military personnel.[92] Bennewitz subsequently reported his findings to the Air Force Office of Special Intelligence (AFOSI) at nearby Kirtland Air force in October 1980. He believed the extraterrestrials presented a threat to the nearby Manzano Nuclear Weapons Storage Area. In an official report signed by Major Thomas Cseh on October 28, 1980 and later released under the Freedom of Information Act, Major Cseh wrote:

> On 26 Oct 80, SA [Special Agent] Doty, with the assistance of JERRY MILLER, GS-15, Chief, Scientific Advisor for Air Force Test and Evaluation Center, KAFB, interviewed Dr. Bennewitz at his home in the Four Hills section of Albuquerque, which is adjacent to the northern boundary of Manzano Base.... Dr. Bennewitz has been conducting independent research into Aerial Phenomena for the last 15 months. Dr. Bennewitz also produced several electronic recording tapes, allegedly showing high periods of electrical magnetism being emitted from Manzano/Coyote Canyon area. Dr. Bennewitz also produced several photographs of flying objects taken over the general Albuquerque area. He has several pieces of electronic surveillance equipment pointed at Manzano and is attempting to record high frequency electrical beam pulses. Dr. Bennewitz claims these Aerial Objects produce these pulses. ...After analyzing the data collected by Dr. Bennewitz, Mr MILLER related the evidence clearly shows that some type of unidentified aerial

> objects were caught on film; however, no conclusions could be made whether these objects pose a threat to Manzano/Coyote Canyon areas.[93]

When AFOSI took no action, Bennewitz approached New Mexico Senator, Harrison Schmitt, who demanded to know why Bennewitz's claims were not being investigated. Frustrated by the lack of official support for his discoveries, Bennewitz issued a detailed report titled Project Beta and continued to accumulate data on extraterrestrial operations in the area.[94]

Based on his intercepted electronic communications, Bennewitz revealed in his Project Beta report the following about the size of the base and the extraterrestrial population:

> The total alien basing area apparently contains several cultures, (all under the designation 'unity') and is approx 3km wide by 8km long and is located in the middle of nowhere on the Jicarilla Indian Reservation west of Dulce, NM. Based on the number of ships presently in this area, the total alien population is estimated to be at least 2,000 and most likely more.[95]

Bennewitz's work had attracted much attention and soon led to a covert effort by AFOSI to discredit him. In a 1989 Mutual UFO Network conference, a prominent UFO specialist, William Moore, caused an uproar when he openly declared that in 1982 he had been co-opted into this effort. He said he began passing on information about Bennewitz's activities to AFOSI and played a role in feeding disinformation to Bennewitz. Moore described the events as follows:

> … when I first ran into the disinformation operation... being run on Bennewitz... it seemed to me... I was in a rather unique position. There I was with my foot... in the door of a secret counterintelligence game that gave every appearance of being somehow directly connected to a high-level government UFO project, and, judging by the positions of the people I knew to be directly involved with it, definitely had something to do with national security! There was no way I was going to allow the opportunity to pass me by

> without learning at least something about what was going on. I would play the disinformation game, get my hands dirty just often enough to lead those directing the process into believing that I was doing exactly what they wanted me to do, and all the while continue to burrow my way into the matrix so as to learn as much as possible about who was directing it and why.[96]

The public declaration by Moore confirmed that Bennewitz had, at least partially, succeeded in electronically monitoring extraterrestrial craft in the area, communicating with extraterrestrials at the Dulce base, and monitoring extraterrestrial control of abductees in the area. This might help explain why AFOSI began what emerged as an intense covert effort to discredit Bennewitz. The basic strategy in the campaign by AFOSI was to suggest that the most egregious aspects of Bennewitz's claims - the Dulce base being a site where humans were abducted for genetic experiments - was disinformation rather than accurate reports of the extraterrestrial presence in the Northern New Mexico area. Indeed Moore argued that by the time he met him in 1982, the bulk of Bennewitz's information was already disinformation fed by AFOSI.[97]

Many UFO researchers despaired of finding the truth of what was happening at Dulce due to the fog of disinformation rumored to be circulating around Bennewitz, and the various activities orchestrated by AFOSI and/or other intelligence services that targeted Bennewitz and his supporters.[98] The dominant view was that Bennewitz was definitely on to something but had succumbed to beliefs that discredited his early and most persuasive work. One UFO researcher claimed that the disinformation was passed on through the intercepted communications: "Where the truth began and ended in the information collected by Bennewitz is debatable but one thing is without doubt true - the content of the intercepted messages certainly caused Bennewitz to become a paranoid and deluded man who eventually suffered a colossal nervous breakdown in 1985."[99] The intensity of his investigations and the official response had a heavy personal toll on Bennewitz causing his nervous breakdown. He later withdrew entirely from any public discussion of the Dulce base and ended his involvement with UFO issues.

Despite his controversial withdrawal from the UFO scene, Bennewitz's credibility as an undisputed electronics genius was not at question, and the extensive database of films, photos and raw electronic communications data of UFO/ET phenomenon, was powerful evidence that something was occurring around the Archuletta Mesa. Veteran UFO researcher William Hamilton thoroughly researched Bennewitz's claims and concluded that Bennewitz was "on the right track in his attempts to locate the underground alien facility in the vicinity of Dulce."[100]

Aside from the raw physical evidence accumulated by Bennewitz, a number of whistleblowers have come forward to give further testimony and even physical evidence of a joint extraterrestrial government underground base at Dulce. They allege that human rights violations happened to abducted civilians. Before analyzing whistleblower testimony concerning the Dulce underground base, I will briefly outline the legal position of whistleblowers when disclosing classified information at national security facilities. This will help explain the difficulty in confirming the professional backgrounds of individuals who have stepped forward to confirm the allegations of massive human rights abuses at joint government-extraterrestrial underground bases.

Whistleblowers and National Security

'Whistleblowers' have been described as courageous employees who often with the zeal of a martyr disclose unethical or criminal government/corporate practices that involve great damage to the public interest.[101] Often the short-term result for whistleblowers is the loss of jobs, reputation, economic security, and even life. A whistleblower can be defined as any employee of any branch of government or corporation who publicly discloses unethical or corrupt practices of a government agency/corporation violating the law and/or damaging the public interest. There are an extensive series of state and federal whistleblower laws affecting those who come forward to disclose such practices and risk their own careers, reputations and physical safety.[102] Employment in government agencies/corporations involving projects with national security implications, guarantees whistleblower protection laws for employees with some important qualifications. This is evidenced by the Basic Federal Whistleblower Statute concerning National

Security Whistleblowers (5 USC 2302).[103] The relevant section of this Statute [5 USC Sec. 2302. (8) (A)] concerns the prohibition of action taken against an employee (whistleblower) because of any disclosure of information that the employee believes is evidence of "a violation of any law, rule or regulation," or "an abuse of authority, or "substantial and specific danger to public health or safety." The relevant section then states the critical qualifying condition: "if such disclosure is not specifically prohibited by law and if such information is not specifically required by Executive order to be kept secret in the interest of national defense or the conduct of foreign affairs."

As evident in the qualifying statement, whistleblowers are not permitted to disclose information if such disclosure compromises national security. This means that if one is employed in a government agency and/or corporation working on a classified project with national security implications, such individuals do not receive protection under Federal Whistleblower statutes for publicly disclosing classified information. Furthermore, if government/corporate employees sign contracts that permit severe penalties for disclosing classified information, such individuals essentially sign away their constitutional rights. They have no legal recourse to prevent the imposition of even the most draconian penalties. Consequently, if employees witness, for instance, egregious human rights abuses committed in the operation of classified projects, they have no legal protection if choosing to disclose this to the general public.[104]

Even more challenging for any whistleblower witnessing abuses at any facility related to extraterrestrial affairs is that the existence of such facilities is very highly classified. This is confirmed in the testimonies of whistleblowers in the first chapter who revealed the extraordinary levels of secrecy surrounding extraterrestrial related activities. In chapter four, I will show how military personnel in extraterrestrial related projects are managed in ways to minimize security leaks by not having on their service records any mention of training or assignments related to extraterrestrial affairs. In some cases, this can even extend to removing from the public record all documentation of any employee at facilities involving extraterrestrial life or technology. So employment and educational records of individuals working at secret underground facilities may be redacted or removed entirely as a standard security procedure to discourage employees from becoming whistleblowers. I will show how this becomes a problem when examining whistleblowers confirming aspects of Bennewitz's testimony.

Military Confrontation at the Dulce Underground Base

Despite the danger in coming forward to reveal the existence of a classified military facility, a number of whistleblowers have testified about the existence of the Dulce base. This helps confirm that such a secret facility is indeed conducting a range of projects that focus on genetic experiments, and human rights abuse of abducted civilians as Bennewitz claimed. A number of whistleblowers have referred to a military confrontation at Dulce between extraterrestrials and U.S. military personnel. The confrontation likely emerged from a conflict over activities being conducted at Dulce, some of which involved human rights abuses.

Phil Schneider claims he worked as a geological engineer in the construction of the Dulce base, and other underground bases in the U.S., and around the globe. In a 1995 lecture, Schneider gave the following details of his background and of a military confrontation at Dulce:

> To give you an overview of basically what I am, I started off and went through engineering school. Half of my school was in that field, and I built up a reputation for being a geological engineer, as well as a structural engineer with both military and aerospace applications. I have helped build two main bases in the United States that have some significance as far as what is called the New World Order [a UN run world secretly controlled by 'Tall Gray' or 'Tall White' extraterrestrials]. The first base is the one at Dulce, New Mexico. I was involved in 1979 in a firefight with alien humanoids, and I was one of the survivors. I'm probably the only talking survivor you will ever hear. Two other survivors are under close guard. I am the only one left that knows the detailed files of the entire operation. Sixty-six secret service agents, FBI, Black Berets and the like, died in that firefight. I was there.[105]

Schneider described the cause of the 1979 military confrontation as little more than an 'accident' arising from drilling for a planned extension of the Dulce base:

> I was involved in building an addition to the deep underground military base at Dulce, which is probably the deepest base. It goes down seven levels and over 2.5 miles deep.... As I was headed down there, we found ourselves amidst a large cavern that was full of outer-space aliens, otherwise known as large Grays. I shot two of them. At that time, there were 30 people down there. About 40 more came down after this started, and all of them got killed. We had surprised a whole underground base of existing aliens. Later, we found out that they had been living on [in] our planet for a long time... This could explain a lot of what is behind the theory of ancient astronauts.[106]

An important difference between Schneider's and Bennewitz's accounts of Dulce is that Bennewitz referred to Dulce exclusively as an extraterrestrial base which he was electronically monitoring. Schneider instead described an extraterrestrial facility underneath a U.S. government facility. He described a seven level U.S. military facility that had 'accidentally' been built on top of an ancient extraterrestrial base. Schneider believed that his job was to simply extend the existing base rather than attacking extraterrestrials for an undisclosed purpose. The unlikelihood that the Dulce facility was 'accidentally' built on an ancient extraterrestrial base suggests that Schneider was only partly informed of the true nature of his mission and what was occurring on the lower levels. The more likely scenario was that Schneider had to assist U.S. military forces to access the innermost layers of the Dulce facility, level 7, that had been closed off and where the true cause of a dispute between extraterrestrials and military personnel lay.

Sometime in 1993 Schneider quit working for his various corporate clients that serviced military contracts. He became convinced of a plot by the "Tall Gray" extraterrestrials to develop a New World Order dominated by the United Nations that they would be secretly controlling. He subsequently began a series of public lectures revealing the activities at the underground bases he helped construct. He also revealed the role of extraterrestrial races in infiltrating national governments and of them being the true architects of a New World Order. Schneider gave a keynote lecture at a MUFON conference in May 1995, and was found dead in his apartment seven months later in January 1996.[107] Circumstances surrounding the death of Schneider and his autopsy report led many to declare that Schneider had been murdered for going public with his knowledge of extraterrestrials and the secret underground base.[108]

As mentioned in chapter one, no public documentation has been made available to confirm Schneider's professional background. If Schneider was telling the truth about his experiences at Dulce the lack of public documentation reveals that he was subjected to a security procedure whereby this would be expunged as a condition of his employment. Despite this lack of public documentation, Schneider's testimony, his clear knowledge of geological engineering, and his mysterious death all support his central thesis that an underground base exists at Dulce. More importantly, his testimony suggests that a military confrontation between extraterrestrials and elite U.S. military forces occurred at the lowest level of this underground facility.

Supporting testimony of the existence of a joint government-extraterrestrial base and a military conflict there in 1979 comes from Bob Lazar. Lazar's background was discussed in the first chapter. To briefly repeat, he worked for a few months in 1988 at the S-4 Nevada facility on reverse-engineering the propulsion and power system of extraterrestrial craft. Lazar revealed that prior to working on the extraterrestrial craft he was required to read 200 pages of briefing documents in preparation for his job.[109] He recalled that the briefing document mentioned a battle between extraterrestrials and humans at a secret base in 1979. He said that the conflict was caused by a security guard who tried to take a weapon into the extraterrestrial area, resulting in fatal wounds to security personnel. Lazar's recollection of the briefing document he read in 1988 is very likely referring to the 1979 Dulce firefight.

Attempts to confirm Lazar's employment and educational background have not been very successful which have led to heated attacks against his credibility.[110] This may be due to a practice claimed to be standard for civilians who work under contract to corporations and/or military/intelligence agencies on classified projects involving extraterrestrials. This practice is the removal of all public records of contracted employees as a security precaution in the event they intentionally or unintentionally publicly disclose what is occurring in such projects. For example, Lazar, found that after leaving the secret S-4 facility (Dreamland) in Nevada in 1988, where his job was to reverse engineer the propulsion and power system of recovered extraterrestrial craft, his birth certificate was no longer available at the hospital where he was born. His school, college and all employment records also disappeared – he simply ceased to officially exist![111] It was only due to the dedicated investigative journalism efforts of George Knapp, a prominent Las Vegas television personality, that some of Lazar's background was eventually verified. Most significant was his employment at the Los Alamos National Laboratory after officials previously denied he had ever worked there.[112]

Another 'whistleblower' that lends credence to the possibility that a firefight had occurred between U.S. military forces and extraterrestrials in a secret underground base was (Dr) Michael Wolf. Wolf's book *Catchers of Heaven* described a firefight between extraterrestrials and elite U.S. military forces that had occurred in 1975 at the Groom Lake, Nevada facility and may have been related to what occurred later at the nearby Dulce:

> The Grays shared certain of their technological advances with military/intelligence scientists, apparently often while prisoner "guests" within secure underground military installations in Nevada and New Mexico. The extraterrestrials have given the U.S. government some of their antigravity craft and a huge amount of fuel (element 115). On May 1, 1975 during one such technology exchange in Nevada, a demonstration of a small extraterrestrial antimatter reactor, the lead Grey asked the Colonel in charge of the Delta Forces guarding the extraterrestrials to remove all their rifles and bullets from the room, (so that they would not accidentally discharge during the energy emissions.) The guards refused, and in the ensuing commotion a guard opened fire on the Grays. One alien, two scientists and 41

> military personnel were killed. One guard was left alive to attest that the ETs apparently used directed mental energy in self-defense to kill the other attacking Delta Forces. Dr. Wolf states that "this incident ended certain exchanges with (the Grays)." [113]

There are important parallels with the 'Dulce war' in the description of the 'Nevada' confrontation described by Wolf, to that described by Schneider. In both cases, a significant number of U.S. military personnel are killed after a violent confrontation with extraterrestrials. These parallels suggest that Wolf was narrating either an entirely different conflict or one in a series of conflicts. Wolf further disclosed in an interview that he had worked at the Dulce laboratory, thereby providing more confirmation for the existence of this secret underground base, key to the claim made by Bennewitz.[114]

As mentioned in the first chapter, there is controversy over Wolf's credibility as a witness. Wolf claims to have been a former scientist and policy maker on extraterrestrial affairs who served from 1979 on the coordinating policy group for extraterrestrial affairs.[115] Wolf claimed that he was being directed by his superiors to participate in a controlled leak of information to the UFO community while providing a fall back of 'plausible deniability' for the government.[116] All public records of Wolf's advanced university degrees and contractual services to different military/intelligence/national security branches of government were allegedly eliminated. This made it very difficult if not impossible to confirm his background and substantiate the startling information he was releasing. He claimed that this removal of public records was 'standard practice' for all civilians employed by either corporations and/or the U.S. military in clandestine projects involving extraterrestrials.[117]

Based on the Schneider, Lazar and Wolf cases I conclude that a standard practice exists for civilians contracted to corporations and/or military whereby their employment and public records are removed as a security precaution against either public disclosure of extraterrestrial related information. Nevertheless, all three were public figures who were interviewed by a number of researchers, and went on the public record with their testimonies. The next alleged testimony I examine is the most controversial of all the whistleblowers to have come forward regarding a joint government extraterrestrial base at Dulce and of a military conflict there in 1979.

In 1987, Thomas Castello, an alleged whistleblower, released 30 photos, video and a set of papers to UFO researchers. Apparently this was physical evidence of the joint U.S. government/extraterrestrial base at Dulce, New Mexico. The collection came to be called the 'Dulce Papers', and provided graphic evidence of the operations of this secret underground facility. The Dulce Papers appeared to provide powerful support to Bennewitz's conclusions regarding activities at the underground base.[118] The Dulce Papers described genetic experimentation, development of human-extraterrestrial hybrids, use of mind control through advanced computers, cold storage of humans in liquid filled vats, and even that humans were a food source for extraterrestrial races. The papers were possible evidence that humans were used as little more than laboratory animals. Responsibility by extraterrestrial races working directly with different U.S. government agencies and U.S. corporations fulfilling 'black budget' military contracts in a joint base. If the papers were genuine, experiments and projects were being conducted involving human rights violations on a scale that exceeded even the darkest chapters of recent human history.

Castello claimed to have worked as a senior security officer at the base before 'quitting' the Dulce facility after a military confrontation occurred in 1979 between elite U.S. military personnel, base security guards, and resident extraterrestrials. Castello claimed he left his Dulce employers in 1979. After the subsequent release of the Dulce Papers in 1987, Castello gave a number of interviews and corresponded with UFO researchers before eventually vanishing from the scene. Castello's claims are outlined in two sources. First, the Dulce papers themselves presumably involving classified material taken from the base. Second, the interviews/correspondence Castello had with a number of UFO researchers. Much of Castello's material has since been circulated on the Internet and has been incorporated in a book titled *The Dulce Wars*.[119] His testimony and evidence therefore provide support for the claims by Schneider, Lazar and Wolf of the military conflict at Dulce in 1979.

Efforts to confirm Castello's employment background and therefore his credibility, as a whistleblower have not been successful. A number of UFO researchers were able to contact Castello before his eventual 'disappearance' in the late 1980s and were able to get answers to a series of questions.[120] According to both William Hamilton and 'Branton', UFO researchers had personally met with Castello and could vouch for his existence and credibility.[121] While the list of contacts and personal interviews with Castello are not extensive, it does appear that he was real. Given the incredible information he disclosed and his limited availability, this does open up the possibility that he was either genuinely frightened of going public or that his testimony was part of a disinformation campaign to discredit the Dulce underground base hypothesis.

It is uncertainty over Castello's background that led to most UFO researchers not taking seriously his claims supporting much of what Bennewitz had earlier reported. Bennewitz was by 1987 associated with a disinformation campaign led by Air Force Intelligence (AFOSI). It is worth exploring in some depth what Castello claimed to have experienced in the Dulce underground base. He provides the most extensive testimony of what may have occurred there.

In the Dulce papers and his personal testimonies Castello claims the existence of a seven level underground facility that jointly houses humans and different extraterrestrial races in Dulce, New Mexico. Castello claims that the humans employed at the base comprised scientists, security personnel, and employees from various corporations who were servicing military contracts.[122] There were four extraterrestrial races claimed to be working at Dulce: the standard 'short' Grays' from Zeta Reticulum (approx 4ft in height); tall Grays from Rigel, Orion (7 ft); and Reptilian species native to Earth; and reptilians from the Alpha Draconis star system (reptilians generally ranging from 6-8 ft). Castello claims that the earth based Reptilians, who he described as the 'working caste', were led by a winged Reptilian species he described as the Draco.[123] He said that the short grays (depicted in movies such as Close Encounters of the Third Kind) are subservient to the Draco Reptilians. Castello says he was employed as a 'Senior Security Technician' at the Dulce facility and that his primary job function was to sort out any security issues between the resident extraterrestrial races and the human employees at the base.[124]

Castello claimed that the different projects at Dulce involved reverse engineering of extraterrestrial technology, development of mind control methods; and genetic experiments involving cloning and creating human-extraterrestrial hybrids. Similar projects have been conducted at Montauk, Long Island and Brookhaven laboratories[125] and have been the subject of a number of other whistleblower testimonies.[126] Significantly, like Schneider, Castello claimed that Dulce was built over an ancient series of natural caverns that were used by extraterrestrials.[127]

Castello says that he directly witnessed the products of the trans-species genetic experiments in the sixth level of the facility. Most disturbing were his claims that abducted humans were subjected to various abuses. He said that a small band of human workers began to cooperate with some Reptilians from the worker caste, who also objected to the abuses occurring at Dulce, in a 'resistance movement'. Eventually, Castello described how an elite Delta force contingent attempted to destroy the 'resistance movement' in 1979:

> Ultimately, it ended when a military assault was initiated via the exit tunnels and they executed anybody on their list, human or reptilian. We fought back, but none of the working caste had weapons, nor did the human lab workers. Only the security force and a few computer workers had flash guns. It was a massacre. Every one was screaming and running for cover. The halls and tunnels were filled as full as possible. We believe it was the Delta Force [because of the uniforms and the method they used] that chose to hit at shift change, an effort that killed as many as named on their list.[128]

Castello claims he quit the facility, taking photos and a video recording eventually distributed to the general public as the Dulce Papers. William Hamilton thoroughly researched Castello's claims and concluded:

> It may be unpalatable to digest or believe Thomas' story. In fact, it seems like part of a living nightmare. There is

> evidence that something strange does go on at Dulce. Does Thomas have the answer? There may be a terrible truth hidden behind the continuing phenomena of UFO sightings, abductions, and animal mutilations. Our government intelligence agencies have had an ongoing watchful eye on all UFO activities for many decades now. This extraordinary phenomenon must have an extraordinary explanation. We may be only one outpost in a vast interstellar empire. [129]

Castello's claims and the evidence he provided supports much of what Bennewitz had concluded from his extensive electronic monitoring and field research. There are also important parallels with what was later claimed by Schneider, Lazar and Wolf.

Abductees Taken to Dulce and Subjected to Human Rights Abuses

Myrna Hansen was not the only person claiming to have been abducted by extraterrestrials and taken to Dulce, where she was subjected to medical experiments, and witnessed various forms of abuses on captive humans. Christa Tilton also claims to be an extraterrestrial abductee. According to Tilton, after the extraterrestrials abducted her into one of their ships, they took her to Dulce where she witnessed U.S. military personnel at the underground facility. A Gray extraterrestrial guided her down through various levels of the facility until she was taken to a room where a human doctor and another Gray extraterrestrial performed some kind of medical procedure:

> My guide smiled at me and told me he would be waiting outside and I would only be there for a few minutes. I began to cry.... The grey alien looked at me and turned around to continue what he was doing. The doctor called for more assistance and it was then that one other grey alien came in. The next thing I knew I was very drowsy. I knew I was being examined internally and when I lifted my head, I saw this horrid grey alien glaring at me with large black eyes. It was then I felt a stabbing pain. I screamed and then the human doctor stood next to me and rubbed something over my stomach. It was cold. The pain immediately subsided. I could

> not believe this was happening to me all over again. I begged for them to let me go, but they just kept on working very fast. After they were finished, I was told to get up and go into this small room and change back into my other clothes. I noticed blood, as if I had started my period. But, I continued to get dressed and when I came out I saw my guide speaking to the doctor in the corner of the room. I just stood there...helpless. I felt more alone then than I ever had in my life. I felt like a guinea pig. After we left that laboratory I was silent. I was angry at him for allowing this to happen to me 'again'. But he said it was necessary. Told me to forget.[130]

Tilton also described seeing humans in tanks as depicted in Castello's video and the Dulce Papers:

> I saw what looked to me to be people of all different types standing up against the wall inside a clear casing-like chamber. I went closer and it looked 'as if' they were wax figures. I could not understand what I was seeing. I also saw animals in cages. They were alive..." [131]

The alleged genetic experiments on abducted humans or those held captive at Dulce received more independent confirmation by (Dr) Daniel Burisch. Burisch claimed to have been secretly taken to Dulce to conduct classified microbiological experiments using extraterrestrial materials. Burisch declined to work in the project but revealed he heard the cries of humans who were detained in the facilities, and threatened by authorities who said they would turn him into a test subject if he didn't participate in the project. Burisch gave an extensive interview on his trip and experience at Dulce:

> … it came as quite the surprise to me that they could possibly be considering the usage of an alien retro-virus recombined with a terrestrial viral genome for possible use in biological-chemical warfare activities - or at least possible use in activities which could move towards biological warfare as applied terrestrially. But this was inconsistent … with my ethical boundaries. It would have exited the ethical boundaries that I place upon myself as a

> scientist… Therefore, my answer was no. And I thought that was it, no more participation.… They agreed to house me in the facility where I went with my cute little orange badge to a residential unit a little further down the tramline and one level below that. They did not change my orange badge when I went one level below. My experience in the time that I think I stayed in a residential unit there was horrifying. You know when you hear human beings screaming in pain? [132]

Burisch's testimony and credentials have been partially corroborated by William Hamilton in a 2006 book. In *Project Aquarius* Hamilton supplies documentary evidence and witness testimony supporting Burisch's claims.[133]

The testimonies of Hansen, Tilton and Burisch support the existence of the classified Dulce facilities and of covert biological projects that likely had military applications. One or more of these classified projects became an area of dispute between extraterrestrial races and clandestine government organizations. This dispute led to military hostilities that became known as the 'Dulce War'. The precise cause of this violent confrontation is unclear due to conflicting explanations of different witnesses examined so far. It may have been a simple mistake as Schneider claims, a misunderstanding as Lazar and Wolf suggest, or egregious human rights abuses as Castello and various abductees claim. What does emerge from the various testimonies is that a violent military confrontation did occur, and it produced a significant number of fatalities involving U.S. military personnel, Dulce security guards, and extraterrestrials.

Based on testimonies and evidence presented so far, it may be concluded that three possibilities stand out as the most likely explanations for what was occurring at Dulce.

1. A top secret joint extraterrestrial-government facility exists at Dulce that is (or was) conducting highly classified biological projects that involve(d) the abduction of human subjects whose rights are (were) severely violated.
2. The Dulce base exists (or existed) but reports of horrific abuses of abducted humans by extraterrestrials were part of a disinformation campaign designed to discredit Paul

Bennewitz and any legitimate research into extraterrestrial activities and secret government projects at Dulce.

3. All the stories about Dulce are disinformation designed to deliberately steer serious investigation away from classified projects elsewhere in New Mexico which Bennewitz had discovered through his electronic intercepts.[134]

The first possibility is supported by the testimonial evidence presented so far which substantiates Bennewitz's main claim of an extraterrestrial base at Dulce. Bennewitz never did realize that Dulce was in fact a joint government extraterrestrial base, and merely thought that the government had agreed to permit untrustworthy extraterrestrials to operate there.[135] The joint nature of the Dulce underground base is revealed by the additional witness testimony by Schneider, Lazar, Wolf, and the abductee, Christa Tilton. It is therefore highly likely that the real goal of the AFOSI disinformation campaign was to steer Bennewitz away from realizing Dulce was a joint government extraterrestrial base performing advanced biological research.

The second possibility needs to be considered. Except for the two abductee testimonies none of the other whistleblowers referred to the kinds of egregious extraterrestrial abuses presented by Castello and his evidence. It is possible that Castello was embellishing a genuine disclosure of a joint extraterrestrial-human base that Bennewitz had unwittingly began accumulating evidence of, with disinformation concerning horrific activities conducted by extraterrestrials. Castello may have been part of a disinformation campaign started by AFOSI (as Moore disclosed in 1989) to misdirect Bennewitz into believing that Dulce was exclusively an extraterrestrial base that was part of a world wide network of extraterrestrial bases abusing human abductees, manipulating the U.S. military, and seeking to take over the planet.[136]

The above scenario is consistent with the way in which disinformation works by exaggerating a factual process (i.e., human rights abuses at a joint government extraterrestrial base) by selectively distorting parts of it (i.e., extraterrestrials involved in human rights abuses).[137] Thus the truth that extraterrestrials were involved in government run genetic experiments involving abductees, was transformed into the idea that Dulce was exclusively an extraterrestrial base where abducted humans were stored in vats, used as a food source and a planetary takeover was underway. This ultimately would discredit those attempting to conduct an objective investigation into what was really occurring at Dulce and elsewhere. The testimonies by Hansen and Tilton, however, give rise to some caution in accepting the above second possibility. Their claims support Castello's testimony suggesting it may be more than simple disinformation.

The third possibility was that Bennewitz's claims were compromised by disinformation intended to steer him and other UFO researchers away from classified military projects elsewhere in New Mexico. This possibility is the least plausible so far given the additional witness testimonies. Nevertheless, in order to further determine the plausibility of each of these possibilities, I now consider the main criticisms made of Bennewitz's and others claims surrounding the Dulce underground base hypothesis.

Critique of the Dulce Underground Base Hypothesis

Ever since Bennewitz first began circulating his claims concerning the Dulce base in the early 1980s, and later physical evidence and personal testimonies provided by Schneider, Castello and others, there has predictably been intense criticism of the evidence supporting the Dulce base hypothesis. These criticisms fall into three categories. First are criticisms of physical evidence such as Bennewitz's intercepted electronic transmissions, communication transcripts, photos, video recordings, and the 'Dulce Papers' provided by Castello; and lack of physical evidence of an underground base in terms of entrances, air vents, etc. Second, are criticisms that focus on the credibility of Bennewitz, Schneider and Castello as reliable sources for the Dulce base hypothesis. Finally, there are criticisms that the whole Dulce underground base hypothesis is a clever disinformation strategy launched by intelligence services such as the Air Force Office of Special Intelligence (AFOSI) to divide the UFO community. I will examine each of these criticisms in turn.

Concerning Bennewitz's evidence, his photographs and films from 1980 clearly demonstrated some anomalous phenomenon acknowledged even by Air Force Intelligence. The difficulty lay in conclusively understanding what these showed.[138] Nevertheless, many UFO researchers believed this to be some of the strongest evidence yet captured on film of UFO's.[139] Bennewitz's electronic communications while again demonstrating something odd was occurring was subject to much controversy and was not conclusive proof. As far as the physical evidence found in the Dulce Papers was concerned, most researchers simply didn't take this seriously, assuming it part of the disinformation campaign earlier waged against Bennewitz. The lack of conclusive proof by way of photos, videos and physical sightings is reminiscent of the entire history of the UFO community's efforts to find sufficient evidence to persuade even the most skeptical of professionals.[140] This suggests that the validity of physical evidence surrounding Bennewitz's electronic records of UFO activity and extraterrestrial communication, as well as the Dulce Papers, will continue to be debated. A clear conclusion over the value of physical evidence provided in proving the existence of the Dulce base is therefore elusive.

Private investigators have explored the terrain where the underground base is allegedly located. The Archuletta Mesa is situated on Jicarilla Apache Indian reservation land. One investigator, Glen Campbell, found that there were no visible security restrictions on the land, no evidence of a military presence, and no concealed entrances, air vents, water intakes from the nearby Navaho river, etc. He subsequently concluded that there was no physical evidence of an underground base. [141] Other field investigators, however, have found evidence of strange occurrences in the area, lending support to the existence of a secret underground base.[142] For instance, Norio Harakaya visited Dulce with a Japanese film production crew in 1990 and concluded:

> I've been to Dulce with the Nippon Television Network crew and interviewed many, many people over there and came back with the firm conviction that something was happening around 10 to 15 years ago over there, including nightly sightings of strange lights and appearances of military jeeps and trucks.[143]

Harakaya's recollection is verified in an incident involving a New Mexico state trooper, Gabe Valdez who was accompanying Bennewitz and an Albuquerque news crew to the Archuletta Mesa,

Dulce. According to interviews conducted by Greg Bishop, Valdez confronted elite Delta forces that suddenly appeared in the Dulce area without any apparent reason:

> The Delta Force set down a few hundred feet away and disgorged a few of their black-clad personnel while Army tank trucks rolled out to refuel them. Still shaken and dubious about approaching the menacing group, Bennewitz and the news people asked Valdez if he knew what was going on. Unnerved but undaunted, Valdez approached the open door of the nearest helicopter. One of the officers shouted that Valdez was out of his jurisdiction, but the single-minded Valdez jumped aboard to take a close-up look at the identifying patches on one of the uniforms before he was threatened with more than a verbal warning and backed off.[144]

Some of the criticisms raised by Campbell might be explained in a number of ways. Castello and Schneider, for example, both described an extensive underground infrastructure that used advanced technology such as a high-speed rail link.[145] According to William Hamilton who conducted a thorough investigation of both Dulce and of claims of an underground ground system: "[t]here appears to be a vast network of tube shuttle connections under the U.S. which extends into a global system of tunnels and sub-cities."[146]

The existence of a secret underground rail system extending also to Dulce would make it possible for entrances to the Dulce base to be concealed in more secure areas. Air circulation and water could be provided in other ways by those possessing the advanced technology to do so. This suggests that criticism of a lack of physical evidence on Jicarilla Apache land supporting a secret underground base is not conclusive, and even conflicts with other testimonies of mysterious military troop movements and anomalous sightings in the area .

The covert disinformation campaign launched by AFOSI against Bennewitz suggests that the physical evidence he had of an underground base in the area, and the public support he attracted, were perceived to be a national security threat. This covert disinformation campaign that began in 1980 suggests that criticisms of the physical evidence provided by Bennewitz, Castello and Schneider, are not conclusive and may themselves be part of an ongoing disinformation campaign. Consequently, criticism of the lack of physical evidence for the existence of an underground base in Dulce fails to dismiss the Dulce base hypothesis.

The second set of criticisms focus on the credibility of the whistleblowers/witnesses who provided evidence or testimony of the Dulce base. Establishing credibility in a field rife with disinformation, intimidation and official efforts to discredit expert witnesses and 'whistleblowers' requires some flexibility in analyzing whistleblower behavioral and/or personality characteristics. A 'nervous breakdown', 'refusal to give interviews', or use of 'cover identities', for instance, may be more a result of covert intimidation than a sign of an individual lacking credibility. Focusing on the mental or health problems encountered by whistleblowers/witnesses advocating the Dulce base hypothesis may amount to little more than veiled personal attacks against the credibility of the principle advocates of the hypothesis. For instance, in an article that is critical of evidence for the Dulce base, the writer Roy Lawhon, glosses over the challenges faced in establishing the credibility of the three principle witnesses/whistleblowers advocating the Dulce Underground base hypothesis - Bennewitz, Castello and Schneider. Lawhon finishes his description of their respective claims with references to a range of personal problems or behaviors each exhibited in a way that appears to be little more than a veiled attack on their credibility.[147] He refers to Bennewitz being "committed for a time to a mental hospital", and then becoming a "reclusive, refusing to talk about UFOs."[148] As mentioned earlier, Bennewitz became the subject of an intense disinformation campaign, public scrutiny, attacks on his credibility, and unusual activities being directed against him that finally led to him having a nervous breakdown. This doesn't affect the quality of his material nor his credibility, but only demonstrates that in intense circumstances, individuals may succumb to the psychological pressure directed against them.

Lawhon repeats unquoted sources that Schneider "had severe brain damage and was also a paranoid schizophrenic." [149] This is probably the most unfair of the criticisms raised by Lawhon.

Schneider spent nearly two years on the lecture circuit (1993-95) candidly revealing his activities while an employee for corporations that built the Dulce and other underground bases. There were ample opportunities for his integrity and mental resilience to be tested, and it appears that he did not disappoint his growing number of supporters.[150] He gave the appearance of a man who knew his life would soon end either from natural causes (he had terminal cancer) or from being murdered. His apparent 'suicide' had the tell tale signs of murder and was not seriously pursued by public authorities.[151] Schneider's testimony and the physical evidence he presented at his lectures represents the most solid whistleblower disclosure available on the existence of the Dulce Base. His scars and injuries may well be physical evidence of a firefight between extraterrestrials and elite U.S. troops having occurred at Dulce in 1979.

Finally, moving on to Castello, Lawhon concludes that Castello "has only provided stories, nothing solid, and has yet to come forward in person." He also says that there "is some doubt as to whether he actually exists."[152] While relatively few researchers can vouch for Castello's existence, that does not exclude the possibility that he was a whistleblower revealing classified information. If so, he would be subject to arrest or other official efforts to 'silence' him, if he publicly emerged. This may explain his mysterious movements and disappearance. His testimony and the Dulce Papers, on their own, lack persuasiveness and may contain embellishments. However, it's worth pointing out that many aspects of his testimony were consistent with what the abductees, Hansen and Tilton, claimed they witnessed. Castello's emergence, if part of an AFOSI disinformation strategy, nevertheless suggests some intelligence agencies were trying to discredit Bennewitz's claims by embellishing some of its key elements. In conclusion, criticisms of the credibility of the principal advocates of the Dulce base hypothesis fail to be persuasive.

The third set of criticisms is best expressed in Greg Bishop's book, *Project Beta.* Bishop focuses on William Moore's 1989 confession at a MUFON conference that he had been co-opted into a covert effort by AFOSI to feed disinformation to Bennewitz in order to discredit him. Bishop elaborates upon the consequences of Moore's confession that Bennewitz had been fed a steady diet of disinformation to arrive at a "science fiction story" about underground extraterrestrial base conducting experiments on abducted humans:

> … with conditioning by repetition and sometimes not-so-gentle prodding from the intelligence community, Bennewitz's science fiction story came to be accepted over time, mostly by UFO buffs and those who thrive on scary rumors … From this mélange of disinformation, Project Beta took shape. [153]

Bishop believes that the purpose of disinformation concerning Dulce was designed to take Bennewitz's attention away from Kirtland Air Force Base where Bennewitz had electronically intercepted some highly classified communications:

> When Bennewitz returned to Albuquerque, he told his Air Force contacts … about his trips out to Dulce and his suspicions that the "alien base" … was probably located there. This was the best news that they had heard in months, since it meant that Bennewitz's attention was starting to turn away from Kirtland. They began to devise a far-reaching plan that would keep him looking permanently at this little hamlet near the Colorado border, and away from the beehive of activity at Kirtland… [154]

While furious that one UFO researcher would actively participate in a disinformation campaign against another researcher, many UFO researchers were quick to accept Moore's story. The most bizarre aspects of Bennewitz's claims, human rights abuses involving extraterrestrial abductions, cold storage of humans and underground vats filled with cattle and human parts were concluded to be disinformation. Bennewitz's claims had been gaining widespread support in the UFO community and had been supported by researchers such as William Hamilton, and the more controversial John Lear.

Some well-established UFO researchers believed that Lear's and Hamilton's claims, reflecting Bennewitz's statements about the Dulce underground base, would damage legitimate UFO research.[155] When it was learned that John Lear had been invited to host the

1989 Mutual UFO Network (MUFON) conference, for instance, prominent MUFON members began to resign in protest.[156] Many UFO researchers did not believe that Bennewitz's electronic interceptions, interpretations of the data, and interviews with abductees, were sufficient proof of an underground extraterrestrial base at Dulce. Bennewitz's claims of extraterrestrials committing gross human rights violations at the base were widely dismissed as little more than disinformation even by those who believed in his integrity and the quality of the hard evidence he had compiled.[157]

The view that disinformation played a major role in Bennewitz developing his views concerning the Dulce base and human rights abuses is easily overruled. He had already compiled an extensive database of information based on his two years of electronic surveillance and interviews with Hansen, prior to approaching AFOSI in October, 1980. Consequently, Bennewitz had already developed many of his views about Dulce **before** AFOSI began to 'allegedly' feed him disinformation. Furthermore, his views were also formed **before** his subsequent meeting with Moore in 1982 who admitted to passing on AFOSI disinformation. It is likely that Bennewitz's observation of UFO/ET activity in the area, electronic monitoring of radio and video transmissions, and his electronic communications, leading up to and including the 'Dulce War', gave him an accurate overall picture of what was occurring in the base. The more likely explanation is that U.S. intelligence services were in damage control mode after Bennewitz's intercepts of electronic communications between extraterrestrial ships and the Dulce base. The even more revealing evidence and testimony provided by Castello, and later by Schneider, became intertwined with disinformation that was actively being fed into the public debate surrounding the Dolce base hypothesis.

Criticism that the most alarming aspects of the Dulce base hypothesis, extraterrestrial human rights abuses, etc., was simply AFOSI disinformation, fails to take into account how disinformation is used as a standard tool by the intelligence community to create confusion and prevent discovery of precisely what is occurring.[158] Bishop's book is arguably the best example of efforts to portray Bennewitz as the unfortunate victim of a military intelligence deception program, dismissing much of the whistleblower testimony supporting Bennewitz.[159] Given the independent nature of the whistleblower and abductee testimony, and the credibility of many of the witnesses, I conclude that a joint government extraterrestrial base did exist at Dulce, and that military conflict occurred there in 1979.

I now return to the three possibilities raised earlier concerning the Dulce underground base hypothesis:

1. A top secret joint extraterrestrial-government facility exists at Dulce that is (or was) conducting highly classified biological projects that involve(d) the abduction of human subjects whose rights are (were) severely violated.
2. The Dulce base exists (or existed) but reports of horrific abuses of abducted humans by extraterrestrials were part of a disinformation campaign designed to discredit Paul Bennewitz and any legitimate research into extraterrestrial activities and secret government projects at Dulce.
3. All the stories about Dulce are disinformation designed to deliberately steer serious investigation away from classified projects elsewhere in New Mexico which Bennewitz had discovered through his electronic intercepts.[160]

Based on the evidence presented thus far, and the lack of conclusive criticism of this evidence, the third possibility can be dismissed. This leads to the conclusion that a secret joint government-extraterrestrial base did exist at Dulce, and that military extraterrestrial conflict did occur over issues most likely involving perceptions of treaty violations by one or both sides. Reports of human rights abuses against civilians abducted for various classified projects at the base, while not conclusive, have sufficient evidentiary support to warrant further investigation by responsible government authorities and human rights organizations. Such abuses appear to have been conducted as part of genetic programs sponsored by government authorities that were assisted by resident extraterrestrials. Stories of extraterrestrials using humans as a food source and similar forms of extreme human rights violations were likely part of the disinformation campaign designed to steer attention away from the U.S. government's role in the abuses occurring at Dulce.

Conclusion: Political Implications of Alleged Human Rights Abuses at Dulce

The whistleblower testimonies examined in this chapter persuasively point to the existence of the Dulce base as a former and/or current joint U.S. government-extraterrestrial underground facility that operated/operates without Congressional and Executive Office oversight. The testimonies further support the view that the 'Dulce war' did involve armed conflict between U.S. military forces, Base Security Personnel, and resident extraterrestrials in 1979. While the precise cause of the military confrontation remains unclear, it appears that one or both sides were not keeping commitments specified in an undisclosed treaty. This 'treaty' most likely was the result of a series of meetings and agreements initiated during the Eisenhower administration, discussed in chapter one. There is cause to believe gross human rights violations may have played a role in sparking the conflict. Disinformation was used to distract researchers from the truth that Dulce was a joint government extraterrestrial facility where U.S. government authorities were fully complicit in human rights violations. Some of these violations involved indefinite detention of captive humans in cells and advanced storage devices (vats) that may have been part of a classified project for long term interstellar travel. Similar human rights abuses may still be occurring in other possible joint government-extraterrestrial bases in the U.S. and other countries around the planet, such as at Pine Gap, Australia.[161]

The immediate political fall out from the 'Dulce Wars' was very likely that it created an indefinite delay in public disclosure of the extraterrestrial presence. The release of the Steven Spielberg movie *Close Encounters of the Third Kind* in 1977 has been long speculated to have been part of an 'acclimation program' to prepare the general public for disclosure of the extraterrestrial presence.[162] NASA sent a 20 page confidential letter to Spielberg outlining what should and shouldn't be in the movie prior to its release. This suggested an unusual degree of official interest in depictions of extraterrestrials and the U.S. government.[163] The 1979 'Dulce War', in which, clandestine authorities in charge of extraterrestrial affairs (the shadow government) ordered an attack on levels of a joint underground base occupied by extraterrestrials would surely have signaled a dramatic shift in attitudes towards the extraterrestrial presence. It also signaled an indefinite hold on full public disclosure.

There is sufficient evidence to justify further investigation into the accuracy of claims surrounding extensive human rights abuses at joint government-extraterrestrial bases that exist(ed) at Dulce and elsewhere in the world. The most effective means of exploring alleged human rights abuses at Dulce would be for a prominent human rights non-government organization such as Amnesty International or Human Rights Watch to initiate an investigation into claims of such abuse. These organizations have extensive experience in performing accurate and confidential investigations in countries historically guilty of gross human rights violations; repressing those stepping forward to reveal such abuses. An investigation by a human rights NGO could provide an opportunity for whistleblowers to step forward and/or pass information concerning alleged human rights abuses at Dulce. This would provide a means of preserving confidentially and preventing criminal charges against whistleblowers for disclosing 'classified information'. In case criminal charges are brought against such whistleblowers by U.S. federal agencies, or they disappear, such individuals could become the focus of 'emergency alerts' that human rights organizations have pioneered over the years to secure release of those revealing 'human rights' abuses.

Another means of exploring alleged human rights abuses at Dulce would be to initiate a Congressionally backed inquiry into such allegations. The full scope of activities at these underground facilities could be examined in terms of possible human rights abuses occurring at U.S. facilities where extraterrestrials work. Comprehensive congressional immunity and protection should be given to all government/military officials and employees of corporations willing to step forward to give information of human rights abuses at bases on U.S. territory and around the globe. Due to high public interest in such alleged abuses, the Congressional inquiry should be open to full media coverage. Whether or not genuine national security considerations merit non-disclosure of such information, this should be put before the Congressional Inquiry for proper consideration and appropriate action.

The 'shadow' government' in charge of managing extraterrestrial affairs has been a factor, either mitigating or causal, in gross human rights abuses occurring in secret bases under its control and/or shared with extraterrestrial races. The role of the 'shadow government' should be investigated and officials made accountable for human rights abuses. Appropriate reforms must be instituted as autocratic states have similarly had to reform their governments as a result of widespread human rights abuses. Human rights NGO's are experienced in conducting such investigations of autocratic regimes. Such action provides a highly desirable means of addressing alleged abuses committed by clandestine groups embedded in national security agencies and functioning as a 'shadow government'.

To deal with the full extent of the alleged human rights abuses committed at joint government-extraterrestrial bases by corporate employees/military personnel, a 'Truth Commission' should be convened. Government/military officials and/or corporate employees directly participating in experiments and projects involving such violations; and/or in the suppression of such information through intimidation of witnesses and whistleblowers, should be investigated. Such a Truth Commission can be modeled on the South African example where blanket amnesty was given to all public officials of the Apartheid era who participated in human rights abuses. The only conditions were that they fully disclose the nature of their activities, and that these abuses were politically motivated rather than personal.[164] Amnesty for officials or employees stepping forward to admit their participation in projects violating basic human rights of U.S. citizens and foreign nationals forcibly held in joint government-extraterrestrial bases is an important means for disclosing the full extent of past secret operations at such bases.

To initiate Congressional and/or Human Rights NGO action dealing with the alleged human rights abuses committed at Dulce, former/current public officials or corporate employees who have first hand knowledge of such abuses committed at Dulce and/or any other joint Government-extraterrestrial facility are encouraged to step forward. A number of whistleblower legal services are available to provide legal counsel for those interested in disclosing their activities, without violating legal/contractual obligations.[165]

Political implications of the human rights abuses at the Dulce base require immediate attention through credible human rights organizations investigating these allegations. Congressionally sponsored inquiries are required on a number of key issues stemming from alleged abuses at Dulce. These include:

a. the U.S. participating in treaties with extraterrestrial races without congressional ratification;
b. military hostilities between U.S. security agencies and extraterrestrial races without the general public or Congress being informed;
c. accountability for human rights abuses committed at Dulce and other bases in the U.S. and elsewhere; and
d. 'black budget' funding of deep black programs such as Dulce, that operate without Congressional or Executive Office oversight.

Is the Dulce type experience limited solely to the U.S. government and U.S. territory? Probably not, due the extensive network of U.S. military bases around the world. Other national governments may have agreed to similar arrangements with extraterrestrials races whereby the human rights of its citizens are traded for advanced extraterrestrial technology. More likely, countries such as Australia, Britain and Canada have permitted the construction of joint U.S. extraterrestrial facilities on their territories, as evidenced by the Pine Gap facility in Australia.

The full extent of events at Dulce may be a watershed in human history. It could well be the first time in recorded history that humanity has had to deal in a politically responsible way with human rights abuses where extraterrestrials are complicit. What makes this possibility particularly worrisome is the role played by various military, intelligence and/or corporate personnel that were clearly involved in such abuses and/or did not take appropriate actions to prevent such abuses. Exposing government policies such as officially sanctioned human rights abuses at joint government extraterrestrial facilities is an urgent priority. A full accounting of events and personnel at all U.S. controlled underground facilities, especially those housing extraterrestrial visitors, is urgently needed.

Table 2. Evidence of a Joint Government ET Base at Dulce

Witness	*Events Claimed to have Witnessed and Supporting Evidence*
Paul Bennewitz	Radio intercepts and photographic evidence of an extraterrestrial base at Dulce. Provided evidence to USAF who implemented a psychological operation to discredit him. Multiple interviews with an extraterrestrial abductee who claimed to have been abused at an underground base at Dulce.
Phil Schneider	Directly involved in the Dulce firefight (1979) with body scars presented as evidence of injuries sustained. Presented a variety of materials and documents to support claims of underground base construction at Dulce and elsewhere. Died in mysterious circumstances after ignoring warnings to stop public lectures.
Bob Lazar	Read a briefing document disclosing a 1979 firefight between extraterrestrials and security personal at a secret base.
Michael Wolf	A firefight occurred in 1975 at another underground base in Nevada. Disclosed that he had also worked at Dulce.
Dan Burisch	Taken to Dulce base for a job interview where he heard abuses of detained civilians. Transported to & from Dulce by high speed underground rail facility.
Thomas Castello	Testimony of employment and defection from the Dulce underground base after witnessing human rights abuses. Provided photos and videos to researchers who interviewed him.
William Moore	Officially sanctioned AFOSI disinformation campaign to discredit Paul Bennewitz while monitoring evidence he collected.
Myrna Hansen	Described under hypnosis being taken into the Dulce underground base by extraterrestrials where she witnessed human rights abuses.
Christa Tilton	Reports being taken to Dulce by extraterrestrials where she witnessed U.S. military personnel, humans stored in vats, and subjected to medical experiments.
Norio Harakaya	Visited Dulce with a Japanese film crew in 1990 and interviewed Dulce residents. Concluded sightings and unusual military activities occurred during the period investigated by Bennewitz.
Gabe Valdez	Confronted Delta Force Personnel intimidating a news crew that was investigating Bennewitz's claims of an underground base at Archuletta Mesa, Dulce.

ENDNOTES: CHAPTER TWO

[74] My most sincere thanks to Hugh Matlock who generously provided the hospitality, intellectual stimulation, thoughtful suggestions and research environment for completing the initial draft of this chapter which was originally published as "The Dulce Report," Exopolitics.org (September 25, 2003).
[75] For documentation on underground military bases and known locations, see Richard Sauder, *Underground Bases and Tunnels: What Is the Government Trying to Hide?* (Adventures Unlimited Press, 1996).
[76] Richard Sauder, *Underwater and Underground Bases* (Adventures Unlimited Press, 2001).
[77] For a copy of the story, go to: http://exopolitics.org/IndianSprings-Project.htm .
[78] Estimates of the size of the annual black budget go as high as 1.7 trillion dollars, see chapter five. For description of how money is annually siphoned from the U.S. economy see Catherine Fitts, "The $64 Question: What's Up With the Black Budget? – The Real Deal," *Scoop: UQ Wire* (23 September, 2002). Available online at: http://www.scoop.co.nz/mason/stories/HL0209/S00126.htm .
[79] See Branton, *The Dulce Wars: Underground Alien Bases and the Battle for Planet Earth* (Inner Light Publications, 1999); and Christa Tilton, *The Bennewitz Papers* (Inner Light Publications, 1994). Discussion forum on Dulce available at: http://groups.yahoo.com/group/Dulce_Base_Investigations .
[80] Greg Bishop, *Project Beta: The Story of Paul Bennewitz, National Security, and the Creation of a Modern UFO Myth* (Paraview Pocket Books, 2005).
[81] See Michael Salla, "Exopolitical Comment # 29– "Review Article: Project Beta: The Story of Paul Bennewitz, National Security, and the Creation of a Modern UFO Myth," *Exopolitics.Org*. May 11, 2005. Http://www.exopolitics.org/Exo-Comment-29.htm .
[82] An online overview of Bennewitz's research is by Chris Lambright, "Paul Bennewitz, electronic recordings, and films of "aerial objects'," (July 1, 1996) available online at: http://www.cufon.org/contributors/chrisl/PB/bennewit.htm .
[83] For some of these images, see Chris Lambright, "Paul Bennewitz, electronic recordings, and films of "aerial objects'," (July 1, 1996) available online at http://www.cufon.org/contributors/chrisl/PB/bennewi2.htm
[84] Paul Bennewitz, Project Beta, is available as an appendix in Greg Bishop, *Project Beta*, and online at: http://web.archive.org/web/20040225165212/http://www.paraarchives.com/documents/p/beta01.htm .
[85] Dr Sprinkle was a psychologist and tenured professor at the University of Wyming who is widely acknowledged as an eminent expert in abduction cases. For discussion of Sprinkle's work with Bennewitz and Hansen, see Greg Bishop, *Project Beta*, 17-23.
[86] See Greg Bishop, *Project Beta,* 20-21. See also Branton, *The Dulce Wars*, chs. 21& 26. Bennewitz refers to the mother and her son in "Project Beta", available in Bishop, Project Beta, 233-59.
[87] Greg Bishop, *Project Beta,* 21.

[88] See Greg Bishop, *Project Beta,* 24-32.
[89] See Greg Bishop, *Project Beta,* 32.
[90] Branton, *The Dulce Wars: Underground Alien Bases and the Battle for Planet Earth* (Inner Light, 1999). Available online at: http://www.bibliotecapleyades.net/esp_dulcebook.htm#menu
[91] See Chris Lambright, "Paul Bennewitz, electronic recordings, and films of "aerial objects'- Part 3" (June, 2003) available online at http://www.cufon.org/contributors/chrisl/PB/bennewi3.htm
[92] In Bennewitz's report, "Project Beta", there are many references to how to militarily defense against extraterrestrial ships suggesting that his communications revealed the hostile relationship that existed between the humans and extraterrestrials. Bennewitz's report, "Project Beta", is available as an appendix in Greg Bishop's, *Project Beta*, 233-59, or online at: http://web.archive.org/web/20040225165212/http://www.paraarchives.com/documents/p/beta01.htm .
[93] Cited online on by World of the Strange, http://www.worldofthestrange.com/modules.php?name=Documents&op=ViewItems&vid=138 .
[94] Bennewitz's report, "Project Beta", is available as an appendix in Greg Bishop's, *Project Beta*, 233-59, or online at: http://web.archive.org/web/20040225165212/http://www.paraarchives.com/documents/p/beta01.htm .
[95] Bennewitz's report, "Project Beta", prologue, is available as an appendix in Greg Bishop's, *Project Beta*, 233-59, or online at: http://web.archive.org/web/20040225165212/http://www.paraarchives.com/documents/p/beta01.htm .
[96] For details on Moore's confession 1989, see http://www.worldofthestrange.com/modules.php?name=Documents&op=ViewItems&vid=144 .
[97] For details on Moore's confession 1989, see http://www.worldofthestrange.com/modules.php?name=Documents&op=ViewItems&vid=144 .
[98] See Chris Lambright, "Paul Bennewitz, electronic recordings, and films of "aerial objects', Part 3" (June, 2003) available online at http://www.cufon.org/contributors/chrisl/PB/bennewi3.htm
[99] "The Aviary," *Think-aboutit.com*, available online at: http://www.think-aboutit.com/ufo/aviary.htm . This is also the conclusion of Greg Bishop, *Project Beta.*
[100] Extract from Bill Hamilton, "Underground Bases and Tunnels," *Cosmic Top Secret* (Inner Light Global Communications, 2002) Available online at: http://www.crowdedskies.com/files/down/cog.html
[101] For discussion of the whistleblower phenomenon, see Myron Peretz Glazer and Penina Migdal Glazer, *The Whistleblowers: Exposing Corruption in Government and Industry* (Basic Books, 1991); and C. Fred Alford, *Whistleblowers: Broken*

Lives and Organizational Power (Cornell University, 2002). For online information go to: http://www.whistleblowers.org .
[102] For detailed discussion of legal definitions and laws concerning whistleblowers, see Stephen M. Kohn, *Concepts and Procedures in Whistleblower Law* (Quorum Books. Westport, Conn. 2000). For online information go to: http://www.whistleblowers.org .
[103] A copy of this statute can be found online at http://www.whistleblower.org/article.php?did=92&scid=96
[104] For further discussion of difficulties confronting whistleblowers concerning extraterrestrial related information, see, Michael Salla, Exopolitical Comment # 32: Whistleblowers, National Security and Unauthorized Disclosure of ETV/EBE Classified Projects available at: http://www.exopolitics.org/Exo-Comment-32.htm.
[105] Schneider's 1995 lecture is available at a number of websites and is titled, "A Lecture by Phil Schneider – May, 1995" One site is http://www.ufoarea.bravepages.com/conspiracy_schneider_lecture.html .
[106] "A Lecture by Phil Schneider – May, 1995," available online at: http://www.ufoarea.bravepages.com/conspiracy_schneider_lecture.html .
[107] Schneider's 1995 lecture is available at a number of websites and is titled, "A Lecture by Phil Schneider – May, 1995" One site is http://www.ufoarea.bravepages.com/conspiracy_schneider_lecture.html .
[108] Cynthia Drayer, "The Death of Philip Schneider, January 17, 1996," available online at: http://www.worldofthestrange.com/modules.php?name=Newsletters&op=ViewItems&vid=69 . For discussion of Schneider's whistleblower testimony, see "Tribute to Phil Schneider," available online at: http://www.apfn.org/apfn/philip.htm .
[109] Jim Marrs, *Alien Agenda* (Harper Paperbacks, 1998) 270-71
[110] One of Lazar's biggest critics is Stanton Friedman. See "My Take on Bob Lazar: The Bob Lazar Fraud," available online at: http://www.v-j-enterprises.com/sflazar.html .
[111] "Billy Goodman Interview with Bob Lazar: Partial transcript, Billy Goodman Happening (December 20, 1989), available online at: http://www.swa-home.de/lazar3.htm See also "George Knapp Interview with Bob Lazar,' On the Record, KLAS-TV, (December 9, 1989). Transcript available online at: http://www.swa-home.de/lazar2.htm.
[112] For references to Knapp and other sources discussing the Lazar case, go to: http://www.anomalies.net/area51/s4/boblazar/ .
[113] Richard Boylan, "Official Within MJ-12 UFO-Secrecy Management Group Reveals Insider Secrets," http://drboylan.com/wolfdoc2.html
[114] Richard Boylan, "Quotations from Chairman Wolf," quoted online at: http://www.drboylan.com/wolfqut2.html
[115] For discussion of PI 40 and other key extraterrestrial management organizations, see Michael Salla, "Political Management of the Extraterrestrial Presence – The Challenge to Democracy and Liberty in America." *Exopolitics.Org*, July 4, 2003. Available online at: http://exopolitics.org/Study-

Paper-5.htm . Also in Michael E. Salla, *Exopolitics: Political Implications of the Extraterrestrial Presence* (forthcoming Dandelion Books, 2004).
[116] See Richard Boylan, "Quotations from Chairman Wolfe," http://drboylan.com/wolfqut2.html .
[117] See Richard Boylan, "Quotations from Chairman Wolfe," http://drboylan.com/wolfqut2.html .
[118] The Dulce papers including a video recording are available on a number of locations on the internet. One site from which they can be downloaded is: http://www.bibliotecapleyades.net/offlimits/esp_offlimits_2.htm .
[119] Branton, *The Dulce Wars: Underground Alien Bases and the Battle for Planet Earth.*
[120] Interviews with Castello are published as chapters 11 & 27, in The *Dulce Wars*, Available online at http://www.bibliotecapleyades.net/esp_dulcebook.htm#menu . See also William Hamilton *Cosmic Top Secret.*
[121] See Branton, *The Dulce Wars*, ch. 27. http://www.bibliotecapleyades.net/esp_dulcebook.htm#menu . See also William Hamilton *Cosmic Top Secret.*
[122] For discussion of the evolution of the system whereby corporations played a primary role in servicing military contracts vis-à-vis extraterrestrial projects, see Michael Salla, Exopolitics: Political Implications of the Extraterrestrial Presence (forthcoming Dandelion Press, 2004), ch 2. Published also as Study Paper #5, www.exopolitics.org .
[123] See Branton, *The Dulce Wars*, ch. 11, Available online at: http://www.bibliotecapleyades.net/branton/esp_dulcebook11.htm .
[124] See Branton, *The Dulce Wars*, ch.11, Available online at: http://www.bibliotecapleyades.net/branton/esp_dulcebook11.htm .
[125] For a detailed discussion of U.S. government sponsored experiments in mind control, see Helmut Lammer & Marion Lammer, *Milabs: Military Mind Control & Alien Abductions* (Illuminet Press, 1999).
[126] See Preston Nichols, *Montauk Project: Experiments in Time* (Sky Books, 1999); Al Bielek and Brad Steiger, *The Philadelphia Experiment and Other UFO Conspiracies* (Innerlight Publications, 1991); Stewart Swerdlow, *Montauk: The Alien Connection* (Expansions Publishing Co. 2002); Wade Gordon, *The Brookhaven Connection* (Sky Books, 2001). For an online interview with Al Bielek, go to http://psychicspy.com/montauk1.html .
[127] Branton, *The Dulce Wars*, ch.11, Available online at: http://www.bibliotecapleyades.net/branton/esp_dulcebook11.htm .
[128] Branton, *The Dulce Wars*, ch.11, Available online at: http://www.bibliotecapleyadcs.net/branton/esp_dulcebook11.htm .
[129] Extract from Bill Hamilton, "Underground Bases and Tunnels," *Cosmic Top Secret* (Inner Light Global Communications, 2002)
[130] Christa Tilton, "Going Under," available online at: http://www.ufocasebook.com/christatilton.html
[131] Christa Tilton, "Going Under," available online at: http://www.ufocasebook.com/christatilton.html

[132] Linda Moulton Howe, "Whistleblower Microbiologist Speaks Out About Alleged "Alien" Named J-Rod," Earthfiles.com (Sept 15, 2003).
[133] Hamilton, *Project Aquarius: The Story of An Aquarian Scientist* (Authorhouse, 2005) . A book review is available online at: http://exopoliticsjournal.com/Journal-vol-1-3-Rev-Salla-Aquarius.pdf .
[134] Advocates of this view include: William Cooper, *Behold a Pale Horse* (Light Technology Publishing, 1991) 222; Greg Bishop, *Project Beta.*
[135] See Bishop, *Project Beta,* 233-59.
[136] See Bishop, *Project Beta,* 32, 233-59.
[137] See the following interview of John Maynard where he discusses how disinformation works in regard to UFOs and extraterrestrial life in the intelligence world, "From Disinformation to Disclosure," *Surfing the Apocalypse,* http://www.surfingtheapocalypse.com/maynard.html . See also Greg Bishop, *Project Beta,* 45-48.
[138] For discussion of Bennewitz's physical evidence, see Chris Lambright, "Paul Bennewitz, electronic recordings, and films of "aerial objects', Part 3" (June, 2003) available online at
http://www.cufon.org/contributors/chrisl/PB/bennewi3.htm
[139] See Chris Lambright, "Paul Bennewitz, electronic recordings, and films of "aerial objects', Part 3" (June, 2003) available online at
http://www.cufon.org/contributors/chrisl/PB/bennewi3.htm
[140] For history of efforts to provide conclusive evidence of the UFO history, see Richard Dolan, *UFOs and the National Security State.*
[141] For lack of physical geological features to support the existence of Dulce, see Glen Campbell, "A Field Trip to Dulce, New Mexico," available online at: http://ufos.about.com/gi/dynamic/offsite.htm?site=http://www.ufomind.com/area51/list/1997/nov/a04%2D001.shtml . See also Roy Lawhon, "Dulce!," available online at: http://ufos.about.com/library/weekly/aa112597.htm .
[142] See Hamilton, *Cosmic Top Secret: America's Secret Ufo Program,* an extract is available online at: http://www.crowdedskies.com/files/down/cog.html .
[143] See Branton, *The Dulce Wars*, ch 5, available online at:
http://eaglenet.enochgraphics.com/dulce/G-HAYAKO.html .
[144] Bishop, *Project Beta,* 160.
[145] For discussion of Maglev transportation and the global underground system, see Richard Sauder, *Underwater and Underground Bases* (Adventures Unlimited Press, 2001). Sauder has a website at: http://www.sauderzone.com .
[146] Extract from Bill Hamilton, "Underground Bases and Tunnels," *Cosmic Top Secret.*
Available online at: http://www.crowdedskies.com/files/down/cog.html
[147] Roy Lawhon, "Dulce!," available online at:
http://ufos.about.com/library/weekly/aa112597.htm .
[148] Roy Lawhon, "Dulce!," available online at:
http://ufos.about.com/library/weekly/aa112597.htm .
[149] Roy Lawhon, "Dulce!," available online at:
http://ufos.about.com/library/weekly/aa112597.htm .

[150] See "Tribute to Phil Schneider," available online at: http://www.apfn.org/apfn/philip.htm .
[151] For documents suggesting he was murdered, see "Tribute to Phil Schneider," available online at: http://www.apfn.org/apfn/philip.htm .
[152] Roy Lawhon, "Dulce!," available online at: http://ufos.about.com/library/weekly/aa112597.htm .
[153] Greg Bishop, *Project Beta*, 152.
[154] Greg Bishop, *Project Beta*, 153.
[155] See Chris Lambright, "Paul Bennewitz, electronic recordings, and films of "aerial objects', Part 3" (June, 2003) available online at http://www.cufon.org/contributors/chrisl/PB/bennewi3.htm .
[156] See resignation letter of MUFON member of Richard Hall, Letter to Walter H. Andrus, Jr. (March 18, 1989). Cited online at: http://www.worldofthestrange.com/modules.php?name=Documents&op=ViewItems&vid=143
[157] See Chris Lambright, "Paul Bennewitz, electronic recordings, and films of "aerial objects', Part 3" (June, 2003) available online at http://www.cufon.org/contributors/chrisl/PB/bennewi3.htm
[158] For an overview of the role of disinformation, see a report by a Senate Commission convened to discuss secrecy, *Report of the Commission on Protecting and Reducing Government Secrecy: 1997.* Available online at: http://www.access.gpo.gov/congress/commissions/secrecy/index.html .
[159] See my review of Bishop's book, "Project Beta: The Story of Paul Bennewitz, National Security, and the Creation of a Modern UFO Myth," at: Http://www.exopolitics.org/Exo-Comment-29.htm .
[160] Advocates of this view include: William Cooper, *Behold a Pale Horse* (Light Technology Publishing, 1991) 222; Greg Bishop, *Project Beta.*
[161] See Timothy Good, *Alien Contact: Top Secret UFO Files Revealed* (Quill 1991) 109-110. For online information on Pine Gap, go to: http://www.mysticaluniverse.com/auzconn/auz2/auz2.html .
[162] See "Disclosure Pattern – 1977," available online at: http://www.presidentialufo.8m.com/disclosure_1977.htm .
[163] See Alex Ioshpe, Close Encounters of the Third Kind, available online at: http://www.geocities.com/Hollywood/Studio/3469/making_enc.html .
[164] See Dorothy Shea, *The South African Truth Commission: The Politics of Reconciliation (*United States Institute of Peace, 2000).
[165] Information on available legal services for whistleblowers can be found at www.whistleblower.org or at www.whistleblowers.com . For more information please contact the author. All communications will be treated as confidential.

Chapter Three

Covert CIA Funding of Extraterrestrial Projects Exposing the 'Black Budget' and the Second Manhattan Project

Introduction[166]

If what I have discussed in the first two chapters is correct, then a vast network of classified projects concerning extraterrestrial life and technology exist. Many of these projects are located in highly classified underground bases that are connected by high speed rail systems in the U.S. and around the planet.[167] This tunnel system would be very expensive. According to Dr Richard Sauder, the "one-time construction cost of an approximately 300 mile-long, deeply buried tunnel system under Grand Mesa, Colorado was estimated at about $4.28 billion. [168] The cost of building and maintaining high speed rail systems such as MagLev around the U.S. involving thousands of miles would be enormous. Even moreso if this involved intercontinental travel under oceans as Sauders has found evidence for![169]

The cost of extraterrestrial related projects around the U.S. and elsewhere around the planet which are located in underground/underwater bases connected by high speed rail systems would be astronomically expensive. The funding for such a network of projects would have to be raised in ways that escape conventional oversight in order to prevent public knowledge of extraterrestrial life and technology. This chapter examines evidence of a vast black budget raised to fund a second Manhattan Project involving extraterrestrial related projects that have been highly classified for over sixty years!

Each year the U.S. Department of Defense (DoD) lists a number of single line items in its budget that have a program number such as 0605236F, code names like CLASSIC WIZARD or vague descriptions such as "special evaluation program." These don't refer to any weapons system known to the general public, Congressional officials or even to defense analysts. These single line items are covers for a 'black budget'. This top secret slush fund is set up by the DoD, with the approval of the U.S. Congress, to fund intelligence organizations such as the CIA, and classified weapons programs by the DoD. The 'black budget' allows intelligence activities, covert operations and classified weapons research to be conducted without Congressional oversight. The justification used is that oversight would compromise the secrecy essential for the success of such 'black programs'. These 'black programs' are typically classified as 'Special Access' or 'Controlled Access Programs' and have a security classification system more rigorous than the 'top secret' classifications for most government agencies. Such programs are known only to those with a 'need to know'.

The 'black budget' funds a covert world of unaccountable intelligence activities, covert military/intelligence operations and classified weapons programs. The conventional view is that this covert world is funded by Congressional appropriations authorizing the DoD to use U.S. Treasury funds for classified projects and intelligence activities that appear as vague single line items on the DoD budget. Subtracting the cost of known weapons systems and programs from the total DoD budget gives Congressional analysts a means of estimating the size and scope of operations of the covert world of 'black projects', without knowing their precise budgets or activities. There is however compelling evidence that the covert world of highly classified projects (aka., "deep black programs") is primarily funded by a black budget created by the CIA rather than the DoD. Rather than being a beneficiary of a Congressionally sanctioned DoD 'black budget', the CIA has its own 'unofficial' black budget that acts as a conduit for funds secretly siphoned into the various military intelligence agencies associated with both the CIA and the DoD, for intelligence activities, covert operations and weapons research.

The CIA has the unique legal ability among all U.S. government departments and agencies to generate funds through appropriations of other federal government agencies and other sources "without regard to any provisions of law" and without regard to the intent behind Congressional appropriations.[170] Every year, billions of dollars of Congressional appropriations are diverted from their Congressionally sanctioned purposes to CIA and DoD based intelligence agencies without knowledge of the public and with the collusion of Congressional leaders. The covert world of 'black programs' acts with virtual impunity, overseen and regulated by itself, funding itself through secret slush funds, and is free of the limitations that come from Congressional oversight, proper auditing procedures and public scrutiny.

In this chapter I unmask the size of the black budget and the covert world of 'deep black' programs it funds. I investigate the mechanisms used to transfer money into the 'black budget'. Following the money trail and official efforts to keep secret the size of the black budget and how it is generated, provides the key pieces of a complex financial and national security jigsaw puzzle.

The key to uncovering the true size of the black budget is the chronic accounting anomalies in the DoD budget. These anomalies reveal over one trillion U.S. dollars annually is being siphoned by the CIA into the DoD for secret distribution to various military intelligence agencies, and the 'deep black' programs they support. Such siphoning, with dubious constitutional status, is made legal by various Congressional enactments, senior Congressional officials, and the Executive Office. The size of the black budget, the secrecy surrounding it, the extent senior Federal officials and agencies go to in targeting individuals and companies threatening to reveal where Congressional appropriations are ultimately going, point to a vast network of 'deep black projects'. This network collectively forms a highly classified second Manhattan Project whose existence, goals and budget are kept secret. The purpose of this new Manhattan Project is covert funding of a network of projects in the U.S. and around the world dealing with extraterrestrial life and technology.

Birth of the Black Budget

In 1947, the National Security Act created the National Security Council and the Central Intelligence Organization (CIA), and it consolidated the U.S. military into one entity, the Department of Defense (DoD). One of the issues that remained unresolved from creation and operation of the CIA was the extent to which its budget and intelligence activities would remain a secret. According to Article 1, sec. 9, of the U.S. Constitution, "No money shall be drawn from the treasury, but in consequence of appropriations made by law; and a regular statement and account of receipts and expenditures of all public money shall be published from time to time." The constitutional mandate requiring transparency in government expenditures conflicted with the need for secrecy concerning Congressional appropriations for the CIA. The solution was for Congress to pass legislation approving the secrecy over the funding mechanisms used for the CIA and its intelligence related activities. The necessary bill was passed with great haste and minimal debate causing considerable concern among those few Congressmen brave enough to openly challenge the constitutionality of the Act.[171] Congressman Emmanuel Celler of New York voted for the bill but protested: "If the members of the Armed Services Committee can hear the detailed information to support this bill, why cannot the entire membership? Are they the Brahmins and we the untouchables? Secrecy is the answer."[172] Celler, like the majority of Congressmen, passed the CIA Act very much like the wealthy father viewing the birth of an illegitimate child, appropriate care would be taken to provide for the child, but there would be no official admission of patrimony or acceptance of responsibility.

The 1949 CIA Act comprised additions to those sections of the 1947 National Security Act that dealt with the creation of CIA. The 1949 CIA Act gave a Congressional stamp of approval to the creation of a 'black budget' as the following sections make clear:

> … any other Government agency is authorized to transfer to or receive from the Agency such sums **without regard to any provisions of law** limiting or prohibiting transfers between appropriations [emphasis added]. Sums transferred to the Agency in accordance with this paragraph may be expended for the purposes and under the authority of sections 403a to 403s of this title without regard to limitations of appropriations from which transferred.[173]

This section meant that funds could be transferred from the appropriations of other government departments earmarked for specific tasks, "without regard to any provisions of law". For example, a Congressional appropriation earmarked for housing subsidies to low-income workers by Housing and Urban Development (HUD), could be legally transferred either to the CIA for covert intelligence activities or through the CIA to a DoD associated intelligence agency for a classified program. HUD employees would find that their relevant housing programs were lacking the necessary funds for relief efforts even though Congress had appropriated these funds for this purpose. Any HUD official smart enough to enquire into the location of the missing funds would be deterred from pursuing the issue. If these officials persisted, they could be summarily dismissed, and then exposed to a variety of CIA activities to silence them.[174]

Despite its legal authority to transfer funds from other federal agencies regardless of the intent of Congressional appropriations, the conventional wisdom was that the major source of appropriations for the CIA came through the DoD. This is apparently what President Truman had in mind when he approved that the "operating funds for the organization [CIA] would be obtained from the Departments of State, War, and Navy instead of directly from Congress."[175] This funding arrangement ostensibly assured that the CIA would be subordinate to the Secretaries of Defense and State who would be in a better position to influence CIA covert activities. Four years after passage of the 1949 CIA Act, the following categories (see Table 3) and sums in the relevant defense force appropriations apparently provided the bulk of the black budget funding of the CIA.

The Congressionally sanctioned method of CIA appropriations meant that the $587 million the CIA acknowledged receiving from DoD for its intelligence operations in 1953 would remain a secret both to rank and file members of Congress, and to the general public. The alleged sum the CIA received from the DoD in 1953 ($4.7 billion in 2008 terms) was, in likelihood, already dwarfed by the funds the CIA was transferring through other government agencies into its black budget.[176]

The constitutional validity of the CIA's black budget and its size was something that did not unduly trouble most Congressmen during the early years of the Cold War. Congress believed that national security considerations concerning the Soviet threat merited such an extraordinary practice. However, it did trouble one U.S. citizen who in 1967 took the CIA to court over the secrecy surrounding the true size of its black budget.

Table 3. The 'Official Black Budget': CIA – Location of Budget Funds Fiscal Year 1953[177]

Appropriation & Service	Project	Total
Maintenance & Operations, Army	Project 1732 Classified project	33 million
	Project 2110 Commercial transportation	163 million
Service-wide Operations, Navy	Activity 10 Contingencies of the Navy	33 million
Ships and Facilities, Navy	Activity 1 Maintenance and operation of the active fleet	70 million
Ordinance and Facilities, Navy	Activity 1 Procurement of ordnance and ammunition	93 million
Contingencies, Air Force	Project 891	33 million
Military Personnel Requirements, Air Force	Project 510 Pay of the Air Force	70 million
Aircraft and Related Procurement, Air Force	Project 120 Aircraft component spares and spare parts	92 million
Total		**587 million**

Legal and Congressional Efforts to Disclose the CIA's Black Budget

William Richardson was a private citizen who realized the inconsistency between the Constitution's requirement that all government appropriations would have "a regular statement and account of receipts and expenditures" published, and the CIA's Act's secrecy provision concerning the CIA budget. In 1967, Richardson made an effort to discover the true size of the CIA's 'black budget' by writing a letter to the U.S. Government Printing Office. He requested a copy of the CIA budget "published by the Government in compliance with Article I, section 9, clause 7 of the United States Constitution."[178] Richardson received replies from the U.S. Treasury that essentially rebuffed his efforts. He decided to start a Federal court action against the U.S. government. He argued that the CIA Act was "repugnant to the Constitution" since it "operates to falsify the regular Statement and Account of all public Money."[179] After three years of legal wrangling, Richardson's case was dismissed by the Pittsburgh Federal Judge, Joseph P. Wilson. Wilson decided that Richardson did not have 'standing' to sue the

Federal government since he was not directly affected by the issue in dispute. In short, Wilson was taking the conservative legal position that a 'generalized grievance' is not a sufficient basis for a private citizen to take a U.S. Federal Agency to court. Richardson appealed and in 1971, succeeded in having his case heard before a full bench of the United States Court of Appeals in Philadelphia (the penultimate legal court in the US). In his legal brief, Richardson claimed:

> Never in the history of this country has so much money been spent without the traditional safeguard of openness and in direct defiance of constitutional provisions.... Billions are spent each year by unknown entities and this amount is spread throughout the Treasury's reporting system to confuse the public and belittle the Constitution.[180]

The nine federal judges ruled in a 6-3 decision in 1972 that Richardson did have legal standing since the Court reasoned that a

> ... responsible and intelligent taxpayer and citizen, of course, wants to know how his tax money is spent. Without this information he cannot intelligently follow the actions of the Congress or the Executive. Nor can he properly fulfill his obligations as a member of the electorate.[181]

Richardson had won an extraordinary, though ultimately short lived, legal victory. He had succeeded in arguing that the 'black budget' was inconsistent with his constitutional obligations and that the CIA Act had doubtful constitutional standing. The 1971 decision of the Court of Appeals is the closest any U.S. court has come to ruling on the constitutionality of the CIA Act. The Court had effectively decided that Congress had no right to deprive American citizens knowledge of the true amount of appropriated money being channeled to the CIA through other government agencies.

The Federal Government immediately appealed to the Supreme Court and in July 1974, the nine Supreme Court Justices ruled in a 5-4 decision, that Richardson did not have the legal standing to challenge the Federal government.[182] Adopting a conservative legal position, the Court argued that Richardson's suit was nothing more than a generalized political grievance by a citizen that needed to be dealt with through the political system, rather than through the legal system. The Supreme Court concluded that it did not need to examine the merits of Richardson's case, since he did not have legal standing to bring the suit to the Court. The Supreme Court thus overturned the earlier ruling of the U.S. Court of Appeals. The immediate consequence was that the black budget would remain a secret for some years yet. Despite the setback, Richardson had demonstrated that the 'black budget' and the CIA Act that created it, had dubious constitutional standing, and only required a challenge from a party with legal standing to possibly have it struck from the statute books.[183]

In the 1970's the black budget and its true size for the first time became a subject of intense congressional scrutiny. In the aftermath of the Vietnam war and the behavior of the intelligence community in sponsoring private wars throughout Indochina and elsewhere, the Senate decided in 1976 to elect a committee to investigate the CIA's covert activities and the black budget of the intelligence community. In its final report, the Senate Select Committee on Intelligence (the Church Committee) found the black budget to be unconstitutional and recommended public disclosure of its size:

> The budget procedures, which presently govern the Central Intelligence Agency and other agencies of the Intelligence Community, prevent most members of Congress from knowing how much money is spent by any of these agencies or even how much money is spent on intelligence as a whole. In addition, most members of the public are deceived about the appropriations and expenditures of other government agencies whose budgets are inflated to conceal funds for the intelligence community.
>
> The failure to provide this information to the public and to the Congress prevents either from effectively ordering priorities and violates Article I, Section 9, Clause 7 of the Constitution.... The Committee finds that publication of the aggregate figure for national intelligence would begin to

> satisfy the Constitutional requirement and would not damage the national security.[184]

Unfortunately, the Church Committee's recommendation was never implemented. The CIA Director (DCI), George Bush, successfully argued for the committee to hold off implementing its decision. The Committee voted 6-5 to hold off and the recommendation was never brought to the whole Senate for a decision.[185]

It would have to wait until the 1990's before Congress would once again take up the issue of the black budget. Ironically, it was Congress that had provided legislation that would be an effective mechanism to end the secrecy surrounding the size of the black budget. The Freedom of Information Act (FOIA) was passed in 1966, making it possible for individuals to gain access to records of any federal government agency by making a written request.[186] All agencies are required to disclose requested records except for information that falls under nine exemptions and three exclusions of the FOIA. The most relevant of these exemptions for the CIA Act was (b)(1) exemption 1 which says: "This exemption protects from disclosure national security information concerning the national defense or foreign policy, provided that it has been properly classified in accordance with the substantive and procedural requirements of an executive order." If an agency refused to release information, the requestor could ask for a Federal judge to adjudicate whether the information did or didn't qualify for the exemption claimed by the agency in withholding the relevant information.

In 1967 when Richardson first took legal action, he did not use the newly passed FOIA in requesting information about the CIA's 'black budget'. He was challenging the constitutional basis of the black budget and CIA Act, rather than arguing that release of the figures would not pose a national security threat. Richardson rightly assumed that the CIA would not release information concerning the black budget on the grounds of national security, and that it could persuasively argue this before a federal judge. This would qualify the CIA for exemption from FOIA.

In 1996, President Clinton introduced a major change in attitude concerning secrecy over the size of the black budget when he argued that its disclosure would not threaten national security.

John Deutsch, the CIA Director at the time, gave Congressional testimony that President Clinton was "persuaded that disclosure of the annual amount appropriated for intelligence purposes would inform the public and not, in itself, harm intelligence activities."[187] President Clinton had effectively undercut the main legal barrier to the CIA indefinitely withholding the size of the black budget from an FOIA request. In 1997 the Federation of American Scientists (FAS) made an FOIA request to the CIA, to disclose the secret combined appropriations for the Intelligence community. This comprises the CIA, National Security Agency (NSA), National Reconnaissance Office (NRO), Defense Intelligence Agency (DIA), National Imagery and Mapping Agency (NIMA), and intelligence branches of the Air force, Navy and Army.[188] The Director of Central Intelligence refused and the case eventually went before a Federal Court. In a last ditch effort to prevent disclosure of the 'black budget' the DCI persuaded both the Senate[189] and the House of Representatives[190] to vote against amendments that would have recommended its disclosure.

The CIA's efforts were to no avail and in 1997 the Federal Judge decided in favor of the FAS that the 'black budget' could be disclosed without harming the national security of the US. In what was the first major crack in the official secrecy surrounding the CIA's budget and its intelligence activities, the CIA subsequently decided to release for the first time the size of its 'official' black budget (appropriations drawn from single line items on the DoD budget). The CIA reserved the right, however, not to disclose this figure in the future. For fiscal year 1997, the combined aggregate appropriations for the Intelligence Community (black budget) was said to be 26.6 billion dollars.[191] For fiscal year 1998, the last year that the CIA complied with FOIA requests, the black budget had risen slightly to 26.7 billion.

The 'official' black budget for the CIA can be estimated by using the percentage of the black budget for the intelligence community that went from DoD appropriations to the CIA as opposed to other intelligence agencies. According to Victor Marchetti and John Marks, the CIA portion of the intelligence black budget was 750 million from 6.228 billion (approximately 12%) for 1973.[192] Victor Marchetti and John Marks put the overall intelligence budget at $6.228 billion for 1973, of which the CIA disposed of $750 million. According to David Wise, author of *The American Police State*:

> In 1975 the entire CIA budget was hidden within a $2 billion appropriation for "Other Procurement, Air Force." The $12 billion total for all U.S. intelligence, much higher than previous estimates, was indicated in the report of the Senate intelligence committee.[193]

Wise's estimate suggests that the proportion of the intelligence black budget that goes to the CIA is closer to approximately 16.7% than the 12.0% estimated by Marchetti and Mark. At the other end, the Federation of American Scientists, using 1998 figures, estimated that the CIA's portion of the black budget was 11.5%.[194] If 12% is taken as the more accurate estimate of the CIA portion of the black budget, this suggests that of the 26.6 billion dollars George Tenet disclosed went to the Intelligence Community from DoD appropriations, approximately $3.2 billion (12%) was the official 'black budget' of the CIA. The 1998 estimate converts to $4.2 billion in 2008 terms. This compares well with the 1953 figure of $587 million that presumably made up DoD appropriations for the CIA black budget, that converts to approximately $4.7 billion in 2008 terms.[195] It appears that much of the mystery surrounding the black budget of the CIA and the intelligence community had been ended once official figures for the CIA were released through FOIA in 1997 and 1998.

I believe that figures released by Tenet in 1997 and 1998 for the 'official black budget' for the intelligence community, and earlier estimates dating from 1953 data, committee reports in the 1970's, is disinformation intended to steer analysts, Congress and the general public away from the true size of the CIA's black budget. The 'unofficial' CIA black budget, in terms of Congressional appropriations and other funds the CIA transfers through other government departments and agencies, far exceeds the 'official' black budget (DoD appropriations earmarked for the intelligence community). The 'unofficial' black budget has been well disguised as a major purpose of the CIA ever since its creation. The CIA acts as a funnel for the combined black budgets of the intelligence community **and** the Department of Defense. This is the reverse of the conventional wisdom behind the 'official' black budget that the DoD funds the CIA. In fact it is the CIA that funds secret projects run by the various military and intelligence services in the DoD. Using the testimony of whistleblowers of other federal government agencies and testimony of DoD Inspector Generals, I argue that billions of dollars are annually extracted from these agencies by the CIA, topped up by revenue from other sources used by the CIA, and then siphoned to the military intelligence agencies within the DoD. These funds are distributed to 'deep black projects' outside of the regular appropriations and oversight process mandated by Congress for 'black projects'.

HUD's Missing Money, Catherine Fitts, Hamilton Securities and the CIA.

In 1989 Catherine Austin Fitts became Assistant Secretary for Housing in Department of Housing and Urban Development (HUD). She began to notice money was not properly tracked as it moved between different HUD departments. There was a lack of proper accounting mechanisms to deal with discrepancies in revenue that indicated fraud at an alarming level.[196] She attempted to put in place some credible financial tracking mechanisms to identify where the money was going and to identify the responsible individuals and HUD departments. After 18 months on the job she was suddenly fired by the Bush administration. Fitts was told the day after she left that her financial reforms through "place-based financial accounting and statements" would also be terminated.[197]

Fitts subsequently created her own investment company, Hamilton Securities Group that used specially created computer software for tracking financial flows in the mortgage industry. In 1993, Hamilton Securities Group won a contract with HUD to manage its $500 billion portfolio. As a result of its innovative computer tracking of finances called 'Community Wizard', Hamilton Securities saved Federal Taxpayers $2 billion and, according to Fitts, "took the world's breath away."[198] Carolyn Betts, a former Hamilton Securities employee said:

> The HUD field office people went absolutely crazy when they saw it. You could go in with a pointer on a map and get to information on expenditures by each HUD program. It was

a pretty beautiful program and would have become unbelievably powerful.[199]

Fitts' innovative program was so successful that it was earning special attention from Congressmen with one chairman of an oversight committee in October 1997 favorably commenting on the "eye-popping" results. [200] Fitts' program had the potential to revolutionize the way in which large multibillion dollar portfolios were managed. Vice President Al Gore's Reinventing Government Initiative gave her firm the Hammer Award for Excellence in Re-engineering Government. Fitts innovation also came to the attention of powerful individuals who viewed it as a threat to the existing way in which finances were tracked in HUD and other federal government agencies. That status quo allowed corporations to reap large profits from government inefficiency.

Fitts' pioneering work came crashing down around her in June, 1996 when a *qui tam* (whistleblower) suit was brought against her firm by a rival HUD contractor who alleged Fitts committed fraud against HUD to the tune of $3.8 million. According to the Federal False Claims Act, a *qui tam* suit has 60 days to be investigated before a federal judge has to reach a conclusion on the substance of the suit and unseal the *qui tam* so that the defendant can respond to the allegations. Instead, the HUD Inspector General together with the federal judge in charge of the case took four years before another judge decided the allegations lacked substance, unsealed the *qui tam* in July 2000. The government then decided to end its role in the case.[201] In the meantime, Fitts' firm was subjected to 18 audits and investigations, multiple subpoenas for thousands of documents, not paid money owed to it by HUD while the 'investigation' was underway, subjected to media leaks and a smear campaign that frightened away potential investors, and ultimately raided by Department of Justice agents in 1998. The raid effectively destroyed the Community Wizard program and put an end to Hamilton Securities' efforts to survive the legal onslaught that involved steep legal costs. In the end, Fitts company went bankrupt and Fitts was emotionally exhausted. She, however, continued to fight for her reputation, repayment from HUD, and exposure of wrong doing by the HUD Inspector General in allowing the *qui tam* law suit to proceed for four years on a 'fishing expedition', while simultaneously leaking false information.[202]

After her experiences in both working with HUD as an employee (1988-1989) and as a contractor (1993-1997) and observing at first hand the chronic state of finances that could not be accounted for under normal accounting rules, Fitts concluded that HUD was being run as a 'criminal enterprise':

> In the summer of 2000, a member of the staff for the Chairman of the Senate appropriation subcommittee (with jurisdiction over HUD ...) confided to me that they believed that HUD was being run as "a criminal enterprise." I responded that I "did not disagree." Reaching that conclusion was a long time coming. It took many years of experience implementing practical and sound reforms to the FHA mortgage system, only to have the system reject any and all efforts to have it become anything other than an integral part of a significant mortgage bubble and a pork and slush fund operation.[203]

The fraudulent movement of finances through HUD were made possible by poor auditing standards that enabled as much as tens of billions of dollars to go annually missing.[204] In a March 2000 report, the HUD Inspector General, Susan Gaffney, reported a high number of 'adjustments' that had to be made to account for $59 billion that could not be located in 1999:

> At the time we discontinued our audit work, a total of 42 adjustments totaling about $17.6 billion had been processed in this manner to adjust fiscal year 1998 ending balances. An additional 242 adjustments totaling about $59.6 billion, were made to adjust fiscal year 1999 activity.[205]

Gaffney argued that the 'adjustments' were caused by HUD's difficulties in reconciling different computer systems. An unnamed official within HUD dismissed the idea of the adjustments being solely problems associated with different computers systems:

> Everything that has transpired at HUD is not an accident, and it sure isn't a computer glitch. When you take the different material violations of the most basic financial-management rules and compare them to the time and effort put in to have first-rate systems, it is impossible to explain it as anything other than significant financial fraud.[206]

Such fraud would not have been possible without collusion at very senior level within HUD. Allegations emerged from an unnamed source in HUD that the Director, Mario Cuomo, knew much about the fate of missing $59 billion for 1999:

> The losses could be far greater than $59 billion, but they don't know for sure because the audit isn't completed. Secretary Cuomo is a very smart control freak, so it's ludicrous to think that he doesn't know what is going on.[207]

Confirmation that losses from HUD were an endemic problem rather than peculiar to 1998 and 1999 comes from the General Accounting Office of Congress that released a report in 2003. It stated that in January 2003, "for the 12th year in a row, the HUD OIG [Office of Inspector General] cited the lack of an integrated financial-management system as a material weakness in its audit of the department's financial statements."[208] In short, billions of dollars were annually missing from HUD and no one knew where the money was going.

Fitts analysis of the fraudulent movement of funds through HUD, her initial firing as an Assistant Secretary, and subsequent difficulties her company had with HUD[209], indicated that she had stumbled on to one of the strategies used by the CIA to generate its secret black budget. Fitts ultimately came to the conclusion that HUD was being run as a money laundering operation to fund black projects.[210] The sums for HUD alone, $59 billion for 1999, were far greater than the official $3.5 billion annual estimated budget of the CIA that came from DoD appropriations. Missing funds from HUD, the alleged participation of the HUD Director in permitting the funds to go missing, and the difficulties suffered by Fitts, point to the CIA being behind the missing HUD funds. The CIA is the only government agency that has the legal authority to co-opt Federal

Agency Directors in permitting billions of dollars to go missing from, or be laundered through, their budgets for transfer into a 'black budget'. It is worth investigating the destruction of Fitts company, Hamilton Securities Group to identify any CIA fingerprints in covering up the secret transfer of HUD funds into what will be argued to be the CIA's 'unofficial' black budget.

According to Uri Dowbenko who has extensively researched the Fitts case in his book, *Bushwacked*, the rival contractor who brought the lawsuit against Fitts, has achieved notoriety for "filing nuisance lawsuits and 'bid protests'" against competitors.[211] The contractor's small mortgage investment firm apparently had, according to Dowbenko, "up to 17 in-house personnel working full time on mountains of paperwork regarding this and other cases."[212] The rival contractor may simply have had a chip on his shoulder from losing the HUD mortgage contract to Fitts' company. Another explanation offered by Dowbenko is that the rival contractor may have been simply a front for more powerful actors threatened by Hamilton's Securities who wished to cripple it through a damaging court process.

According to Dowbenko, more revealing was the behavior of the federal judge in charge of Fitts' case who eventually presided over the case. According to court transcripts, the initial judge had indicated in 1996 that it would be inappropriate to extend the seal [on the *qui tam*] without evidence and that unless evidence was produced he would not extend the seal again. The case was then transferred to another federal judge of the District of Columbia's District Court. According to Uri Dowbenky, the new judge "managed to illegally keep a *qui tam* lawsuit sealed for almost 4 years. That could be a 'judicial' record."[213] The judge had given multiple 60-day extensions to further investigate the allegations that he claimed were not limited to the False Claims Act limit of 60 days that applied to Department of Justice investigations, since the HUD Inspector General had independent subpoena power and chose to continue the investigation.[214] Extending the *qui tam* in this highly dubious manner meant that it was kept sealed thus preventing Hamilton from responding to the allegations, and thus prolonging an elaborate 'fishing expedition' that would financially exhaust Hamilton Securities.

A significant background fact about federal judge presiding over the Hamilton case was that he was the General Counsel for the CIA before being appointed as a federal judge to the District of Columbia District Court by Ronald Reagan in 1985. The federal judge's CIA background and the continued extensions of the *qui tam* case that had questionable legal standing and which was finally unsealed and dropped by a new Federal judge appointed to the case after his retirement in 2000, according to Dowbenky, point to a CIA covert program to destroy Hamilton Securities.

One conclusion from Dowbenky's research is that Fitts company was targeted since it threatened to undermine and even expose the way the CIA secretly extracted congressional appropriations from, or laundered funds through, HUD and other government agencies.[215] The CIA was using its unique legal status of being able to **lawfully transfer** Congressional appropriations or 'laundered money' through other federal government agencies, to fund projects administered by the intelligence community, and to destroy any individual or company that threatened to reveal such a process.

The wide extent of chronic auditing irregularities for most government agencies suggested that it was not just HUD that was used by the CIA as vehicle for siphoning money into its 'unofficial' black budget. A Senate Committee on government reform investigated the auditing practices of federal government agencies in 2001. Committee Chairman, Senator Fred Thompson, released a report which found that ineffectual auditing practices were endemic and led to billions of dollars annually going missing from most government agencies.[216] Rather than restricting itself to the appropriations through the DoD (the 'official' black budget), something Congress was aware of and tolerated, the accounting irregularities of many government agencies were possible evidence that the CIA was accumulating a sizable portion of its 'actual' black budget through other government agencies.

The Ultimate Beneficiary of the CIA 'Black Budget': The Intelligence Community and the Second Manhattan Project

The covert role of the CIA in destroying Hamilton Securities suggests that the $59 billion missing from HUD in 1999 was some of the money transferred to the CIA's 'unofficial black budget'. The 'legal' status of such a secret transaction on the basis of national security meant that the CIA could do this and be sure that senior officials in HUD and the Department of Justice would cooperate in keeping these transfers a secret. The legal onslaught suffered by Hamilton Securities was indicative of a covert CIA operation. This involved cooperation by senior officials in HUD, the DOJ, a federal judge and a former HUD contractor, in destroying a domestic U.S. company that had developed technology that threatened to reveal where the missing HUD money was really going.

Estimates of the CIA's 'official' black budget have been shown earlier to be in the vicinity of $3.5 billion and thought to be extracted from DoD appropriations. If the CIA was the recipient of the missing HUD money, this meant that the CIA was in fact a conduit for appropriated federal funds and non-appropriated funds being channeled through HUD and the CIA. Rather than the CIA being a recipient of DoD funds, as commonly thought, the CIA was more likely secretly funding intelligence activities and covert operations conducted through the intelligence community associated with the DoD. It is worth exploring how the CIA could be siphoning money to those elements of the intelligence community associated with the DoD, and how these funds could in turn be used by the DoD and the intelligence community to fund a large number of 'deep black projects' that operate outside of the oversight system developed for regular classified projects funded by Congressional appropriations. These regular classified programs are 'waived' Special Access Programs in the DoD, and 'waived' Covert Access Programs in the CIA. I turn now to examine events surrounding the inception of the CIA and its relationship with the DoD in jointly running and funding the intelligence community associated with the DoD.

The end of the Second World War witnessed the dissolution of the CIA's predecessor, Office of Strategic Services (OSS) that had been established in June 1942, and headed by a former civilian, William Donovan.[217] Donovan put together an assortment of adventurers, intellectuals, and military personnel that carried out a number of intelligence activities and covert operations during the war that had limited success. The OSS, however, was not trusted with the most sensitive war intelligence by the two main U.S. military intelligence services - the Office of Naval Intelligence

(ONI) and the Army's G-2. The war's end meant that foreign intelligence and covert operations were again dominated by the different military services, the State Department and the FBI (the FBI had extensive operations in Latin America) who would be very protective when it came to their most sensitive intelligence data.

The post-war structure of the national security system was debated, and the military services were on the record as being opposed to the formation of a civilian agency that would play a leading role in foreign intelligence gathering or covert operations.[218] Indeed, the idea of the different military intelligence services being headed by a civilian agency would have been quite a challenge for President Truman and his advisors to argue. This was due to the major role played by U.S. military intelligence in successfully conducting the war, and the peripheral role played by the OSS. Despite the wartime experience and the conventional wisdom that the military was more than capable of handling intelligence related activities, the passage of the National Security Act in 1947, led to the formation of a unified defense bureaucracy, the Department of Defense, three main military services (US Army, Navy and Air Force), and the creation of the National Security Council and the CIA.[219] The CIA became the formal head of the U.S. intelligence Community responsible for coordinating and providing leadership on all intelligence related activities. This meant that an organization based on the wartime model of a relatively small organization that conducted covert operations (the OSS) would be formally responsible for all U.S. intelligence activities both military and civilian. This represented a major shift for the different military services yet they acquiesced to Truman's request, but did so in a way that meant the DoD through its various associated intelligence services maintained considerable bureaucratic power in running the intelligence community in association with the CIA.

Up until 2005, the Director of the CIA (DCI) was the formal head of the Intelligence Community comprising the CIA, the National Security Agency, National Reconnaissance Office, the various military intelligence agencies and intelligence services of civilian agencies such as the FBI and the State Department.[220] A new position of Director of National Intelligence (DNI) was established in 2005 after passage of the Intelligence Reform Act in 2004.[221] The DNI formally took over functions previously performed by the DCI.

It would now be the DNI, rather than the DCI, who would formally head the intelligence community and give the daily intelligence briefing to the President. Nevertheless, the DCI was still the formal head of the CIA, a large government agency. The DNI's power was far more limited with only a relatively small office, and few resources to effectively head the U.S. intelligence community.

While the CIA has historically been the junior partner to the DoD when it comes to intelligence activities and covert operations, it has one major bureaucratic advantage over the DoD. This concerns 'black budget' allocations for highly classified projects. It would be far easier for the Congress to accept the idea of an 'official' black budget sanctioned by law, if a civilian agency was formally in charge of this unusual budgetary mechanism. It would require an extraordinary degree of trust by Congress that such a budgetary mechanism was not being abused. Congress was quite adamant that all appropriations to the DoD would be spent in ways consistent with the law, i.e., Congressional resolutions and enactments.[222] This is what distinguished American style democracy from an authoritarian police state. This meant that the DoD's power to create a 'black budget' would be circumscribed by relevant Congressional provisions governing the 'unacknowledged' Special Access Programs ('black projects') this funded.[223] The CIA provided ideal cover for creation of an 'unofficial' black budget that could legally launder and transfer funds through, non-DoD federal government agencies. The recipient of black budget funds was not the CIA as Congress intended in the CIA Act, but 'deep black projects' institutionally located within different branches of the intelligence community, the military services, Department of Energy, and select private corporations.

An important source of information about how the CIA has used black budget funds for covert actions is Colonel Fletcher Prouty. Prouty was Chief of Special Operations for the Joint Chiefs of Staff from 1955 to 1964 where he was responsible for military support of the CIA's covert operations. He was so alarmed by what he witnessed that in 1972, he wrote a book exposing the CIA's influence in the U.S. and the world.[224] According to Prouty, the CIA siphoned off funding and resources from the Pentagon and other government agencies for covert operations that were not approved by either the executive or legislative branches of government. More disturbingly, the CIA had embedded its assets and agents in virtually all Federal government departments, including the military, so it could gain institutional support for its covert operations without any kind of oversight or accountability. Prouty believe that the rapid growth in CIA covert operations since 1949 represented a major threat to constitutional government, and professional military standards.

The CIA's activities exclusively benefited the interests of what Prouty described as a "Power Elite" that essentially formed an unelected secret government that used visible government institutions and personnel for its goals.[225] The personnel recruited by the Power Elite to manage its interests made up a "Secret Team" that according to Prouty were:

> … security cleared individuals in and out of government who receive secret intelligence data gathered by the CIA and the National Security Agency (NSA)…. Membership on the Team, granted on a "need-to-know" basis, varies with the nature and location of the problems that come to its attention. The Secret Team has very close affiliations with elements of power in more than three-score foreign countries and is able when it chooses to topple governments, to create governments, and to influence governments almost anywhere in the world.[226]

The "Power Elite", through its specially recruited Secret Team, was ultimately in charge of the CIA's vast global network of resources, personnel and covert operations that exploited other branches of the U.S. government, and could topple national governments. The Power Elite was also ultimately responsible for how the CIA would raise black budget funds to support covert operations and "deep black projects". As in all CIA covert operations, a suitable cover was required to hide the real way funding was raised.

The CIA's 'official' black budget is the cover for how the large network of deep black projects run by members of the U.S. intelligence community, military services, Department of Energy and select private corporations are really funded. The CIA could provide for sufficient funding for an extensive number of 'deep black projects' entirely separate from regular DoD appropriations earmarked for the intelligence community. Congressional budget analysts and the general public are not aware of how different branches of the U.S. military, the intelligence community, Department of Energy and private corporations were secretly housing classified projects funded by CIA siphoned funds.

A secret funding arrangement between the CIA and the different military services in a manner that bypassed budgetary restraints on DoD associated activities would offer considerable mutual advantages to the CIA and the DoD. Both could create deep black projects outside the normal Congressional appropriation system and the regular DoD oversight process. The CIA has the legal power to secretly transfer appropriations from other government agencies, and moving these funds to whatever operations it deemed necessary. The 1949 CIA Act describes this power as follows:

> The sums made available to the Agency may be expended without regard to the provisions of law and regulations relating to the expenditure of Government funds; and for objects of a confidential, extraordinary, or emergency nature, such expenditures to be accounted for solely on the certificate of the Director.[227]

As the clause makes clear, the CIA Director may use funds from the black budget "without regard to the provisions of law." This means that the DCI has enormous power in funding 'deep black programs' and disregarding any legal or budgetary restrictions where the DCI deems a project to be of "extraordinary" or "emergency nature". The DCI would be able to prevent the Inspector General of the CIA - an independent official appointed by Congress - from conducting a thorough audit of the CIA's budget and exposing the actual size of the black budget. The relevant statute from the CIA Act is worth quoting since it is a unique restriction not found in the case of the power of Inspector Generals of other federal agencies:

> The Director may prohibit the Inspector General from initiating, carrying out, or completing any audit, inspection, or investigation, or from issuing any subpoena, after the Inspector General has decided to initiate, carry out, or

> complete such audit, inspection, or investigation or to issue such subpoena, if the Director determines that such prohibition is necessary to protect vital national security.[228]

The above clause directly contradicts the relevant federal statute that governs Inspector Generals in other government departments and agencies: "Neither the head of the establishment nor the officer next in rank below such head shall prevent or prohibit the Inspector General from initiating, carrying out, or completing any audit or investigation, or from issuing any subpoena during the course of any audit or investigation."[229]

Another advantage from having the CIA act as the unofficial funding source, was that the various military services, intelligence agencies, Department of Energy, and private corporations would be able to provide physical and personnel infrastructure for deep black projects funded by the CIA's black budget.[230] Some of these funds would 'legally' come from the appropriations of other government departments and agencies originally intended for other purposes. This enabled the DoD associated intelligence services to circumvent the Congressional requirement that no appropriations for DoD activities be expended "unless funds therefore have been specifically authorized by law". [231] In essence, the DoD and DCI were collaborating in circumventing Congressional intent designed to prevent DoD ever using funding sources outside of the Congressional appropriation process.

A further mutual advantage was that the CIA could play a significant consultative role in the various DoD associated intelligence agencies in both intelligence activities and covert operations. Such operations would be outside the regular oversight process in Congress, the Executive Office and even the DoD. This would enable security professionals within the military intelligence agencies, rather than political appointees in Congress, the Executive Office and DoD to make key decisions in the oversight of the 'deep black projects' that could run on whatever 'unofficial' black budget funding the CIA could raise. The only restraint was the willingness of directors of different government agencies to allow a portion of their budget allocations to go to the CIA and DoD entities in the intelligence community. The directors would also be expected to cover up the movement of significant sums of money that the CIA had raised elsewhere and was 'laundering' through these agencies. Most disturbingly, there is a growing body of evidence that a portion of the funds laundered through government agencies such as HUD by the CIA comes from organized crime and the drug trade.[232]

Organized Crime, Drugs, and the CIA

Allegations of links between the CIA and the drug trade first came to public attention in the 1970's when a number of public officials came forward with evidence of such links. One of these was a former police officer in the Los Angeles Police Department (LAPD), Michael Ruppert. In 1977, as a result of his official investigation into the drug trade in Los Angeles, Rupert uncovered evidence that the CIA was playing an active role in bringing drugs into New Orleans and Los Angeles. When Rupert disclosed this information to his superiors in the LAPD, he became a target for surveillance, harassment and burglaries that eventually led to his resignation.[233]

Another key official is a retired Drug Enforcement Agency agent, Celerino Castillo III, who was the lead DEA agent in Guatemala and discovered that the CIA was involved in the drug trade to raise finances for its covert operations. In a written statement to the House Permanent Select Committee on Intelligence Castillo gave detailed information on a number of drug running operations that involved cooperation between the CIA and organized crime cartels.[234] Celerino claimed:

> The key to understanding the "crack cocaine" epidemic, which exploded on our streets in 1984, lies in understanding the effect of congressional oversight on covert operations. In this case the Boland amendment(s) of the era, while intending to restrict covert operations as intended by the will of the People, only served to encourage C.I.A., the military and elements of the national intelligence community to completely bypass the Congress and the Constitution in an eager and often used covert policy of funding prohibited operations with drug money.[235]

Another prominent official was Marine Colonel James Sebow, the third in command of the El Toro Airbase, California, who discovered evidence that C-130 cargo flights coming into the airbase from Central America were filled with drugs. Sebow communicated his finding to the base commander, Col Joseph Underwood, and then found himself along with Col Underwood, subject to investigations for minor offenses, relieved of command and threatened with Court Martial if he did not cooperate with the investigation. On January 22, 1991, Sebow was found dead, apparently by suicide, but an investigation by family members and supporters revealed evidence that he was in fact murdered for what he had discovered.[236] On the day before his death, Sebow's widow recalled a conversation Sebow had with Col Underwood who had stopped by for a visit:

> Underwood stopped by and repeatedly tried to talk Jimmy into accepting an early retirement to avoid a court-martial. Jimmy objected strongly. At this, Underwood became quite angry. Sally stated, "I have never seen such a vicious face as Joe's when Jimmy said he would not retire and would take the entire matter to a court-martial if necessary. Underwood jumped up and said, "You'll never go to a court-martial, and I mean ***never***!"[237]

The events surrounding Sebow's death support allegations that he had uncovered a CIA supported drug running operation into the US, and was murdered to prevent this from being exposed.

In the July 12, 1985 personal notes of Oliver North, used by his legal defense during his various trials and Congressional hearings over his role in selling U.S. weapons to Iran to fund the Nicaraguan Contras, North referred to a meeting involving a number of NSC and CIA officials. At the meeting, $14 million was mentioned as the funds the Contra rebels would raise from the drug trade.[238] North's admission did not get serious press coverage despite the apparent confirmation that the CIA was complicit in the use of drugs as revenue for covert operations.[239] It can be inferred that North's efforts were an amateurish effort by an NSC 'basement team' to raise revenue for NSC covert operations. His efforts were modeled on a far more successful covert activity by the CIA to use revenue from the drug trade.

The best known case of an alleged link between the CIA and the drug trade emerged from the pioneering investigative journalism of Gary Webb in 1996 who published the "Dark Alliance" series in the San Jose Mercury during Summer 1996.[240] Webb presented a compelling case that the CIA played a role in allowing drug money to be used to fund the Contra rebels in Nicaragua. While Webb's series was focused on the proceeds of drug activities going to the Contras, his conclusion that the CIA colluded in this endeavor supported broader allegations of the CIA having used the drug trade to finance covert operations.

Webb's series of articles generated intense national interest until the publication of an 'independent' investigation by the Washington Post on October 4, 1996, claimed that there was insufficient evidence to support Webb's allegations.[241] The New York Times and Los Angeles Times followed up on October 20 with equally critical articles.[242] Criticisms began to mount and eventually led to the editors of the San Jose Mercury apologizing for 'errors' in Webb's Dark Alliance series, and had Webb transferred to a less prominent news bureau.[243] Webb resigned in disgust in November, 1997, ending a nineteen year career as a journalist.

One of the two writers of the Washington Post article, had previously received assignments with the CIA fuelling allegations he was a CIA asset. This raised the possibility that the Post had been co-opted into a covert campaign to undermine Webb's work. The critical stories in the New York Times and Los Angeles Times relied on similar 'unnamed sources' to the Post article further raising the possibility that Webb had become a victim of a covert CIA operation through the 'establishment' newspapers to discredit his findings.[244] In January 1998, the Inspector General of the CIA released a report exonerating the CIA of any role in the drug trade.[245]

So far I have demonstrated the existence of a black budget created by the CIA that circumvents Congressional intent on the use of appropriations of different federal departments and agencies. This includes the laundering of funds possibly gained from organized crime and the drug trade. It is worth estimating the size of the CIA's black budget and what it is used for.

Estimating the Size of the CIA's 'unofficial' Black Budget

Using Fitts estimates of money missing from HUD, and knowledge of the appropriations process, a more accurate figure of the CIA's 'unofficial' black budget that feeds the intelligence community associated with DoD can be estimated. It should be emphasized that it is only the CIA that has Congressional authority to draw appropriations through other government agencies 'without regard to any provisions of law' or 'intended use of appropriations'. This means that money missing from the Congressional appropriations of other agencies would be initially siphoned through the CIA and no other intelligence agency. Other agencies in the intelligence community gather their appropriations through the DOD which generates the 'official' black budget through fictitious line items on its annual budget. Consequently, it can be concluded that 'appropriated money' channeled through HUD and other agencies is going into the CIA's 'unofficial' black budget. In turn, this money goes directly into deep black programs located within the military services, intelligence community, Department of Energy, and private corporations.

The CIA's 'unofficial' black budget would therefore not appear on the DoD budget as single line items but would be annually moved through the DoD budgetary mechanisms in a way to prevent financial tracking. A description of this process appears *Blank Check: The Pentagon's Black Budget,* by Tim Weiner:

> One way the form [Form 1080, Voucher for Transfer Between Appropriations and/or Funds] is used to allow money to flow from the Treasury to the Army, or from one Army account to another, is for an officer to fill out the 1080. The bursar then signs the form and issues a Treasury check. The 1080 vouches that the money has been used to pay for the costs of authorized programs. It creates an audit trail - a paper path showing money flowing.[246]

An estimate of the size of the CIA's black budget, would therefore be unaccounted movement of funds through the DoD. According to an investigative journalist, Kelly O'Meara, the use of a range of accounting mechanisms such as "unsupported entries," "material-control weakness," "adjusted records," "unmatched disbursements," "abnormal balances" and "unreconciled differences" are evidence of large sums of money being moved through the DoD without being accounted for.[247] Since the Inspector General of DoD has a certain degree of independence, traces of the CIA black budget could appear in auditing anomalies using some of the terms O'Meara describes. David K. Steensma, Acting Assistant Inspector for auditing DoD, wrote in a 2002 report that "DoD processed $1.1 trillion in unsupported accounting entries to DoD Component financial data used to prepare departmental reports and DoD financial statements for FY 2000."[248] Elaborating on the significance of the DoD Inspector General's reports, O'Meara has written:

> [T]he deputy IG [Inspector General] at the Pentagon read an eight-page summary of DOD fiduciary failures. He admitted that $4.4 trillion in adjustments to the Pentagon's books had to be cooked to compile the required financial statements and that $1.1 trillion of that amount could not be supported by reliable information. In other words, at the end of the last full year on Bill Clinton's watch, more than $1 trillion was simply gone and no one can be sure of when, where or to whom the money went.[249]

According to the Office of the Inspector General, the accounting irregularities for fiscal year 1999 were even larger, totaling up to 2.3 trillion dollars; and for fiscal year 1998, 1.7 trillion dollars (see table 4).

The Inspector General's reports are important evidence that trillions of dollars were siphoned through the Department of Defense (DoD) during the fiscal years 1998-2002.[250] Using the Inspector General reports of accounting anomalies, it can be estimated that Fitts and O'Meara's estimates of missing money from the DoD closely approximates the CIA's 'unofficial' black budget. Consequently, the CIA black budget annually approximates 1.1 trillion dollars to 1.7 trillion – a truly staggering figure when one considers that the DoD budget for 2009 will be approximately 515 billion dollars.[251] Even the vast funding of DoD in terms of personnel, weapons systems and research into 'conventional weapons systems', is dwarfed by covert funding up to three times larger than the entire conventional DoD funded military system.

Table 4. Department of Defense (DoD) – Unsupported Accounting Entries 1998-2003

Fiscal Year	Unsupport -ed Entries USD	Source	Highlighted Quotes
2002	Not disclosed due accounting irregularities	Independ-ent Auditor Report	"DoD financial management and feeder systems cannot currently provide adequate evidence to support various material amounts on the financial statements. Therefore we did not perform auditing procures to support material amounts on the financial statements."[252]
2001	Not disclosed due accounting irregularities	Independ-ent Auditor Report	"We did not obtain sufficient, competent evidentiary matter to support the material line items on the financial statements ... the scope of our work was not sufficient to enable us to express, and we do not express, an opinion on these financial statements"[253]
2000	1.1 trillion	Office of Inspector General, Audit	"Of the $4.4 trillion in department-level accounting entries, $2.8 trillion were supported with proper research, reconciliation, and audit trails. However, department-level accounting entries of $1.1 trillion were unsupported or improper."[254]
1999	2.3 trillion	Office of Inspector General, Audit	"... department-level accounting entries of $2.3 trillion were made to force financial data to agree with various sources of financial data without adequate research and reconciliation, were made to force buyer and seller data to agree in preparation for eliminating entries, did not contain adequate documentation and audit trails, or did not follow accounting principles."[255]
1998	1.7 trillion	Inspector General Statement	"... final statements were more untimely than ever and a record $1.7 trillion of unsupported adjustments were made in preparing the statements."[256]

The vast size of the estimated CIA 'unofficial' black budget strongly suggests a collective effort by the CIA, the military services, the intelligence community, and the Department of Energy to fund a network of highly classified projects so large as to dwarf the original Manhattan project conducted at Los Alamos National Laboratories during the Second World War.[257] The original Manhattan project aimed to develop an atomic bomb for use in the war against Nazi Germany. The network of projects funded by the CIA's black budget aims to develop a range of advanced weapons systems and intelligence capabilities for use against an adversary whose existence and identity still remains classified.[258] I will henceforth refer to this network of highly classified projects as the second Manhattan Project - 'Manhattan II' is the ultimate beneficiary of the CIA's 'unofficial' black budget.

Oversight of the CIA's 'Unofficial' Black Budget & Manhattan II

Considering the vast size and unconventional funding source for Manhattan II, it is worth exploring how oversight of both the CIA's 'unofficial' black budget and of Manhattan II has evolved. It is worth investigating to whom program managers for projects funded by the CIA's unofficial black budget answer. The vastness and secrecy surrounding Manhattan II from its inception sometime during the Truman administration places it outside of the conventional political process where the appointment of key civilian leaders is subject to partisan politics. Partisan politics could compromise the secrecy of Manhattan II and the black budget that funds it.

The conventional political process has little direct influence on the appointment of senior military personal. They undergo a process of first being recommended to the President by the relevant DoD promotions boards, then appointed by the President, and finally confirmed by the Senate. While the military leadership of the DoD is outside the partisan political arena, this is not the case for the appointment of civilians who take on key positions as Secretaries, Deputy Secretaries, and Undersecretaries of the different military services in the DoD with each new administration.

Senior military officials may be generally aware of Manhattan II without having detailed knowledge of the black budget that funds it or the deep black projects within it. To have detailed knowledge, one must belong to an inner sanctum of national security officials, or 'Secret Team' as Fletcher Prouty refers to it:

> One of the most powerful weapons in the most political and powerful capitals of the world is that of exclusion. To be denied the "need to know" status, like being a member of the Team, even though one may have all the necessary clearances, is to be totally blackballed and eliminated from further participation. Politically, if you are cut from the Team and from its insider's knowledge, you are dead.[259]

It is likely that the politically appointed leaders of the DoD have little substantive knowledge of Manhattan II. They likely have as their chief task, ensuring secrecy of Manhattan II and of the CIA generated 'black budget' that feeds it. Thus, the Secretary of Defense would play no formal oversight of Manhattan II, far less of the black budget that sustains it. Nor is Manhattan II controlled by the Joint Chiefs of Staff and the Directorates for Intelligence (J-2) and Operations (J-3) that are responsible for intelligence and operational functions of the DoD. This is vividly illustrated in the case of Admiral Tom Wilson, the former head of intelligence J-2, in the Joint Chiefs of Staff. When Wilson was advised of the existence of black projects related to extraterrestrial technology, he asked for information. He was told, "Sir, you don't have a need to know. We can't tell you."[260] According to a reliable source, "the primary people who denied Wilson were not even DoD personnel, but rather private contractors, mainly attorneys."[261] As Prouty would say, Wilson was not part of the "Secret Team" straddling military and corporate worlds approved by the Secret Government (or "Power Elite") to have access to such information.

It is also unlikely that either the Director of the CIA (DCI) or the Director of National Intelligence (DNI) is made fully aware of the extent of the 'unofficial' black budget, the activities used to raise money for it, and the second Manhattan project it funds. The DCI, like all agency and department heads appointed by the President and confirmed by the Senate, is subject to the partisan political process. Up to the Carter administration, the tradition was that the appointment of a DCI would not be politicized. However, President

Gerald Ford effectively abandoned this tradition with the appointment of George Bush as DCI in 1975.[262] President Carter appointed Admiral Stansfield Turner as the new DCI in 1977. He in turn was replaced as DCI by William Casey, appointed by President Reagan in 1981.

Given the partisan political nature of the DCI since Bush, it is likely that much of the budgetary authority of the DCI was secretly delegated to a body that formally plays the key oversight role for the 'unofficial' black budget, and the covert Manhattan II projects it funds.[263] The delegated powers derived from the Truman administration in the form of Executive orders and/or National Security Council directives not published in the U.S. Federal Gazette required for all Executive orders.[264] These unpublished Executive orders and NSC directives thereby remain secret. They have been reconfirmed and gradually expanded by subsequent presidential administrations. The result is that ultimate oversight of the black budget and of Manhattan II remained firmly outside of the conventional oversight process.

Effective oversight of Manhattan II, comes from an 'executive committee' established to make it immune to partisan politics. This ensures that strict secrecy can be preserved, and politically motivated leaks prevented. The power and resources delegated to this 'executive oversight committee' for Manhattan II by the Executive Office, and its role in ensuring that 'black budget' funds are correctly used and kept secret from the general public, justifies a description of it as a 'shadow government'.[265]

Conclusion : Covert Funding of Extraterrestrial Projects

The method used in guiding my analysis in this chapter is to follow the money trail created by the CIA's black budget. This enables a number of important insights to be drawn about the institutions playing key roles in generating, protecting and distributing black budget funds. Critical in this analysis has been the experience of individuals and companies such as Catherine Fitts and Hamilton Securities, who experienced what evidence indicates was a CIA orchestrated covert campaign to discredit financial tracking reforms. These reforms threatened to make more transparent the financial flows of HUD and other government agencies. The systematic accounting problems experienced by HUD and other agencies points to the existence of an unofficial black budget over one trillion dollars annually. The size of the black budget and the CIA activities used to generate funds for it, point to a vast secret network of projects funded outside normal Congressional appropriation processes. What follows is a discussion of some of the primary conclusions that can be drawn, and arguments made concerning the CIA's 'unofficial' black budget and the Manhattan II project it funds.

It is worth repeating that the CIA is legally authorized by Congress to transfer, "without regard to any provisions of law", funds from other government agencies for the generation of a black budget. There is much evidence that the CIA uses this power to disregard law to complement whatever funds it can generate through Congressional appropriations, with funds gained through the drugs trade and organized crime. These funds are then laundered through different government agencies, departments and private corporations. The total annual sum of the black budget is best estimated through accounting anomalies in the main departmental recipient of all black budget funds, the DoD. Funds in the vicinity of 1.1 trillion dollars (and possibly as high as 1.7 trillion) finance a network of classified intelligence activities and covert operations that collectively form a second Manhattan Project.

The oversight of the Manhattan II project occurs outside of conventional oversight system that can be easily compromised by partisan politics. The oversight system that has evolved has been very successful in dividing different functions for Manhattan II in ways that balance institutional rivalries between national security organizations without compromising secrecy. Thus, the CIA generates the black budget, and transfers these funds to projects institutionally located in the military services, intelligence community, and Department of Energy. These different government and military entities in turn, hire private contractors and/or provide necessary military resources for these covert programs. The programs are housed in national laboratories, military bases, private corporations, or at other classified locations. The program managers of each of the classified projects associated with Manhattan II answer directly to an 'executive committee' outside the regular oversight process of DoD, CIA, Congress, the Executive Office, the newly created office of the Director of National Intelligence, and even the Joint Chiefs of Staff.

The respective intelligence, defense and appropriations committees in the U.S. Congress provide legitimacy for Manhattan II and the black budget that funds it by not revoking the budgetary powers allocated to the CIA through the 1949 CIA Act. Finally, the Executive Office through the National Security Council issues the necessary executive orders/NSC directives to coordinate the functions and activities in all the branches of government in order to secretly run Manhattan II. Each branch of the national security system plays an important role in Manhattan II, without being fully in control. This ensures a division of powers according to different functions required for Manhattan II. Effective oversight of Manhattan II, however, comes from an 'executive committee' that is immune to partisan political process, outside of the public arena, and whose oversight power and control of resources makes it a 'shadow government'.

It needs to be emphasized that the 'unofficial' black budget and Manhattan II Project have legally evolved in ways responding to a national security contingency yet to be revealed to the American public. The classified adversary for this elaborate secret system is arguably a 'potential threat' that warrants an extraordinary network of covert programs dwarfing the original Manhattan Project. Annually the network consumes between 1.1 to 1.7 trillion dollars in a non-transparent manner.

The 'potential threat' driving Manhattan II is an undisclosed extraterrestrial presence subject to agreements and joint projects that cause it to remain highly classified. Manhattan II can, therefore, be finally exposed as a vast network of covert projects related to the extraterrestrial presence. In particular, it funds projects associated with the reverse engineering of extraterrestrial vehicles, developing advanced technologies based on information supplied by extraterrestrials, the creation of deep underground bases, and the creation of fleets of alien reproduction vehicles. Some of these covert projects arise out of secret agreements with extraterrestrials examined in chapter one which lead to a number of global problems. The importance of Manhattan II in responding to the extraterrestrial presence is such that the CIA has, evidently, used organized criminal networks and the drug trade as sources of funding.

It is unclear when the full scope and impact of Manhattan II will be disclosed to the American public. Disclosure of Manhattan II has tremendous public policy consequences. These include increased loss of trust in federal government agencies, loss of morale among senior agency officials instructed to cover up black budget transactions, non-transparency in the flow of government appropriations, targeting of policy makers and business leaders who discover the fraudulent accounting, and money laundering occurring with the black budget. These consequences warrant serious examination of the need for maintaining the secrecy of Manhattan II and for the 'unofficial' black budget that funds it.

Finally, the extraterrestrial presence toward which Manhattan II is directed towards requires immediate declassification. There are inherent dangers in depicting extraterrestrials as a 'potential threat' in a non-transparent and unaccountable manner where the general public plays no role. Not only does such a depiction carry unacceptable strategic risk for an effective national security policy to extraterrestrial life (to be examined in chapter five), it is totally outside of the moral/legal restrictions likely to emerge from vigorous public debate in democratic societies. Maintaining an enormous black budget to fund a network of covert projects as a policy imperative, does not address the moral, legal and strategic issues required for a comprehensive policy response to an extraterrestrial presence.

ENDNOTES: CHAPTER THREE

[166] I wish to acknowledge Hugh Matlock for his hospitality, intellectual stimulation and research facilities for the completion of the first version of this chapter. Many thanks to Art Miller for his assistance in printing and distributing an earlier version. I wish to further thank Mike Schaefer and an anonymous reader for alerting me to errors in an earlier version of this chapter.
[167] See Richard Sauder, *Underwater and Underground Bases* (Adventures Unlimited Press, 2001): 102-29.
[168] See Richard Sauder, *Underwater and Underground Bases*, 129.
[169] Sauder, *Underwater and Underground Bases*, 143-216.
[170] 50 United States Code (U.S.C.) 403j(b). For an online database of all federal statutes codified in the USC, go to: http://www.access.gpo.gov/uscode/index.html.
[171] See Tim Weiner, *Blank Check: The Pentagon's Black Budget* (Warner Books, 1990) 118
[172] 95 *Congressional Record* 1945 (1949). Also quoted in Weiner, *Blank Check*, 119
[173] 50 U.S.C. 403f(a)
[174] This occurred to Catherine Austin Fitts whose work in detailing the black budget will be examined later.
[175] Cited in Fletcher Prouty, *The Secret Team*, http://www.ratical.org/ratville/JFK/ST/STchp3ii.html .
[176] The American Institute for Economic Research provides an online conversion program at: http://www.aier.org/colcalc.html .
[177] Data comes from a declassified CIA document detailing its projected budget for fiscal year 1953, "Location of Budgeted Funds for Fiscal Year 1953," CIA, 15 February, 1952, available online at: http://www.fas.org/sgp/othergov/cia1953bud.pdf .
[178] Quoted in Weiner, *Blank Check,* 218.
[179] Quoted in Weiner, *Blank Check,* 219.
[180] Quoted in Weiner, *Blank Check,* 220-21.
[181] Quoted in Weiner, *Blank Check,* 222. *Richardson v. U.S.* 465 F. 2d 844, 853, United States Court of Appeals for the Third Circuit, 1972.
[182] For the courts ruling as well as dissenting opinions, see U.S. v. Richardson (418 U.S. 166) 167-202.
[183] For further discussion see "The CIA's Secret Funding and the Constitution," 84 *Yale Law Journal* 613 (1975).
[184] See Senate Select Committee on Intelligence, *Whether Disclosure of Funds for the Intelligence Activities of the United States Is in the Public Interest*, Report No. 95-274, 94th Congress, 2nd Session, June 16, 1977 (Government Printing Office, 1977). Also quoted in Weiner, *Blank Check,* 137-38
[185] See Weiner, *Blank Check,* 138.

[186] FOIA was enacted in 1966 as Title 5 of the United States Code, section 552. For online information, see http://www.usdoj.gov/04foia/referenceguidemay99.htm .
[187] See "FAS Sues CIA for Intelligence Budget Disclosure," http://www.fas.org/sgp/foia/ciafoia.html
[188] For a copy of the lawsuit, see "FAS Sues CIA for Intelligence Budget Disclosure," http://www.fas.org/sgp/foia/ciafoia.html . For a website describing the Intelligence Community, go to http://www.intelligence.gov/ .
[189] See Intelligence Authorization Act for Fiscal Year 1998, Amendment No.416 Congressional Record: June 19, 1997 (Senate) p. S5963-S5978]; Available online at: http://www.fas.org/sgp/congress/s858.html
[190] "House Debate on Intelligence Budget Disclosure," Intelligence Authorization Act for Fiscal Year 1998, Congressional Record: July 9, 1997 (House)] p. H4948-H4985. Available online at: http://www.fas.org/sgp/congress/hbudg.html
[191] See "Statement of the Director of Central Intelligence Regarding the Disclosure of the Aggregate Intelligence Budget for Fiscal Year 1997," http://www.fas.org/sgp/foia/victory.html
[192] Marchetti and Marks, *The CIA and the Cult of Intelligence* (Alfred Knopf, 1974) 61, 81.
[193] Wise, *The American Police State* (Random House, 1976) 185.
[194] See Federation of American Scientists, http://www.fas.org/irp/agency/budget1.htm .
[195] The American Institute for Economic Research provides an online conversion program at: http://www.aier.org/colcalc.html .
[196] See Mari Kane, "On the Money Trail: The dangerous world of Catherine Austin Fitts," *North Bay Bohemian*, September 5-11, 2002: http://www.metroactive.com/papers/sonoma/09.05.02/fitts-0236.html
[197] See Kane, "On the Money Trail," *North Bay Bohemian* (September 5-11, 2002). Available online at: http://www.metroactive.com/papers/sonoma/09.05.02/fitts-0236.html
[198] See Kane, "On the Money Trail," http://www.metroactive.com/papers/sonoma/09.05.02/fitts-0236.html
[199] See Kane, "On the Money Trail," http://www.metroactive.com/papers/sonoma/09.05.02/fitts-0236.html
[200] See Uri Dowbenky, "HUD Fraud, Spooks and the Slumlords of Harvard," *Bushwacked: Inside Stories of True Conspiracies* (National Liberty Press, 2003) 1-18. Available online at: http://www.conspiracydigest.com/bushwhacked.html
[201] Paul M. Rodriquez, "Mortgage Scandal - HUD Gives Up With Fitts," *Insight On the News,* available online at: http://www.insightmag.com/main.cfm?include=detail&storyid=161204 . However, a civil suit by John Ervin & Associates was allowed to continue by the government even though it had the ability to end the case since it found no evidence of wrong doing. This effectively meant that Ervin Associates would continue to tie up Hamilton Securities and Catherine Fitts in the court system.

[202] See Fitts, "Summary of Events As of February, 2001: http://www.solari.com/media/summary.html

[203] Catherine Austin Fitts, "Experience with FHA-HUD Background Information for Unanswered Questions," June 2003. Available online at: http://solari.com/gideon/fhalist.htm

[204] See Kelly Patricia O'Meara, "Why Is $59 Billion Missing From HUD?" *Insight on News* (Nov 6, 2000). Available online at: http://www.insightmag.com/main.cfm?include=detail&storyid=246245

[205] Susan Gaffney , "Audit Results for the Department of Housing and Urban Development," Testimony before a hearing of the Subcommittee on Government Management, Information, and Technology (March 22, 2000 1999). Available online at: http://www.whereisthemoney.org/59billion.htm and http://www.hud.gov/offices/oig/data/reform.pdf .

[206] Quoted in Kelly Patricia O'Meara, "Why Is $59 Billion Missing From HUD?" *Insight on News* (Nov 6, 2000). http://www.insightmag.com/main.cfm?include=detail&storyid=246245

[207] Quoted in Kelly Patricia O'Meara, "Why Is $59 Billion Missing From HUD?" *Insight on News* (Nov 6, 2000). http://www.insightmag.com/main.cfm?include=detail&storyid=246245

[208] "HUD's Financial Woes Continue," *Insight On the News* (April 18, 2003). Available online at: http://www.insightmag.com/news/421370.html

[209] For discussion of the difficulties encountered by Fitts' company, see Paul Rodriquez, "Thankless Task," *Insight on the News* (May 21, 2001). Available online at: http://www.insightmag.com/main.cfm/include/detail/storyid/210955.html

[210] Catherine Fitts, "The Myth of the Rule of Law or How Money Works: The Destruction of Hamilton Securities." *SRA Quarterly: Third Quarter Commentary* (London, 2001) 2. Available online at: http://www.solari.com/gideon/q301.pdf

[211] Dowbenky, *Bushwacked: Inside Stories of the True Conspiracy* (National Liberty Press). Available online at: http://www.conspiracydigest.com/bushwhacked.html .

[212] Dowbenky, *Bushwacked*, available online at: http://www.conspiracydigest.com/bushwhacked.html .

[213] Dowbenky, *Bushwacked*, available online at: http://www.conspiracydigest.com/bushwhacked.html .

[214] See Fitts, "Summary of Events," http://www.solari.com/media/summary.html

[215] Fitts' own conclusion was that the CIA was indeed involved in the destruction of Hamilton, but her view was that HUD was being used to launder money from the illicit drug trade. Catherine Fitts, "The Myth of the Rule of Law or How Money Works," *SRA Quarterly,* 5.

[216] Report of Senator Fred Thompson, Chairman, Committee on Governmental Affairs, on Management Challenges Facing the New Administration (US Senate, 2002) available online at: http://www.senate.gov/~gov_affairs/vol1.pdf .

[217] For history of OSS, See Michael Warner, "Office of Strategic Services," http://www.cia.gov/cia/publications/oss/foreword.htm

[218] See State Department history of Intelligence Services, http://www.state.gov/www/about_state/history/intel/intro.html .
[219] See 50 U.S.C. 401
[220] The Intelligence Community website is: http://www.intelligence.gov/
[221] Intelligence Reform Act available online at: http://thomas.loc.gov/cgi-bin/query/D?c108:2:./temp/~c108vQo59t .
[222] 10 USC114. Available online at: http://www4.law.cornell.edu/uscode/10/stApIch2.html
[223] The relevant Congressional statutes for SAPs is 10 U.S.C.119
[224] L.Fletcher Prouty, *The Secret Team: The CIA and its Allies in control of the United States and the World* (Skyhorse Publishing, [1972) 2008).
[225] Fletcher Prouty, *The Secret Team* [Preface, "The Secret Team II," 1997] *xxxv-xxxvi.*
[226] Fletcher Prouty, *The Secret Team,* 3.
[227] 50 U.S.C.403j (b)
[228] 50USC403q (b)(3)
[229] 5a U.S.C.3(a)
[230] For discussion for how the CIA could recruit personnel for its covert projects see Prouty, *The Secret Team,* 313-30.
[231] 10 U.S.C.114. Available online at: http://www4.law.cornell.edu/uscode/10/stApIch2.html
[232] See Gary Webb, *The Dark Alliance* (Seven Stories Press, 1998). For online information on the connection between the CIA and the drug trade, see Michael Rupert's 'From The Wilderness' website: http://www.fromthewilderness.com .
[233] For a brief summary of Rupert's background, see "Opening Remarks of Michael C. Rupert for the Senate Select Committee on Intelligence," available online at http://www.fromthewilderness.com/free/ciadrugs/ssci.html
[234] "Written Statement of Celerino Castillo III (D.E.A., Retired) to the House Permanent Select Committee on Intelligence," April 27, 1998. Celerino's statement is available online at: http://www.fromthewilderness.com/free/ciadrugs/contra1.html .
[235] Castillo, "Written Statement," available at: http://www.fromthewilderness.com/free/ciadrugs/contra1.html .
[236] See David Zucchino, The suicide files: Death in the military----last of a four part series," *The Philadelphia Inquirer*, December 22, 1993. Available online at: http://www.whatreallyhappened.com/RANCHO/POLITICS/MENA/suicide4.html. See also Gary Null, "The Strange Death of Col Sabow," available online at: http://www.garynull.com/documents/sabow.htm
[237] Gary Null, "The Strange Death of Col Sabow," http://www.garynull.com/documents/sabow.htm

[238] Lawrence E. Walsh, Final Report of the Independent Counsel for Iraq/Contra Matters, Vol. 1. (United States Court of Appeal for the District of Columbia Circuit, 1993) ch. 21. Available on line at: http://www.fas.org/irp/offdocs/walsh/chap_21.htm .
[239] See Michael Ruppert, "A CIA Confession: Oliver North Exposed," *From the Wilderness*, October 21, 1998. Available online at: http://www.fromthewilderness.com/free/ciadrugs/volii.html
[240] Webb subsequently wrote the book, *Dark Alliance* (Seven Stories Press, 1998).
[241] See Robert Suro and Walter Marcus, "The CIA and Crack: Evidence is Lacking of Alleged Plot," *Washington Post*, October 4, 1996. See also Webb, *Dark Alliance*, 448-50.
[242] See "Tale of CIA and Drugs Has Life of Its Own," *New York Times*, October 20, 1996. The Los Angeles Times articles ran over three days beginning October 20. See also Webb, *Dark Alliance*, 452-55.
[243] See Webb, *Dark Alliance,* 461-65.
[244] Webb, *Dark Alliance,* 450-52.
[245] Inspector General, CIA, "Report of Investigation: Allegations of Connections Between CIA
and The Contras in Cocaine Trafficking to the United States (Office of Inspector General Investigations Staff, CIA, January 29, 1998) Vols 1-2. Available online at: http://www.cia.gov/cia/reports/cocaine/report/index.html
[246] Weiner, *Blank Check,* 178-79.
[247] Kelly Patricia O'Meara, "Government Fails Fiscal-Fitness Test," *Insight on the News* (April 29, 2002). Available online at: http://www.insightmag.com/news/246188.html .
[248] David K. Steensma, "Agency Wide Financial Statements. The Department of Defense Audit Opinion." (February 26, 2002) The Report can be viewed online at: http://www.dodig.osd.mil/Audit/reports/fy02/02-055.pdf .
[249] Kelly Patricia O'Meara, "Rumsfeld Inherits Financial Mess," *Insight on the News* (Aug. 10, 2001). Available online at: http://www.insightmag.com/main.cfm?include=detail&storyid=139530 . Another media report on the 1.1 trillion missing dollars is Tom Abate, Military waste under fire $1 trillion missing – Bush plan targets Pentagon accounting, *San Francisco Chronicle* (May 18, 2003. Available online at: http://www.ratical.org/ratville/CAH/DODtrillions.html#p6 .
[250] See Fitts, "Real Deal, Saving Tennessee," Scoop UQ Wire (July 4, 2002). Available online at: http://www.scoop.co.nz/mason/stories/HL0207/S00031.htm#a . Fitts has a website with a number of resources describing how more than a trillion dollars are annually unaccounted for in a number of government agencies. Go to http://www.solari.com .
[251] "Fiscal 2009 Department of Defense Budget is Released," *Defense Link*, February 04, 2008. Available online at: http://www.defenselink.mil/releases/release.aspx?releaseid=11663 .

---

[252] Independent Auditor's Report on the Department of Defense Fiscal Year 2002 Agency-Wide Principal Financial Statements (1/15/03) Project D2002FI-0104.000, part III, p. 225, http://www.dodig.osd.mil/Audit/reports/
[253] Independent Auditor's Report on the Department of Defense Fiscal Year 2001 Agency-Wide Financial Statements (02/26/02), Report No. D-2002-055, http://www.dodig.osd.mil/Audit/reports/
[254] Office of the Inspector General, Compilation of the FY 2000 DoD Agency-Wide Financial Statements -- Report No. D-2001-181(PDF)-Project No. D2001FI-0018.003 http://www.dodig.osd.mil/Audit/reports/ .
[255] *Department of Defense,* Office of the Inspector General – Audit, "Department-Level Accounting Entries for FY 1999" Report No. D-2000-179 (PDF) http://www.dodig.osd.mil/Audit/reports/ .
[256] Testimony: Statement of Eleanor Hill, Inspector General, Department of Defense, Before the Subcommittee on Readiness and Management Support Senate Armed Services Committee, United States Senate on Defense Financial Management (04/14/99) http://www.dodig.osd.mil/Audit/reports/
[257] See Leslie R. Groves, *Now It Can Be Told: The Story of the Manhattan Project* (Da Capo Press, 1983).
[258] For an intriguing description of what the black budget funds and the 'classified adversary', see Catherine Fitts, "The $64 Question: What's Up With the Black Budget? – The Real Deal," *Scoop: UQ Wire* (23 September, 2002). Available online at: http://www.scoop.co.nz/mason/stories/HL0209/S00126.htm . For a more conventional assessment of potential future adversaries, see Judy Chizek, "Military Transformation: Intelligence, Surveillance and Reconnaissance" (Congressional Research Service, Library of Congress, May 2002). Available online at: http://www.fas.org/irp/crs/RL31425.pdf
[259] Prouty, *The Secret Team,* 4.
[260] Steven Greer, *Hidden Truth, Forbidden Knowledge* (Crossing Point Publications, 2006) 158.
[261] Richard Dolan, "The Admiral Wilson UFO Story," available online at: http://www.ufodigest.com/news/0808/wilson.html .
[262] *John Helgerson, CIA Briefings with Presidential Candidates* (Central Intelligence Agency, 1996,) ch. 5, available online at: http://www.cia.gov/csi/books/briefing/cia-8.htm .
[263] See Harold Relyea, "Presidential Directives: Background and Overview," available online at: http://www.fas.org/irp/crs/98-611.pdf .
[264] For an overview of Presidential Directives and executive power to create new bodies and delegate authority without Congressional approval, see Harold Relyea, "Presidential Directives: Background and Overview" (Congressional Research Service, Library of Congress, February 2003) Available online at: http://www.fas.org/irp/crs/98-611.pdf .
[265] For discussion of the shadow government and its evolution, see Michael Salla, *Exopolitics: Political Implications of the Extraterrestrial Presence*, ch. 2. Available online at: http://exopolitics.org/Study-Paper-5.htm .

Chapter Four

Managing U.S. Personnel in Extraterrestrial Related Projects

Introduction[266]

The evidence concerning UFO crashes that are extraterrestrial in origin, and their covert retrieval by highly specialized teams involving joint military and government personnel, is extensive and persuasive. Evidence has been accumulated by pioneers of UFO crash research such as Leonard Stringfield, and more recently by Dr Robert Wood and Ryan Wood.[267] Understanding the highly classified procedures established to manage the retrieval of crashed UFOs received a significant boost with the public emergence of the Special Operations Manual – SOM1-01 in 1994.[268] SOM1-01 provides an important analytical framework for understanding, and answering questions about, classified procedures used for locating, isolating and recovering crashed UFOs that are extraterrestrial in origin. Significantly, SOM1-01 described the classified government entity created for the managing crash retrieval operations. Known as the Majestic-12 Group, it evolved out of the "Majestic 12 Operation" created by President Truman on September 24, 1947.[269]

In addition to SOM1-01 providing such information, there are the testimonies of a number of whistleblowers who claim to have participated in UFO crash retrieval operations or participated in a number of highly classified extraterrestrial related projects. I will concentrate on two whistleblowers, Clifford Stone and Dan Sherman. Their respective testimonies give important insights into the nature of 'black projects' designed to facilitate UFO crash retrievals, and the procedures used for managing personnel recruited into extraterrestrial related projects.

In this chapter, I use both SOM1-01 and whistleblower testimonies of Stone and Sherman to outline the main procedures used in UFO crash retrievals. The main goal is to identify key elements of how personnel are covertly managed when recruited into extraterrestrial related projects. I contrast the testimony of Stone with key elements in SOM1-01, in order to better understand how

SOM1-01 is applied in practice, and to help substantiate Stone's testimony of being covertly employed as a telepathic interface in UFO crash retrieval operations. I will also use Sherman's testimony concerning his employment as an "intuitive communicator" in another extraterrestrial related project, as a means of corroborating Stone's claims with regard to his covert training and UFO crash retrieval duties. Finally, I provide ten key principles from Stone's and Sherman's testimonies for understanding how personnel are recruited, trained and managed by the Majestic-12 Group for extraterrestrial related projects in general, and crash retrieval operations in particular.

Authenticity of SOM1-01 as a 1954 document

There continues to be debate over the genuineness of SOM1-01. One approach is to analyze it as a historic document that can be authenticated by comparing its chief elements to similar documents produced in the 1950's, and to identify possible anachronisms. The idea is that if it is shown that SOM1-01 was created in 1954 without any modern anachronisms, then it is extremely unlikely that its public emergence forty years later would be the product of a modern hoaxer. The more likely possibility is that it is a genuine document that was leaked for reasons related to government or military personnel dissatisfied with the pace of official disclosure of an extraterrestrial presence. Both Dr Robert Wood and Ryan Wood take this approach. They have provided a number of persuasive arguments for the authenticity of SOM1-01 as a document produced in 1954 replicating the standards used in that era for similar government issued documents.[270] Significantly, they find it devoid of modern anachronisms, and have yet to find any evidence for it being a hoax. In the latest edition of *Top Secret/Majic*, Stanton Friedman is in agreement with the Woods' analysis suggesting the authenticity of SOM1-01 as a document produced in 1954.[271] Furthermore, in his most recent book, Friedman concludes that the SOM1-01 document "is very likely genuine."[272]

A contrasting approach is taken by UFO researchers such as Jan Aldrich, a former Assistant Adjutant for the U.S. Army. Aldrich points to significant departures from standard military manuals that are developed in a meticulous fashion to eliminate discrepancies. In 1996, Aldrich identified 50 discrepancies in SOM1-01 that in his view indicate the kind of 'sloppiness' found in a fraudulent document. [273] He dismissively speculates that SOM1-01 was produced by an "Air Force buck Sgt., with some training in military intelligence," together with some friends cutting and pasting from Army manuals.[274] He therefore concludes that it is highly unlikely that SOM1-01 is genuine. Aldrich overlooks that such discrepancies may not be evidence of a fraudulent document, but evidence of a significant departure from the normal military procedure for creating such manuals. Such a departure might result in the kind of "sloppy" formatting and discrepancies that would stand out for (former) military professionals skilled in the preparation of similar manuals.

The discrepancies in SOM1-01 from standard military manuals can be explained by the highly classified security procedures created not only for managing UFO crash retrievals, but for creating manuals such as SOM-01 itself. Indeed, I will reveal the existence of a parallel organization to the conventional military that borrows military personnel for a variety of ad hoc duties that are overseen by a covert management group mentioned in SOM1-01 – Majestic-12 Group. SOM1-01 describes the history of this group as follows:

> 4. Operation Majestic 12 was established by special classified presidential order on 24 September 1947 at the recommendation of Secretary of Defense James V. Forrestal and Dr. Vannevar Bush, Chairman of the Joint Research and Development Board. Operations are carried out under a Top Secret Research and Development – Intelligence Group [Majestic-12 Group] directly responsible only to the President of the United States.

Documents such as the Eisenhower Briefing Document, the Truman Memo, and the Cutler-Twining Memo confirm that the Majestic-12 [or MJ-12] Group was created by Presidential Executive Order as a highly classified part of the executive branch of government that recruits extensively from the military, but is not itself a military department.[275]

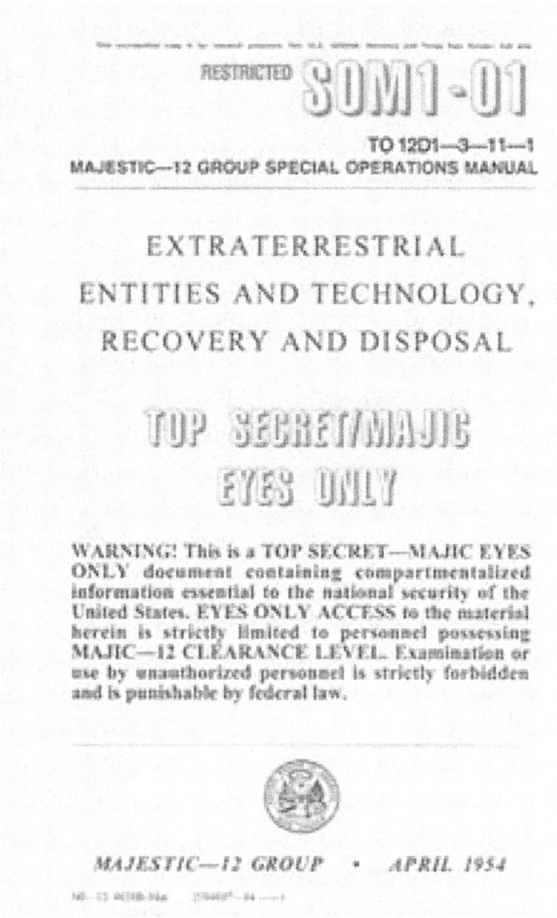

RESTRICTED SOM1-01

TO 12D1—3—11—1

MAJESTIC—12 GROUP SPECIAL OPERATIONS MANUAL

EXTRATERRESTRIAL ENTITIES AND TECHNOLOGY, RECOVERY AND DISPOSAL

TOP SECRET/MAJIC EYES ONLY

WARNING! This is a TOP SECRET—MAJIC EYES ONLY document containing compartmentalized information essential to the national security of the United States. EYES ONLY ACCESS to the material herein is strictly limited to personnel possessing MAJIC—12 CLEARANCE LEVEL. Examination or use by unauthorized personnel is strictly forbidden and is punishable by federal law.

MAJESTIC—12 GROUP • APRIL 1954

Figure 1. Cover of Special Operations Manual

The Majestic-12 Group sits at the apex of an extensive network of government-military-corporate organizations and joint projects engaged in classified activities concerning extraterrestrial technologies and extraterrestrial life forms. The Majestic-12 Group is functionally equivalent to the "Power Elite" that Col Fletcher Prouty believes to sit at the apex of a world wide network of covert operations conducted by the CIA.[276] According to Prouty, the CIA acts as a recruiting agency for personnel and resources from any government agency or military department required for these covert operations.

Chief among these classified activities controlled by Majestic-12 is overseeing the location, retrieval and reverse engineering of crashed UFOs that are extraterrestrial in origin. This extensive network of classified organizations and projects was described in chapter three as a second Manhattan Project. Manhattan II is funded by a set of covert mechanisms that are extra-constitutional in nature, and estimated to be over one trillion dollars annually.

The development of manuals such as SOM1-01 may not be a product of military professionals in the normal course of their duties. Instead such manuals are likely produced by military personnel co-opted into MJ-12 classified projects on an ad hoc basis due to their skills, who then revert back to their normal military duties. A more informed speculation to Aldrich's about the production of SOM1-01 may therefore be offered. SOM1-01 likely emerged from a 'master sergeant' and other individuals with the necessary security clearance and experience in UFO crash recoveries, being asked by their superiors in the Majestic-12 Group to prepare a crash retrieval manual using existing army manuals as templates.

This explanation accounts for the number of discrepancies found in SOM1-01 when compared with the normal standard for a military manual, but does not dismiss the authenticity of SOM1-01 as a government issued manual produced in 1954. If this is the case, then the discrepancies found in SOM1-01 can be explained as a function of the peculiar system used to create it. This explanation provides an answer to the apparent genuineness of SOM1-01 as implied by its authenticity as a 1954 document (confirmed by Robert and Ryan Wood, and supported by Friedman); while containing numerous discrepancies as identified by Aldrich and others. In short, discrepancies in SOM1-01 as a 1954 document suggest its genuineness as a product of the covert system that created it, rather than evidence of it being a modern fraud. Consequently, I will use SOM1-01 as a reference tool for helping corroborate the testimony of a whistleblower, Clifford Stone, who claims to have directly participated in UFO crash retrieval operations and Project Moon Dust.

Clifford Stone's Claims Regarding UFO Crash Retrieval Operations

Staff Sergeant Clifford Stone served in the U.S. Army for a 22 year period from 1969 to 1990. He claims that he was recruited into an elite UFO retrieval team due to his natural ability to telepathically communicate with extraterrestrial biological entities (EBEs).[277] He claims that he was picked out during his childhood by the U.S. military and had an Air Force Captain regularly visit him on a weekly basis who encouraged Stone to pursue his interest in UFOs, and eventually influenced his decision to join the military. Upon joining the Army Stone found himself starting a very untypical military career in a highly classified project he subsequently learned was called Project Moon Dust.[278] Stone says he was initially given training in Nuclear, Biological and Chemical Warfare at Fort MacCallum, Alabama; and then given regular army assignments until called away to perform his UFO crash retrieval duties when required. A mysterious 'Colonel' was the individual who supervised Stone while performing his covert duties. Stone claims that when required for UFO retrievals he was typically called out for temporary duty (TDY) to serve between three days to a week, but in some international cases these could take longer with one month being the longest. His army service record refers to him only performing clerical duties as a typist; and has no reference to his alleged training for, or assignments with, UFO crash retrieval teams. Finally, Stone described how his effort to retire from the Army in 1989 (after twenty two years of service) was opposed by the 'Colonel' who said his crash retrieval services were still required.

Some support for Stone's claims of having worked in covert UFO retrieval projects is extensive documentation Stone uncovered to support the existence of classified UFO crash retrieval teams associated with Project Moon Dust, and of crash retrieval operations in various countries.[279] Stone began, in the late 1970's to use Freedom of Information Act (FOIA) requests to uncover information disclosing the existence of Project Moon Dust that was created to recover debris of UFOs. In addition, Stone's military service was characterized by his dogged determination to disclose UFO information even though this was highly unusual for someone engaged in full time military service. His efforts were not viewed favorably and even opposed by his Army superiors. His FOIA activities led to punishments such as censure, being confined to base, relocation to foreign US bases, and the failure to progress in rank beyond Staff Sergeant. Stone's conflict with Army authorities over his FOIA requests, and the actual documentation on Project Moon

Dust, is circumstantial evidence for his claim that he was secretly recruited into covert UFO retrieval teams without the knowledge of his military superiors.

Stone's use of FOIA was particularly important since this would be a logical legal instrument used by an individual who desired to disclose the nature of his activities without making unauthorized disclosures of classified information. Stone's FOIA research led to him being acknowledged by UFO researchers such Major Kevin Randle who favorably referred to his "pioneering research."[280] Stanton Friedman also described Stone as a "dedicated researcher" who brought into the public arena "a multitude of government documents, many never before published."[281] Both Randle and Friedman subsequently distanced themselves from Stone when he publicly announced that he worked with UFO crash retrieval teams, and did not have the documentation to verify this. To help substantiate Stone's claims, I now examine them in relation to SOM1-01 to find parallels and consistencies in terms of procedures and policies. If Stone's claims are consistent with SOM1-01, then this helps confirm his testimony. Also, such consistency would help identify the security procedures used to manage personnel recruited into covert UFO crash retrieval projects.

Contrasting Clifford Stone's UFO Crash Retrieval Claims with SOM1-01

Stone claimed that he was part of a highly classified advance team for crash retrievals that would check for biological or radioactive contamination. This was combined with his most important duty which was to be the telepathic interface in case communication was required with any extraterrestrial biological entity (EBE) found at the crash scene. Stone claimed that these operations were led by an individual who wore civilian clothes whose rank he was never told but whom he called 'Colonel'. The 'Colonel' would take charge of retrieval operations, and lead the debriefing sessions. This appears to be very odd given the propensity for operations involving military personnel to be led by military officers where rank dictates authority. However, the 'Colonel' and the covert team Stone was recruited into appeared to be one of the "Special Teams" described in SOM1-01 as follows:

> 4.a. The recovery for scientific study of all materials and devices of a foreign or extraterrestrial manufacture that may become available....
> 4.b. The recovery for scientific study of all entities and remains of entities not of terrestrial origin which may become available...
> 4.c. The establishment of Special Teams to accomplish the above operations.

These special teams would not require any distinguishing uniforms specifying rank since they were given "Top priority" at UFO crash retrieval locations:

> 24d. OPNAC Team personnel will be given TOP Priority at all times regardless of their apparent rank or status. No person has the authority to interfere with the OPNAC Team in the performance of its duties by special direction of the President of the United States.

The "special direction" mentioned in 24d almost certainly refers to a classified Executive Order never released to the general public. In addition, Stone claimed that he sometimes traveled internationally to perform crash retrievals that were led by the 'Colonel'. This is consistent Stone's overseas assignments and with the following SOM1-01 passage:

> 4.e. Establishment and administration of covert operations to be carried out in concert with Central Intelligence to effect the recovery for the United States of extraterrestrial technology and entities which may come down inside the territory of or fall into the possession of foreign powers.

This is an important passage since it explicitly refers to the prominent role of the CIA in crash retrieval operations. The passage provides a clue into the identity of the mysterious civilian, 'the Colonel', that directed operations when Stone was present. The 'Colonel' was very likely a CIA agent directing what is clearly a covert operation. Such a scenario is supported by Colonel Fletcher Prouty's observations concerning the leading role played by the CIA in covert operations. According to Prouty, the CIA's covert operations are extensive, draw personnel from all branches of government, and dwarf its intelligence functions.[282] He wrote that by 1961, "the CIA had succeeded in building such a broad base within the bureaucracy of the U.S. Government that any meaningful reference to the CIA must take into consideration the existence of this vast infrastructure."[283] Stone's testimony of his 'special team' being led by a civilian who took charge of the crash retrieval operations despite the possibility of high ranking military personnel at the scene, is consistent with SOM1-01, and the observations of Prouty concerning the CIA's leading role in covert operations.

Stone further claimed that the 'Colonel' allowed him to read a three inch thick booklet that contained information on 57 known types of extraterrestrial biological entities (EBEs):

> That information was from a little publication that they had that the person I called the Colonel always carried [with] him. … It was a little booklet that he carried, actually a little thick booklet, a loose leaf notebook type situation. But the intent of cataloguing the different species was so that they could render the best first aid they could in identifying which species they had at any given location.[284]

Stone claims he first saw the Heinz 57, "EBE Guidebook" in 1979 and said that it contained much information on each of group of EBEs in terms of their physiology, food requirements and medical information. He claims he could read the Guidebook when he was serving on the retrieval teams up until 1989. Stone says that the Guidebook was to be used in case First Aid had to be administered to any EBEs found at crash sites. We can now compare his claims with a passage from SOM1-01:

> 24. b. Injured or wounded entities will be treated by medical personnel assigned to the OPNAC Team. If the team medical personnel are not immediately available. First Aid will be administered by Medical Corps personnel at the initial site. Since little is known about EBE biological functions, aid will be confined to the stopping of bleeding, bandaging of wounds and splinting of broken limbs. No medications of

> any kind are to be administered as the effect of terrestrial medications on non-human biological systems are impossible to predict.

Stone's testimony is consistent with the first aid assistance described in SOM1-01. As part of the advance team attending crash retrieval sites, Stone would have a "need to know" when it came to administrating first aid to injured EBEs. Stone's testimony however indicates that knowledge of EBE physiology had considerably advanced since 1954 when no substances were prescribed for dealing with EBE injuries by SOM1-01 since the effects were "impossible to predict". By 1979, however, a medical manual was made available to detail what substances could or couldn't be administered. This indicates that in the 25 years since SOM1-01 was crafted, a great deal of information had been acquired on EBE physiology. This is consistent with the number of crash retrieval operations that have been estimated to have occurred over these years, and the knowledge gained through them.[285]

In a July 2005 interview I had with Stone, he describes the code word he would receive for leaving his normal duties to go on TDY assignment with the Project Moon Dust crash retrieval team:

> The code word that was used with me was "the general sends his regards". I didn't know if there was a general involved or not since I never saw the general. I was told "bags to go", so you grab your DA-50 bag, all your equipment will be packed and you kiss your wife and your children good bye and you left. You never knew if you were going to see them again. There were accidents where people didn't return.[286]

This reveals how his crash retrieval duties would be conducted without knowledge of his immediate army superiors. As far as they were concerned, Stone would be called away to perform TDY duties or training, and would then have to return to complete his normal military duties. The following quote describes the nature of the security clearance required by Stone when called away from his normal Army duties to participate in crash retrieval operations.

> Well any time I needed a security clearance, I had whatever security clearance to do whatever it was they wanted me to

> do. You were debriefed afterwards and you sign the non-disclosure agreement, but it's not supposed to work that way. It's supposed to be that they give you that on a one time basis, on a "need to know" and that's where it stops short of getting the actual clearance and being fully briefed into the job.[287]

I can now evaluate Stone's statements concerning being called away through the use of secret codes and the issuance of temporary security clearances in terms of SOM1-01: "Contact with EBEs by military personnel not having MJ-12 or OPNAC clearance is to be strictly limited to action necessary to ensure the availability of the EBEs for study by the OPNAC Team."[288]

This supports Stone's claim of being clearances on a one time "need to know" basis, where he was not given the higher security clearance of MJ-12 personnel. The use of codes to summon Stone to his covert duties would be a means of maintaining "absolute top secrecy" as required by section 4.f in SOM1-01: "The establishment and maintenance of absolute top secrecy concerning all the above operations."

Stone's reference to getting the "actual clearance and being fully briefed into the job" involved completing training at what he described as "the school:"

> I was not aware of where it was located, what was taught. I got to meet some people who went there and to me they were scary. It was like, you know, even enlisted people were above reproach. I mean, it was like "your station in life is less than mine because I know secrets that no one else knows." It's hard to explain but there's something sinister about the people when they came back from the school.[289]

The "school" was something for those interested in making more of a commitment to working with MJ-12 and experiencing the career advancement such covert work would bring. The existence of elite military courses concerning extraterrestrial life and technology was supported by the leaking of a U.S. Air Force Academy textbook in the early 1970s. Titled, "Introductory Space Science, Volume II, Department of Physics, USAF," the textbook was used by the Air

Force Academy, at Colorado Springs, Colorado to introduce future pilots to the ideas of extraterrestrial life and technology.[290] The Air Force Academy pulled the textbook from its teaching program after much controversy arose subsequent to its leaking.

Finally, Stone claims that during his first recovery operation for Project Moon Dust in 1969 he was assigned to guarding a captured EBE. The EBE revealed to Stone during their telepathic communication that it intended to escape. Stone claims that the EBE would have been terminated by security in making such an attempt. The scenario described by Stone was given credence by Major George Filer, a former USAF intelligence officer, who testified that an extraterrestrial had been shot and killed after attempting to escape from McGuire Air Force Base in 1978.[291] In order to ensure the EBE's safety, Stone decided to help the EBE escape. This extraordinary claim that extraterrestrials can be terminated out of security concerns is corroborated in the following section of SOM1-01:

> 24.c. In dealing with any living Extraterrestrial Biological Entity, security is of paramount importance. All other considerations are secondary. Although it is preferable to maintain the physical well-being of any entity, the loss of EBE life is considered acceptable if conditions or delays to preserve that life in any way compromise the security of the operation.

Like many whistleblowers revealing classified information concerning UFOs, there is controversy over inconsistencies between Stone's testimony, and lack of documentary evidence to verify his alleged training and service in covert projects. Stone claims that all his covert training for, and duties with crash retrieval operations, were not recorded in his military records. The exclusion from military records of all reference to training and deployment for crash retrieval operations is consistent with a policy of maintaining "absolute top secrecy" as detailed in section 4.f of SOM1-01. Sanitizing the training and service records of personnel associated with crash retrieval teams would be a means of maintaining the 'absolute secrecy' required for these operations.

The absence in Stone's military records of any reference to covert projects related to EBEs replicates what occurred for Dan Sherman. Sherman claims that his covert training for telepathic communication with EBEs, and his actual service in that capacity was not recorded on his military service record. I will now examine Sherman's background to provide a means of contrasting and corroborating Stone's UFO crash retrieval testimony.

Dan Sherman and Project Preserve Destiny

Dan Sherman served with the US Air Force for twelve years (1982-1994) and received a number of awards including the Commendation Medal and the Achievement Medal. He was recruited into a classified program, "Project Preserve Destiny" (PPD), that was conducted under the auspices of the National Security Agency (NSA).[292] The training was for Sherman to become an "intuitive communicator" with EBEs. Essentially, Sherman would learn to telepathically interface with EBEs and pass on this information through a secure computer system to his handlers within the NSA. Sherman's training for PPD was conducted at the same time while training for a conventional military career in electronic intelligence (ELINT), which itself was classified. Significantly, Sherman was told that he suited to the task since he was identified early in his childhood by the military as someone that was capable of communicating with EBEs. He claims that his desire to join the Air Force was stimulated by a Major Roberts stationed at nearby Beale Air Force base who regularly visited Sherman's home when he was between 10-11 and talked to Sherman about how great life was in the Air Force.

Sherman claimed that extraterrestrial projects were embedded within regular classified projects with high national security significance. This was more than enough, according to Sherman, to prevent any prying Congressman from discovering the existence of extraterrestrial projects. Once the Congressman was given minimal details about the classified project that acted as a cover, this satisfied his/her curiosity and deterred further questions. Sherman described how his ELINT training acted as a cover for his participation in PPD. In his book, *Above Black*, Sherman revealed how he was recruited and trained in a way unknown to his normal ELINT military trainers. The training occurred over the same period as his normal training in ELINT. He describes his contrasting training experiences as follows:

> I remember my day of ELINT school being fun because I had a lot of people to interact with.... The first day of PPD school could not, in any way, be described as fun. By my second day of attending PPD school I was sick and tired of it and I didn't want to go anymore. The novelty of being an "intuitive communicator" had worn off.[293]

When he was subsequently assigned to the NSA, Sherman worked on a specially designed computer where he could perform both his normal ELINT work, and also work as an intuitive communicator when required with EBEs. The individuals responsible for Sherman's training and subsequent covert work within the NSA were officers with the rank of Captain who would not operate through the normal chain of military command either within the USAF or within the NSA. The responsible organization appeared to be a parallel system that operated through but was not part of the NSA.

According to Fletcher Prouty, the NSA along with the CIA is one of the principle intelligence agencies used by the "Secret Team" for covert operations.[294] Personnel recruited into the Secret Team come from all branches of government and military, and are given need-to-know access to the covert operation to which they are assigned. These operations will be institutionally located wherever necessary to ensure their success.[295] In the case of extraterrestrial affairs, Secret Team personnel are loyal not to the service they are assigned to, but to the MJ-12 Group (what Prouty terms the "Power Elite"). The NSA captain that Sherman reported to was likely not a career NSA officer, but one of the "Secret Team" members assigned to the NSA to direct PPD as a covert operation on behalf of the MJ-12 Group.

Sherman worked on PPD for almost three years. He says that when he asked to leave PPD he was denied, and told that he would be forcibly re-enlisted regardless of his wishes. Sherman claims he was so angry and determined to leave, that he came up with a strategy that would lead to his departure: "Anyone who has a dire need to rid themselves of the military can use this method, but I don't advise it... However, I knew this was the only method I could use that would completely shut out the authority of my PPD chain of command."[296] Significantly, Sherman's military record does not reflect his training as an intuitive communicator, or his subsequent work as a telepathic interface with EBEs. Nor is there any record of who the officers were that he reported to in performing his intuitive communicator work. Sherman's experience offers an independent means of corroborating the testimony of Clifford Stone.

Table 5. Comparative Experiences between Clifford Stone and Dan Sherman

Dan Sherman (Project Preserve Destiny)	Clifford Stone (Project Moon Dust)
Recruited due to innate telepathic skills recognized during childhood;	Recruited due to innate telepathic skills recognized during childhood
Inspired to join the Air Force by a Major Roberts who regularly talked to him between the ages of 10-11	Inspired to join the Air Force by a Captain who visited his home on a weekly basis
PPD duties overseen by succession of captains outside of the normal chain of command	Crash retrievals overseen by a civilian (the Colonel) outside of the normal chain of command
Covert training occurred without the awareness of normal military commanders	Covert training occurred without the awareness of normal military commanders
Employment occurred without normal military commanders being aware that he was performing duties for a covert agency operating through the USAF/NSA	Employment occurred without normal military commanders being aware that he was performing duties for a covert agency operating through the US Army
Military records have no details of either the training or service he performed in relation to communication with EBEs.	Military records have no details of either the training or service he performed in relation to UFO crash retrievals.
Experienced great difficulty in being released from PPD due to relatively few individuals that could replace him.	Experienced great difficulty in retiring from Army due to the 'Colonel' stating that his services were still required.

The seven elements in Table 5 appear in both the testimonies of Sherman and Stone, and suggest that they were recruited into projects overseen by the Majestic-12 Group. MJ-12 had created a system for recruiting personnel that would be a very effective means of maintaining secrecy.

Sherman's whistleblower testimony offers important corroborating support for Stone's claims for having worked on UFO crash retrieval teams. Combined with a number of consistencies with SOM1-01, Stone's highly specific FOIA requests on Project Moon Dust, his long military service, it can be concluded that Stone's testimony is very likely an accurate reflection of his experiences while working on UFO crash retrieval teams.

Conclusion: Identifying the Procedures Used in MJ-12 Group Projects & UFO Crash Retrieval

The similarities in Stone's and Sherman's whistleblower testimonies suggest that a common set of procedures is used for recruiting, training and employing individuals for MJ-12 Group projects involving extraterrestrial life or technologies. The procedures for MJ-12 Group personnel appears to be primarily oriented towards maintaining total secrecy by minimizing the impact of unauthorized disclosures by individuals recruited into MJ-12 Group projects. The security procedures that can be identified in Stone's and Sherman's testimonies appear to be generic for a range of MJ-12 Group projects including UFO crash retrieval operations and/or activities related to extraterrestrial life. From the above analyses of their testimonies, the following key security procedures are used for managing personnel in MJ-12 Black Operations.

The above security procedures reveals the effectiveness of the system developed by the MJ-12 Group in recruiting, training and employing individuals on covert projects such as UFO crash retrievals involving extraterrestrial technologies and/or EBE communications. The "MJ-12 Group Personnel Security Procedures for Black Operations" leaves no paper trail, minimizes the number of individuals aware of MJ-12 projects, and provides no means for personnel to substantiate their claims regarding training and employment in MJ-12 Group projects. Also great pressure is exerted on recruited individuals to remain loyal to their covert program supervisors. Finally, great effort is made to keep MJ-12 Group projects separate to regular military activities.

Table 6. MJ-12 Group Personnel Security Procedures for Black Operations

No.	Personal Management Procedures
1	Individuals are identified during childhood as having unique skills (e.g., telepathic communication) that can be of use to MJ-12 Group projects, and are cultivated for specific tasks, such as telepathic interface, in UFO crash retrievals;
2	Individuals are encouraged to join a particular branch of the military and pursue a conventional military career that provides a suitable cover for MJ-12 Group projects;
3	Individuals are contacted by officials outside of the normal chain of military command and recruited into the MJ-12 Group project.
4	Training occurs in addition to the normal military duties performed by the individual, and without the awareness of normal military commanders.
5	Deployment and work with the MJ-12 Group project occurs without the awareness of normal military commanders.
6	Clearances for MJ-12 Group projects are given on an ad hoc temporary basis, unless the individual completes further training or commits more fully to the project.
7	Individuals are prevented from learning about and/or forming friendships with others involved in MJ-12 Group projects.
8	Military service records contain no mention of an individual's training, activities, awards or clearances that are associated with MJ-12 Group projects.
9	The lack of paper trail or awareness by normal military commanders of participation in MJ-12 Group projects leaves individuals subject to manipulation by MJ-12 Group.
10	Significant efforts are made to persuade individuals to make a greater commitment to MJ-12 Group projects by attending more advanced training, and not leaving MJ-12 Group service.

It is highly likely that something similar to the above set of ten principles was used in the development of SOM1-01. This would account for the number of alleged discrepancies in SOM1-01 when compared to standard Army manuals. The discrepancies of SOM1-01 were likely a result of the ad hoc manner that those familiar with crash retrieval operations, were coordinated by the MJ-12 Group in producing SOM1-01. Its creators, out of security concerns, were not able to share the manual with other military professionals to exclude possible discrepancies, which is a normal part of the drafting process for new Army manuals.

The ten security procedures above appear to be outside the guidelines used for the most classified programs in U.S. military. Unacknowledged Waived Special Access Programs (SAPs) [or Controlled Access Programs in the case of the intelligence community] are reported only to the heads of Defense or Intelligence committees of the U.S. Congress in verbal reports.[297] No documents or written records are supplied to Congress since waived SAPs officially do not exist. Nor would personnel participating in such programs be permitted to keep records of their participation in waived SAPs in terms of their military or agency records.

The key difference between waived SAP's and the MJ-12 Group projects, however, is that the latter occur outside of the normal chain of command within the U.S. military and/or intelligence community. This suggests that a parallel system exists that siphons off military personnel for MJ-12 Group projects when needed, without the awareness of regular military commanders. Prouty elaborates how this occurs in terms of the leading role played by the CIA:

> The CIA maintains hundreds of U.S. military units for its own purposes. Many of these units become involved in this type of operation [covert operations]. After these cover units have been in existence for several years the military has a hard time keeping track of them. The military system is prone to try to ignore such abnormalities, and the CIA capitalize on this to bury some units deep in the military wasteland. The CIA also maintains countless paramilitary and pseudobusiness organizations that weave in and out of legitimacy and do business much as their civilian counterparts would.[298]

Evidence for the existence of a parallel system of classified projects outside of the regular chain of military command and intertwined with private corporations was earlier illustrated in the case of Vice Admiral Tom Wilson. In 1997, Dr Steven Greer and former Astronaut Dr Edgar Mitchell had a private meeting with Admiral Wilson about classified extraterrestrial related projects. At the time, Wilson was J-2, head of Intelligence for the Joint Chiefs of Staff.

Greer claimed that he passed on to Wilson details of a "secret document that had a list of the code names and projects names dealing with the extraterrestrial connected projects." [299] When Wilson checked to determine if the projects existed, he was denied access. According to Greer:

> Once Admiral Wilson identified this group, he told the contact person in this super-secret cell: "I want to know about this project." And he was told, "Sir, you don't have a need to know. We can't tell you." Now, can you imagine being an admiral, J-2, the head of intelligence for the Joint Chiefs of Staff, at the Pentagon, and being told, "We not going to tell you"? Well, he was shocked and angry.[300]

Significantly, "the primary people who denied Wilson were not even DoD personnel, but rather private contractors, mainly attorneys."[301] The covert extraterrestrial projects Greer had the code names for, involved a network of private and military personnel that were most likely part of the CIA's vast network of military and business assets.

The existence of a parallel governmental system using military personnel for its own purposes has been suspected for some time as illustrated in comments quoted so far by Col Prouty. It's worth repeating that Prouty was Chief of Special Operations for the Joint Chiefs of Staff from 1955 to 1964 where he was responsible for military support of the CIA's covert operations. Another source is Senator Daniel Inouye who at the 1987 Iran-Contra Senate hearings said: "There exists a shadowy Government with its own Air Force, its own Navy, it's own fundraising mechanism, and the ability to pursue its own ideas of the national interest, free from all checks and balances, and free from the law itself." Given the evidence provided by Stone and Sherman, and corroborating testimony such as Admiral Wilson's experience, Prouty's revelations and Inouye's observations, it can be concluded that MJ-12 Special Group projects are outside the control of the regular chain of command within the U.S. military.

Overall, MJ-12 Group may be considered to be a parallel branch of government that runs an extensive network of projects involving personnel recruited from the military sector while maintaining extraordinarily high levels of security. When combined with contents outlined by the SOM1-01 manual, the testimonies of Clifford Stone and Dan Sherman provide an overview of the procedures used to manage personnel involved in UFO crash retrievals and other MJ-12 Group projects. SOM1-01, and the Stone and Sherman testimonies provide clear insight into how UFO crash retrieval operations have been conducted for over five decades and successfully kept out of the public arena. Most importantly, their testimonies show how extraterrestrial related projects have historically recruited and managed personnel. It is these management policies that have enabled the secrecy system concerning extraterrestrial life to remain in place for so long.

ENDNOTES – CHAPTER FOUR

[266] This chapter is a revised version of a presentation at the 4th Annual UFO Crash Retrieval Conference, November 10, 2006 Las Vegas, Nevada, that was later published in the *Exopolitics Journal* 2:2 (2007): 79-96.
[267] See Ryan Wood, *Majic Eyes Only* (Wood & Wood Enterprises, 2006); and Leonid Stringfield, Status Reports 1-VII. Information available at: http://www.www.nicap.org/bios/stringfield.htm .
[268] Reprinted in The Majestic Documents (Wood & Wood Enterprises, 1998) 133-86; also available online at: http://209.132.68.98/pdf/som101_part1.pdf .
[269] The Truman memo is available online at: http://209.132.68.98/pdf/truman_forrestal.pdf . An official 1954 document, the Cutler Twining memo, refers to a scheduled meeting for the MJ-12 Special Studies Project: http://209.132.68.98/pdf/cutler_twining.pdf .
[270] See Robert Wood, "The Authenticity of the Special Operations Manual," in *Majic Eyes Only*, 264-67.
[271] See Friedman's discussion of SOM1-01 in *Top Secret/MAJIC* (Marlowe and Company, 2005) 161-66.
[272] Stanton Friedman, *Flying Saucers and Science: A Scientist Investigates the Mysteries of UFOs* (New Page Books, 2008) 286.
[273] Jan Aldrich, "Special Operations Manuel 1-01," Parts 2 & 3, http://www.virtuallystrange.net/ufo/updates/1996/dec/m18-003.shtml , http://www.virtuallystrange.net/ufo/updates/1996/dec/m18-008.shtml .
[274] Jan Aldrich, "Special Operations Manuel 1-01," Part 4, http://www.virtuallystrange.net/ufo/updates/1996/dec/m19-004.shtml
[275] For discussion of the authenticity of these documents and their proving the existence of a Majestic-12 Group, see Stanton Friedman, *Top Secret/MAJIC,* 56-102,
[276] L.Fletcher Prouty, *The Secret Team: The CIA and its Allies in control of the United States and the World* (Skyhorse Publishing, [1972) 2008]) [Preface, "The Secret Team II," 1997] *xxxv-xxxvi.*
[277] Clifford Stone's views are summarized from an extensive interview I conducted with him in July 2005 that was published in successive editions of the *Exopolitics Journal* . These are available online at: http://exopoliticsjournal.com/Journal-vol-1-1-Stone-pt-1.pdf & http://exopoliticsjournal.com/Journal-vol-1-2-Stone-pt-2.pdf.
[278] He provides documentary evidence for the existence of Project Moondust in his book, Clifford Stone, *UFOs Are Real: Extraterrestrial Encounters Documented by the U.S. Government* (SPI Books, 1997).
[279] This documentation is available in his two books, *UFOs are Real* and *UFO's: Let the Evidence Speak for Itself* (C. Stone, 1991).
[280] Kevin Randle, *Project Moondust: Beyond Roswell- Exposing the Government's Continuing Covert UFO Investigations and Cover-Ups* (Avon Books, 1998) 151.

[281] Friedman's quote is extracted from the preface to Stone's, *UFO's Are Real,* xii.
[282] Fletcher Prouty, *The Secret Team: The CIA and its Allies in Control of the United States and the World* (Skyhorse Publishing, 2008) 65-110.
[283] Prouty, *The Secret Team,* 33.
[284] Part two of July 2005 interview with Clifford Stone, http://exopoliticsjournal.com/Journal-vol-1-2-Stone-pt-2.pdf .
[285] See Ryan Wood, *Majic Eyes Only.*
[286] Part one of July 2005 interview with Clifford Stone, http://exopoliticsjournal.com/Journal-vol-1-1-Stone-pt-1.pdf .
[287] Part one of July 2005 interview with Clifford Stone, http://exopoliticsjournal.com/Journal-vol-1-1-Stone-pt-1.pdf .
[288] Section 23.b. SOM1-01 .
[289] Part two of July 2005 interview with Clifford Stone, http://exopoliticsjournal.com/Journal-vol-1-2-Stone-pt-2.pdf .
[290] Extract from the USAF manual is available online at: http://www.ufoevidence.org/documents/doc1532.htm .
[291] See "Testimony of Major George A. Filer III," available online at: http://www.topsecrettestimony.com/Witnesses/AllWitnesses/MajorGeorgeAFilerIII/tabid/256/Default.aspx .
[292] Sherman describes his experiences and provides parts of his service record in *Above Black: Project Preserve Destiny – Insider Account of Alien Contact and Government Cover-Up* (One Team Publishing, 1998).
[293] Sherman, *Above Black,* 49.
[294] Prouty, *The Secret Team,* 3.
[295] Prouty, *The Secret Team,* 313-29.
[296] Sherman, *Above Black,* 140.
[297] For an overview of the classification system, see *Report of the Commission on Protecting and Reducing Government Secrecy: 1997.* Available online at: http://www.access.gpo.gov/congress/commissions/secrecy/index.html .
[298] Prouty, *The Secret Team,* 103.
[299] Steven Greer, *Hidden Truth, Forbidden Knowledge* (Crossing Point Inc., 2006) 158.
[300] Steven Greer, *Hidden Truth, Forbidden Knowledge*, 158.
[301] Richard Dolan, "The Admiral Wilson UFO Story," available online at: http://www.ufodigest.com/news/0808/wilson.html .

Part B – Responding to U.S. Government Policies on Extraterrestrial Life & Advanced Technology

Secret U.S. government policies concerning extraterrestrial life have been developed and implemented since the Second World War era. In addition to exposing these policies, they need to be substantively critiqued. Key policies developed in response to extraterrestrial life have major weaknesses. The secrecy system concerning extraterrestrial life does not help in adequately addressing policy weaknesses since they remain hidden from public scrutiny. The three chapters in Part B deal with weaknesses in some of the public policies implemented to respond to extraterrestrial life. Some of these weaknesses threaten human sovereignty. Pointing out the deficiencies in the current policies and advocating alternatives, will help persuade policy makers to move forward with extraterrestrial disclosure as a strategic imperative.

Chapter five analyses the strategic doctrine known as 'power politics' that has been used to develop national security strategy towards extraterrestrial life. I point out that 'power politics' fails to recognize the importance of an informed citizenry as a restraint on irresponsible policy choices. Political disclosure will help inform the public so responsible global defense policies can be developed in response to genuine national security threats involving extraterrestrial life.

Chapter six examines the dangers of using space weapons against Extraterrestrial Civilizations. There has long been a covert effort to shoot down extraterrestrial vehicles. Evidence points to 'successes' in a limited number of cases. This chapter discusses the inherent flaw in conceptualizing extraterrestrials as a potential external security threat. I point out that emphasis needs to be placed on the internal security threat posed by some extraterrestrial groups. This requires a strategic doctrine based on political transparency and public accountability when it comes to dealing with the security threat posed by some extraterrestrial groups.

Finally, chapter seven examines the policy of suppressing the emergence of a civilian spacecraft industry that uses advanced technologies similar to those used by extraterrestrial civilizations.

Preventing the emergence of a civilian spacecraft industry is a poor public policy choice that impedes humanity's technological creativity, and promotes the interests of vested interest groups promoting antiquated energy sources such as fossil fuels.

Chapter Five

The Failure of Power Politics as a Strategic Response to Extraterrestrial Life

Introduction[302]

I have so far presented witness testimonies that different extraterrestrial groups have appeared before senior national security officials of the U.S. to offer a variety of technologies, programs and forms of assistance. As discussed in the first chapter, these national security officials decided to enter into secret agreements with extraterrestrials who offered technologies with military applications. In responding to the presence of extraterrestrial life, senior officials in national security organizations of major nations have secretly implemented public policies and an overall strategic response. In developing an adequate national security response, U.S. policy makers deliberately adopted a strategic policy similar to 19th century Prussia/Germany. Under the leadership of its powerful Chancellor, Otto Von Bismarck, Prussia transformed itself from a mid-size Germanic principality vulnerable to its more powerful European neighbors, to a unified German Empire that quickly became a leading European power. Senior officials in the U.S. planned to emulate the role of Prussia/Germany by developing a strategy for coordinating Earth's system of sovereign states under the leadership of the U.S. in order to adequately respond to the extraterrestrial presence.

The assistance of extraterrestrial visitors offering to develop 'human capacities' and protecting the global environment through advanced spiritual teachings was refused. Policy makers viewed subordinating 'technology acquisition' to 'spiritual development' as a strategically dangerous choice. There was little support among policy makers for the idea that humanity's acquisition of advanced technology had outstripped its ethical capacities to prevent the destructive use of such technology. Furthermore, there was great uncertainty surrounding the extraterrestrial presence in terms of distinguishing friend from foe. There has subsequently been a secret effort to develop a vast network of compartmentalized 'black projects' for an advanced planetary defense system capable of ensuring the sovereignty of major countries and humanity in general. As discussed in chapter three, the network of projects rivaling the first Manhattan Project, has been financially supported by a 'Black Budget'. In the U.S. alone this is estimated to be over one trillion dollars annually, and constitutes a second 'Manhattan Project'.

This chapter analyses the strategic implications of 'power politics' modeled on Bismarck's Prussia/Germany, and the secret defense system put in place to respond to the extraterrestrial presence. I reveal the complete exclusion of the general public from extraterrestrial affairs, and from playing any significant role in planetary defense. Rather than viewing the general public as a strategic asset in developing a successful response to extraterrestrial life, policy makers viewed the general public as a strategic liability. The public would remain uninformed about extraterrestrial life. The role of the general public became a passive one of merely remaining a provider of basic resources for the extensive network of compartmentalized black projects designed to provide a successful response to extraterrestrial life.

I will show in this chapter the inherent flaw in a power politics strategy that relegates the general public into a passive role in any global defense system. There is a need for full disclosure of extraterrestrial life, so that global humanity can play an active role in global defense by developing human capacities in a range of critical areas. These include: 'consciousness raising'; galactic history and education; health; poverty; and incorporation of environmentally friendly extraterrestrial technologies.[303] These areas of assistance offered by extraterrestrial civilizations have hitherto attracted only marginal interest by national security officials. In cooperating with extraterrestrial civilizations interested in assisting global humanity in these 'consciousness raising' and 'friendly technology' capacity areas, grass roots organizations and individuals will have a significant strategic impact on how extraterrestrial life is managed and global defense established. This will ultimately enable human society to be better prepared to respond to any contingencies created by extraterrestrials currently acting to subvert human sovereignty and freedom.

I will further propose that the strategic doctrine underpinning the global defense of the planet vis-à-vis the extraterrestrial presence is unbalanced and skewed towards a military and technological response. There is a need to balance military/technological projects with grass roots human capacity building. Finding this balance will enable policy makers and the general public to deal with a range of global problems. These problems currently provide a cover for subversion of human affairs by some extraterrestrial groups seeking to control the Earth's population and resources. Chapter one revealed the scope and nature of secret agreements with extraterrestrials, these provide the opportunity for such subversion to occur. To ignore the failure of power politics as an appropriate strategic response to the extraterrestrial presence is to invite the same sequence of policy mistakes that led to the First World War. This time, however, the conflict may be at an interplanetary level. Such a conflict would directly threaten human sovereignty and freedom.

The Strategic Dilemma – Finding Strategic Allies Among Extraterrestrial Races

Official confirmation of an extraterrestrial presence occurred during the Second World War era.[304] Policy makers from the U.S. and major allied states were presented with an unprecedented dilemma. How should they respond? They had learned conclusively of the existence of extraterrestrials with advanced technologies outdating by centuries the most advanced weapons systems of the successful allied states. More disturbingly, the extraterrestrials possessed advanced mental and psychic powers with the potential of subtly influencing even the most sophisticated policy makers during communications, let alone an unprepared general public.

In chapter four, I analyzed the case of Sergeant Dan Sherman who revealed his participation in 'Project Preserve Destiny', a secret U.S. National Security Agency communication project that used psychics for establishing telepathic contact with extraterrestrial civilizations.[305] Sherman reported on his telepathic communications with extraterrestrials races such as the 'Grays' and the difficulty in training to have accurate telepathic communications with them. According to another whistleblower, Lt. Col. Philip Corso, extraterrestrials use telepathy for both communication and navigation purposes.[306] The unanswered question here was "how might extraterrestrials use these abilities to unduly influence unsuspecting individuals and public officials?"

The appearance of these technologically and mentally advanced extraterrestrials was complicated by the fact that there appeared to be a number of civilizations competing against one another in monitoring and/or interacting with the Earth. The intentions, activities and agendas of these extraterrestrial civilizations could not be conclusively determined. Many appeared to be friendly, some unfriendly and others neutral.[307] This presented an enormous policy dilemma for national security officials who were assessing the global policy environment at the end of the Second World War. Which of the extraterrestrial civilizations could policy makers cooperate with in learning more about extraterrestrial life in general and developing an appropriate strategic response?

Policy makers needed to first identify and categorize the different extraterrestrial civilizations. There were those with whom cooperative agreements involving technology and resources would ultimately be made. This was done with the awareness that this group of extraterrestrials were possibly strategic competitors for control of Earth's resources. There was a second group of extraterrestrial visitors that appeared ethically advanced and offered non-military forms assistance. They mainly interacted with willing private citizens. Finally, there were a third group of extraterrestrials that largely monitored events on Earth. They appeared to be neutral over who controlled the Earth's resources and ultimately controlled humanity's destiny.

There was a major difference in policy between extraterrestrial civilizations over the exchange of extraterrestrial technology that had weapons applications. Some extraterrestrials were willing to trade technology with military applications for permission to conduct a biological program aimed at genetically enhancing their race. The race commonly known as 'Grays' claimed to come from Zeta Reticulum and said they had overused reproductive cloning procedures to the extent that their genetic makeup had suffered.[308] In contrast, as briefly mentioned in chapter one, 'human looking' extraterrestrials appeared that were willing to assist in the 'consciousness raising' of the planet's population and developing environmentally friendly technologies. These human looking extraterrestrials offered no technology of military significance, and instead requested the dismantling of nuclear weapons that they considered extremely dangerous.[309]

The strategic dilemma here for policy makers in making a choice, was compounded by what appeared to be a complex web of relationships, many friendly, some neutral, and others hostile, between the different extraterrestrial civilizations. There are a number of distinct extraterrestrial civilizations visiting Earth who can be distinguished on the basis of whether or not they have participated in secret agreements described in chapter one.[310] To complicate matters further, researchers point to a diversity of factions within each extraterrestrial civilization making it difficult to conclusively know their long-term goals and agendas.[311] The diversity of extraterrestrial factions and wars between them has historical support in terms of Sumerian cuneiform texts recording activities of the ancient Anunnaki (an extraterrestrial race from the mysterious planet Nibiru) that played a role in human colonization of the Earth.[312]

The diversity of extraterrestrial relationships and factions made it difficult to assess the strategic implications of working with any one civilization since these extraterrestrial relationships appeared to be fluid. There was evidence, for example, that a hidden and indigenous Earth race of 'Reptilians' was cooperating with a more dominant winged Reptilian race from Alpha Draconis, with a history of both conflict and cooperation with the Grays.[313] The Grays' relationship with these Reptilian races needed to be taken into account in any agreement since technology exchanges would impact on the relationship between humans and the hidden indigenous Reptilian presence on Earth.

It can be inferred that prior to reaching agreement with national governments based on technology exchange for genetic experiments, the Grays had reached agreements with Reptilians who have had a long-term presence on Earth, perhaps predating the human presence.[314] This means that any agreement with the Grays would implicitly involve permission or cooperation with the Reptilian race that has historically exercised a powerful influence, if not secret control, over key national institutions.[315] Indeed, researchers such as Jim Marrs, William Bramley and David Icke claim that there has been a secret extraterrestrial control system in place for thousands of years.[316]

In what was a momentous, though secret, policy decision for the entire planet, the national security organizations of the U.S. and other major governments decided to form a strategic alliance with the Grays and the Reptilian extraterrestrials.[317] The goal of this alliance was to enable clandestine national security organizations to effectively build an extensive network of 'black projects' aimed at providing an adequate defense infrastructure for the planet using extraterrestrial technologies and information. These secret agreements have led to the construction of an extensive number of underground bases around the planet linked by highly advanced transportation systems and complete support services.[318] Some of these are joint human-extraterrestrial underground bases in locations such as Dulce, New Mexico, and Pine Gap Australia.[319]

In chapter two, it was claimed that both Grays and Reptilians worked alongside human workers at the Dulce joint underground base under contract by various corporations, and supervised by U.S. special military forces. Ordinary civilians were subjected to extensive human rights violations. The alliance meant that other races that were more inclined towards assisting humanity in dealing with social and environmental problems were sidelined due to their lack of strategic significance for policy makers dealing with extraterrestrial affairs. The model that national security organizations in the U.S. used to develop a 'successful strategy' was based on Realpolitik or 'power politics'. 'Power politics' was successfully used by 19th century Prussia in developing its military and industrial capacity while uniting the Germanic principalities. Unification was achieved without its European neighbors allying themselves to prevent Prussia's rapid expansion in influence and power.

'Power Politics', the United States & the Extraterrestrial Presence

'Power politics' refers to the Realpolitik practiced by a variety of national leaders since Cardinal Richelieu, Chief Minister of France (1624-42), but most successfully by Otto Von Bismarck, Prussia's last Prime Minister and Germany's First Chancellor (1862-

90).[320] Bismarck's power politics was based on two assumptions about the nature of international politics. First, states should use all means at their disposal to advance their national 'interests'. And second, a 'balance of power' was the key to preserving peace and stability, and states needed to respect this while competing over their respective national interests.[321] Ethical and/or universal principles were at best irrelevant to the practice of power politics; or, at worst, recipes for national disaster.[322] 'Power politics' was an extension of the political philosophy of the medieval Italian theorist, Nicolo Machiavelli, who proposed a set of principles designed to extend a Sovereign's rule.[323] Machiavelli argued that morality had no inherent value other than its usefulness for attaining one's ultimate goal: political power.

Power politics meant navigating through the competing interests of other states in a way that gradually increased one's national interests at the expense of one's competitors without provoking these competitors to ally themselves to prevent a change of the status quo. In the case of Prussia during the middle part of the 19th century, this meant expanding Prussia's influence in Europe at the expense of Austria and France. This had to be done without provoking a reaction by Britain and Russia that could lead to alliances threatening Prussia's national interests. In a relatively short time after coming to office, Bismarck's Prussia successively defeated Austria (1866) and France (1870-71) in two short wars. Prussia succeeded in uniting the northern German principalities in 1866 in a Confederation dominated by Prussia (1866), and then absorbing all the principalities in the German Empire in 1871 under Prussia's King Wilhelm I and with Bismarck as Chancellor. Bismarck's ability to maneuver between Prussia's national competitors in a way that gradually increased Prussia's/Germany's interests without provoking a major backlash among competitors became a model for how a state could strategically use its assets to become the dominant actor in a regional system.

Bismarck's power politics has been used as an exemplary model in developing the strategy for how national security agencies in the U.S. and other major states would respond to the extraterrestrial presence. The individuals most responsible for developing the power politics strategy was Dr Henry Kissinger, a well-known advocate of realpolitik in his controversial public career.[324] Kissinger served in the Army Counterintelligence Corps from 1943-46. At the close of World War II, he stayed on active duty in occupied West Germany. He was assigned to the 970th Counter Intelligence Corps Detachment, where he played a key role in 'Operation Paperclip' – the recruitment of German scientists who had worked on advanced technologies. Kissinger's counter-intelligence work marked him out in military intelligence circles as someone who had the keen intellect and strategic thinking abilities that could handle the most important strategic policy issue facing the US - how best to respond to extraterrestrial life.[325] Kissinger subsequently went on to serve in key consulting positions with key national security committees in the Eisenhower administration that dealt with covert operations and responding to extraterrestrial life.[326]

Kissinger was a protégé of Nelson and David Rockefeller who ensured that Kissinger rose to prominent leadership positions in the secret committees developed to manage extraterrestrial affairs, i.e., the Majestic 12 /PI 40 Group.[327] This is confirmed in various whistleblower accounts of Kissinger's leadership role. According to William Cooper, who served on the briefing team of the Commander of the Pacific Fleet, he saw documents revealing Kissinger as one of the directors of a 1955 Study Group that helped set policy on extraterrestrial life.[328] Another whistleblower source for Kissinger's leadership position in extraterrestrial affairs was Colonel Steve Wilson who claims he served on UFO crash retrieval operations.[329] Wilson described Kissinger as the overseer of MJ-12/PI-40.[330]

Along with his consultancy and leadership roles in the MJ-12 Group and NSC committees involved in covert operations, Kissinger also featured prominently in national and international organizations. These included the Council on Foreign Relations, the Trilateral Commission and the Bilderberg Group where he has served on executive committees.[331] In chapter four I described how personnel are managed in extraterrestrial affairs through various covert operations managed by the MJ-12 Group. It is therefore important to acknowledge Kissinger's leading role in covert operations since the 1950s. This was revealed by Prouty who wrote: "Henry Kissinger is the titular head of the intelligence community's clandestine operations reaction faction. His appearance as a one-man power center is simply due to the fact that he fronts for the Secret Team and the secret intelligence community."[332]

In sum, the strategic response that the U.S. took vis-à-vis the extraterrestrial presence was a version of power politics, and it was Kissinger who was largely responsible for this. This meant that U.S. policy makers viewed other states and the different extraterrestrial factions as respectively strategic allies and/or competitors for Earth's resources and population. The goal of power politics adopted by the U.S. under Kissinger's tutelage was for the U.S. to build upon its post-Second World War status as the most powerful nation on the planet, and to lead the way in a secret coordinated global response to the extraterrestrial presence.[333]

Practitioners of power politics sought to identify those extraterrestrials they could best work with in promoting their respective national interests. Meanwhile, they would maintain a balance of power that would prevent a 'war of the worlds' or war between major states over extraterrestrial issues. Ethical or universal principles such as 'galactic brotherhood', 'universal peace' and 'cosmic law' were either irrelevant, or viewed as recipes for disaster in terms of national interests and global defense. Those extraterrestrial groups that practiced these ethical/universal principles were, in some cases, simply ignored. Working with such groups would not advance the national interests of the major states in the opinion of policy makers. In other cases these ethically advanced extraterrestrials were regarded as strategic competitors for the loyalty of the planet's citizenry. Sophisticated counterintelligence methods were implemented to limit the appeal of ethically advanced extraterrestrial civilizations to private citizens. This involved discrediting and debunking evidence confirming private citizen contact with extraterrestrial civilizations in what appeared to be a Galactic version of COINTELPRO.[334] Extraterrestrial civilizations willing to enter into agreements concerning joint basing rights, trading extraterrestrial technology, experiments on human genetic material, and behavior modification techniques, thus became secret allies of the U.S.

Policy makers applying power politics in dealing with extraterrestrials viewed their 'national interests' in a narrow restrictive way in terms of the military, industrial and scientific capacities required for building an effective military deterrent to any possible undesirable extraterrestrial intervention in human affairs. It was seen that this would be the best means of protecting national interests of the U.S. and other major states. Solid evidence for this power politics strategy comes in the whistleblower testimonies of those who participated in clandestine reverse engineering programs for weapons development not disclosed to the general public and elected public officials.[335]

In the case of the emergence of the U.S. as the dominant global nation, agreements would be made with those extraterrestrial civilizations that would assist U.S. strategic objectives. Military conflicts would occur with those extraterrestrials from which strategically significant assets could be won. In chapter one, it was revealed that the Eisenhower administration met with and reached agreements with extraterrestrials. I also described the full extent of those agreements in terms of activities and collaborative projects between various U.S. military corporate entities and various extraterrestrial groups.

Despite agreements being reached with extraterrestrials, as I explained in the first chapter, there was resentment among some military officials over their terms. For example, Col Phillip Corso, wrote: "We had negotiated a kind of surrender with them [ETs] as long as we couldn't fight them. They dictated the terms because they knew what we most feared was disclosure."[336] Corso's comment is very significant since he served in important committees in Eisenhower's National Security Council that dealt with extraterrestrial affairs.[337] His comments describe the tension inherent in secret agreements whose terms were not well known, and sanctioned extraterrestrial activities that were constitutionally dubious. Chapter two described the existence of joint facilities such as the secret Dulce base in New Mexico, where extraterrestrials participated in human rights violations. A deadly firefight occurred in 1979 for reasons that are still not clear, but clearly indicated the tenuous nature of secret government-extraterrestrial agreements. Both the U.S. and the extraterrestrials have apparently violated these agreements/treaties. The extraterrestrial race known as the 'grays' secretly abducted and experimented with more human subjects than they were reporting to military-intelligence authorities.[338]

Partly due to violations of secret agreements, the U.S. military began targeting extraterrestrial vehicles with advanced weapons technology and capturing their ships and occupants.[339] There is evidence that the High frequency Active Auroral Research Program can be used as a particle beam projector capable of generating a global shield. High-speed ions are projected into the magnetosphere thereby destroying the electronic systems of any craft attempting to enter the Earth's atmosphere.[340] This secret limited warfare with unannounced extraterrestrial visitors became a means of gaining extraterrestrial technology not being achieved through negotiated agreements. So, like Bismarck's Prussia/Germany, power politics practiced by the U.S. and its major allies would seek a balance of power with extraterrestrial visitors. This would simultaneously ensure no major interplanetary war, and only limited military conflicts with specified extraterrestrial visitors. The result would be a gradual strengthening of the U.S. strategic position and its technological capabilities without precipitating global catastrophe.

At the global level, there continues to be efforts to coordinate the use of military force through multilateral institutions as occurred with the U.N. sanctioned intervention in Iraq/Kuwait in 1991; or NATO's military intervention in Kosovo in 1999. The power politics strategy was that global humanity through the U.S. and other major nations would be able to deal with the extraterrestrial presence through a position of strength. The ultimate goal is the construction of a 'planetary fortress' against unwanted extraterrestrial intervention and/or subversion.

There is clear evidence that the power politics conducted by the U.S. and its allies in response to extraterrestrials has as a major component the construction of a global surveillance system and exotic weapons systems over both the planet's skies and oceans. The Low Frequency Active sonar waves used by the U.S. Navy to monitor sub-ocean activities ostensibly of submarines, but more accurately of extraterrestrial vehicles, are having a damaging effect on the planet's cetaceans.[341] Lawsuits were filed in the U.S. to put a stop to the Navy's testing. It remains questionable whether the Navy would voluntarily stop such testing. The U.S. Navy secretly has a need to monitor extraterrestrial activity in the world's oceans since these are perceived as a potential threat. In a book titled *The Antilles*

Incident, a U.S. Navy Captain revealed how Underwater Submersible Objects (USO) are secretly tracked by Naval headquarters.[342] His destroyer class ship was directed to a specific location in the mid-Atlantic where it engaged with a USO over a period of several days. The U.S. Navy destroyer fired weapons at the USO which had no effect. Several crewmen were taken by the USO. Upon return to port, the Captain and crew were debriefed not to talk about the incident, and the Captain was reassigned to the Pentagon.

In addition to a surveillance system in the world's oceans, there would be a global electromagnetic shield around the planet. A prototype for this global shield is the High frequency Active Auroral Research Program (HAARP) which can be used as a particle generator to send ions into the magnetosphere that quickly surround the earth, in an electromagnetic shield to prevent entry of extraterrestrial craft.[343] Former Los Alamos physicist, Dr Douglas Beason has revealed the rapid development of "Directed Energy Weapons" that can send electromagnetic pulses anywhere on the earth for surveillance or destructive purposes.[344] Earth would to all intents and purposes become a planetary fortress. The strategic consequences of 'planetary fortress' policy would be that the only extraterrestrial groups permitted to 'show themselves' to the global population are those that serve the 'national interests' of the U.S. and major states. The choice would be made by a restricted group of policy makers managing extraterrestrial affairs. This would limit the quantity and quality of extraterrestrial interactions in a post-Contact world to those permitted by policy makers who have developed secret agreements with specific extraterrestrial civilizations. It could therefore be predicted that the actual conditions of a mass contact event would be contrived or spun in a way that served the interests of elite policy makers and the extraterrestrial groups they work with.[345]

In a book titled, *An Introduction to Planetary Defense: A Study of Modern Warfare Applied to Extra-Terrestrial Invasion,* Dr Travis Taylor and his co-authors present a case for how the planet can defend itself against extraterrestrials.[346] They present a statistical argument for the existence of advanced extraterrestrial life and the likelihood that they will someday visit the Earth. They consider the probability that these advanced extraterrestrials might try to take over the planet using their more advanced technologies. Dr Taylor, et al., then present a response based on weapons development, long term defense strategy, asymmetric tactics to be used, suggestions on organization, funding, and counter intelligence responses.

Given that Dr Taylor and his co-authors have decades of contractor experience with the Department of Defense, their book gives the lay person a clear idea of how defense strategists might seriously approach the issue of extraterrestrial life and national defense. Their book gives a hypothetical argument for the existence of extraterrestrial life. It does not cite evidence that extraterrestrials are currently visiting Earth and that some have even entered into secret agreements with the U.S. government. Nevertheless, their book shows how defense strategists would justify a rapid weapons development program, over decades if necessary, in order to reach some kind of military parity with advanced extraterrestrial life. This is precisely the long term defense strategy that underscores a power politics approach to extraterrestrial life.

The Failure of Power Politics & Centralized Global Defense against Extraterrestrial Intervention & Subversion

Power politics based on the Prussian/German historical experience appears very understandable and even laudable as the basic strategy to preserve humanity's sovereignty and independence in response to more technologically developed extraterrestrial races. Historic models such as the conquest of the Americas are testimony to the danger of making unwarranted assumptions about the benevolent intentions of more technologically advanced visitors to one's national shores.[347] The Brookings Report to NASA in 1960 pointed to the potential for civilizational collapse with the appearance of more technologically advanced extraterrestrial societies: "Anthropological files contain many examples of societies, sure of their place in the universe, which have disintegrated when they had to associate with previously unfamiliar societies espousing different ideas and different life ways."[348] There has been a strategic policy of advancing national interests by dealing with extraterrestrial civilizations in terms of concrete assistance for a rapid program of military modernization and political coordination among major states. This appears at first glance a sensible way of moving forward in dealing with the diversity of unknown extraterrestrial actors and possible threats they pose to human sovereignty.

There is evidence that much of the apparent hostility behind the Cold War was contrived to mask the true strategic cooperation occurring between major powers and the need to keep this secret from their respective general publics.[349] A key assumption in this cooperative strategy was that global general public would not be able to deal with the social, political and economic consequences of the extraterrestrial presence. Premature disclosure was viewed as risking the disintegration of societal infrastructure. This led to the rapid modernization program based on extraterrestrial technology and agreements becoming highly classified state secrets. This excluded the general public from gaining any official information on the extraterrestrial presence. Elected public officials were informed only to the extent that they held key cabinet or legislative positions that were critical in passing policies that affected the network of compartmentalized black projects, and the black budget that funded them.[350]

This paralleled the power politics practiced by Bismarck's Prussia/Germany where the German Empire was democratic in name only and where the parliament could only pass non-binding decisions rather than control the policy making process. The German parliament and population therefore could not act as a restraint on the aspirations of the reckless new German Emperor, Wilhelm II, once the cautious Bismarck was forced to retire in 1890. This ultimately proved disastrous and was directly responsible for the buildup in European tension that led to the First World War. This exposed the inherent strategic flaws in power politics. Excluding the German population from having real influence in the policy making process was to remove the only viable restraint to reckless national leadership in a centralized political system.

The conventional explanation for the First World War was that it was caused by the reckless policies of Wilhelm II, and that the more cautious Bismarck would never have allowed the war to occur.[351] This explanation disguises the deeper cause which was the centralized policy making process that Bismarck encouraged that eliminated any checks and balances in the way power politics was conducted at the national level. While such a system might work with cautious policy makers such as Bismarck at the helm, it would be disastrous with more irresponsible policy makers. History has demonstrated that power politics is inherently flawed as a strategic doctrine since it encourages a centralized political system where there are few restraints on irresponsible leaders and their policies.

It appears that a similar situation is now occurring in the way leadership is exercised over the management of the extraterrestrial presence in the U.S. Kissinger's more cautious power politics style based on his own strategic understanding of extraterrestrial life is being challenged by a new generation of leaders. This new generation of policy makers managing extraterrestrial affairs is bolder and less risk averse than Kissinger's generation. The horrors of the Second World War and the need to prevent this happening again was still fresh in the minds of policy makers.

A number of whistleblowers discuss the leadership style of a national security group described as 'the cabal' who have a xenophobic hatred of the extraterrestrial visitors and are intent on military confrontation. According Daniel Salter, a former counter intelligence agent for the National Reconnaissance Office, "a renegade force called the Cabal is responsible for attacking and retrieving extraterrestrial entities and craft."[352] Just as Bismarck's influence over German foreign policy was eclipsed by a new generation of risk taking leaders under Wilhelm II, so too Kissinger's approach to extraterrestrial management is now being eclipsed. This will lead to a more dangerous period where poor policy choices can lead to military adventurism by 'renegade forces' within the extraterrestrial management system. This was reflected in the military adventurism of the neo-conservative Bush administration over the more cautious foreign policy pragmatists in the U.S. Republican party.[353] This kind of military adventurism transplanted into extraterrestrial affairs poses a long-term threat to human freedom sovereignty. In short, the power politics strategy that has dominated the extraterrestrial management system, has laid the foundation for a devastating breakdown in the way the extraterrestrial presence is managed.

The failure of power politics as a coherent strategy for responding to the extraterrestrial presence stems from dismissal of the role of an informed general public in managing the extraterrestrial presence. In particular, there is a dismissal of the idea that human 'capacity building' in the sense of empowering citizens to be more responsible and active in responding to important global issues, provides a vital asset in dealing with extraterrestrials. This inherent flaw in a power politics approach to extraterrestrial life is based on the assumption that the general public offers a 'soft target' which extraterrestrial races could easily subvert. In the calculations of policy makers, such subversion would threaten any technological modernization program underway and a coordinated response to the extraterrestrial presence.

Policy makers have believed that the creation of a secret compartmentalized national security system would be the best safeguard against extraterrestrial subversion. Meanwhile the military, technological and scientific capacities to respond to the extraterrestrial presence would be developed. In short, a secret compartmentalized national security system forms a 'hard target' for subversion in contrast to the general public as a 'soft target' for subversion. There is evidence that in the U.S. this secret compartmentalized national security system forms a second 'Manhattan Project' that dwarfs the first Manhattan project and the construction of atomic weapons.[354]

Unfortunately, whistleblower testimonies have demonstrated the fallacy of assuming a secret compartmentalized national security system forming a hard target for extraterrestrial subversion. Extraterrestrial subversion has occurred in: the military-intelligence community; corporations that secretly fulfill contracts dealing with the extraterrestrial presence; and in key educational and research institutions.[355] For example, Clifford Stone soon after the start of his military service testified to seeing a Gray extraterrestrial in the basement of the Pentagon flanked by two military personnel before being rendered unconscious by it.[356] This points to Gray extraterrestrials playing undisclosed roles in sensitive military installations. Another military whistleblower, Charles Hall described how he regularly witnessed senior Air Force generals and officials in the presence of Tall White extraterrestrials at Nellis Air Force base.[357] The Air Force generals could be easily manipulated due to their desire to acquire advanced technologies at virtually any cost. The "Tall Whites" use of advanced mind control techniques against

Hall, suggested they could similarly manipulate senior Air Force officials.

Another whistleblower, Phil Schneider, a former civil engineer employed in black projects involving the construction of underground bases provided detailed testimony of the extent of extraterrestrial subversion in a range of public lectures before he was found dead in controversial circumstances.[358] Further whistleblower testimonies have provided researchers with information of the historic and contemporary role played by extraterrestrial visitors in subverting human affairs.[359] Aside from whistleblower testimonies, there are also 'conspiracy theory' researchers such as Jim Marrs, William Bramley, David Icke, Lynne Picknett and Clive Prince, who describe how extraterrestrials have been able to subvert the policy making community at the highest levels.[360] They argue this has occurred not only in the contemporary era but also historically.

Extraterrestrial subversion in the contemporary era has been made possible by the secrecy and compartmentalization surrounding all aspects of the extraterrestrial presence. Furthermore, there is evidence that advanced technology involving mind control, implants, drugs, and psychotronics have been used to control humans.[361] Testimonies from individuals who participated in classified compartmentalized government projects occurring at Montauk, Long Island, point to the pervasive use of these technologies. They also describe the time travel and cloning technologies used by some visiting extraterrestrials at Montauk.[362] Such technologies provides the opportunity for extraterrestrial subversion of a centralized decision making process. It requires compromising only a few key policy makers to subvert the whole national security system. Indeed, centralizing decision making concerning national security is discretely encouraged by extraterrestrial groups desiring to subvert the decision making process. The extraterrestrials which enter into secret agreements may have as their ultimate goal the subversion of the entire national security system of a leading nation such as the U.S. They may be feigning cooperation when their real purpose is to subvert, rather than gain assistance in areas of particular interest to extraterrestrials. Cooperating in the network of secret compartmentalized black projects provides the opportunity for this extraterrestrial subversion to occur quietly. This has tremendous long-term costs for human sovereignty and freedom.

Dealing with the problem of extraterrestrial subversion of the decision making process requires an extensive set of checks and balances. This is essential in a robust democratic process based on transparency, openness and accountability. In contrast, a secret compartmentalized national security system has few checks and balances. The transparency, openness and accountability necessary for identifying and eliminating extraterrestrial subversion of human society has not been possible. This is due to the continued secrecy policy surrounding the extraterrestrial presence. The democratic processes that add a series of checks and balances to prevent irresponsible government policies, have not been allowed to develop for national security organizations responding to the extraterrestrial presence. This absence of democratic processes has facilitated, rather than curbed, extraterrestrial infiltration and subversion of the national security system.[363]

A further flaw in the power politics strategy is that extraterrestrial civilizations with no interest in providing technologies with weapons development potential were deemed strategically irrelevant. They were not permitted to openly assist in human capacity building, and individuals who came into contact with them were thoroughly discredited.[364] This greatly limited, as a significant actor in human affairs, extraterrestrial civilizations whose behavior appeared far more ethical. These 'ethically advanced' extraterrestrials were more intent on building human capacities than providing technological assistance with military applications for national security organizations. Their core belief that humanity's technological development had outstripped its ethical capacity to prevent the destructive uses of such technology, created great friction among policy makers.[365] Furthermore, it appeared that the majority of extraterrestrial visitors shared this more ethical perspective about humanity's ability to wisely integrate advanced technology. Those extraterrestrials that participated in technology exchange agreements appeared to be a minority whose motives are highly questionable.[366]

A power politics approach has led to the unfortunate situation wherein the only extraterrestrials officially allowed to interact with human societies are those participating in the secret agreements serving the national interests of major states in building military, industrial and scientific capacities. Judging from extensive testimonies surrounding human abductions results have been mixed. Some researchers argue that these abductions have a beneficial impact. Others argue that abductions consistently violate the rights of civilians forced to participate in these extraterrestrial programs.[367] Dan Sherman claims to have resigned from the U.S. Air Force after learning about the invasive procedures used in abductions.[368] Furthermore, there is persuasive evidence that extensive extraterrestrial violations of human rights have occurred at joint extraterrestrial-government bases as described in chapter four, indicating a high degree of official/corporate complicity.

Interactions with extraterrestrial civilizations intent on human capacity building have been limited to isolated events and have not been permitted to more broadly impact on human society.[369] The most famous example is George Adamski whose contacts with the Venusians were supported by reliable witnesses, photographs, films and even physical samples.[370] Another well known case is Eduard "Billy" Meier who has extensive photographic, video and audio evidence of visiting extraterrestrials from the Pleiades since 1975.[371] Columbian contactee, Enrique Castillo, allegedly met with 'Pleiadian' extraterrestrials from 1973-1976 and developed a number of initiatives to expand awareness of the extraterrestrial visitors in South America.[372] Another example is James Gilliland in Washington State, US, who has also provided extensive photographic, film and sound evidence of visiting extraterrestrials.[373] Extraterrestrial interactions with Adamski, Meier, Castillo and Gilliland provide an example of the type of consciousness raising and education that this group of extraterrestrials would introduce in their 'capacity building' of human society.

The power politics underlying strategic response to the extraterrestrial presence has led to a secret centralized compartmentalized global defense policy. This policy does not adequately use humanity's best asset against extraterrestrial subversion and intervention, an informed and empowered global citizenry. Such a self-empowered citizenry would have positive impact on how the extraterrestrial presence is managed, and in creation of a viable global defense to respond to any extraterrestrial contingency. An informed global citizenry offers possibilities of a balanced global defense using all available strategic assets to counter any extraterrestrial subversion and undesirable intervention. Power politics consequently fails to be a suitable strategic response to the extraterrestrial presence. An alternative is urgently required.

Developing an Alternative Strategy for Responding to Extraterrestrial Life

At the moment, the U.S. and other major global states have secret agreements with different extraterrestrial races that lead to the exchange of technologies with military applications. All commercial applications are released at a rate with only marginal impact on the global population, ostensibly because dual-use extraterrestrial technologies might aid rogue states in regional conflicts. Col. Phillip Corso, former head of the Foreign Technology Desk in the Army's Research and Development department, claims that he led a top-secret clandestine project to reverse engineer extraterrestrial technology recovered from the 1947 Roswell crash.[374] He wrote that his project successfully leaked a number of these reverse engineered extraterrestrial technologies for both the military and civilian sectors. Corso claims that the rapid technological advances over the last 50 years, in fiber optics, integrated circuit chips, night-vision equipment, and super tenacity fibers such as Kevlar were a direct result of these clandestine projects.

A highly centralized and secret compartmentalized system has been put in place to deal with the extraterrestrial presence and technology, and is funded by revenues that escape the normal budgetary auditing and accountability of government funded projects. [375] The purpose of the secret, centralized and compartmentalized system created in response to the extraterrestrial presence, is to develop an effective defense system against undesirable extraterrestrial intervention that threatens national or human sovereignty. It is therefore worth exploring if there is a viable alternative to such a secret, centralized and compartmentalized defense system that can enhance human sovereignty and freedom.

During the early years of the Eisenhower administration when a group of 'ethically advanced' extraterrestrials met with U.S.

government officials appointed to deal with the extraterrestrial presence, the extraterrestrials offered to assist with a number of environmental, technological, political and socioeconomic problems. The sole condition was that the U.S. dismantle its nuclear arsenal.[376] When the government officials declined, this group of extraterrestrials subsequently withdrew and played no role in the government's clandestine program to reverse engineer extraterrestrial technology for advanced weaponry.

These 'ethically advanced' extraterrestrials have subsequently concentrated their efforts to consciousness raising of the general public. They have warned of the hazards of nuclear and 'exotic' weapon systems reverse engineered from extraterrestrial technology. Furthermore, ethically advanced extraterrestrials have limited the environmental impact of clandestine projects; encouraged the development of alternatives to using fossil fuel as an energy source; and prepared the general populace for eventual disclosure of extraterrestrial life.[377] None of these areas of assistance were judged to be strategically significant from the perspective of policy makers dealing with extraterrestrial affairs. They based their policies on the power politics advocated by Kissinger and others, and simply excluded ethical principles promoted by some extraterrestrial groups.

Some former military and government 'whistle blowers' have revealed the activities of clandestine government agencies and interests opposed to incorporating extraterrestrial technology into the public arena.[378] These 'grass roots' areas of assistance do however have strategic significance in terms of organizing a grass roots social defense against undesirable extraterrestrial intervention and/or subversion in human affairs. This form of social defense is even more relevant given the likelihood that some extraterrestrial visitors have already infiltrated/subverted military-intelligence organizations and severely compromised national security systems.[379] A global population fully aware of different extraterrestrial civilizations, and equipped with the grass roots technology to provide for its own needs, would be able to provide another level of planetary defense. Furthermore, an aware and self-empowered population would be able to provide a means for a more democratic system that provides checks and balances to the way in which the extraterrestrial presence is managed.

The failure of power politics as a successful strategy for responding to the extraterrestrial presence leads to irresponsible policies on extraterrestrials being passed. This is due to the absence of checks and balances that preclude undesirable extraterrestrial influences in a genuinely democratic decision making process. Developing an aware and empowered humanity requires that the global population begins working in those 'non-strategically significant' areas that national security organizations have dismissed. What is urgently required is an action program whereby the grass roots citizenry begin working with those extraterrestrial races interested in human capacity building. As human capacities are developed in collaboration with such races, greater awareness of the full complexity of the extraterrestrial presence in terms of the activities and agenda of different races will be generated. Developing human capacities will help prevent irresponsible policy making by a more bold assertive generation of leaders who may have been compromised in the centralized compartmentalized national security system dealing with extraterrestrial affairs. Strengthening grass roots social defense against undesirable extraterrestrial intervention and subversion in global affairs is the best means of maintaining human sovereignty and independence, in a world slowly awakening to the truth of the extraterrestrial presence.

ENDNOTES: CHAPTER FIVE

[302] I wish to acknowledge Hugh Matlock for his hospitality, intellectual stimulation and research facilities for the completion of the first version of this chapter which was published online at http://www.exopolitics.org/Study-Paper-7.htm .

[303] See Michael Salla, "A Report on the Motivations and Activities of Extraterrestrial Races – A Typology of the Most Significant Extraterrestrial Races Interacting with Humanity" available online at: http://www.exopolitics.org/Report-ET-Motivations.htm

[304] For reference to the extraterrestrial presence in the Second World War era, see Michael Salla, *Exopolitics: Political Implications of the Extraterrestrial Presence* (Dandelion Books, 2004) 109-48. Originally published as: "Foundations for Globally Managing Extraterrestrial Affairs – The Legacy of the Nazi Germany-Extraterrestrial Connection," Exopolitics.org, July 27, 2003. Available online at: http://www.exopolitics.org/Study-Paper-6.htm

[305] Dan Sherman, *Above Black: Project Preserve Destiny Insider Account of Alien Contact & Government Cover-Up* (Oneteam Publishers, 1997). See also his website at: www.aboveblack.com

[306] See Philip Corso, *The Day After Roswell* (Pocket Books, 1997).

[307] For the different motivations of extraterrestrial races, see Michael Salla, "A Report on the Motivations and Activities of Extraterrestrial Races – A Typology of the Most Significant Extraterrestrial Races Interacting with Humanity" available online at: http://www.exopolitics.org/Report-ET-Motivations.htm .

[308] For discussion of the Grays and their activities on Earth, see Courtney Brown, *Cosmic Voyagers* (Onyx Books, 1997).

[309] See Michael Salla, "Extraterrestrials Among Us," *Exopolitics Journal*, 1:4 (2006): 284-300.

[310] See Michael Salla, "A Report on the Motivations and Activities of Extraterrestrial Races – A Typology of the Most Significant Extraterrestrial Races Interacting with Humanity" available online at: http://www.exopolitics.org/Report-ET-Motivations.htm

[311] For information on different relationships between and within extraterrestrial civilizations, see Courtney Brown, *Cosmic Explorers* (Signet 2000).

[312] See Zecharia Sitchin, *The Wars of Gods and Men: Book III of the Earth Chronicles* (Avon 1999) and Joseph Farrell, *The Cosmic War: Interplanetary Warfare, Modern Physics and Ancient Texts* (Adventures Unlimited Press, 2007).

[313] Evidence of the cooperation between the different Reptilian species and the Grays is found in whistleblower testimony of the Dulce underground base discussed in chapter two. See also Branton, *The Dulce Wars: Underground Alien Bases and the Battle for Planet Earth* (Inner Light Publications, 1999); and Val Valerian, *Matrix II: The Abduction and Manipulation of Humans Using Advanced Technology* (Leading Edge Research Group, 1989/90). Online information available at http://www.trufax.org/catalog/m2.html.

[314] R. A. Boulay, *Flying Serpents and Dragons: The Story of Mankind's Reptilian Past* (Book Tree, 1999).
[315] For discussion of the Reptilian presence, see Jim Marrs, *Rule by Secrecy: The Hidden History That Connects the Trilateral Commission, the Freemasons, and the Great Pyramids* (Perennial, 2001); and David Icke, *The Biggest Secret: The Book That Will Change the World, Bridge of Love Publications,* 2nd ed. (January 1999).
[316] See Jim Marrs, *Rule By Secrecy* (Perennial, 2000); William Bramley, *Gods of Eden* (Avon Books, 1990); and David Icke, *Children of the Matrix: How an Interdimensional Race has Controlled the World for Thousands of Years-and Still Does* (David Icke Books, 2001).
[317] See chapters one and two.
[318] See Richard Sauders, *Underwater and Underground Bases* (Adventures Unlimited Press, 2001).
[319] See chapter two and also Whitley Strieber, "The Mystery of Pine Gap," http://www.unknowncountry.com/mindframe/opinion/?id=64
[320] For description of power politics and how it historically developed from the national policies of Cardinal Richelieu, see Henry Kissinger, *Diplomacy* (Touchstone Books, 1995).
[321] Hans Morgenthau, *Politics among nations : the struggle for power and peace* (Alfred Knopf, 1985)
[322] Henry Kissinger, *Does America Need a Foreign Policy* (Touchstone Book, 2001)
[323] Nicolo Machiavelli, *The Prince* (Bantam 1984).
[324] For Kissinger's own views about realpolitik see, *Diplomacy*. For controversy over Kissinger's policies, see Seymour M. Hersh, *The Price of Power: Kissinger in the Nixon White House* (Summit Books, 1983).
[325] For evidence of the relationship between the Army's Counterintelligence Corp and the extraterrestrial presence, see the following declassified report from 22 July 1947 concerning the Roswell incident. http://209.132.68.98/pdf/ipu_report.pdf
[326] See Michael Salla, *Exopolitics*, 59-108. Originally published as "Political Management of the Extraterrestrial Presence – The Challenge to Democracy and Liberty in America," www.exopolitics.org (July 4, 2003).
[327] See Michael Salla, *Exopolitics,* 59-108. Originally published as "Political Management of the Extraterrestrial Presence – The Challenge to Democracy and Liberty in America," www.exopolitics.org (July 4, 2003).
[328] William Cooper, *Behold a Pale Horse* (Light Technology Publishing, 1991) 210-11.
[329] Wilson's background and controversy over his credentials were discussed in chapter one.
[330] See online interview with Dr Richard Boylan, at http://www.drboylan.com/mj12org2.html
[331] See Daniel Estulin, *The True Story of the Bilderberg Group* (TimeDay, 2007)
[332] Fletcher Prouty, *The Secret Team: The CIA and its Allies in control of the United States and the World* (Skyhorse Publishing, [1972) 2008]) 89.

[333] For description of how the major allied states cooperated after the second world war era, see Michael Salla, *Exopolitics,* 109-48. Originally published as: "Foundations for Globally Managing Extraterrestrial Affairs – The Legacy of the Nazi Germany-Extraterrestrial Connection," Exopolitics.org, July 27, 2003. Available online at: http://www.exopolitics.org/Study-Paper-6.htm

[334] See Michael Salla, "GALACTIC COINTELPRO - Exposing the Covert Counter-Intelligence Program against Extraterrestrial Contactees," *Exopolitics Journal,* 2:3 (2008): 167-89. Available online at: http://exopoliticsjournal.com/vol-2-3.htm

[335] See Phillip Corso, *The Day After Roswell.*

[336] Phillip Corso, *The Day After Roswell*, 292.

[337] Corso served in the Operations Coordinating Board which was associated with MJ-12, the control group managing extraterrestrial affairs, see chapter 11.

[338] See chapter one.

[339] This is supported in the extensive secret crash retrieval operations that have been conducted. See Ryan Wood, *Majic Eyes Only* (Wood Enterprises, 2006). See also Richard Boylan, "Quotations from Chairman Wolf, http://www.drboylan.com/wolfqut2.html ; also Richard Boylan, "Colonel Steve Wilson, USAF (ret.) Reveals UFO-oriented Project Pounce," http://drboylan.com/swilson2.html .

[340] See Nick Begich and Jeanne Manning, *Angels Don't Play This HAARP: Advances in Tesla Technology* (Earthpulse Press, 1995) Brother Jonathan, "What Is HAARP? What it looks and Sounds Like," Brother Jonathan News 12/15/00 http://www.brojon.org/frontpage/bj1203.html
http://news.nationalgeographic.com/news/2003/10/1008_031008_whalebends.htm l

[342] Donald Todd, *The Antilles Incident* (Book World Inc., 1998).

[343] See Brother Jonathan, "What Is HAARP? What it looks and Sounds Like," Brother Jonathan News 12/15/00 http://www.brojon.org/frontpage/bj1203.html

[344] Douglas Beason, E-bomb: How America's New Directed Energy Weapons Will Change the Way Future Wars Will Be Fought (De Capo Press, 2006).

[345] For discussion of contact scenarios, see the final chapter, "The Race for First Contact - Shaping Public Opinion for the Open Appearance of Extraterrestrial Races." An earlier version is available online at: http://www.exopolitics.org/Exo-Comment-9.htm

[346] Travis Taylor, Bob Boan, R.C. Anding, and T. Conley Powell, *An Introduction to Planetary Defense: A Study of Modern Warfare Applied to Extra-Terrestrial Invasion* (Brown Walker Press, 2006).

[347] For discussion of how the Conquest of the Americas relates to the extraterrestrial presence, see Michael Salla,
"Inviting Extraterrestrial Intervention: Collapse of the 'Berlin Wall' or 'Conquest of the Americas'? Exopolitics.Org (Nov 27, 2003) http://www.exopolitics.org/ET-Intervention&Berlin-Wall.htm

[348] *Brookings Institute, Proposed Studies on the Implications of Peaceful Space Activities for Human Affairs,* (1960) 215. For an online overview of the Brookings Report, go to: http://www.enterprisemission.com/brooking.html .
[349] See Michael Salla, *Exopolitics,* 109-48. Originally published as "Foundations for Globally Managing Extraterrestrial Affairs – The Legacy of the Nazi Germany-Extraterrestrial Connection," Exopolitics.org (July 27, 2003) http://www.exopolitics.org/Study-Paper-6.htm
[350] For discussion of the black budget and network of black operations it funds, see chapter three.
[351] See Kissinger, *Diplomacy.*
[352] See Daniel Salter, *Life With a Cosmic Clearance* (Light Technology Publishing, 2003) 128. See also Richard Boylan, "Quotations from Chairman Wolf," http://www.drboylan.com/wolfqut2.html
[353] See Patrick J. Buchanan, *Day of Reckoning: How Hubris, Ideology, and Greed Are Tearing America Apart* (Thomas Dunne Books, 2007).
[354] See chapter three.
[355] See M. Salla *Exopolitics,* 149-90. First published as "Responding to Extraterrestrial Infiltration of Clandestine Organizations Embedded in Military, Intelligence and Government Departments," www.exopolitics.org , May 30, 2003.
[356] Testimony of Sergeant Clifford Stone, in Steven Greer, ed., Disclosure, 332.
[357] See Charles Hall three volume series, *Millennium Hospitality.* Online information available at: http://exopolitics.org/charles-hall.htm .
[358] Phil Schneider's gave a 1995 lecture that is available at a number of websites and titled, "A Lecture by Phil Schneider – May, 1995" One site is http://www.ufoarea.bravepages.com/conspiracy_schneider_lecture.html
[359] See chapter two, and Val Valerian, *Matrix II: The Abduction and Manipulation of Humans Using Advanced Technology* (Leading Edge Research Group, 1989/90). Online information available at http://www.trufax.org/catalog/m2.html
[360] Jim Marrs, *Rule by Secrecy: The Hidden History That Connects the Trilateral Commission, the Freemasons, and the Great Pyramids* (Perennial, 2001); David Icke, *The Biggest Secret: The Book That Will Change the World, Bridge of Love Publications,* 2nd ed. (January 1999); William Bramley, *Gods of Eden* (Avon, 1993); and Lynne Picknett & Clive Prince, *The Stargate Conspiracy: The Truth About Extraterrestrial Life and the Mysteries of Ancient Egypt* (Berkley Pub Group, 2001).
[361] See Alex Constantine, *Psychic Dictatorship in the USA* (Feral House, 1995); and Nick Begich, *Controlling the Human Mind: The Technologies of Political Control or Tools for Peak Performance* (Earthpulse Press, 2006).
[362] See Preston Nichols, *Montauk Project: Experiments in Time* (Sky Books, 1999); Al Bielek and Brad Steiger, *The Philadelphia Experiment and Other UFO Conspiracies* (Innerlight Publications, 1991); Stewart Swerdlow, *Montauk: The Alien Connection* (Expansions Publishing Co. 2002); Wade Gordon, *The Brookhaven Connection* (Sky Books, 2001). For an online interview with Al Bielek, go to http://psychicspy.com/montauk1.html .

[363] See Michael Salla, *Exopolitics*, ch 4. An earlier version of this chapter is available online at: http://www.exopolitics.org/Study-Paper-4.htm .
[364] See Michael Salla, "GALACTIC COINTELPRO - Exposing the Covert Counter-Intelligence Program against Extraterrestrial Contactees," *Exopolitics Journal* 2:3 (2008): 167-89.
[365] See chapter one for the debate generated by requests of extraterrestrials to end nuclear testing, and public disclosure.
[366] See Michael Salla, "A Report on the Motivations and Activities of Extraterrestrial Races – A Typology of the Most Significant Extraterrestrial Races Interacting with Humanity" available online at: http://www.exopolitics.org/Report-ET-Motivations.htm .
[367] For positive encounters see John Mack, *Abduction: Human Encounters with Aliens* (New York: Ballantine Books, 1994); and Mack, *Passport to the Cosmos: Human Transformation and Alien Encounters* (Three Rivers Press, 2000). For more sinister encounters see David Jacobs, *The Threat: Revealing the Secret Alien Agenda* (Simon and Schuster, 1998). Budd Hopkins, *Missing Times* (Ballantine Books, 1990);
[368] Dan Sherman, *Above Black,* 134-38.
[369] See Michael Salla, "GALACTIC COINTELPRO - Exposing the Covert Counter-Intelligence Program against Extraterrestrial Contactees," *Exopolitics Journal* 2:3 (2008): 167-89.
[370] See Lou Zinsstag and Timothy Good, *George Adamski: The Untold Story* (Ceti Publications 1983).
[371] The most famous of these were the Billy Meier's visitations, which were supported by extensive photographic evidence. See Gary Kinder, *Light Years: An Investigation into the Extraterrestrial Experiences of Eduard Meier* (Atlantic Monthly, 1987).
[372] Enrique Castillo, *UFOs: A Great New Dawn for Humanity* (Blue Dolphin Publishers, 1997)
[373] Gilliland is author of, and has a website at: Becoming Gods II: Interdimensional Mind Earth Changes & The Quickening UFOs Their Origins and Intentions (Self-Mastery Earth Institute, 1997) website is: http://www.eceti.org/
[374] Corso, *The Day After Roswell.*
[375] See chapter three.
[376] See Michael Salla, "Eisenhower's 1954 Meeting With Extraterrestrials," available online at: http://exopolitics.org/Study-Paper-8.htm . See also: Bill Cooper, Beyond a Pale Horse.
[377] For more detailed discussion of 'helper extraterrestrials', see Michael Salla, Exopolitics, 1-58.
378 See Steven M. Greer, *Extraterrestrial Contact : The Evidence and Implications* (Crossing Point Publications, 1999).
[379] See M. Salla, *Exopolitics*, 149-90. First published as Michael Salla, "Responding to Extraterrestrial Infiltration of Clandestine Organizations Embedded in Military, Intelligence and Government Departments," May 30, 2003, www.exopolitics.org .

Chapter Six

The Folly of Using Space Weapons against Extraterrestrial Civilizations

Introduction

In one of its first major policy changes after coming into power in January 2001, the Bush administration signaled its intent to withdraw from the Anti-Ballistic Missile Defense Treaty with Russia. The ABM Treaty had been intended to prevent the deployment of weapons in space and enjoyed major international support since its ratification in 1972 by the Nixon administration. In a May 2001 speech, President Bush argued that the 30 year old ABM Treaty was outdated and that the U.S. must formally move beyond its constraints to deal with new security threats:

> We need a new framework that allows us to build missile defenses to counter the different threats of today's world. To do so, we must move beyond the constraints of the 30-year-old ABM Treaty. This treaty does not recognize the present, or point us to the future. It enshrines the past. No treaty that prevents us from addressing today's threats, that prohibits us from pursuing promising technology to defend ourselves, our friends and our allies is in our interests or in the interests of world peace.[380]

The Bush administration gave its formal notice to withdraw on December 13, 2001, and promptly withdrew six months later. The Bush administration thus formally embarked on realizing some of the goals of the Strategic Defense Initiative that had first been promoted by the Reagan administration in March 1983. Reagan had envisaged the development of space based intercept systems that could be used to destroy large scale ballistic missile attacks on the United States. Reagan's SDI floundered as the Cold War wound down and the Democrat controlled U.S. Congress aimed to use the anticipated 'peace dividend' to improve social programs.

Furthermore, many prominent scientists argued against the cost of developing SDI's futuristic weapons systems. In July 1999, the Clinton Administration passed the National Missile Defense Act calling for a more limited anti-ballistic missile system:

> It is the policy of the United States to deploy as soon as is technologically possible an effective National Missile Defense system capable of defending the territory of the United States against limited ballistic missile attack (whether accidental, unauthorized, or deliberate) with funding subject to the annual authorization of appropriations and the annual appropriation of funds for National Missile Defense.[381]

The Bush administration quickly moved to formally deploying an antiballistic missile system as part of the National Missile Defense Program.

In May 2005, the US Air Force formally requested permission from the Bush administration for a national security directive so that it could "secure space to protect the nation from attack." The Air Force request moves the Bush Administration closer to approving the weaponization of space and sparking an arms race in space with the US major strategic competitors, Russia and China. These developments towards deploying weapons in space received a surprising objection when a former Canadian Defense Minister addressed a UFO Conference in Toronto. He linked the deployment of space weapons not to possible ballistic missile attacks by rogue nations or terrorist groups, but as a means of targeting UFOs that were piloted by extraterrestrial visitors.

Paul Hellyer and Opposition to the Weaponization of Space

On September 25, 2005, the Honorable Paul Hellyer, a former Canadian Minister for National Defense gave a speech in Toronto addressing the weaponization of space.[382] For the 82 year old Hellyer, his speech reaffirmed his long standing opposition to any governmental efforts to develop weapons that could be targeted against or used in Space. While Defense Minister in the Lester Pearson administration from 1963-67, Hellyer had officially rebuffed initiatives from the Johnson administration to approve an anti-ballistic missile defense system. In a 2003 article he wrote: "It is almost 40 years since U.S. secretary of defense Robert McNamara asked me if Canada would be interested in helping develop an anti-ballistic missile defense for North America. I was able to say, "Thanks, but no thanks," which was the position of the Pearson government and one that I fully endorsed."[383]

During his 2005 speech, Hellyer also addressed the UFO phenomenon and described his time as Minister for Defense where the occasional UFO sighting report crossed his desk. He claims to never have had time for what he considered to be a "flight of fancy", but nevertheless retained an interest in the UFO phenomenon. While Minister for Defense, he was guest of honor at the opening of the world's first UFO landing pad at Alberta, Canada in 1967. He thought it an innovative idea from a progressive Canadian community willing to pay for his helicopter ride, but did not give much thought to UFOs as having serious policy implications.

Hellyer's position on UFOs dramatically changed after watching the late Peter Jennings documentary special, "Seeing is Believing" in February 2005. Hellyer decided to read a book that had been idly sitting on his book shelf for two years. Philip Corso's, *The Day After Roswell*, sparked intense interest for Hellyer in terms of its policy implications, and Corso distinguished service in the U.S. Army and the Eisenhower administration. Corso who reached the rank of Lt Colonel, named real people, institutions and events in his book that could be checked. Intrigued by the policy implications, Hellyer decided to confirm whether Corso's book was real or a "work of fiction". He contacted a retired United States Air Force General and spoke to him directly to verify Corso's claims. The unnamed General simply said: "every word is true and more."[384] Hellyer then proceeded to discuss the "and more …" with the general and claimed he was told remarkable things concerning UFOs and the extraterrestrial hypothesis that interplanetary visitors have been here since at least 1947. Hellyer then privately asked a number of 'officials', some occupying senior positions, about Corso. He again received confirmation that Corso's claims were accurate.[385] Finally convinced that the UFO phenomenon was real Hellyer decided to come forward and publicly speak about some of the "most profoundly important policy questions that must be addressed."[386]

Among the profound policy questions raised by Hellyer was the designation by the U.S. military of visiting extraterrestrials as an 'enemy'. According to Hellyer, this had led to the development of "laser and particle guns to the point that they can be used against the visitors from space."[387] It is this targeting of visiting extraterrestrials that concerns Hellyer, and he asks "is it wise to spend so much time and money to build weapon systems to rid the skies of alien visitors?"[388] Hellyer poignantly raises the key policy question: "Are they really enemies or merely legitimate explorers from afar?"[389] Hellyer's question raises profound importance in understanding the relationship between visiting extraterrestrial civilizations and the recent effort to deploy weapons in space. Significantly, Hellyer's stated position on deploying weapons in Space and opposition to the possible military targeting of extraterrestrials is in stark contrast to the man who initially convinced him of the reality of extraterrestrial visitors: Lt. Col. Philip Corso.

Colonel Philip Corso's Support for the Strategic Defense Initiative & Weaponization of Space

In his book, *The Day After Roswell*, co-authored with William Birnes, retired Lt. Col. Philip Corso declared that extraterrestrials were abducting civilians, violating U.S. airspace, and destroying aircraft sent to intercept them. Corso viewed the extraterrestrials as a direct threat to U.S national security and declared: "For over fifty years, now, the war against UFOs has continued as we tried to defend ourselves against their intrusions."[390] Elsewhere in *The Day After Roswell*, Corso describes the national security threat posed by UFOs and the need for a military weaponization program to target and shoot down UFOs conducting such violations. He specifically championed President Reagan's Strategic Defense Initiative (SDI). Corso believed that SDI was the appropriate response to extraterrestrial intrusions, and that the US and USSR both knew what SDI's true purpose was:

> We [US & USSR] both knew who the real targets of SDI were… It was the UFOs, alien spacecraft thinking themselves invulnerable and invisible as they soared around the edges of our atmosphere, swooping down at will to

> destroy our communications with EMP bursts, buzz our spacecraft, colonize our lunar surface, mutilate cattle in their own horrendous biological experiments, and even abduct human beings for their medical tests and hybridization of the species. And what was worse we had to let them do it because we had no weapons to defend ourselves.[391]

A number of UFO researchers have claimed that these bellicose statements towards extraterrestrial visitors were introduced by Corso's co-author William Birnes, and that Corso was not as anti-extraterrestrial as *The Day After Roswell* suggests. That is not accurate as a reading of Corso's original notes make clear. His original notes were first published in Italy and contain many similar statements revealing the depth of Corso's animosity towards visiting extraterrestrials.[392] For example, in terms of violating U.S. air space, Corso wrote: "They have violated our air space with impunity and even landed on our territory. Whether intentional or not, they have performed hostile acts. Our citizens have been abducted and killed." [393] Corso went on to fully describe the nature of the interaction between extraterrestrial visitors and the general population:

> … the aliens have shown a callous indifference concerning their victims. Their behavior has been insidious and it appears they might be using our earth and manipulating earth life. Skeptics will excuse them that possibly they are benevolent and want to help, however, there is no evidence they have healed anyone or alleviated human ailments. On the other hand, they have caused pain, suffering and even death.[394]

Corso here reveals the depth of his animosity towards extraterrestrials and the information he had received on their intrusive activities. His statements reveal that he had a skeptical view of the 'benevolence' of visiting extraterrestrials. Corso endorsed comments such as General Douglas Macarthur's claim in 1955 that the "nations of the world will have to unite, for the next war will be an interplanetary war." In terms of cooperation between the US and Russia (former USSR) to deal with the extraterrestrials,

Corso wrote: "The U.S. and USSR are aligning their space programs against a common enemy."[395]

Consequently, it can be concluded that there is no ambiguity in Corso's belief that extraterrestrials are a genuine threat to US. national security and that weaponization of space was an urgent policy priority to deal with the "extraterrestrial enemy". If alive today, Corso would no doubt be a strong supporter of the current U.S Air Force plans to weaponize space, and build a global defense shield that could target extraterrestrial visitors. In short, Corso has consistently demonstrated strong support for military solutions to the presence of visiting extraterrestrials that in his view were performing abductions and other 'intrusive activities' that posed a direct threat to U.S. national security.

Do Extraterrestrials Pose a National Security & Global Threat?

The question that can now be raised is whether extraterrestrials do genuinely pose a national security threat to the U.S. or the earth more generally. This question is made very complex by the amount of conflicting data on the extraterrestrial presence from a variety of whistleblower and witness sources whose testimony is more difficult to verify when compared to the case of the highly decorated Corso. Answering such a policy question first requires that one understand the nature of the "national security threat" posed by extraterrestrials. Second, one needs to identify any groups of extraterrestrials that may be performing intrusive actions that fall into the category of 'threat'. Finally, one has to identify extraterrestrials performing non-intrusive activities that do not appear to be a threat to the national security of the U.S. or other countries.

In the first chapter I examined testimonies that the U.S. has entered into agreements with extraterrestrial races. I have referred to considerable circumstantial and testimonial evidence pointing to President Eisenhower being actively involved in meeting with and reaching agreements with extraterrestrial races.[396] Col Corso, who served in the Eisenhower administration, alludes to such agreements in various passages in *The Day After Roswell*. For example, he wrote: "We had negotiated a kind of surrender with them [extraterrestrials] as long as we couldn't fight them. They dictated the terms because they knew what we most feared was disclosure."[397]

I have already described some of the ever growing number of whistleblowers describing the various agreements reached with extraterrestrials. These witnesses saw direct evidence of the agreements during their participation in projects or assignments with the highest possible security classifications. These agreements involved the exchange of technology or information by extraterrestrials in exchange for the right to establish bases on U.S. territory. The existence of such bases is explicitly revealed by Corso in his private notes. After describing the various intrusive activities performed by the extraterrestrials, Corso went on to make the following startling claim: "The above are acts of war which we would not tolerate from any worldly source. It also appears they do not tolerate any such acts on our parts on their bases."[398] The implication here is that the extraterrestrials have bases, likely on U.S. territory as alleged by other whistleblowers, and the U.S. government was powerless to fully monitor these bases.

Extraterrestrials that have entered into these agreements or 'negotiated surrender' as Corso claims; have performed activities in the form of abductions, genetic experiments and aerial activities that lead to great suspicion as to their ultimate agenda. Corso repeatedly pointed out that such intrusive actions amounted to an act of war and justified a concerted military response by U.S. authorities. It needs to be pointed out that prior to these agreements, most human-extraterrestrial interactions appeared to be of the benevolent 'space brother' category that emerged in the 1950's. [399] Individual 'contactees' were exposed to a variety of positive extraterrestrial experiences that inspired a rapid growth in public interest in the benevolent 'space brothers'. There is reason to believe that the abduction phenomenon that emerged into the public consciousness with the famous Betty and Barney Hill case in 1961 was a direct result of agreements reached with extraterrestrials. That is not to say that negative experiences with extraterrestrials or 'abductions' didn't happen before the agreements. The agreements enabled these abductions to increase at a rate which went far beyond whatever government authorities originally approved.

The Secret Government, MJ-12 & Classified Agreements with Extraterrestrials

The government authority that would be responsible for making the alleged covert agreements is generally known by UFO researchers as Majestic-12 or MJ-12 Group. Documentary evidence for the existence of such a secret organization emerged in 1987 with the discovery of a memo from President Eisenhower's Special Assistant, Robert Cutler, to General Nathan Twining. The memo referred to a scheduled meeting for July 16, 1954 and referred to the "MJ-12 Special Studies Project". The memo was found in the national archives and has been shown to be genuine.[400] In another document 'leaked' to UFO researchers and known as the Eisenhower Briefing Document, Majestic-12 is described as having operational control of the UFO phenomenon:

> Operation Majestic-12 is a Top Secret Research and Development/Intelligence operation responsible directly and only to the President of the United States. Operations of the project are carried out under control of the Majestic-12 (Majic-12) Group which was established by special classified executive order of President Truman on 24 September, 1947.[401]

The Briefing Document remains controversial, but exhaustive archival analysis by researchers strongly point to its authenticity.[402]

The Briefing Document listed 12 prominent military officials and national security experts as its members among whom included Gordon Gray who occupied a number of senior defense positions including Secretary to the Army for President Truman from 1949-1950. He was later President Eisenhower's Special Assistant for National Security (1958-61). Significantly, Gray was appointed by President Truman to be the first director of the Psychological Strategy Board (PSB) established in 1951 and declared to be part of the CIA. In 1953, the PSB was replaced by the more powerful Operations Coordinating Board (OCB). It's worth going into detail of the history and activities of both these organizations since they are related to management of the UFO phenomenon. Furthermore, each organization involved Col Corso, a military intelligence specialist, in various covert operations while serving in the Eisenhower administration. It is likely that service on these Boards gave Corso the background information that formed his developed views on extraterrestrials and support for the weaponization of Space.

The Psychological Strategy Board (PSB) was created "under the NSC to coordinate government-wide psychological warfare strategy". [403] The PSB was formally succeeded by the more powerful Operations Coordinating Board established by Executive Order 10483 on September 2, 1953 with the following charter:

> ...the Operations Coordinating Board shall (1) Whenever the President shall hereafter so direct, advise the agencies concerned as to... the execution of each security action or project so that it shall make its full contribution to the attainment of national security objective views and to the particular climate of opinion the United States is seeking to achieve in the world...

Initially, the OCB was based at the State Department and while formally authorized to report to the National Security Council (NSC) and implement NSC decisions, it was formally independent from the NSC. On February 25, 1957, Executive Order 10700 formally incorporated the OCB into the NSC, which meant the NSC had greater oversight and control of the OCB. The OCB was officially 'abolished' by President Kennedy with Executive Order 10920 on February 18, 1961 that revoked Executive Order 10700.

Both the Psychological Strategy Board (PSB) and the Operations Coordinating Board (OCB) were interagency committees that were responsible for covert operations in the Truman and Eisenhower administrations, and reported directly to the National Security Council. Both the PSB and OCB specialized in psychological warfare through the use of propaganda, mass media, and disinformation. These would prove to be the very tools used to deny or ridicule the UFO phenomenon in the U.S. and suggests that both the PSB and OCB played a key role in this.

There has been speculation that the OCB played a critical role in managing the UFO phenomenon, and secretly continues to play this role though with another name.[404] Corso's original notes provide evidence supporting this UFO management role played by both the PSB and the OCB. According to his military records, Col Corso was assigned to both the Psychological Strategy Board and Operations Coordinating Board when serving with the Eisenhower administration from 1953-1956. Corso received numerous security clearances some of which gave him access to UFO information. In his original notes, Corso writes:

> During my military career at one time or another, I counted nine clearances above "Top Secret" granted to me. These included cryptographic, satellite, code and intercept, special operational clearances and the "Eyes Only" category of special White House (NSC) matters. They made available to me all matter within the government which included "UFO" information.[405]

Consequently, Corso's service on both the PSB and OCB, and his access to UFO related information is evidence that both these bodies played critical roles in managing the UFO phenomenon through covert psychological operations. Furthermore, the OCB was not abolished by Kennedy in 1961 as generally thought since the revoking of Executive Order 10700 effectively made the OCB independent of the NSC rather than abolishing it. Executive Order 10920 only removed the OCB out of control and scrutiny of the Kennedy administration. This made the OCB once again an independent interagency governmental organization with significant power through the covert psychological programs it managed, and an important implementing mechanism for the even more mysterious Majestic-12.

Due to its clandestine nature and unaccountable status, Majestic-12 and covert organizations such as the Operations Coordinating Board that manage UFO affairs are referred to as the 'shadow' or 'secret government'. President Clinton when asked by famed Washington Post correspondent Sarah McClendon why he didn't do more to have the truth about UFOs disclosed, he confided: "Sarah, there's a secret government within the government, and I don't control it."[406] There is growing evidence that over the decades since its formation as a set of committees embedded in the NSC, the 'secret government' has morphed into a quasi-governmental entity that is outside the control of any branch of the U.S. government. This has occurred with the increased privatization of the research and development of extraterrestrial technology. Such a morphing process is supported by the testimony of Ben Rich, former CEO for the Lockheed's Skunk Works, who privately confirmed:

> There are 2 types of UFOs -- the ones we build and ones 'they' build. We learned from both crash retrievals and actual "hand-me-downs." The Government knew and until 1969 took an active hand in the administration of that information. After a 1969 Nixon "purge", administration was handled by an international board of directors in the private sector.[407]

Consequently, the 'secret government' is a quasi-governmental entity that controls and makes policy decisions over how to deal with extraterrestrials; whether they constitute a 'threat' or not; and develops agreements with some extraterrestrial civilizations.

The 'Internal' versus 'External' Security Threat by Visiting Extraterrestrials

There is intense debate over whether extraterrestrials involved in abductions and other intrusive activities described by Corso (commonly described as 'Grays' from Zeta Reticulum) have a covert 'take-over' agenda. Researchers such as Dr David Jacobs (author of *The Threat*) believe the 'Grays' have a covert plan to take-over human society by engineering a superior hybrid race.[408] On the other hand, researchers such as Dr John Mack (author of *Passport to the Cosmos*) believes the star visitors have a 'transformative' agenda designed to blend together the best characteristics of extraterrestrials and humanity.[409] While this is an important debate, it glosses over one of the key features of the extraterrestrial presence - classified agreements between extraterrestrials and the 'secret government'. In considering the 'transformative' vs. 'take-over' debate, it is vital to consider all the data and come up with a nuanced response that takes into account different extraterrestrial races performing activities. Visiting extraterrestrials need to be distinguished on the basis of them either being inside or outside the secret network of agreements reached with the 'secret government'.[410]

The key policy issue is not whether we should establish communication with extraterrestrials to resolve differences that lead to confrontations over the number of abductions or other intrusive activities reported by Corso and others. The key issue is the precise nature of the agreements reached with extraterrestrials, and how these are conducted in a covert and unaccountable manner. As far as the abduction phenomenon is concerned, it is very likely that these were made possible by, or accelerated as a result of, covert agreements by secret government authorities with one or more extraterrestrial civilizations.

Consequently, the national security threat posed by extraterrestrials is a covert one that exists through the classified agreements established by secret governments with some extraterrestrial races. The motivation of extraterrestrials that have entered into these agreements is very questionable and gives considerable cause for suspicion as to their overall intent. Certainly the great number of abductions that have occurred give rise to the 'take over' scenario promoted by Dr Jacobs and other researchers. Once one considers the vast secret infrastructure created to develop extraterrestrial technologies and the illicit funding required for such an infrastructure, it becomes clear that the national security threat posed by extraterrestrials is INTERNAL rather than EXTERNAL.[411] Corso's depiction of extraterrestrials as an external military threat to the U.S. is therefore not accurate.

Extraterrestrials that have entered into agreements with secret government authorities are complicit in the creation of national security system based on secrecy, unaccountability and illicit funding. This directly threatens US. national security both in terms of a covert take-over by extraterrestrials, and an erosion of the constitutional principles upon which the U.S. is based. The real national security threat posed by some extraterrestrial visitors is a result of the desire of the 'secret government' to acquire and develop extraterrestrial technologies at any cost. This is even if the desire for technology acquisition means giving permission to a limited number of abductions and other intrusive actions.

On the other hand, extraterrestrials who have not entered into such technology exchange agreements with secret government authorities have behaved in ways that display great respect towards individuals they have contacted. This is evidenced in the extensive number of 'contactee' or 'space brother' reports from the 1950's, right up to the modern era. These extraterrestrials that typically look human in appearance reflect great respect for human free will and follow what appears to be a clear directive for non-interference in human affairs. Extraterrestrials that are trying to assist humanity, as described by these alleged contactees, are secretly being targeted by space weapons in order to capture their technology or the EBEs themselves. This also includes Grays from Zeta Reticulum who are involved in abductions that have reached agreements with the secret government. It does appear that the relationship between the Grays and the 'secret government' is a complex one where some whistleblowers report on military confrontations between them in terms of the extent to which either or both have violated the terms of their secret agreements.[412]

Conclusion: The Use of Space Weapons is an Inappropriate Policy for Extraterrestrial Visitors

In terms of the deploying space weapons, the deliberate targeting of extraterrestrial visitors needs to be exposed. This requires briefing legislative officials in the U.S. and elsewhere so that a more appropriate policy response can be developed. There is a need to put a halt to the current U.S. policy of targeting extraterrestrial vehicles through the deployment of space based and other advanced weapons systems. As Hellyer pointed out in his September 2005 speech: "Are they really enemies or merely legitimate explorers from afar?" What makes this policy issue complex from the perspective of whistleblowers such as Corso, who is representative of many military officials briefed about the extraterrestrial presence, is that they believe that the weaponization of space is appropriate. This policy is justified, in Corso's and other military officials' views, on the basis of the intrusive activities of extraterrestrials.

The abduction phenomenon and related intrusive activities needs to be understood in terms of the highly classified agreements reached between the 'secret government' and extraterrestrials. It should be pointed out that military officials such as Corso did not appear to be briefed about friendly extraterrestrials and the latter's non-intrusive activities. Instead, Corso was given information on abduction related activities and other extraterrestrial intrusions that lead to the psychological framework for the creation of 'enemy images'. This process is described by Sam Keen in *Faces of the Enemy* which clearly outlines how the creation of enemy images has been a vital aspect for fighting successful wars.[413] In short, what has emerged over the last 50 years or so is the creation of an 'extraterrestrial enemy' that justifies the development and deployment of space weapons according to Corso and other military officials. This takes us to the warnings of Dr Carol Rosin, a former spokeswoman to Dr Werner Von Braun, about a contrived extraterrestrial threat being the basis of a public disclosure of extraterrestrial life.[414] Such a contrived threat would direct public perceptions towards extraterrestrials as unfriendly and a security threat. A more nuanced assessment based on the 'internal' versus 'external threat' posed by extraterrestrials is needed.

Consequently, in response to the profound policy question raised by Hellyer of whether weaponization of space is an appropriate policy response to the extraterrestrial visitors, the answer is NO. There is no need for a military response to the extraterrestrial visitors. It is clear that extraterrestrials who pose a credible 'national security threat' do so by virtue of their involvement in a series of secret agreements that make possible a covert take over of the vast infrastructure of extraterrestrial related projects that exist in the U.S., and other countries. This covert extraterrestrial threat requires a POLITICAL solution rather than a MILITARY solution –public disclosure of extraterrestrial life.

With public disclosure of extraterrestrial life, there can be the necessary transparency and accountability to ensure that any technology exchange agreements with extraterrestrials are conducted in a responsible way, and do not make human society prone to a covert 'take-over' by extraterrestrials. It is very likely that the abduction phenomenon would cease to be a problem once transparency and accountability were brought into play. Extraterrestrial visitors performing such activities could be closely monitored and persuaded from continuing any activities that violated individual human rights. 'Persuasive mechanisms' would come in a variety of ways: rigorous public debate over extraterrestrial activities; educating extraterrestrials about human rights standards; and the anticipated support of many extraterrestrial civilizations in monitoring and countering violations by other extraterrestrials.

The Honorable Paul Hellyer called for an urgent public debate over the appropriateness of current military policies directed towards extraterrestrial visitors. The current policy advocated by Corso of weaponizing space and targeting extraterrestrial vehicles, is supported by many former and current military officials 'in the loop' about the extraterrestrial visitors. The development and use of space based weapons against extraterrestrial visitors will be shown to be a poor policy choice once the true history of 'secret government' and extraterrestrial agreements is revealed. As a former Minister of Defense, Hellyer is very familiar with the importance of policy questions concerning the use of military weapons in resolving international political problems. He is to be congratulated for bringing to the public's attention the "profoundly important policy questions that must be addressed" with regard to the weaponization of space and the alleged targeting of extraterrestrial visitors.[415]

ENDNOTES - CHAPTER SIX

[380] "Speech by President George W. Bush," National Defense University, Washington, May 1, 2001. Transcript available at: http://www.fas.org/nuke/control/abmt/news/010501bush.html .
[381] Cited in "National Security Presidential Directive/NSPD-23," available online at: http://www.fas.org/irp/offdocs/nspd/nspd-23.htm .
[382] "Exopolitics Toronto: A Symposium on UFO Disclosure and Planetary Direction," http://www.exopoliticstoronto.com/archives.html .
[383] Paul Hellyer, "Missile Defense: It Was Wrong Then and It's Wrong Now," *Globe and Mail*, May 15, 2003. Available online at: http://www.commondreams.org/views03/0515-10.htm .
[384] For more details on Hellyer's speech and to view it online, go to: http://tinyurl.com/3fv2f7.
[385] Hellyer disclosed the existence of these officials in a private conversation with the author in November 8, 2005, but chose not to reveal further details of them due to their need for anonymity.
[386] Cited from 2005 Exopolitics Toronto lecture presentation available online at: http://tinyurl.com/3fv2f7 .
[387] Cited from 2005 Exopolitics Toronto lecture presentation available online at: http://tinyurl.com/3fv2f7 .
[388] Cited from 2005 Exopolitics Toronto lecture presentation available online at: http://tinyurl.com/3fv2f7 .
[389] Cited from 2005 Exopolitics Toronto lecture presentation available online at: http://tinyurl.com/3fv2f7 .
[390] Philip Corso, *The Day After Roswell* (Simon & Schuster, 1997) 290.
[391] Corso, *The Day After Roswell*, 292.
[392] Philip Corso, *L'Alba Di Una Nuova Era* [Dawn of a New Age] tr. Maurizio Baiata (Pendragon, 2003). I thank Maurizio Baiata for permission to quote extracts based on his translation of Corso's original notes.
[393] *Dawn of a New Age*, 77.
[394] *Dawn of a New Age*, p. 98.
[395] *Dawn of a New Age*, 78.
[396] See Chapter one. For further discussion of testimonial and circumstantial evidence of such a meeting, see Michael Salla,. "Eisenhower's 1954 Meeting With Extraterrestrials: The Fiftieth Anniversary of First Contact?" Exopolitics.Org (February 12, 2004): http://www.exopolitics.org/Study-Paper-8.htm
[397] *The Day After Roswell*, 292.
[398] *Dawn of a New Age*, p. 77
[399] See William Hamilton, "California Contactees," available on line at: http://www.geocities.com/Area51/Shadowlands/6583/et031.html .
[400] See Stanton Friedman, *Top Secret/Majic* (2005): 86-102
[401] *Majestic Documents*, 128. See also www.majesticdocuments.com

[402] See Friedman, *Top Secret/Majic,* 56-85.
[403] Cited in *Foreign Relations of the United States*, 1964-1968, vol. XII , Western Europe, pp. XXXI-XXXV, April 16, 2001. Available online at: http://www.fas.org/sgp/advisory/state/covert.html .
[404] See "A Nation Deceived," http://www.mega.nu:8080/ampp/roundtable/emchurch.html .
[405] Corso, *Dawn of a New Age,* 31.
[406] See http://www.presidentialufo.com/newpage17.htm .
[407] Cited in "Formal announcement from William Louis ("Bill") McDonald, Sr.:", http://www.stealthskater.com/Documents/Andrews_02.doc .
[408] David Jacobs, *The Threat: Revealing the Secret Alien Agenda* (Simon and Schuster, 1999).
[409] John Mack, Passport to the Cosmos (Thorsons, 2000).
[410] See chapter one. See also Michael Salla, "The Motivations and Activities of Extraterrestrial Civilizations," http://www.exopolitics.org/Report-ET-Motivations.htm .
[411] See chapter three. An earlier version was published as Michael Salla, "The Black Budget Report," *Scoop Magazine*, January, 2004, available online at: http://www.scoop.co.nz/stories/HL0401/S00151.htm .
[412] See chapter four. An earlier online version was published as Michael Salla, "The Dulce Report," at: http://www.exopolitics.org/Dulce-Report.htm .
[413] See Keen, *Faces of the Enemy: Reflections of the Hostile Imagination* (Harper Collins, 1991).
[414] See Carol Rosin interview, available online at: http://www.illuminati-news.com/ufos-and-aliens/html/carol_rosin.htm .
[415] Cited from 2005 Exopolitics Toronto lecture presentation available online at: http://tinyurl.com/3fv2f7

Chapter Seven

U.S. Government Suppression of a Civilian Spacecraft Industry

Introduction[416]

In 1955, Otis T. Carr, a protégé of Nikola Tesla began a highly visible public effort to develop a prototype civilian spacecraft that could be mass produced in kits and sold to the public. If successful, Carr would have developed the world's first civilian spacecraft and would have revolutionized the aviation industry. The vehicle was to be powered by a generator drawing electrical energy from the environment and stored in special coils. The stored electrical energy would have produced an antigravity effect for propulsion.[417] Carr claimed to have been taught all he knew about electromagnetic energy and antigravity principles by the famous Yugoslav inventor Nikola Tesla. He had resided in a New York hotel where Carr worked part time while completing his studies. Tesla had publicly stated in 1915 that he knew how to build an antigravity flying vehicle: "My flying machine will have neither wings nor propellers. You might see it on the ground, and you would never guess that it was a flying machine. Yet it will be able to move at will through the air in any direction with perfect safety."[418] Tesla's flying vehicle would be powered by electrical energy drawn from the earth's atmosphere. Frustrated by lack of industry support, Tesla revealed his radical ideas to the young Carr over a three year period.

Tesla taught Carr how electromagnetic energy could be freely harnessed from the abundant electrical energy in the atmosphere. The possibility that electrical energy could be freely acquired without expensive power plants, conductive wires, relay stations, telephone poles and significant power loss, challenged conventional power companies. Tesla was told that his radical ideas would not be funded. J.P. Morgan and other industrialists were not be able to meter the free electrical energy that could be easily drawn from the atmosphere. Indeed, Tesla's ideas challenged the foundations of the global economy and monetary system.

Inspired by the aging Tesla, Carr set about testing Tesla's principles in 1937 when he began creating model spacecraft.[419] Carr eventually became convinced that he could develop a civilian spacecraft that could travel into the upper atmosphere, to the moon and even achieve the speed of light. All this could be achieved by following Tesla's advice of tapping into the electrical energy in the atmosphere to power the spacecraft, storing such energy in a special "regenerative coil" for interplanetary flights.

Otis Carr claims to build the world's first civilian spacecraft

Carr founded a company, OTC Enterprises, Inc, in 1955 in Maryland, and set about raising necessary funds and skilled personnel for building models. These could be tested to validate a full scale prototype. These models ranged in sizes. They included a six foot version to test the feasibility of his ideas for a planned 45-foot prototype spacecraft. In November 1959 Carr successfully patented his design for a full scale civilian spacecraft he called OTC-X1.[420] It had a circular design that made it look like a flying saucer (see figure 2.).

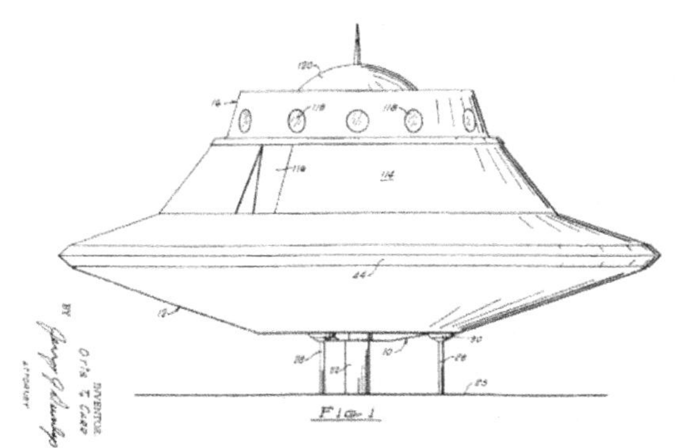

Figure 2. Patent Office Schematic of OTC-X1

In order to gain a patent for his design from a skeptical Patents Office, he claimed his OTC-X1 was an amusement device. The introduction to his patent claims: "This invention relates generally to implements in amusement devices, and more particularly to an improved amusement device of the type where the passengers will receive the impression of riding in an interplanetary spacecraft."

In a 1959 radio interview Carr described the various tests conducted for developing his prototype civilian spacecraft:

> "We plan to build a prototype model as a demonstration device. Now I would like to state that certain models have been built by me and tested. Each one has been airborne. One was lost entirely in space. We had a control system and this one didn't function. This has already been done."[421]

The OTC-X1 would be powered by a number of capacitor like objects Carr called "Utrons". In an earlier 1957 interview, Carr described the Utrons as "a storage cell for electrical energy. In operation it generates electricity at the same time it puts out electromotive force. This is the central power system for our space craft."[422] The Utrons would supply a series of counter rotating magnets the energy they required for overcoming the Earth's gravitational field. Carr described this process as follows:

> [W]e have capacitor plates and electro-magnets as a part of this system. Now this is counter-rotating, the electro-magnets rotate in one direction and the accumulator, the batteries rotate in another. The capacitor plates rotate in conjunction with the battery so that we have a clockwise and counter clockwise rotation. Now the third system is the cabin that maintains the crew. This does not rotate, it is fixed due to the fact the two bodies are rotating clockwise and counter clockwise. Therefore the system causes the craft to escape from the gravity pull. The craft itself due to this system still has internal gravity because it still has the same weight that it had in the beginning.

Carr's design would create an entirely new gravitational field inside the craft. This effectively created a zero mass environment inside his craft that would suspend the normal laws of inertia. This zero mass environment would enable the spacecraft to achieve light speed velocity.[423] It would also enable occupants to withstand tremendous accelerations and changes in directions without being pulverized by immense g-forces inside the craft. Carr detailed the intricate electromagnetic propulsion system of his spacecraft in his 1959 patent. Carr stated that all electrical power would be extracted from the atmosphere and be stored in sufficient quantities in "regenerative coils" to power the craft during interplanetary travel: "We are able here, the first time to our knowledge, to use atmospheric electricity as a recharging system. This is done as a part of operational principal of the craft."[424]

Carr demonstrated a small model in an interview as reported in Fate Magazine:

> Otis T. Carr, president of OTC Enterprises, Inc., detailed his claims in an interview and demonstration of a crude model of a circular motion machine which he said is the principle of a "free energy circular foil" space craft he can build, if someone puts up the money. He said the machine can be adapted to devices of any size to produce continuous power absolutely free of dissipation. Its immediate application, Carr said, would be in a space craft - which would be able to fly among the planets in controlled flight. It could land or take off as desired on the earth, the moon or any planet in the earth's solar system, he said.[425]

Carr scheduled a test for his six foot model in April 1959 for an audience of approximately 400 people in Oklahoma City. Technical difficulties and a sudden illness contracted by Carr led to the test being cancelled. A 1959 article published in *Fate Magazine* described the failed test as follows:

> The serious field of UFO's and flying saucer research received a setback at Oklahoma City in late April when a highly publicized launching attempt by O.T.C. Enterprises of Baltimore, Md., resulted in failure. Hundreds of persons had been invited to Oklahoma City by Otis T. Carr to watch him "launch a six-foot prototype model of the O.T.C. X-1, a space craft which works on 'utron' energy." Those who were there came away disappointed. The flying saucer did not fly.[426]

All that was shown to the public were three dimensional illustrations of his design. Carr was nowhere to be found. Long John Nebel, a famous New York radio host, located Carr at the nearby Mercy hospital where he had been admitted for eight days due to a lung hemorrhage. Mysteriously, Carr had become ill on the eve of what should have been a major publicity coup for him. Carr's spacecraft project was becoming increasingly shrouded in mystery and controversy.

Those present were dissatisfied and some complained that they were not even shown the model to be tested:

> I don't know what's going on but I feel they never had any intention of trying to launch the model. I could not see any plans in sight for the model and, in fact, I understand, that a Mr. Maywood Jones presented only what he called "three-dimensional illustrations" of Carr's ideas.[427]

Many accepted public criticisms that Carr was promoting his OTC-X1 in order to create interest for his planned amusement park ride at Frontier City in Oklahoma City:

> One Oklahoma City television reporter expressed the general feeling of the townspeople: "This thing will never leave the ground. And I feel that a great deal of the ballyhoo they're giving out is tied in with the ride at Frontier City. I have tried constantly to get in to see the saucer model, but they've kept it hidden." [428]

With growing hostile public opinion in Oklahoma, Carr decided to move his center of operations to Apple Valley, California in late 1959. To prevent any further public debacles, he decided not to announce any test flights in advance. With new financial backing and a large production plant, Osbrink, at his disposal, Carr proceeded with his plans to develop and test his spacecraft. Major Wayne Aho, a former Army Combat Intelligence Officer during World War II, and Carr's chief pilot, proclaimed that he would "fly to the moon in a flying saucer on December 7, 1959."[429] Little was subsequently heard of Carr's efforts and plans to test his full scale 45-foot prototype. No public reports exist of any subsequent tests.

In raising revenue for his spacecraft program, Carr was experiencing increasing problems with the U.S. Securities and Exchange Commission that had placed an injunction against Carr, ordering him to cease selling unregistered stock".[430] On June 2, 1960, Carr told a California audience of 300 that it was a "treacherous misstatement of fact to say or infer that we [OTC Enterprises] are coming to California to raise money in stock sales."[431]

In January, 1961 the Attorney General of New York, Louis J. Lefkowitz, claimed Carr had swindled $50,000. He was charged with "the crime of selling securities without registering the same."[432] Carr was sentenced to a 14 year prison term. At the same time, *True Magazine* labeled Carr a hoaxer, thereby effectively ending any remaining public sympathy for him. After serving part of his term, Carr was released from prison, and disappeared from the public arena. Suffering ill health and cut off from supporters, he lived in obscurity until his death in 1982. Apparently, the bold development of a civilian spacecraft industry had ignominiously failed. Its pioneer, a protégé of the great Nikola Tesla, was publicly disgraced as a felon having apparently hoaxed members of the general public with his wild tales of building a civilian spacecraft while actually promoting an amusement park ride.

The true history of what happened with Carr and his effort to develop a civilian spacecraft industry would remain secret for almost another 50 years. It is only the public emergence of one of Carr's trusted technicians that the truth would finally be told of what had really happened with the world's first civilian spacecraft effort.

Ralph Ring Emerges to Reveal Carr's successful development of the OTC-X1

In March 2006, a largely unknown individual came forward to reveal that he was one of three pilots of a successful test of Carr's full scale prototype of the OTC-X1.[433] Ralph Ring claims to be a technician who was recruited into Carr's team attempting to build a 45-foot prototype spacecraft after Carr had relocated in California in 1959. Ring at the time was a talented inventor who had grown frustrated with corporate sector disinterest in innovative principles concerning electromagnetic energy. He had earlier helped the famous French oceanographer Jacques Cousteau develop the aqualung, and later worked at a government-funded research organization called Advanced Kinetics.

In a series of public interviews and presentations, Ring described the conditions of leaving Advanced Kinetics. He claims to have resolved two complex engineering problems involving electromagnetism. Confident of a job promotion, Ring was instead told by the director that they were government funded corporation and "we're paid to look for the answers, but not to find them!"[434] In frustration, Ring left and met with Carr in late 1959, and was quickly impressed with his ideas, including a plan to build a civilian spacecraft. In his first public interview, Ring described Carr as follows:

> He was an unquestioned genius. Tesla had recognized his quality immediately and had taught him everything he knew. He was inspired, and – like Tesla – seemed to know exactly what to do to get something to work. He was a private man and was also very metaphysical in his thinking. I think the fact that he was not formally trained in physics helped him. He was not constrained by any preconceived ideas. As crazy as it sounds now, he was determined to fly to the moon and really believed it could be done. I believed it. We all did.[435]

Ring directly participated in the testing of smaller models of the OTC-X1 craft developed by Carr. He described how these had been successfully tested and exhibited unique characteristics when achieving certain rotational speeds:

> ...the metal turned to Jell-o. You could push your finger right into it. It ceased to be solid. It turned into another form of matter, which was as if it was not entirely here in this reality. That's the only way I can attempt to describe it. It was uncanny, one of the weirdest sensations I've ever felt.[436]

Most importantly, Ring claims that the 45-foot OTC-X1 prototype developed by Carr was completed and successfully tested back in 1959. Ring says he was one of three pilots on the craft which flew 10 miles instantaneously. Ring described how Carr had been able to maintain communications with the three man team piloting the

OTC-X1 who were instructed to complete a series of tasks, before returning to the launch site. When asked if the OTC-X1 had flown to its destination, Ring said:

> Fly is not the right word. It traversed distance. It seemed to take no time. I was with two other engineers when we piloted the 45' craft about ten miles. I thought it hadn't moved – I thought it had failed. I was completely astonished when we realized that we had returned with samples of rocks and plants from our destination. It was a dramatic success. It was more like a kind of teleportation. [437]

Ring described how the test flight had been able to change the flow of time:

> What's more, time was distorted somehow. We felt we were in the craft about fifteen or twenty seconds. We were told afterwards that we'd been carefully timed as having been in the craft no longer than three or four minutes. I still have no complete idea how it worked. [438]

The most remarkable part of Ring's testimony concerns the unique navigation system used by the pilots to control the movements of the OTC-X1. According to Ring, this navigation system used the conscious intent of the pilots rather than conventional technology.

> The Utron was the key to it all. Carr said it accumulated energy because of its shape, and focused it, and also responded to our conscious intentions. When we operated the machine, we didn't work any controls. We went into a kind of meditative state and all three of us focused our intentions on the effect we wanted to achieve. It sounds ridiculous, I know. But that's what we did, and that's what worked. Carr had tapped into some principle which is not understood, in which consciousness melds with engineering to create an effect. You can't write that into equations. I have no idea how he knew it would work. But it did. [439]

Success of the first test of the full scale OTC-X1 meant that planning for flights into outer space and to the moon was now proceeding in earnest. Ring said Carr and his crew worked round the clock to complete the testing program before announcing the results to the general public.

The most dramatic part of Ring's testimony concerns what happened two weeks after the successful test of the OTC-X1. He said that Carr's operation was closed down by the FBI and other government agencies in a secret raid involving seven or eight truckloads of armed government personnel. The FBI told Carr that his project was being closed "because of your threat to overthrow the monetary system of the United States of America."[440]

Indeed, Carr's successful testing of a civilian spacecraft, had it been allowed to go ahead, would have revolutionized the energy sector and the aerospace industry. The conventional energy industry using fossil fuels to generate electric power and the aviation industry would have become redundant overnight. Large U.S. corporate interests in the energy sector would have lost substantial investments. Lack of corporate profits would throw countless thousands out of work. The financial effect of a civilian spacecraft industry using electrical energy from the atmosphere for power would indeed have placed enormous pressure on the U.S. monetary system possibly causing its collapse.

In a series of interviews and public presentations, Ring claims FBI agents confiscated all the equipment including the OTC-X1 prototype. They debriefed all of Carr's employees, warned them to remain silent on what had happened, and made Carr sign non-disclosure agreements. Ring's testimony, if true, reveals what really happened with Otis Carr's radical civilian spacecraft project. Rather than Carr being a fraud who deceived a number of investors funding his radical civilian spacecraft ideas, Carr had been successful. His success so threatened entrenched interests in the energy sector, that his operation was shut down with the full approval and knowledge of a select number of government agencies concerned with the financial impact on the U.S. monetary system. Carr himself was forced to endure trumped up charges designed to discredit him, and end his bold effort to develop a civilian spacecraft industry.

How Credible is Ralph Ring's Testimony?

How much evidence exists to substantiate Ring's testimony? Ring is a very likable and sincere individual who has impressed audiences with his genuineness and frankness. Bill Ryan and Kerry Cassidy, founders of Project Camelot, a website featuring video interviews of whistleblowers, were the first to interview Ring in March 2006.[441] After a series of interviews, they conclude: "There is no doubt in our minds that Ralph Ring is 100% genuine. Everyone who has met him and heard his story in person is in full agreement."[442] This is something I can personally verify since I was able to hear Ring present his ideas at the International UFO Congress in 2007. I was also able to personally interview him later in Hawaii when he accepted an invitation to attend a conference I co-organized.[443] I agree with Ryan and Cassidy that Ring's personal qualities make him very credible. He appears to be motivated by a simple desire to tell the truth about events that happened almost 50 years ago that could have revolutionized life on the planet.

Ring has provided a number of photographs of the OTC-X1 developed by Carr. These photographs had previously not been published. The photos showed that Carr had indeed succeeded in building a number of models including the 45 foot prototype spacecraft (see Figure 3).[444] The photos dispel the view that Carr had not succeeded in developing a full scale prototype spacecraft. Ring's photos are material evidence that he did indeed collaborate with Carr on the OTC-X1, as he claims.

Figure 3. Full Scale Version of OTC-X1

Perhaps most significant is what occurred to Ring soon after coming forward to reveal his experiences with Otis Carr in March 2006. Bill Ryan describes what happened:

> Shortly afterwards, Ralph went into hospital for a routine knee replacement operation. He accidentally received the wrong treatment, and nearly died three times. At the time of writing (July 2006) he has just recently emerged, very frail, from intensive care - but is determined to tell his story. Prior to that he had enjoyed perfect health for 71 years.[445]

In his presentations at a number of conferences Ring described how he had been taken by ambulance to a hospital 25 miles away, bypassing a hospital adjacent to where he was staying.[446] Ring hovered perilously close to death as a result of the 'mistreatment' and the long ambulance ride. Was the "accidental" application of another patient's medication, and the "bypassing" of nearer hospitals part of a covert attempt on Ring's life? The circumstances are certainly suspicious and indicate an effort to silence Ring. This series of "accidental" events that almost took Ring's life soon after his public emergence provides circumstantial evidence in support of his claims.

Public Policy Implications

We can now draw together the different elements concerning Otis Carr's OTC-X1 project and Ralph Ring's testimony. Carr's successful development of a fully operational civilian spacecraft using radical electromagnetic propulsion and navigation systems led to a brutal response by federal government agencies. Agencies led by the FBI raided Carr's construction facilities, confiscated equipment, intimidated employees into silence, and publicly discredited Carr through trumped up charges orchestrated from the U.S. Stock and Securities Commission. Ring's public testimony and photographic evidence he provided of the existence of Carr's OTC-X1, give confidence that elements inside the U.S. Government suppressed a wholly civilian owned spacecraft industry. Several motives for this suppression appear.

The first and principal motive for the government suppression was to protect U.S. industrial interests in the energy sector that would have been threatened by knowledge of how to draw free electrical energy from the atmosphere. U.S. corporations dominate the energy sector around the planet, and the appearance of "free energy" technologies would wreak havoc on their stock value. This would impact negatively on the entire U.S. economy.

A second and related motive for this suppression is the impact of "free energy" technologies on the U.S monetary system – the explanation given by FBI agents for raiding Carr's plant. The development of free energy technologies would make redundant the conventional energy sector owned by U.S. corporations possibly leading to a collapse of the U.S. dollar.

A third possible motive is preventing the development of a civilian spacecraft industry that could travel into outer space and other planets with minimal or no government regulation. Such a civilian spacecraft industry could enable travel to nearby planets to confirm whether intelligent life forms have ever resided or continue to reside on the moon, Mars and elsewhere in our solar system. There is evidence that intelligent extraterrestrial life has been discovered on the moon and other planets but this is being suppressed by major governments.[447] Many analyses of NASA photographs of the moon and Mars reveal artificial structures and anomalous phenomenon under intelligent control. Despite widespread public interest in these, NASA refuses to seriously investigate such evidence and many have concluded a cover up is underway.[448]

A fourth motive to suppress Carr's OTC-X1 project was to keep secret technology already being developed in classified projects. Carr's work was not deemed important enough to be classified so that he and his technicians could continue to work on developing his ideas of a spacecraft that could travel to the moon at light speed. His project was shut down, Carr discredited and his technicians intimidated into silence. There is an obvious explanation for this response by involved government authorities.

The reason for the treatment given to Carr and his technicians was that government authorities had no need for Carr's ideas on how to develop a spacecraft capable of light speed, and which could tap into free electrical energy available in the Earth's atmosphere. Responsible government authorities would also have no need for the unique navigation system developed by Carr for his OTC-X1 that used a mind-technology interface between the pilots and the spacecraft. This was not because government authorities were not interested in these ideas. These authorities already had a classified project for an antigravity craft capable of near light speed and powered by electrical energy drawn from the natural environment.[449] This is supported by the testimonial evidence concerning agreements with extraterrestrial life, and the retrieval of crashed extraterrestrial vehicles discussed in chapters one and four. The principles for near 'light speed' space flight were likely so well known that the efforts of civilian inventors were simply not needed in classified antigravity projects. The conclusion is that in the 1950's, the U.S. government already had a number of operational spacecraft that were capable of attaining near light speed, and could draw electrical energy from the Earth's atmosphere that could be stored for space travel.

A final possible motive for the closing down of Carr's spacecraft program is that an exclusive group of quasi-governmental or "shadow government" authorities with strong ties to corporations did not want to alert regular military and/or government authorities of the existence of such advanced technology. I earlier described an interview Dr Steven Greer and former Apollo Astronaut Edgar Mitchell had with Vice Admiral Tom Wilson in 1997 when Wilson was J-2, head of the Intelligence division of the Joint Chiefs of Staff. When advised of certain Special Access programs involving possible extraterrestrial technology, Wilson was denied access to these since he did not have a "need to know".[450] Such unprecedented action, restricting a sitting head of intelligence of the Joint Chiefs of Staff, demonstrates that a group of "shadow government" authorities keeps advanced technologies away from regular military and governmental authorities. The existence of such a "shadow government" has been suggested by a number of prominent U.S. politicians. It's worth repeating Senator Daniel K. Inouye's comment: "There exists a shadowy Government with it's own Air Force, its own Navy, it's own fundraising mechanism, and the ability to pursue its own ideas of the national interest, free from all checks and balances, and free from the law itself."[451] Shutting down Carr's civilian spacecraft program would deny regular military and governmental authorities knowledge and access to such advanced technology. This would place the regular military at great disadvantage in monitoring what is occurring in deep black projects involving advanced technology controlled by shadowy government agencies outside of the regular chain of command.

Carr's mysterious illness prior to his public testing of his six foot model in 1959, and the near death of Ralph Ring in 2006 after his coming forward to reveal his testimony, suggest covert government operations to prevent public demonstration and knowledge of advanced technologies. Covert government agencies have been historically observed to be targeting inventors and researchers working on advanced technologies.[452] Discrediting, silencing or terminating inventors and/or whistleblowers appears to continue.

Conclusions

In 1959/1960, Otis Carr and his team had succeeded in developing the world's first civilian spacecraft. This notable achievement was brutally suppressed, and Carr was incarcerated on trumped up charges in 1961. The collusion of some elements of the U.S. government in suppressing the emergence of a civilian spacecraft industry emerges as a key historical fact. U.S. corporations in the energy sector, aware of Carr's ambitious program, were likely a key factor in this suppression.

The implications of Ring's testimony and Carr's achievements are momentous for humanity. Rather than a felon who hoaxed the general public with radical ideas of civilian spacecraft, Carr was a heroic inventor who succeeded, against tremendous odds in building the world's first civilian spacecraft. Carr and his team of collaborators need to be acknowledged and honored for their pioneering efforts. Congressional inquiries should be immediately launched to fully investigate what happened to Carr. The FBI and other government agencies involved in raiding Carr's facilities and confiscating equipment should reveal what occurred. The precise role of U.S. corporations complicit in these repressive actions also need to be thoroughly investigated. Appropriate legislation needs to be developed to prevent future instances of pioneering inventors being targeted by government agencies acting at the behest of vested interest groups.

The technological revolution that will emerge with a thorough investigation of Carr's accomplishments must be embraced rather than hidden from the general public. Shadowy governmental agencies and corporations responsible for suppressing the public emergence of such technology, even to the extent of denying it to regular military forces, need to be revealed and made accountable. Humanity is on the threshold on a remarkable achievement, the development of an inexpensive civilian spacecraft industry that can achieve travel to planets in our solar system and the stars. Vested financial interests and quasi-governmental groups hoarding such technology can no longer be allowed to hold back this remarkable achievement.

ENDNOTES – CHAPTER SEVEN

[416] Great thanks to Jack Davis for his proof reading and editing of an earlier version of this chapter. Ralph Ring's testimony initially emerged through Bill Ryan and Kerry Cassidy from Project Camelot who made available his interview in video format, and supplied a number of his documents online. They deserve great credit for their efforts to bring to the public the testimony of Ring, and of whistleblowers and researchers who cast light on many exotic topics. Their website is http://www.projectcamelot.net .

[417] The principle of stored electrical energy producing anti-gravity effects was patented by the inventor Thomas Townsend Brown and has been subsequently called the Biefeld-Brown Effect. See Thomas Valone, *Electrogravitics II: Validating Reports on a New Propulsion Methodology* (Integrity Research Institute, 2005).

[418] Nikola Tesla, interviewed in *The New York Herald Tribune*, October 15, 1911

[419] See 1957 Interview with Long John Nebow where Carr describes how he began creating models of his ideas: http://www.keelynet.com/gravity/carr4.htm .

[420] US Patent # 2,912,244, Amusement Device (November 10, 1959).

[421] Transcript of Radio Interview: "Long John" Nebel & Otis Carr, *et al.* (WOR Radio, NY, 1959). Available online at: http://www.rexresearch.com/carr/1carr.htm.

[422] Cited at: http://www.keelynet.com/gravity/carr4.htm .

[423] The mainstream scientific view that the speed of light presents and insurmountable obstacle to the physical presence of extraterrestrial visitors has been increasingly challenged by new theories concerning faster than light speed travel. See James Deardorff, et al., "Inflation-Theory Implications for Extraterrestrial Visitation," *Journal of the British Interplanetary Society*, 58 (2005): 43-50. Available online at: http://www.ufoevidence.org/news/article204.htm

[424] Cited from 1957 Interview with Long John Nebow, available at: http://www.keelynet.com/gravity/carr4.htm .

[425] Original source: Gravity Machine? *FATE magazine* (May 1958) p. 17. Online copy available at: http://www.keelynet.com/gravity/carr1.txt .

[426] W. E. Du Soir, "The Saucer that didn't Fly," *FATE magazine,* (August 1959) p. 32. Cited online at: http://www.keelynet.com/gravity/carr3.htm .

[427] Du Soir, "The Saucer that didn't Fly." Cited at: http://www.keelynet.com/gravity/carr3.htm .

[428] Du Soir, "The Saucer that didn't Fly." Cited at: http://www.keelynet.com/gravity/carr3.htm .

[429] Cited online at: http://www.keelynet.com/gravity/carr3.htm. Biographical information on Wayne Aho is available at: http://www.answers.com/topic/wayne-sulo-aho .

[430] Cited from Project Camelot website:
http://www.projectcamelot.net/ralph_ring.html
[431] Du Soir, "The Saucer that didn't Fly." Cited at:
http://www.keelynet.com/gravity/carr3.htm .
[432] Cited in OTIS T. CARR, PLAINTIFF IN ERROR, v. STATE OF OKLAHOMA, DEFENDANT IN ERROR. Case No. A-12907. January 11, 1961. Available Online at: http://tinyurl.com/4uqog5 .
[433] Ring first met with Bill Ryan and Kerry Cassidy in March 2006 to reveal his remarkable story.
[434] Ralph Ring, conference presentation at the International UFO Congress, Laughlin, Nevada, 2007. DVD available at:
http://www.ufocongress.com/index.php/category/2007-ufo-congress/ .
[435] Cited from Project Camelot interview with Ralph Ring:
http://www.projectcamelot.net/ralph_ring.html
[436] Cited from Project Camelot interviews with Ralph Ring,
http://www.projectcamelot.net/ralph_ring.html
[437] Cited from Project Camelot interviews with Ralph Ring,
http://www.projectcamelot.net/ralph_ring.html
[438] The citation from Project Camelot refers to 15 minutes, in a private conversation with Ralph Ring on March 25, 2007, he corrected this to 15 seconds:
http://www.projectcamelot.net/ralph_ring.html .
[439] Cited from Project Camelot interviews with Ralph Ring,
http://www.projectcamelot.net/ralph_ring.html
[440] Ralph Ring, conference presentation at the International UFO Congress, Laughlin, Nevada, 2007.
[441] More information on Project Camelot available at:
http://www.projectcamelot.net
[442] Cited from Project Camelot interviews with Ralph Ring,
http://www.projectcamelot.net/ralph_ring.html
[443] Ralph Ring spoke at the May 11-13, 2007 Earth Transformation Conference. Details available online at: http://earthtransformation.com/speakers-2007.htm
[444] Photos available online at: http://projectcamelot.org/ralph_ring.html
[445] Cited from Project Camelot interviews with Ralph Ring,
http://www.projectcamelot.net/ralph_ring.html
[446] Ring's first conference presentation was at the International UFO Congress at Laughlin, Nevada in March 2007. This was followed by a similar presentation at the Earth Transformation Conference at Kona, Hawaii in May 2007.
[447] See Michael Salla, *Exopolitics: Political Implications of the Extraterrestrial Presence* (Dandelion Books, 2004); Steven Greer, *Disclosure: Military and Government Witnesses reveal the Greatest Secrets in Modern History* (Crossing Point Press, Inc., 2001).
[448] See Richard C. Hoagland, *The Monuments of Mars: A City on the Edge of Forever*, 5th Edition (North Atlantic Books, 2003); and Fred Steckling, *We Discovered Alien Bases on the Moon* (G.A.F. International, 1990).

[449] For discussion of antigravity technology and government classification of such principles, see Nick Cook, *The Hunt for Zero Point* (Broadway Books, 2001).
[450] Steven Greer, *Hidden Truth, Forbidden Knowledge* (Crossing Point, Inc., 2006) 158-59.
[451] Inouye made this claim at the Iran-Contra hearings conducted by the U.S. Senate. Cited online at:
http://www.sourcewatch.org/index.php?title=Shadow_Government
[452] See G. Cope Schellhorn, "Is Someone Killing Our UFO Investigators," http://www.metatech.org/ufo_research_magazine_evidence.html

Part C –Exopolitics as a New Paradigm for Understanding Extraterrestrial Life

Exopolitics is a new discipline seeking to understand public policy issues associated with extraterrestrial life. An exopolitical perspective helps greatly in identifying the hidden extraterrestrial policies that underlie many contemporary international issues. The primary challenge confronting practitioners of exopolitics is to prepare the general public for the exposure of secret government policy concerning extraterrestrial life. This requires first explaining the main concepts and approaches that make up exopolitics, and the unique perspective it brings to international public policy issues. The three chapters that make up Part C. seek to achieve this goal.

Chapter eight explains how exopolitics is an emerging academic paradigm that examines public policy issues concerning extraterrestrial life. The chapter points out that one does not need to believe in the existence of extraterrestrial in order to develop exopolitics ideas and approaches. A number of historic documents adopt exopolitics approaches despite qualifying statements about an absence of empirical evidence proving the existence of extraterrestrial life.

The following chapter examines the evolution of the exopolitics concept from the flying saucer conspiracies of the 1950's through to the explicit exopolitical models that have been more recently developed. Key individuals and organizations involved in the evolution of the exopolitics concept are described. This chapter shows how exopolitics is quickly evolving into a paradigm that can challenge the status quo of secrecy concerning extraterrestrial life.

Chapter ten provides an exopolitical perspective on false flag operations. The chapter shows how exopolitics underlies major international public policy issues. Examining the 911 false flag operation from a conventional public policy perspective is shown to be deficient. Only an exopolitical perspective accurately brings out the full scope of the principal actors and processes behind false flag operations such as the 911 attacks.

Chapter Eight

Exopolitics: Discipline of Choice for Public Policy Issues Concerning Extraterrestrial Life

Introduction[453]

The existence of extraterrestrial life has long been a subject of intense speculation and fierce public debate. Speculation has focused on the more than 200 billion solar systems known to exist in the Milky Way, and similar figures for other galaxies, that might harbor advanced extraterrestrial life. This is exemplified in estimates of extraterrestrial life in the galaxy provided by Project OZMA participants (forerunner to Search for Extraterrestrial Intelligence - SETI), who in a 1961 meeting agreed on the Drake equation. They came up with the initial figure of 10,000 technological civilizations scattered throughout the galaxy.[454] Such estimates have allowed futurists and science fiction authors to speculate on what such life would be like, and how it may impact on human society at some future date. Scientific speculation has taken the form of estimating the possibilities of advanced extraterrestrial life evolving in our galaxy, and the levels of scientific advancement that these would have reached. The Russian Astronomer Nikolai Kardashev, for example, speculated that advanced extraterrestrial civilizations could be distinguished by the quantity of energy they used. This could occur at a planetary level (Type I), stellar level (Type II) or galactic level (Type III).[455]

Public debate concerning extraterrestrial life has focused upon extensive visual sightings, radar trackings and photographs of Unidentified Flying Objects (UFOs) that appear to be under intelligent control. Many UFO sightings have been acknowledged by government officials as not explainable in terms of known aircraft or natural phenomena, and have even been reported to outperform the most advanced aircraft possessed by industrialized nations. For example, former Chairman of the Joint Chiefs of Staff in the U.S., General Nathan Twining, made the following declaration about the "flying disks" phenomenon in September 1947: "The phenomenon reported is something real and not visionary or fictitious."[456] Such comments by similar senior military or government officials have led to the extraterrestrial hypothesis that UFOs are extraterrestrial in origin, as a possible explanation.[457] More recently, a growing number of former government, military and corporate officials have come forward to disclose direct experience of UFOs and extraterrestrial life, and of government suppression of corroborating data.[458]

While speculation and debate continues around the subject of extraterrestrial life and its relation to UFO sightings, there has been growing controversy about how to approach the growing pool of data available in the public domain, primarily through the Internet. The data comprises many thousands of accounts by both private individuals; and former corporate, military and government officials; who have made available personal testimonies, photos, videos and documentation concerning extraterrestrial life. National governments have also significantly contributed to the growing pool of open source data available. The U.S. government, for example, has made available many documents through Freedom of Information Act requests that are now available on the internet. Similarly, governments such as France and Britain in 2007 and 2008 placed thousands of UFO case files on the internet.[459]

One approach to the public database has been to focus primarily on evidence concerning UFOs, and to subject this to rigorous scientific analyses to determine its credibility. Another more recent approach gaining popularity has been to focus on the public policy implications of evidence concerning extraterrestrial life. These respective approaches are generally known as 'UFOlogy' and 'exopolitics'. The supporters of each approach advocate distinct methodologies for dealing with the data available in the public domain. In this chapter, I contrast these two approaches to UFO-related data in terms of their suitability for comprehensively understanding the public policy implications of extraterrestrial life.

UFOlogy and Emphasizing Scientific Study of Physical Evidence

The field of UFOlogy is generally accepted to have started with sightings of what were initially called 'flying saucers' by Kenneth Arnold in June 1947. The frequency of flying saucer reports in the U.S. quickly led to a classified study by the U.S. Air Force with the initial assistance of the Federal Bureau of Investigation in 1948. Documents have emerged to confirm that the

Air Force commissioned technical specialists at its Air Technical Division at Wright Patterson Air Force Base to conduct a detailed investigation. The resulting investigation of approximately 300 cases produced a highly classified study called 'The Estimate of the Situation' in September 1948, whose initial conclusion reportedly supported the extraterrestrial hypothesis. The Estimate and its remarkable conclusion was moved all the way up the Air Force hierarchy to the desk of the Chief of Staff, General Hoyt Vandenberg who, according to unconfirmed reports, rejected it and made clear that support for the extraterrestrial hypothesis was not an acceptable conclusion for reasons related to national security.[460] According to Captain Edward Ruppelt, who in 1952 set up and was in charge of Project Blue Book, the official USAF investigation of the UFO phenomenon: "The general said it would cause a stampede....How could we convince the public the aliens weren't hostile when we didn't know ourselves? ... the general ordered the secret analysis burned. But one copy was held out - Major Dewey Fournet and I saw it in 1952."[461]

If accurate, Ruppelt's statement suggests that the extraterrestrial hypothesis was not a neutral scientific problem to be determined by technical specialists, but an issue of utmost national security concerns. Clearly, the public policy implications of extraterrestrial life, trumped any neutral scientific study of the phenomenon. It could not be assumed that the findings of any genuine investigation of UFOs would be released to the general public. The subsequent official U.S. Air Force study of UFOs,

Project Blue Book, was dogged by criticisms by UFO researchers that important evidence was being overlooked. The most well-known critic was Major Donald Keyhoe who wrote a number of books concerning 'flying saucers'.[462] He eventually became the head of the National Investigative Committee for Aerial Phenomenon (NICAP) which was created in 1956 to initiate civilian investigations of UFO's and to pressure the USAF to conduct more thorough investigations. Keyhoe and NICAP employed well-credentialed scientists, engineers and former officials to build an impressive database confirming the reality of UFOs and the support this gave to the extraterrestrial hypothesis. Regardless of Keyhoe's and NICAP's efforts, USAF and official government attitudes were dismissive, and even recommended debunking of UFO reports on national security grounds.

The 1953 CIA-sponsored Robertson Panel delivered a report, the Durant Report, that recommended ridiculing the flying saucer phenomenon and the possibility of extraterrestrial life, for national security reasons. The Report stated:

> The "debunking" aim would result in reduction in public interest in "flying saucers" which today evokes a strong psychological reaction. This education could be accomplished by mass media such as television, motion pictures, and popular articles.... Such a program should tend to reduce the current gullibility of the public and consequently their susceptibility to clever hostile propaganda.[463]

Subsequent debunking by government and military officials culminated in Keyhoe and some UFO researchers concluding that a government conspiracy existed to cover up information. Keyhoe's 1955 book, *The Flying Saucer Conspiracy,* detailed the extent to which the U.S. military was silencing personnel from revealing what they had seen and withholding corroborating physical evidence.[464]

Other UFO researchers, in contrast, insisted that the government had merely "fouled up" its study of UFOs, and that no government conspiracy existed. The consensus between the two groups of UFO researchers was that more emphasis would be given to establishing the scientific merit of UFO evidence, to counter the debunking efforts of government officials and members of the public. Public policy implications of the data confirming the reality of UFOs and the likelihood of the extraterrestrial hypothesis would be put off to some future date when evidence would be sufficiently overwhelming to remove all possible doubt.

As a field of study, UFOlogy therefore concentrated on scientific analysis of physical data associated with UFOs, and minimized speculation on the origins of UFOs and the extraterrestrial hypothesis. This is best demonstrated in a famous definition by Dr Allen Hynek, who defined the scientific study of UFOs as follows:

> We can define the UFO simply as the reported perception of an object or light seen in the sky or upon the land the appearance, trajectory, and general dynamic and luminescent behavior of which do not suggest a logical, conventional explanation and which is not only mystifying to the original percipients but remains unidentified after close scrutiny of all available evidence by persons who are technically capable of making a common sense identification, if one is possible.[465]

Leading UFOlogists such as Dr Hynek were not receptive to the idea that government entities were systematically tampering with evidence and intimidating individuals into silence. Any government 'cover-up' was limited to maintaining silence on evidence confirming UFOs, and not admitting to blunders in official studies of UFOs. Thus the government 'cover-up' or 'foul-up', according to UFOlogists, could be overcome by more detailed scientific studies.

The view that a 'hard' cover-up existed in terms of systematic evidence tampering and intimidating witnesses by draconian security measures was dismissed. The idea of a 'hard cover-up' would seriously undermine the merit of the scientific method championed by UFOlogists for getting to the truth. Leading UFOlogists were scientists with backgrounds in engineering, astronomy, meteorology, physics, and/or image analysis. They were "technically capable of making a common sense identification", and dismissed the 'hard cover-up' idea as unsubstantiated conspiracy theory.[466] Consequently, neither the UFO data that pointed to the existence of extraterrestrial life, nor evidence of a high level government cover-up on national security grounds, would be discussed in terms of its public policy implications.

UFOlogy as a field of study was not receptive to analyses of the public policy implications of extraterrestrial life which was regarded as premature and too speculative. Instead, a number of ad hoc public policy measures were adopted in terms of briefings of government officials and the mass media of the need for serious scientific study of UFOs given the quality of evidence. This attitude has not appreciably changed over the sixty-year period of UFO investigations by official and private entities. It is best exemplified in documents such as "The Best Available Evidence" which was circulated in a confidential policy initiative by Laurence Rockefeller to brief the Clinton Administration of UFOs in the early 1990s.[467] More recently in November 2007, a Press Conference at the National Press Club in Washington DC chaired by former Arizona Governor Fife Symington, focused exclusively on expert witness sightings of UFOs. [468] The extraterrestrial hypothesis was deliberately excluded from discussions by Symington and the organizers.

The Brookings Report and Public Policy Implications of Extraterrestrial Life

While UFOlogists avoided analysis of the public policy implications of extraterrestrial life, official documents would slowly emerge detailing such implications. Undoubtedly the most important document to publicly emerge is the 1961 Brookings Institute study commissioned by NASA on behalf of the U.S. Congress. Titled "Proposed Studies on the Implications of Peaceful Space Activities for Human Affairs," the Brookings Report devoted several sections to discussing the public policy implications of extraterrestrial life. The Brookings Report delivered to the U.S. Congress in April 1961, described the potential impact of extraterrestrial life or 'artifacts' being found on nearby planetary bodies. The Report stated:

> While face-to-face meetings with it [extraterrestrial life] will not occur within the next 20 years; artifacts left at some point in time by these life forms might possibly be discovered through our space activities on the moon, Mars, or Venus.[469]

The Report described the unpredictability of societal reactions to the discovery of extraterrestrial artifacts:

> Evidences of its [extraterrestrial] existence might also be found in artifacts left on the moon or other planets. The consequences for attitudes and values are unpredictable, but would vary profoundly in different cultures and between groups within complex societies; a crucial factor would be the nature of the communication between us and the other beings.[470]

The Report also mentioned, as cited earlier, that devastating societal effects could also result from contact with more technologically advanced off world societies.[471] The Brookings Report went on to raise the possibility of suppressing any announcement of extraterrestrial life or artifacts for national security reasons: "How might such information, under what circumstances, be presented or withheld from the public?"[472] Significantly, the Brookings Report pointed out that "of all groups, scientists and engineers might be the most devastated by the discovery of relatively superior creatures, since these professions are most clearly associated with mastery of nature."[473]

The Brookings Report provides the first officially sanctioned analysis of the public policy implications of discovering extraterrestrial life and/or artifacts. The Report confirms the unpredictability of societal responses around the globe, and raises the possibility of societal collapse. The clear conclusion is that the discovery of extraterrestrial life and/or artifacts would be of the utmost national security concern. Furthermore, the Brookings Report alluded to the possible desirability of withholding from the public any discovery concerning extraterrestrial life and/or artifacts on national security grounds. It should be pointed out that the Brookings Report itself, while not a classified document, was mysteriously withheld from the general public until 1993 when it was discovered at a Federal Archive in Little Rock, Arkansas.[474] The conclusions of the Brookings Report and its non-availability for over thirty years, helps confirm that an official effort was well underway to discourage discussion of the public policy implications of extraterrestrial life.

The Brookings Report together with the Durant Report make it possible to identify ten significant public policy questions concerning extraterrestrial life that are raised by these official documents:

1. Is an official cover-up of extraterrestrial life justified on national security grounds?
2. To what extent would official disclosure of extraterrestrial life destabilize global society?
3. What segments of American and global society would be most affected by disclosure of extraterrestrial life?

4. To what extent are the tools of psychological warfare such as debunking and discrediting of witnesses, to be used on the American and global public to dismiss the seriousness of data concerning UFOs and extraterrestrial life?
5. To what extent is the mass media used to promote a cover-up of extraterrestrial life?
6. What is the constitutional standing of classified executive orders concerning extraterrestrial life?
7. To what extent does the public's 'right to know' impact on official efforts to limit information on extraterrestrial life on a 'need to know' basis?
8. To what extent would a cover-up of information on extraterrestrial life involve draconian national security measures?
9. To what extent should scientific principles or technologies gained from extraterrestrial life be shared with the general public?
10. Should public policy decisions concerning extraterrestrial life or technologies be decided in secretly appointed committees veiled from public scrutiny or made transparent in a highly visible public process?

These public policy questions and the issues they address arise directly out of officially sanctioned investigations, the Durant Report and the Brookings Report. The related public policy issues do not require acceptance of data confirming the reality of extraterrestrial life, only the *possibility* that extraterrestrial life exists.

Consequently, there is an important need to systematically study such public policy issues using a range of disciplinary approaches incorporating both quantitative and qualitative methods on the publicly available evidence on extraterrestrial life and UFOs. This needs to be done in a way that satisfies two constituencies who strongly differ over the question of whether the minimum threshold of evidentiary support for the reality of extraterrestrial life has been attained. The first constituency comprises individuals and groups who do not accept that a minimum threshold of evidence has been reached to prove that extraterrestrial life exists beyond all reasonable doubt. Prominent examples include supporters of Search for Extraterrestrial Intelligence (SETI), who argue that the possibility of extraterrestrial life is sufficient to justify the investment of appreciable resources in seeking evidence through radio transmissions. Such individuals and groups largely accept the pioneering work of Frank Drake and his SETI colleagues in calculating the likelihood of extraterrestrial life existing in the Milky Way galaxy.[475] Many advocates of SETI, however, openly challenge the evidence proposed by UFO researchers as having proved the existence of extraterrestrial life.[476]

A second constituency is individuals and groups who argue that a minimum evidentiary threshold has been reached but that the general public and many scientists are not aware of this. This group believes that vigorous education programs are needed to inform the public of the available evidence, much of which has been ignored by the mass media, universities and public officials. More importantly, this second constituency argues that public policy analysis needs to proceed using the available evidence.

Exopolitics and Public Policy Concerning Extraterrestrial Life

Historically there have been a number of attempts to address key public policy issues concerning evidence of extraterrestrial life from the perspective of inadequate official investigations and governmental suppression of UFO data.[477] These public policy issues have arisen in an ad hoc manner in the context of proposed or ongoing UFO investigations without any attempt to systematically address these policy issues.[478] This has primarily resulted in attempts by UFO researchers to get national governments to initiate official investigations and to create the necessary governmental bodies to achieve this task. This is exemplified in the 1978 UN General Assembly Decision to set up a United Nations agency to investigate UFO reports and the possibility of extraterrestrial life. Paragraph 2 of UN General Assembly Decision 33/426 states:

> [T]he General Assembly invites interested Member States to take appropriate steps to coordinate on a national level scientific research and investigation into extraterrestrial life, including unidentified flying objects, and to inform the Secretary-General of the observations, research and evaluation of such activities.[479]

While lauded at the time as a great achievement by UFO researchers, to date the UN has not implemented this decision, nor made any effort to study the public policy issues associated with the evidence.

The closest the international community has come to examining public policy issues related to extraterrestrial life is the study of governmental, military and commercial activities concerning outer space. Studies of outer space have focused on issues such as space weapons, space debris, satellites, national space programs, and space tourism. This has led to introduction of the term 'astropolitics' as a new scholarly discipline to cover space policy issues. The term itself was first used in 1994 in a cavalier manner to refer to the hidden politics of astrophysics.[480] A more serious approach began in 2003 with the creation of an astropolitics journal which describes its aims and scope as dedicated "to interdisciplinary analysis of civil, commercial, military, and intelligence space activities."[481] To date, *Astropolitics: The International Journal of Space Politics & Policy,* has not included any articles examining evidence concerning UFOs or the extraterrestrial hypothesis.[482] This glaring omission demonstrates how astropolitics, as currently defined and understood, is not interested in addressing public policy issues associated with available evidence of extraterrestrial life. Consequently, up until recently, there has been no attempt to systematically study public policy issues concerning extraterrestrial life.

'Exopolitics' has been proposed as a distinct disciplinary approach that attempts to provide a systematic study of extraterrestrial life. The first reference to 'exopolitics' as a distinctive approach to studying public policy issues associated with extraterrestrial life appeared in a seminal 2000 paper by Alfred Webre, J.D., where he wrote:

> No mainstream politicians have defined extraterrestrial presence as a live political or public policy issue. No sizable number of citizens of any terrestrial nation are moved to call upon their local politicians or the political process to connect with the extraterrestrial presence, or study it, or even acknowledge it officially… Exopolitics is a fundamental organizing, mediating, social, and governmental process in our interplanetary and interdimensional space.[483]

The need for systematic discussion of public policy issues concerning extraterrestrial life by establishing a new discipline called 'exopolitics' was more formally proposed in a January 2003 paper where I argued that evidence concerning extraterrestrial life would:

> ... lead to the birth of a new field of public policy, 'exopolitics', which can be defined as the policy debate over the choices governments and populations need to make in formulating and implementing legislative and policy responses to the presence of ETs in human affairs."[484]

More recently, a definition has been proposed for helping better formalize exopolitics as a branch of political science:

> *Exopolitics is the study of the political actors, institutions and processes associated with extraterrestrial life.*[485]

The advantage of this definition is that it makes it possible for exopolitical discussion of public policy issues without necessarily accepting that extraterrestrial life has been discovered and/or is covered up for national security reasons. This helps offset criticism that exopolitics makes *a priori* assumptions that extraterrestrial life exists which might be directed at alternative definitions of exopolitics. So, for example, the Brookings Report can be cited as a document making a number of exopolitical statements concerning public policy implications of extraterrestrial life, without accepting the reality of extraterrestrial life. Similarly, SETI researchers speculating about protocols for dealing with contact with extraterrestrial life are implicitly analyzing exopolitical themes.[486] Finally, proponents of "astropolitics" who are focused on public policy issues concerning outer space, may also incorporate exopolitical themes as they seriously consider the policy implications of possible extraterrestrial life.[487]

Most supporters of exopolitics accept that the existence of extraterrestrial life has been abundantly demonstrated by a vast and ever-growing pool of evidence accumulated over the last sixty years provided by eyewitnesses, whistleblowers, scientists, 'experiencers' and leaked government documents. Consequently, most advocates of exopolitical analysis claim it is finally time to focus on public policy aspects of this accumulated evidence. This is exemplified in the case of Paul Hellyer, the former Defense Minister of Canada, who has spoken at a number of exopolitical events on what he describes as some of the "most profoundly important policy questions that must be addressed."[488]

Alternatively, it is possible, as already mentioned, for public policy aspects of extraterrestrial life to be analyzed without necessarily accepting the veracity of evidence supporting such life. Consequently, while exopolitical analysis often proceeds from accepting the persuasiveness of evidence establishing the reality of extraterrestrial life and/or artifacts, exopolitics does not require such an acceptance as a necessary condition. A sufficient condition for exopolitical study is acceptance that the *possible* existence of extraterrestrial life has significant public policy implications.

Most exopolitical analysts contrast their approach with UFOlogists who continue to advocate accumulating more evidence to provide a scientific argument for proving to determined skeptics that UFOs are real and that the extraterrestrial hypothesis is a legitimate focus of scientific inquiry. Exopolitics analysts conclude that much of the skepticism concerning UFOs and extraterrestrial life crosses the conceptual boundary between objective criticism and debunking.[489] This has led to claims that the debunking performed by critics of UFOlogy and exopolitics, is part of the debunking and ridiculing effort recommended by the Durant Report, and implicitly legitimated by the Brookings Report. In short, the discussion of public policy issues concerning extraterrestrial life is itself subjected to debunking as evidenced in the 30 years of secrecy surrounding the Brookings Report and its findings. This has prevented the development of the field of exopolitics for over five decades since UFO research began in 1947.

The attempt to raise public policy discussion of extraterrestrial life has led to much debate and controversy. Supporters of exopolitics have been subjected to sustained criticisms for proposing serious public policy discussion of the available evidence. Many 'UFOlogists' remain highly critical of exopolitics as an emerging disciplinary approach to public policy issues concerning extraterrestrial life. UFOlogists and other skeptics have difficulty grasping that exopolitics is the forerunner to a legitimate academic discipline that can be anticipated to be eventually established in every major university for the systematic study of such policy issues. Critics of exopolitics often tend to focus on some of the pioneers of exopolitical thought in terms of their methods and ideas, rather than identifying the merits of demarcating the conceptual boundaries for a scholarly approach to public policy issues concerning extraterrestrial life.[490]

Exopolitics as the Discipline of Choice

The present historical situation is in some ways analogous to the 19th century where there was much debate on how to prepare individuals for studying public policy issues in relation to careers in international diplomacy, public office and/or as university professors. Gentlemen drawn from the Aristocratic class formed a unique pool of amateur scholars who emphasized classical studies as the best preparation for dealing with public policy issues. They recommended the historical works of Cicero, Josephus, Herodotus, Thucydides and other ancient authors; and requisite training in Latin, classical Greek or similar ancient languages.[491] Amateur 'gentlemen scholars', as they have been described, prescribed ample leisure time for study of public policy issues and criticized those who required remuneration from their studies. Nevertheless, largely out of the History departments of many universities, the new discipline of Political Science began to emerge in the 1860s; and these were staffed by salaried professionals trained in the latest methods of political scholarship and pedagogy.[492] Political science developed as an academic discipline since it fulfilled a functional need: the need was to systematically study public policy issues, and how individuals could be trained to professionally deal with these.

Political science is now the discipline of choice for those wanting to systematically study public policy issues and to be professionally trained to work with these in various careers. Similarly, exopolitics will be the discipline of choice for those desiring to study public policy issues associated with extraterrestrial life, since it also fulfills a functional need. The functional need is to understand how extraterrestrial life impacts on public policy issues, and to professionally train individuals to deal with these. Exopolitics will be first established in departments of political science as a legitimate sub-field, as is currently the case with 'international politics', 'foreign policy', 'comparative politics', 'political economy', etc., in many political science departments. The precursor to such academic studies is the Exopolitics Certification Program created with faculty drawn from the Exopolitics Institute.[493] Eventually, exopolitics will emerge as a distinct department with an interdisciplinary focus spanning public policy issues relating not only to political science, but to *exo*science, *exo*religion, *exo*diplomacy, etc.

Debunkers, UFOlogists, SETI researchers and other critics of exopolitics are poor students of history not to have observed how academic disciplines and sub-fields develop to fulfill functional needs. Such individuals are remiss in not observing how exopolitics will fill the functional need for the systematic study of public policy issues concerning extraterrestrial life. The choice of the word 'exopolitics' to represent this nascent academic discipline has long-term strategic value due to the functional need it fills. Exopolitics will complement the still emerging discipline of astropolitics that focuses on the politics of outer space which is likely to emerge into a rubric for exopolitics and associated disciplinary approaches to outer space. Exopolitics is the term of choice to deal with the public policy issues identified earlier, and others that arise from documents and evidence concerning extraterrestrial life and technologies.

Both UFOlogy and SETI will become redundant as fields of study since the functional needs each serves will quickly be settled once the existence of extraterrestrial life is accepted. The reality of UFOs will be moot once they have been publicly identified as 'extraterrestrial', 'interdimensional' or 'extratemporal' in origin. UFOs that are extraterrestrial origin will no longer form a unique conceptual category of unidentified flying objects, but will become identified as extraterrestrial vehicles (ETVs). Similarly, continued efforts to "search for extraterrestrial intelligence" will also become redundant. Discerning the existence of extraterrestrial life through radio communications will cease to have much of a functional need once such life has been confirmed. Finally, proponents of astropolitics will be forced to incorporate much of the hitherto ignored evidence concerning extraterrestrial life given the obvious implications for outer space affairs.

Those devoted to UFOlogy, SETI and astropolitics are missing a great opportunity to contribute to establishing legitimate conceptual parameters for exopolitical study. Experts in these fields of study can assist in bringing clarity to the public policy implications of a phenomenon they are also interested in. Exopolitics is here to stay as the discipline of choice for understanding the public policy implications of extraterrestrial life. Exopolitics as a new branch of knowledge will revolutionize academic studies and the world as we know it.

ENDNOTES – CHAPTER EIGHT

[453] Grateful thanks to Dana Tomasina for proof-reading an earlier version of this article published in the *Exopolitics Journal* 2:4 (July 2008): 268-83. An earlier version also appeared in *World Affairs: The Journal of International Affairs,* 12:2 (Summer 2008).
[454] See Frank Drake, "The Drake Equation: A Reappraisal," in *First Contact: The Search for Extraterrestrial Intelligence*, eds. Ben Bova & Byron Preiss (Bryon Preiss, 1991) 115-17.
[455] Kardashev, N. S. "Transmission of Information by Extraterrestrial Civilizations," *Soviet Astronomy*, 8:2 (1964) 217-21.
[456] "Letter From General N.F. Twining to Commanding General, Army Air Forces, 23 September 1947." Available online at: http://everything2.com/index.pl?node_id=679398
[457] For comments by former military and government officials concerning UFO's see Don Berliner with Marie Galbraith and Antonio Huneus, *UFO Briefing Document: The Best Available Evidence* (UFO Research Coalition, 1995) 153-208.
[458] See Steven Greer, Disclosure: Military and Government Witnesses Reveal the Greatest Secrets in Modern History (Crossing Point Inc., 2001). Website: www.disclosureproject.com
[459] France's UFO files are available online at: http://www.cnes-geipan.fr . The UK's Ministry of Defense UFO files are available online at: http://www.mod.uk/DefenceInternet/FreedomOfInformation/PublicationScheme/SearchPublicationScheme/UnidentifiedAerialPhenomenauapInTheUkAirDefenceRegion.htm
[460] For detailed analysis of what occurred with the initial "Estimate of the Situation," See Michael Swords, "Project Sign & Estimate of the Situation," *Journal of UFO Studies*, 7. Available online at: http://www.ufoscience.org/history/swords.pdf
[461] Donald Keyhoe, *Aliens from Space* (Signet Books, 1973) 14.
[462] Donald Keyhoe's first book was *The Flying Saucers are Real* (Fawcett Gold Medal, 1950).
[463] Cited from online version of Robertson Panel at: http://www.cufon.org/cufon/robertdod.htm
[464] Donald Keyhoe, *The Flying Saucer Conspiracy* (Henry Holt & Co. 1955).
[465] Allen Hynek, *The UFO Experience: A Scientific Inquiry* (Henry Regnery Company, 1972), 10.
[466] Allen Hynek, *The UFO Experience,* 10.
[467] See Don Berliner, et al., *UFO Briefing Document.*
[468] For media coverage of the November 12, 2007 National Press Club Conference on UFO's go to: http://cficoverage.wordpress.com/
[469] Brookings Report, 215. For an overview of the Brookings Report, go to: http://www.enterprisemission.com/brooking.html

[470] Brookings Report, 215.
[471] Brookings Report, 215.
[472] Brookings Report, 215.
[473] Brookings Report, 225.
[474] See Richard Hoagland and Mike Bara, *Dark Mission: The Secret History of NASA* (Feral House, 2007) 81.
[475] See Frank Drake, "The Drake Equation: A Reappraisal," in *First Contact,* eds. Bova & Preiss, 115-17.
[476] See Isaac Asimov, "Terrestrial Intelligence," & Arthur C. Clarke, "Where Art They" in *First Contact,* eds., Bova and Preiss, 29 & 310.
[477] See Donald Keyhoe, *Aliens from Space.*
[478] For discussion of an evolution in approaches to public policy issues concerning extraterrestrial life, see Michael Salla, "The History of Exopolitics: Evolving Political Approaches to UFOs and the Extraterrestrial Hypothesis" *Exopolitics Journal* 1:1 (2005) 1-17. Available online at: http://exopoliticsjournal.com/Journal-vol-1-1.htm .
[479] See UN General Assembly Decision 33/426, 1978 . Available online at: http://www.ufoevidence.org/documents/doc902.htm
[480] Eric J. Chaisson, *The Hubble Wars: Astrophysics Meets Astropolitics in the Two-Billion-Dollar Struggle over the Hubble Space Telescope* (Harper Collins, 1994)
[481] See aims and scope of, *Astropolitics: The International Journal of Space Politics & Policy,* http://www.informaworld.com/smpp/title~content=t713634457
[482] The only article that made any significant reference to extraterrestrial life was John Hickman, "Problems of Interplanetary and Interstellar Trade," *Astropolitics: The International Journal of Space Politics & Policy,* 6:1 (2008): 95-104.
[483] First published in June 2000 and republished in the Exopolitics Journal 2:2 (2007): 142-50. http://exopoliticsjournal.com/vol-2/vol-2-2-Exp-Webre.htm
[484] See, Michael Salla, "The Need for Exopolitics, Implications of Extraterrestrial Conspiracy Theories for Policy Makers and Global Peace," *www.Exopolitics.Org* (January 2003): http://exopolitics.org/Study-Paper1.htm . Paper published as chapter one in *Exopolitics: Political Implications of Extraterrestrial Life* (Dandelion Books, 2004).
[485] This is a revised version of a standard definition I proposed in 2005 in an earlier version of chapter nine, "The History of Exopolitics" *Exopolitics Journal* 1:1 (2005) 1-17.
[486] See Michael Michaud, "A Unique Moment in Human History," in *First Contact,* eds., Bova and Preiss, 243-61.
[487] To a limited extent, this was done in an article by John Hickman, "Problems of Interplanetary and Interstellar Trade," *Astropolitics: The International Journal of Space Politics & Policy,* 6:1 (2008): 95-104.
[488] See chapter six.
[489] See chapter eleven.
[490] For example, see Kevin Randle, Exopolitics, available online at: http://kevinrandle.blogspot.com/2005/11/exopolitics.html

[491] See Michael Parenti, "Patricians, Professionals and Political Science," *American Political Science Review*, 100:4 2006) 499. Available online at: http://www.apsanet.org/imgtest/APSRNov06Parenti.pdf

[492] See Michael Parenti, "Patricians, Professionals and Political Science," *American Political Science Review*, 100:4 2006) 499. Available online at: http://www.apsanet.org/imgtest/APSRNov06Parenti.pdf

[493] See: http://exopoliticsinstitute.org/certificates/

Chapter Nine

The Evolution of Exopolitics: A Transformative Paradigm in the Study of UFOs and Extraterrestrial Life

The study of extraterrestrial life has long been handicapped by the use of the term Unidentified Flying Object (UFO). Introduced into widespread public use by Captain Edward Ruppelt in 1952, the UFO term eventually replaced the more popular 'flying saucer' initially used to describe what was being sighted by individuals.[494] The 'flying saucer' term immediately connoted the idea of extraterrestrial life flying in technologically advanced spacecraft. The scientific community desired a more neutral way of describing what was increasingly witnessed or recorded by large numbers of individuals in both private and official capacities. The main handicap of the UFO term, however, was that it framed the phenomenon being sighted and tracked by countless thousands of individuals as primarily unidentified. This overlooked evidence that the phenomenon being sighted and recorded had indeed been identified by a select group of national security officials. They had implemented a policy to keep this information away from the general public and most public officials. The UFO term subsequently became part of a national security policy implemented to debunk reports and evidence of extraterrestrial life. For example, an official could truthfully claim that "UFOs do not pose a security threat" and were therefore unimportant from a national security perspective. In reality, the official was fully aware that "Identified Flying Objects" in the form of technologically advanced spacecraft posed a security threat. The UFO term has therefore had the unfortunate side effect of implicitly assisting a national security policy to keep the truth of extraterrestrial life from the general public. A new term is therefore needed for describing the possibility of extraterrestrial life visiting or residing on Earth in technologically advanced spacecraft, and that term is exopolitics.

I pointed out in chapter nine how Exopolitics is a term increasingly used by many UFO researchers and activists as a consequence of a number of websites, books and conferences that have taken distinctive approach to the UFO phenomenon and the possibility of extraterrestrial life visiting or residing on Earth. By the end of 2008 there had been over ten international conferences that explicitly focused on exopolitics[495]; three books written about exopolitics;[496] the establishment of a non-government organization dedicated to exopolitics[497]; a respected international journal (World Affairs) that devoted an issue to exopolitics,[498] an Exopolitics Journal,[499] and an Exopolitics Certification Program.[500] This chapter describes the concept of exopolitics and its history in terms of early pioneers who began to focus on the political aspects of the UFO phenomenon and the possibility of extraterrestrial life. This has culminated in the term 'exopolitics' coming into widespread use. This will help identify some of the leading ideas in the exopolitics field and the challenges ahead as exopolitics is increasingly used with multiple meanings and different evidentiary sources.

I begin by defining exopolitics, its foundations and pioneers in the field, as a distinct political approach to the UFO phenomenon and extraterrestrial life. A clear definition enables one to identify who among the early UFO researchers first began pursuing exopolitical issues. I proposed in chapter eight the following as a standard definition for exopolitics: *"Exopolitics is the study of the political actors, institutions and processes associated with extraterrestrial life."*

This makes it possible to distinguish between the term 'exopolitics' and the concept of exopolitics. While the term 'exopolitics' is relatively new, being coined in 2000, and coming into widespread usage in 2003; the concept of exopolitics has been implicit in terms such as the "Flying Saucer Conspiracy", "UFO Cover Up", "Cosmic Watergate", etc., that have been a standard part of UFO literature for over six decades .

Exopolitics is distinct to UFO research which is focused on the empirical analysis of UFOs. It avoids inquiries into extraterrestrial life until sufficient empirical evidence on UFO sightings has been amassed to indubitably substantiate an extraterrestrial presence. As cited earlier, Dr Allen Hynek defined the scientific study of UFOs as "the reported perception of an object or light seen in the sky or upon the land the appearance, trajectory, and general dynamic and luminescent behavior of which do not suggest a logical, conventional explanation..."[501]

Visiting extraterrestrial life was first officially proposed as the most valid explanation for UFO/Flying Saucer sightings by a classified study initiated by the U.S. Air Force in 1948. As mentioned earlier, the classified study of approximately 300 cases produced an 'Estimate of the Situation' in September 1948, concluding that these were interplanetary in nature. The study's remarkable conclusion was rejected by USAF Chief of Staff, General Hoyt Vandenberg. He made clear that acceptance of visiting extraterrestrial life was not an acceptable conclusion for reasons related to national security concerns.[502] The rejection of the initial Estimate of the Situation and the subsequent destruction of the initial report found its way to private UFO investigators such as Major Donald Keyhoe who concluded that it was evidence of a cover up at the highest level of the U.S. military and government. Keyhoe was confidentially told the following by Capt Edward Ruppelt about Gen Vandenberg's decision to reject the original Estimate of the Situation.[503]

Keyhoe's subsequent writings and investigation of how the explanation of visiting extraterrestrial life was being deliberately undermined by military and national security agencies mark the birth of exopolitics as a distinctive approach to the UFO phenomenon. Keyhoe's approach was an exopolitical analysis of the key agencies and individuals behind the UFO cover-up is a seminal source of exopolitical thought. I will describe exopolitics in terms of four phases that independently continue to the present day.

Exopolitics – Phase 1 (1948-): The Flying Saucer Conspiracy

The foundations of exopolitics lies in a number of researchers that began seriously exploring evidence of a high level conspiracy by various government agencies and military departments to hide the truth about UFOs and extraterrestrial life. These researchers and their books emerged in the early 1950's as it became clear that military departments and national security agencies were not genuine in their efforts to seriously investigate UFO sightings and evidence supporting the existence of extraterrestrial life. This accelerated as news about Vandenberg's 1948 rejection of the original Estimate of the Situation was leaked.

A critical event in this process was the January 1953 Robertson Panel. A group of scientists chaired by Dr H. P. Robertson and covertly funded by the CIA, recommended that UFO sightings be debunked due to the potential for these events to be manipulated by 'foreign powers' in a way that would undermine U.S. national security. The panel recommended an "educational program" to deter the general public from demanding a serious investigation of UFO sightings. As cited earlier, the program involved debunking UFO reports through the mass media.[504]

The Robertson panel was followed in March 1954 by the secret passage of Joint Army Navy Air Force Policy (JANAP) 146, making it an offense for military servicemen or airline pilots to disclose information about UFO sightings that had been reported and were subject to an official 'investigation'.[505] Another critical document was the Brookings Report that was prepared by the Brookings Institute for a NASA committee in 1960. In a section titled, "The Implications of a Discovery of Extraterrestrial Life," the Report describes the devastating societal effects that might emerge from any announcement of such a discovery:

> The knowledge that life existed in other parts of the universe might lead to a greater unity of men on Earth, based on the "oneness" of man or on the age-old assumption that any stranger is threatening.... Whether earthmen would be inspired to all-out space efforts by such a discovery is a moot question. Anthropological files contain many examples of societies, sure of their place in the universe, which have disintegrated when they had to associate with previously unfamiliar societies espousing different ideas and different life ways; others that survived such an experience usually did so by paying the price of changes in values and attitudes and behavior.[506]

The Brookings Report outlines the national security implications of humanity openly associating with technologically advanced extraterrestrial life. The Report lends support to a secret national security policy of covering up evidence that extraterrestrial life is visiting and/or based on Earth.

It is the political cover up of UFO related information verifying extraterrestrial life that has led to the notion of a 'flying saucer' or UFO conspiracy. Authors and books commenting on the UFO conspiracy come from two complementary but distinct sources: researchers and 'experiencers'. Each takes a distinctive approach to exopolitics based on the ways in which information is gained and evaluated. The first focuses on political processes surrounding the study of UFOs and extraterrestrial life. The second approach comprises the political processes used by extraterrestrial civilizations themselves.

The first approach is based on the systematic study of the best evidence available from UFO cases in order to formulate conclusions about the reality of the phenomenon, and the existence of a UFO cover up. This approach involves seminal UFO researchers such as Donald Keyhoe who wrote a number of books identifying a political cover up of the evidence substantiating the existence of the UFO phenomenon as real, and of evidence supporting extraterrestrial life. Keyhoe was an especially significant researcher, since he began as a skeptic. As a consequence of his field investigations he became convinced of the reality of the UFO phenomenon and extraterrestrial life. Keyhoe did not use the term 'exopolitics' but choose instead to use the term 'flying saucer conspiracy' to highlight the hidden political and national security processes at work, keeping from the general public the truth of extraterrestrial life. Keyhoe's most important books displaying his implicit promotion of the exopolitics concept were *The Flying Saucer Conspiracy* (1955); *Flying Saucers Top Secret* (1960); and *Aliens From Space* (1973). In these books, Keyhoe meticulously outlines how the various military departments and national security agencies are involved in a conspiracy at the highest level to systematically cover up evidence supporting UFO sightings and extraterrestrial life.

Keyhoe used a wide range of sources for his conclusions. Using the friendships and networks from his military days, he was able to secure information 'leaked' to him by military officials concerning UFO sightings. He also was able to access a great amount of data gained from field researchers who investigated sightings from civilians, military and the aviation industry. Keyhoe also headed the National Investigating Committee for Aerial Phenomena (NICAP) in 1959 and meticulously based his exopolitical or "UFO conspiracy" ideas on the solid empirical evidence that had been discovered. Such evidence was systematically discredited, debunked or ignored by military departments, national security agencies and government institutions.

Keyhoe focused on various ways in which the truth about the UFO reports, especially of the giant UFO's (or 'motherships') reported in 1953/54, might have led relevant US authorities to conclude that disclosure would cause widespread panic and loss of confidence in US military authorities.[507] This Keyhoe believes may be the real reason for the cover up. In his final book, *Aliens From Space*, Keyhoe firmly identifies the CIA and U.S. Air Force as the two key institutions behind the cover up and responsible for discrediting UFO researchers and witnesses, and for sabotaging initiatives with Congress for having the UFO phenomenon seriously studied. In particular, Keyhoe described events surrounding efforts by the National Investigations Committee for Aerial Phenomenon (NICAP) to initiate congressional hearings in 1961. NICAP compiled the best UFO sightings in a confidential report to Congressional representatives for a planned hearing in the Science and Astronautics Committee in the House of Representatives.[508] The planned congressional hearing was aborted after the shock resignation of Admiral Hillenkoetter, former Director of the CIA, from the Board of Governors of NICAP in early 1962. The confidential NICAP report was eventually published as *The UFO Evidence,* documenting 700 cases supporting the reality of the UFO phenomenon.[509] Keyhoe was convinced that Hillenkoetter's resignation was caused by high level government intervention preventing the House committee hearing from going ahead.

Keyhoe's ideas of a UFO conspiracy became more widespread among UFO researchers after the publication of the Condon Report in 1969, widely dismissed by UFO investigators as a whitewash designed to permit the USAF to drop serious investigations of UFO sightings.[510] Termination of Project Blue Book on the grounds that UFO sightings had no scientific value or national security concerns was for many, evidence that a government conspiracy did exist. Its role was to down play the significance of the UFO phenomenon by dismissing or discrediting evidence as recommended in the 1953 Robertson Panel.

The ideas of a national security cover-up and 'conspiracy' at the highest level of government were subsequently taken up by a number of authors who objectively analyzed UFO sightings and leaked statements reports. Timothy Good's *Above Top Secret: The Worldwide UFO Cover Up* (1987) stands out as one of the most influential and well written exposes of how the UFO phenomenon has been systematically covered up in major countries to hide the truth about the extraterrestrial life. Another significant book on the UFO 'cover up' is Richard Dolan's, *UFO's and the National Security State* (2000). Dolan's book offers a detailed analysis of how the UFO phenomenon had been systematically covered up in the U.S. at the highest level by military and national security agencies. Good's and Dolan's analyses offer insight into the key agencies and departments responsible for covering up evidence supporting the reality of UFOs and extraterrestrial life.

The second approach to the UFO conspiracy concerns individuals who claim to have directly experienced extraterrestrial contact. They offer startling evidence for the existence of extraterrestrial life in terms of their extraordinary experiences. These 'experiencers' or 'contactees' claim that a systematic government/military effort exists to discredit these 'contactees' and corroborating witnesses, and to debunk the evidence confirming extraterrestrial life. There have been a great number of alleged 'contactees' who were very prominent in the 1950s and 1960s but fell into disfavor as a result vigorous debunking of the evidence and discrediting of witnesses by the general media, USAF and UFO researchers.

Some of these early contactees - George Adamski, Daniel Fry, Howard Menger, and George Van Tassel - described how government agencies and military departments kept this information from getting into the public realm. Much of the evidence for the veracity of these contactee reports continues to be strongly contested, but some researchers find the evidence to be persuasive. For example, veteran UFO researcher, Bill Hamilton, examined the cases of a number of "California contactees" and argued that there was much merit in these cases which conventional researchers chose to ignore.[511] These early contactees related much information about the politics, philosophy, economics and law practices of extraterrestrial civilizations among themselves, and with developing worlds such as earth. The contactees' experiences suggested that government agencies were not willing for information allegedly gained directly from extraterrestrial civilizations to get into the public arena. A sophisticated counter-intelligence program, Galactic COINTELPRO, was subsequently waged to disrupt and neutralize the national security threat posed by contactees.[512]

More recently, contactees such as Billy Meier, Sixto Paz Wells, 'Adrian' and Carlos Diaz, have supplied much evidence to substantiate their extraterrestrial contacts. Extensive photographs and independent witness sightings have been offered to substantiate these claims, and a number of investigators have concluded favorably over the authenticity of each contactee's claims.[513] Nevertheless, controversy continues over the authenticity of these cases, and evidence supplied by contactees substantiating the extraterrestrial hypothesis (ETH) and a government conspiracy to cover up the evidence. These contactees' reports allegedly give an idea of the political processes used by extraterrestrials themselves in their relations with one another and with Earth. If their experiences are genuine, it can be concluded that a conspiracy to cover up the political processes used by extraterrestrials allegedly monitoring and interacting with the Earth does exist.

Exopolitics: Phase 2 (1974-): FOIA, Leaked Documents and Cosmic Watergate

Exopolitical research went through another stage of development with the passage of the Freedom of Information Act by the U.S. Congress in 1974 (revised from the original 1966 version). This focused on documentary evidence of UFOs, and an associated political process to cover this up.[514] The passage of FOIA led to the emergence of organizations such as the Citizens Against UFO Secrecy (CAUS) with the goal of using the legal process to extract documentary evidence relevant to UFO sightings and the UFO cover-up. Formed in the late 1970s by Peter Gersten, together with W.T. Zechel and Brad Sparks, CAUS achieved most public prominence for launching lawsuits against the National Security Agency (NSA) and the Central Intelligence Agency (CIA).[515] These lawsuits resulted in a limited number of documents being released proving conclusively that UFOs are an issue raising deep national security concerns for these two agencies. On the whole, CAUS and other individuals engaged in FOIA research found government agencies and military departments very evasive and unhelpful in responding to legitimate FOIA requests. Lawrence Fawcett's and Barry Greenwood's 1984 book, *Clear Intent*, discusses in detail much of the FOIA activity of CAUS, its lawsuits, and its success in exposing the political process for covering up evidence concerning UFOs and extraterrestrial life.

Another significant book that discusses how UFO evidence is covered up by key government and military institutions is Clifford Stone's 1997 book, *UFOs are Real.* Stone examines key documents gained through FOIA requests that demonstrate the existence of various classified programs and incidents that deal with the UFO phenomenon, and the agencies and military departments involved. He persuasively demonstrates that government agencies will lie to investigators over UFO information.

One of the most astonishing exopolitical developments was the leaking of a number of documents known as the Majestic Documents that were initially sent to Jaime Shandera in 1984 and publicly announced in 1987 by William Moore.[516] These documents emerged from the efforts of UFO researchers such as Shandera, Moore and Tim Cooper to liaise with 'insiders' in order to get information for a possible documentary.[517] Dr Robert Wood achieved considerably success in demonstrating that these documents are authentic and/or replicas of historic documents. Another researcher, Stanton Friedman, examined the leaked "Majestic Documents" and proposed the existence of a "Cosmic Watergate" created to maintain secrecy over evidence supporting the extraterrestrial hypothesis (ETH). Friedman, through detailed historical scholarship, provides compelling authentication for a number of Majestic Documents.[518] He concludes in favor of the authenticity of documents describing the creation of the Majestic 12 Group for controlling evidence related to extraterrestrial affairs. These documents include the "Eisenhower Briefing Document" describing the history of crashed extraterrestrial vehicles (ETVs) and captured extraterrestrial biological entities (EBEs); and the "Special Operations Manual" that outlines recovery procedures for ETVs and EBEs.[519]

Collectively, the Majestic Documents describe key actors, institutions and processes associated with an extraterrestrial presence known to exist since at least 1947. The leaked Majestic Documents offer surprising evidence of a comprehensive government cover up of UFOs and extraterrestrial life. In conclusion, research through FOIA and leaked government documents constituent an important stream of exopolitical research into the government cover up of evidence supporting extraterrestrial life.

Exopolitics: Phase 3 (1992) Political Activism and the UFO Cover Up

Operation Right to Know (ORTK) was active from 1992-1995 in organizing demonstrations for the right of the general public to learn the truth about UFOs and for full public disclosure to occur. Sponsored by Ed Komarek and Mike Jamieson, ORTK organized the first UFO protest in Washington D.C. in June 1992.[520] ORTK 'shocked' the traditional UFO community by employing political activism rather than the more traditional scientific study of the UFO phenomenon. It organized 10 demonstrations in the U.S. and Britain before disbanding in 1995. ORTK was a significant expression of political activism aimed against the political cover-up of the UFO phenomenon.[521] ORTK laid the foundation for subsequent efforts to mobilize broad mass based action for ending the "Cosmic Watergate".

At the same time ORTK became active, another more clandestine effort was underway to promote UFO disclosure. This was orchestrated by Laurence Rockefeller in 1993 and comprised a confidential effort to have President Clinton briefed on UFO issues so he could take the initiative for full public disclosure. Rockefeller's initiative involved contacting Clinton's science advisor, Dr Jack Gibbons, and sending him the most persuasive evidence for the reality of the UFO phenomenon. Rockefeller later organized an informal round table meeting of a number of prominent UFO researchers including Dr. Scott Jones, Dr. John Mack, Dr. Bruce Maccabee, Dr. Leo Sprinkle, Linda Moulton Howe, and Dr. Steven Greer who convened to share information with staffers from Gibbons' office.[522] The Rockefeller initiative began to lose support after Gibbons became opposed to it and warned President Clinton about cooperating with the initiative. After a briefing by Laurence

Rockefeller, allegedly to both President Clinton and Hillary Clinton in August 1995, the initiative collapsed due to concerns that pursuing a pro-disclosure policy would present insurmountable political problems for President Clinton. The best available UFO evidence submitted to Dr Gibbons and to President Clinton in the form of case studies was eventually distributed to members of Congress and other legislative bodies, and finally published as *The Best Available Evidence*.[523]

An independent and complementary initiative for political disclosure began with Dr Steven Greer. In contrast to the Rockefeller initiative and to the earlier briefing report prepared by NICAP in 1961-64 that relied on the best case sightings of UFO's for initiating legislative investigations, Greer focused instead on whistleblower testimonies. Greer had begun systematically interviewing a number of 'whistleblowers' who claimed to have participated in classified projects involving extraterrestrial technologies and/or extraterrestrial biological entities (EBEs). Aside from cooperating with the Rockefeller initiative to brief Dr Gibbons and President Clinton about UFOs, Greer began a more public effort to brief senior Clinton officials such as CIA Director James Woolsey, based on Greer's 'deep throat' sources. Greer built an impressive database of testimonies by whistleblowers who outlined how military authorities and national security agencies were systematically covering up evidence confirming both the reality of the UFO phenomenon and extraterrestrial life.

Greer's database eventually led to the beginning of the Disclosure Project, with a Press Conference in May 2001 featuring prominent officials from a range of military, government and corporate entities disclosing their knowledge of UFOs & extraterrestrial life.[524] Greer's Disclosure Project combined both witnesses and whistleblowers who had seen UFO's and/or played a role in the control of this information. This replicated the work of UFO researchers such as Donald Keyhoe. Greer's Project also featured individuals who claimed to have participated in classified projects such as UFO crash retrievals and reverse engineering ETVs (extraterrestrial vehicles).

Greer's Disclosure Project was unique in political activism to end UFO secrecy. It highlighted the role of whistleblowers who had participated in classified projects involving EBEs (extraterrestrial biological entities) and reverse engineering of ETVs. His focus on whistleblowers of highly classified projects involving EBEs or ETVs, led to him being criticized by many UFO researchers attacking the lack of documentation substantiating the extraordinary claims made by such whistleblowers. Nevertheless, the credentials, integrity and consistency of many of these whistleblowers convinced many that there exists a highly classified network of projects involving EBEs and ETVs that are hidden from the public in a Cosmic Watergate.

Another expression of political activism aimed against UFO secrecy was the candidature of Stephen Bassett in the 2002 Congressional elections. Bassett ran for a House seat in Maryland and attempted to raise the UFO secrecy issue into the political mainstream. While Bassett was not the first to run on an explicit UFO platform in Congressional elections or an electoral campaign, he was the first candidate to make it onto the November ballot in Congressional elections after openly promoting the UFO subject. Bassett ran on the slogan of shifting UFO debate "from lights in the sky" to "lies on the ground." Bassett like many UFO researchers/activists before him, was convinced by the extensive data of a political cover up. He was destined to play an important role in the promotion of Exopolitics as a distinct approach to UFO data.

In conclusion, those engaging in various forms of political activism to end the UFO cover up were implicitly promoting an exopolitical approach to the data on UFOs and extraterrestrial life. While the term 'exopolitics' had not yet come into use, the above individuals all implicitly understood the concept of exopolitics as a political process associated with a cover up of evidence concerning UFOs and extraterrestrial life.

Exopolitics Phase 4: – Exopolitics Emerges as a Distinct Approach to UFO Evidence

Exopolitics as a distinct approach to UFO data grew out of all three phases described above; political analysis and activity focused on processes covering up evidence substantiating the reality of UFOs and extraterrestrial life. The term exopolitics had not yet come into general usage. It was in 2000 that the exopolitics term was first seriously used, and only the years after 2003 that the 'exopolitics' term began to enjoy widespread coverage.[525]

Those explicitly supporting exopolitics as a distinct disciplinary approach to extraterrestrial life, contrast it to the empirical study of UFO sightings focusing on improved investigative techniques and analysis of the best available evidence substantiating the reality of the UFO phenomenon and extraterrestrial life. While UFO studies has been dominated by physical scientists with an affinity for quantitative analysis of empirical UFO data, exopolitical researchers tend to have social science backgrounds where qualitative analysis of UFO and extraterrestrial life data occurs more often. It is therefore no surprise that those explicitly supporting the 'exopolitics' term have social science backgrounds.

There are two ways of defining exopolitics as a distinct approach to data on UFOs and extraterrestrial life. The first, more conventional approach, concentrates on political processes associated with extraterrestrial life insofar as these impact on global politics. This approach reflects what occurred in the first three phases of the historical development of exopolitics as I discussed earlier. The second way of defining exopolitics involves examination of political processes among extraterrestrial civilizations themselves and how this relates to human affairs.

I was the first to explicitly define exopolitics in terms of conventional political processes associated with extraterrestrial life in global politics with a set of online study papers beginning in January 2003. These culminated in the first published exopolitics book, '*Exopolitics: Political Implications of the Extraterrestrial Presence* (2004). This book defined exopolitics as the "policy debate over the choices governments and populations need to make in formulating and implementing legislative and policy responses to the presence of ETs in human affairs."[526] In my book, I proposed that extensive data concerning extraterrestrial life should be ranked in terms of degrees of persuasiveness, and the strongest data analyzed in terms of its exopolitical implications. The book further offers an exopolitical analysis based on key political actors, institutions and processes that explicitly deal with extraterrestrial life.

My book offers an overview of different sources of evidence; the political institutions and processes created to globally manage information on UFOs and extraterrestrial life; and analysis of conventional international politics from the perspective of extraterrestrial life. My reliance on whistleblower and other evidentiary sources such as the Majestic Documents led to much controversy with conventional UFO researchers who widely dismiss the credibility of whistleblower testimonies concerning classified projects involving ETVs and EBEs. In chapter eleven I will show how such criticisms often cross the line between objective criticism and debunking demonstrating the methodological biases against whistleblower testimony.

Furthermore, there continues to be debate over the authenticity of the Majestic Documents and their use for understanding how data on UFOs and extraterrestrial life is systematically removed or discredited.[527] My subsequent debates with many veteran UFO researchers demonstrates that there is a clear dividing line between us. I believe that "Cosmic Watergate" involves systematic manipulation and removal of documentation and evidence substantiating whistleblower testimonies; whereas many UFO researchers demand documentation and hard evidence to substantiate whistleblower testimonies.[528] This ongoing debate involves different disciplinary approaches to the extensive data on UFOs and extraterrestrial life.

The takes me to the second way of defining exopolitics. The first person to use the term 'exopolitics' was Alfred Webre, J.D., who in 2000 wrote an e-book or 'online treatise' that was 22,000 words in length and was freely downloaded from the internet. His e-book was titled "Exopolitics: Towards a Decade of Contact."[529] Webre subsequently expanded his e-book and had it published in 2005 as: *Exopolitics: Politics, Government, and Law in the Universe*. Webre had been employed in 1977 as a futurist at the Stanford Research Institute (SRI). His project to establish communications protocols with extraterrestrials, sponsored by President Carter's White House, was abruptly cancelled by SRI due to Pentagon pressure.

In his online e-book, Webre defined Exopolitics as: "the study of political process and governance in interstellar society". His definition of exopolitics was based on his research findings on the existence of a 'universe society' of extraterrestrial races highly organized in a universal federation. Their adopted policy of non-interference with regard to humanity had placed Earth under a 'quarantine' due to humanity's propensity for using destructive weapons in resolving geo-political problems. Webre's approach to exopolitics mirrored the information released by early 'contactees' such as Adamski, Menger and Van Tassel describing the politics, law and economic systems of visiting extraterrestrial races. Webre did not use these contactee reports in developing his analysis. Instead, he used a means of reasoning described in his e-book as the "intuitive method of knowledge":

> A more appropriate approach to Universe society is the intuitive method of knowledge. This intuitive approach to our Universe is not what the contemporary human scientific establishment wants you to pursue. Since time immemorial, our human culture has used intuition to survive. Our User's Guide uses the inductive, intuitive method to build a working model of what the Universe is really like.

In his 2005 book, Webre elaborates further on his "intuitive method" of psychic information gained through methods such as "scientific remote viewing". Webre has been a major source of (exo)political activism to prevent the weaponization of space and to stimulate the United Nations in taking a proactive stance in preparing the world community for extraterrestrial life.[530] Webre's earlier focus on the "intuitive method of knowledge" has been more recently strengthened by his inclusion of whistleblower and experiencer testimonies that point to the existence of a flourishing interstellar society with organized political processes. Webre's approach to exopolitics promises to be very significant in the future as the existence of extraterrestrial life is more widely accepted; and the political processes used by extraterrestrial civilizations receive greater scrutiny. Greater use of "intuitive methods" of information gathering and communication, the extraterrestrial approach, will occur in the future to gain a more comprehensive database on extraterrestrial life.

Another pioneer explicitly supporting the exopolitics term is Stephen Bassett who organized a series of "Exopolitics Expos" in the Washington DC metropolitan area in April 2004 and 2005.[531] Bassett's Exopolitics Expos were the first UFO conferences that were explicitly focused on the exopolitical implications of the UFO cover-up and extraterrestrial life. Basset emphasized at the conferences his earlier Congressional campaign slogan: "it is not about lights in the sky, it is about lies on the ground." Bassett assembled a line up of distinguished speakers from UFO research as well as pioneers in exopolitics research providing a unique opportunity for the general public to witncss the emergence of exopolitics as a distinct approach to the UFO phenomenon and extraterrestrial life.

In addition to Webre, Bassett and I, who gave the 'exopolitics' term its initial impetus, there are a growing number of UFO researchers, organizers and activists supporting exopolitics research. These include veteran UFO researcher Paola Harris who investigated and supported the credibility of key whistleblowers such as Col Philip Corso, Sgt Clifford Stone and (Dr) Michael Wolf. Harris has explicitly come out in support of the exopolitics term and sponsored a number of exopolitics seminars in Italy. By early 2007 she had published her first book that explicitly discussed exopolitics. [532] She also became International Director for the Exopolitics Institute in 2006, and is a course instructor in the Exopolitics Certification program.[533]

There have also been more conferences explicitly promoting exopolitics. These include Dr Roberto Pinotti, a long time Italian UFO researcher, who is the organizer of the First Annual Symposium on Exobiology and Exopolitics at the University of Calabria, Italy in October, 2005. And also the Exopolitics Toronto Symposium organized by Victor Viggiani and Mike Bird on September 25, 2005, that featured a former Minister of Defense for Canada, Paul Hellyer. [534] Hellyer confirmed the authenticity of Col Corso's testimony on UFOs and extraterrestrial life, and referred to government management of this information as the "most successful cover up in the history of the world."[535] I, along with the assistance of other exopolitics pioneers, launched an Exopolitics Institute for political study and activism in extraterrestrial affairs, and an *Exopolitics Journal*.[536] Finally, an Exopolitics Certification program was launched through the Institute offering the general public a means for a more formal education in exopolitics.[537]

Conclusion: Reframing Debate on Extraterrestrial Life and the Challenge of Exopolitics

Evidence supporting the existence of extraterrestrial life is multifaceted and overwhelming in scope. Detailed analysis of the actors, institutions and processes associated with extraterrestrial life is needed. The UFO term needs to be discarded as insufficient to this task due to the way it primarily frames public debate on extraterrestrial life in terms of a phenomenon that is "unidentified". This overlooks what evidence conclusively suggests are technologically advanced spacecraft that have been identified, and this information is kept from the general public on the basis of national security concerns. Widespread use of the UFO term implicitly supports the Cosmic Watergate concerning extraterrestrial life. Transforming public debate over evidence concerning extraterrestrial life requires introducing new terminology. A global educative program based on an exopolitics approach to extraterrestrial life is needed.

Exopolitics is a term that will continue to gather support as the cover up of evidence substantiating extraterrestrial life becomes more difficult to maintain with a global population becoming ever more informed. As exopolitics grows in popularity there is likely to be three main debates among researchers attracted to this newly defined science.

First will be the debate over how to best to define exopolitics. One approach will be my definition in terms of national and global political processes concerning extraterrestrial life. Another approach will be Webre's definition which focuses on the political processes and institutions of extraterrestrial civilizations *themselves.* As more reliable data emerges concerning extraterrestrial life, it is likely that these two approaches will merge. Until then, it is my view that exopolitics research should begin with the global actors, processes and institutions concerning evidence of extraterrestrial life visiting or residing on Earth.

A second debate concerns accepted usage of the UFO term. Many veteran UFO researchers desire to preserve current approaches to the study of UFOs as a physical science. They eschew framing it and the underlying phenomenon of extraterrestrial life in an overt political framework. This will require understanding how an exopolitics approach has been implicit in the pioneering research of seminal UFO investigators such as Donald Keyhoe. This will be important as many contemporary UFO researchers attempt to marginalize exopolitics as 'fringe UFO research' with no historical roots. Efforts to analyze UFOs and extraterrestrial life have historically addressed political factors. This, however, has been secondary to the primary goal of accumulating sufficient empirical evidence to persuade scientific skeptics. A more politically oriented approach to UFO research and extraterrestrial life, will lead to much debate between UFO and exopolitics researchers.

The third debate will be in identifying the appropriate methodology for evaluating the evidentiary sources used in exopolitics research. A social science methodology is often used by exopolitical researchers to evaluate available data. This is due to exopolitical researchers observing a deliberate "secret government" effort to remove, tamper and destroy evidence, and intimidate witnesses. This leads to debate with UFO researchers who wish to exclusively use physical science methodologies where hard evidence and documentation is used to support any claim. UFO researchers downplay the extent to which a secret government exists and interferes with evidence substantiating extraterrestrial life. The debate over an appropriate methodology will again lead to much debate between UFO and exopolitics researchers.

The fourth debate concerns different methods respectively used in astropolitics and exopolitics as emerging academic disciplines. As explained in chapter eight, astropolitics focuses on the politics of outer space and to date has eschewed any examination of evidence concerning extraterrestrial life. As evidence for extraterrestrial life is more widely accepted, astropolitics authors will predictably begin to cover similar areas as exopolitics researchers but will predictably attempt to restrict discussions on the basis of competing methodologies. This will lead to disputes over the best methods and scope of formal academic studies of extraterrestrial life and its policy implications. Exopolitics researchers will be able to draw upon a more diverse database of evidentiary material concerning extraterrestrial life. In contrast, astropolitical researchers will be using a more restricted database. This will likely lead to much debate over which database, the 'exopolitical' or 'astropolitical', is more useful for policy makers.

In addition to debates over how to define and research exopolitics, there will also be a fundamental public policy debate, what I call the "challenge of exopolitics". This concerns the secret policy debate over how and when to disclose the truth of extraterrestrial life and associated government agreements concerning such life. Possible negative reactions of the general public in terms of societal collapse, and a loss in trust and confidence in governmental institutions are central to this policy debate. The challenge of exopolitics requires transcending the historical agreements that contribute to present public policy and eventual public responses to extraterrestrial life.

ENDNOTES – CHAPTER NINE

[494] See Edward J. Ruppelt, *The report on unidentified flying objects* (Doubleday, 1956).
[495] Stephen Basset organized the 2004 and 2005 Exopolitics Annual Expos in the Washington DC area; an Exopolitics Symposium was organized at the University of Toronto on Sept 25, 2005, further conferences that focused on exopolitical issues were held in Hawaii from 2006, 2007 and 2008 that were co-organized by Dr Michael Salla and Angelika Whitecliff, further conferences organized by Stephen Bassett dealing with exopolitics were held in 2007 and 2008. A number of symposia/conferences on Exopolitics were held in Italy from 2006-2008 that were sponsored respectively by Dr Roberto Pinotti and Paola Harris.
[496] The three books are Michael Salla, *Exopolitics: Political Implications of the Extraterrestrial Presence* (Dandelion Books, 2004); Alfred Webre, *Exopolitics: Government, Politics and Law in the Universe* (Universe Books, 2005); and Paola Harris, *Exopolitics: How Does One Speak to a Ball of Light* (Authorhouse, 2007).
[497] The "Exopolitics Institute" was launched on July 4, 2005. Main website is: www.exopoliticsinstitute.org .
[498] *World Affiars: The Journal of International Issues* 12: 2 (Summer 2008).
[499] The "Exopolitics Journal" was launched on October 1, 2006. Main website is: http://exopoliticsjournal.com .
[500] The Exopolitics Certification Program was launched in 2006/2007, see: http://exopoliticsinstitute.org/certificates .
[501] Allen Hynek, *The UFO Experience* (1972), p. 10.
[502] See Michael Swords, "Project Sign & Estimate of the Situation," http://www.ufoscience.org/history/swords.pdf
[503] See Donald Keyhoe, *Aliens from Space* (1973) 14.
[504] Cited from online version of Robertson Panel at: http://www.cufon.org/cufon/robertdod.htm
[505] See: http://www.cufon.org/cufon/janp146c.htm
[506] Brookings Institute, *Proposed Studies on the Implications of Peaceful Space Activities for Human Affairs*, (1960) 215. For an online overview of the Brookings Report, go to: http://www.enterprisemission.com/brooking.html .
[507] See the *Flying Saucer Conspiracy* (1953).
[508] See Keyhoe, *Aliens from Space*, 76-86.
[509] NICAP, *The UFO Evidence* (1964), ed. Richard Hall.
[510] See "The Condon Report: A Whitewash," http://mimufon.org/1960%20articles/CondonRptWhitewash.htm
[511] William Hamilton, "California Contactees", http://www.geocities.com/Area51/Shadowlands/6583/et031.html
[512] See Michael Salla, "GALACTIC COINTELPRO - Exposing the Covert Counter-Intelligence Program against Extraterrestrial Contactees," *Exopolitics Journal,* 2:3 (2008): 167-89. Available online at: http://exopoliticsjournal.com/vol-2-3.htm .

[513] See Gary Kinder: *Light Years: An Investigation into the Extraterrestrial Experiences of Eduard Meier* (1987); John Mack, *Passport to the Cosmos* (Three Rivers Press, 1999) and Randolph Winters, *The Miami Contacts* (The Pleiades Project, 1995) VHS.
[514] For Congressional Guide to FOIA, go to: http://www.fas.org/sgp/foia/citizen.html
[515] See website for more details: http://www.caus.org .
[516] Website with documents is: www.majesticdocuments.com .
[517] See Robert Collins and Richard Doty, *Exempt from Disclosure* (Peregrine Publications, 2005).
[518] *Top Secret/Majic* (1996).
[519] See Stanton Friendman, *Flying Saucers and Science* (New Page Books, 2008).
[520] See online report at: http://www.presidentialufo.com/washington_demonstration.htm
[521] For more info go to: http://www.destinationspace.net/ufo/editorial/ORTK.asp .
[522] For discussion of the Rockefeller initiative, see: http://www.presidentialufo.com/part1.htm .
[523] Don Berliner, *UFO Briefing Document: The Best Available Evidence* (2000).
[524] For more information, go to: www.disclosureproject.com
[525] Alfred Webre introduced the term 'exopolitics' in 2000. It received widespread coverage due to a series of articles I published through my website Exopolitics.Org . Since its launch in January 2003, Exopolitics.Org has been the most popular exopolitics website in terms of visitors and search engines up to the date of rating.
[526] Michael Salla, *Exopolitics* (2004) 2. Also available online at: http://www.exopolitics.org/Study-Paper1.htm
[527] See Stanton Friedman, *Top Secret/MAJIC* (Marlowe and Company, 2005).
[528] Go to: http://www.exopolitics.org/Exo-Comment-32.htm
[529] Archived copy available at: http://web.archive.org/web/20010129030900/www.universebooks.com/exoone.html
[530] See Institute for Cooperation in Space, http://www.peaceinspace.com
[531] Bassett continued to hold similar conferences in September 2007 and April 2008 though with different titles that didn't explicitly incorporate the exopolitics term.
[532] This was titled *Exopolitics: How Does One Speak to a Ball of Light* (Author House, 2007), see: http://www.paolaharris.com/books.htm http://www.paolaharris.com/final_exopolitics.htm
[533] See http://exopoliticsinstitute.org/board.htm
[534] Visit: http://www.exopoliticstoronto.com
[535] Cited in Michael Salla, http://www.exopolitics.org/Exo-Comment-38.htm
[536] Visit: www.exopoliticsinstitute.org and www.exopoliticsjournal.com .
[537] Go to: http://exopoliticsinstitute.org/certificates/index.htm .

CHAPTER TEN

False Flag Operations and 9-11: an Exopolitical Perspective

Introduction[538]

On the sixth anniversary of the '9-11' attacks, significant numbers of American citizens continue to doubt official versions of the attacks and the adequacy of the 9-11 Commission Report. According to a Zogby poll released on September 4, 2007, 31.2% of respondents believed that key members of the Bush administration either let it happen (26.4%) or made it happen (4.8 %).[539] Most significant was that a staggering 67.2% of respondents believe that the 911 Commission should have investigated the mysterious collapse of World Trade Center Building 7. An earlier Scripps Howard/Ohio University national survey conducted in August 2006, found that 36% of Americans believe 9-11 was an 'inside job' with government agencies complicit in what occurred.[540] There has been a steady stream of authors, journalists, researchers and media personalities coming forward to declare that 9-11 was an 'inside job'. Some of the more prominent include the theologian Dr David Ray Griffin author/editor of a number of books on 9-11 including *The New Pearl Harbor Revisited: 9/11, the Cover-Up, and the Exposé* (2008), Michael Ruppert author of *Crossing the Rubicon: The Decline of the American Empire at the End of the Age of Oil* (2004), and actor Charlie Sheen who went public with his views on March 2006.[541] Finally, a website was created by a committee of scholars criticizing official explanations and also arguing that 9-11 was an 'inside job'.[542]

With the ever growing number of those claiming 9-11 was an inside job and that there was an official cover up, it comes as no surprise that many now view the 9-11 attacks as part of an historical pattern of governments using 'false flag' operations to overcome opposition to their policy objectives. A false flag operation is best described as a covert operation conducted by "governments, corporations, or other organizations, which are designed to appear as if they are being carried out by other entities."[543]

An increasing number of books and videos are now discussing historic false flag operations in relation to 9-11. The more prominent include David Griffin's, *The New Pearl Harbor* (2004 & 2008); Barrie Zwicker's, *Towers of Deception: The Media Cover-up of 9/11 (2006)*; and Alex Jones video, *TERRORSTORM: A History of Government Sponsored Terrorism* (2006). Griffin, Zwicker and Jones examine historic 'false flag' operation to present the historical context for analysis of events surrounding 9-11 and the contrived "war on terror". In historic 'false flag' operations such as the burning of the Reichstag in 1933, the 1953 Iranian coup, the Gulf of Tonkin incident in 1964, intelligence operatives from governments staged events that would be blamed on targeted groups in a way that would facilitate government polices to increase their power or topple foreign governments. More controversially, Griffin argues that the 1941 Pearl Harbor attack was a false flag operation and that this demonstrates the magnitude to which false flag operations can be conducted.[544]

Zwicker and Jones discuss how the Nazis directly benefited by covertly orchestrating the burning of the Reichstag and blaming it on communists. Similarly, they describe how U.S. and British policies directly benefited by false flag operations aimed at the popular nationalist Prime Minister of Iran, Muhammad Mossadeq, who was accused of pro-communist sympathies. This led to a coup in 1953 whereby the Shah of Iran was able to assume dictatorial powers that reversed the controversial nationalization policies of Mossadeq. The 1964 Gulf of Tonkin incident according to Zwicker, Jones and Griffin was another false flag operation whereby communist North Vietnam was blamed for two attacks on U.S. warships. Documents later released conclusively showed that the second attack never occurred. They also describe failed false flag incidents such as the attack on the USS Liberty by the Israeli Airforce in 1967 during the six day war. They claim that the sinking of the Liberty would have put great pressure on the U.S. to enter the war in support of Israel which planned to shift responsibility to Egypt.

Griffin, Zwicker, and Jones have all cited the Operation Northwoods documents that showed the Joint Chiefs of Staff had approved false flag operations in the early 1960s that involved terrorist attacks against American infrastructure and even cities.

These covert actions would have been blamed on Cuba and used to justify a military invasion but were never approved by the Kennedy administration.[545] Griffin, Zwicker and Jones use this and other cases as evidence that false flag operations have a long history in the covert actions of many governments including the US.

Having persuasively presented evidence that governments have in the past used false flag operations, Griffin, Zwicker and Jones turn their attention to the 9-11 attack; and, to varying degrees, a number of other 'terrorist attacks' in Britain, Spain and Bali. In all these cases, Griffin, Zwicker and Jones present evidence that these were false flag operations. They cite historic documents, interview whistleblowers, identify inconsistencies in official versions, and circumstantial evidence that all point to these recent terrorist attacks being false flag operations. In terms of the 9-11 attack in the U.S. and the July 7, 2005 (7-7) attack in Britain, they examine security drills that led to much confusion on the part of security forces that permitted security lapses that may have allowed the attacks to occur. Zwicker and Jones argue that such drills are a characteristic of false flag operations where it is critical to have security forces not involved in such covert operations stand down. They present persuasive evidence that the war on terror is contrived with the goal of depriving citizens in the U.S. and western democracies of their civil liberties, and to neutralize domestic opposition to the war in Iraq.

Who was really behind 9-11 and other terrorist attacks, and why?

With regard to the question of who was really behind 9-11 and other terrorist attacks, a number of 9-11 authors provide what they believe to be the real factors driving the contrived war on terrorism. I will concentrate on four that represent the major thrust of 9-11 arguments: Griffin, Zwicker, Jones, and Ruppert and simply refer to them collectively as the '9-11 authors'. To varying degrees the 9-11 authors point to efforts led by the U.S. and Britain to capture the oil resources of 'rogue nations' such as Iraq in order to gain control of the oil industry. By capturing Iraq, driving oil prices up, corporate interests in the U.S. and Britain stand to make enormous short term profits. As the supply of oil reaches peak production, an idea most strongly championed by Ruppert, this ensures that US/British corporate interests are in the driver's seat for benefiting in the long term from skyrocketing oil prices as industrializing nations such as India and China generate increasing demand for oil. Control over the vital oil industry would therefore enable U.S. corporate dominance in global financial markets well into the next generation. This would make China and India, potential future competitors to U.S. global dominance, more subservient to U.S. policies.

The 9-11 authors argue that it is not just oil interests seeking to benefit from wars in Iraq, but also the armaments industries in the U.S. which are by far the world's largest weapons suppliers. Essentially, U.S. corporate contractors need a contrived war on terrorism to continue to sell their military products to the Pentagon which needs to conduct punitive missions against rogue nations. The ultimate rationale for the arms industry is driven by corporate greed to take advantage of security threats to maintain a perpetual war economy that is funded at the expense of the ordinary tax payer. Eisenhower's famous farewell address warning of the dangers of the military-industrial complex is most commonly cited as evidence of such a danger.

In addition to U.S. financial dominance and corporate greed, the 9-11 authors offer their ultimate rationale for the contrived war on terrorism. This is the theory of Pax Americana that what drives U.S. policy is the need to establish U.S. hegemony around the planet. Griffin, Jones, Ruppelt and Zwicker argue that by the former Bush administration claiming that 'rogue states' are 'harboring terrorists', and developing Weapons of Mass Destruction (WMD) that would be given to the terrorists, the U.S. has the rationale to launch preemptive wars and establish control over nations opposed to U.S. dominance. They cite neo-conservative figures associated with the New American Century Project as exponents of this imperialist agenda to establish U.S. global dominance.[546] Consequently, the war on Iraq was justified using the WMD thesis that Saddam Hussein was allied with terrorist groups that he would have used as proxies to launch such weapons on the US. While U.S. global hegemony would be justified on the need to make the world safe for democracy, the true rationale according to 9-11 authors is to make the world profitable for key U.S. corporations allied with the oil and armaments industries.

The assessments of the 9-11 authors of false flag operations as being rooted in the greed of the oil and armaments industries, and the imperialist designs of neo-conservatives continues to attract much support. Many disenchanted with official explanations for terrorist attacks on the U.S. and Britain; the spinning of the intelligence data used to justify the war on Iraq; and the enormous profits generated by corporations involved in the oil and armaments industries agree with the 911 authors. This is understandable since Griffin's, Zwicker's and Jones' analysis of false flag operations is helpful in identifying the catalyst for government policies that result in diminished civil liberties and dampen domestic opposition to preemptive wars ostensibly aimed to "protect democracy." In reality such policies provide windfall profits for large U.S. corporations. The analyses of the 9-11 authors focus on U.S. imperialism. These analyses help identify the enormous influence neo-conservatives had in the former Bush administration in dictating official government policy. There is however a missing perspective in the analyses of the 9-11 authors focusing on the trifecta of the oil industry, the military-industrial complex, and U.S. imperialism. A perspective that provides a deeper level of analysis for what is really driving U.S. policies in the Middle East and elsewhere around the planet. The 9-11 authors are missing the exopolitical perspective.

Understanding the Exopolitical Perspective

I have shown in the two proceeding chapters that exopolitics is a distinct disciplinary approach to extensive evidence that extraterrestrial civilizations are visiting the Earth. This book has furthermore revealed how this evidence is systematically covered up by both government agencies and military departments in the U.S. and other major nations. The cover-up has been described by veteran UFO researchers as a "Cosmic Watergate."[547] Thomas Kuhn's *The Structure of Scientific Revolutions* (1962) suggests that our understanding of science periodically undergoes a paradigm shift. Exopolitics represents a paradigm shift in political thinking about the underlying forces driving domestic and international affairs.

Not only is evidence of extraterrestrial visitation in the contemporary era being covered up; but, perhaps more significantly, evidence of an historic extraterrestrial presence that has sponsored past human civilizations is also covered up. This means that both the knowledge and technology of extraterrestrials currently visiting the Earth, and historic evidence of earlier extraterrestrial visitations, have become paramount national security concerns that are kept hidden from the general public. The true extent of the national security implications concerning public disclosure of an extraterrestrial presence is revealed in a Brookings Institute study for NASA in 1960 claiming that public discovery of an extraterrestrial intelligence could lead to the collapse of Western civilization.[548] The impact of an extraterrestrial presence and its implications for politics, science, economy and culture, could very quickly lead to a collapse of vital institutions for every country on the planet thereby threatening the sovereignty of major nations. Furthermore, according to a number of former military whistleblowers, UFOs have disabled or destroyed U.S. nuclear missiles on a number of occasions.[549] This partly reveals the secret concern of policy makers over extraterrestrial visitors. In short, the national security implications of an extraterrestrial presence trumps every other national security issue, and is the Rosetta Stone for understanding the true dynamics underlying global politics and international finance.[550]

Evidence for the cover-up of an extraterrestrial presence is extensive and persuasive. Hundreds of credible whistleblowers have emerged from the military, government and corporate sectors to describe the cover up various aspects of UFOs and the extraterrestrial hypothesis. The testimonies of many of these government whistleblowers are available through private organizations such as the Disclosure Project.[551] Furthermore, leaked classified documents have disclosed critical features of the national security system created to deal with extraterrestrial life. Many of these documents are available through the popular "Majestic Documents" website.[552] Numerous websites, books and organizations have presented the evidence and testimonies of thousands of witnesses, 'experiencers', researchers and whistleblowers revealing the extent of extraterrestrial visitation to Earth.

The 9-11 authors fail to identify a number of key exopolitical factors behind false flag operations. These factors have to do with the political management system created for extraterrestrial affairs; the technology and knowledge about extraterrestrials that are located on the territory of different foreign governments; and with the 'black budget' needed to finance covert operations based on acquiring extraterrestrial technologies and information. Given the highly classified nature of extraterrestrial affairs, all these activities occur without any congressional or legislative oversight in the U.S. and other major nations such as Britain, Russia and China. I will now examine five exopolitical factors that need to be considered when analyzing false flag operations in general.

Five exopolitical factors and False Flag Operations

The first factor is the existence of a covert web of interlocking governmental and military agencies in the U.S. and around the world created to manage extraterrestrial affairs. Often described as the 'secret government', this organization operates in parallel with the more conventional political system comprising elected representatives and appointed government officials. This is similar to Lewis Lapham's distinction between the "provisional government" and the "permanent government" wherein the former comprises elected officials while the latter comprises special interest groups drawn from corporations, military and educational sector.[553] Individuals in the conventional system of government, Lapham's "provisional government", are only briefed on the basis of "need to know" and not due to their rank or position. Consequently, it has been demonstrated that sitting Presidents can be kept out of the loop as occurred in the cases of presidents Carter and Clinton.[554] As mentioned earlier, President Clinton reportedly said to senior White House reporter Sarah McClendon: "Sarah, there's a secret government within the government, and I have no control over it."[555] The 'secret government' managing extraterrestrial affairs sits at the apex of the unelected "permanent government" and has been described as MJ-12 or PI-40.[556]

Major false flag operations such as 9-11 almost certainly involve the 'secret government' using such operations as part of its broader agenda in managing extraterrestrial affairs. It is very unlikely that transitions in the "provisional government", such as the 2000 election of George Bush and the appointment of neo-conservatives to prominent positions would be capable of producing false flag operations on the order of 9-11. The ascendancy of neo-conservatives to high government positions would not be sufficient to enable false flag operations to proceed due to the potential opposition of many career bureaucrats and government officials. Only a more long term and secretive management system that exists outside of the rotation of elected political officials could hope to rein in career bureaucrats and government officials. Consequently, given the magnitude of the 9-11 attacks, this could only have occurred with the assent of the secret (or permanent) government that used neo-conservatives appointed to senior positions in the Bush administration (the 'provisional government') as the instruments for achieving the former's policy goals. The uncritical support of major governments such as Britain and Australia in subsequent policies adopted by the Bush administration, is due to the 'secret governments' of these nations coordinating their policies in a global management system created for extraterrestrial affairs. This involves many quasi governmental organizations such as the Trilateral Commission, the Bilderberg Group, and the Council of Foreign Relations that supply the resources and leadership for dictating long term secret government policies around the planet.[557]

The second factor to consider for false flag operations is the need by the secret government to maintain exclusive control of all extraterrestrial technology and evidence found around the world. This involves the removal of any physical evidence of extraterrestrial visitation from the public realm, and the relocation of this to the classified scientific laboratories of the U.S. or other major nations. There are numerous instances of extraterrestrial vehicles crashing around the planet. These have been documented and analyzed in a recent book by Ryan Wood's, *Majic Eyes Only*.[558] In all these cases, governments are expected to comply either through inducements or sanctions with these covert efforts led by the secret government which is global in scope. National leaders who do not comply run the great risk of being removed from office.

For example, the 1979 coup that removed the Prime Minister of Granada, Sir Eric Gairy, was a false flag operation. It was designed to prevent Gairy from getting the United Nations to seriously move forward in investigating the UFO issue. Gairy was instrumental in Grenada's sponsorship of the only United Nations Resolution dealing with UFOs (passed in 1978). He was scheduled to meet with UN Secretary General on 13 March 1979, to discuss further UN initiatives on UFOs based on extraterrestrial material recovered in Grenada.[559] On the same day of his meeting, his government was removed from power in a revolutionary coup led by Maurice Bishop. Gairy's case suggests that false flag operations resulting in coups led by disgruntled elites may be a result of a policy of forcing out of office non-compliant national leaders to the global system covering up UFO/extraterrestrial information. Such leaders are replaced by more compliant individuals who can be easily discredited or removed in the future.

The third exopolitical factor is the need to gain control of any territory that once hosted ancient civilizations that contain artifacts providing valuable information or technology left by extraterrestrials. These ancient civilizations have buried within their ruins much information and even technology gained through extraterrestrial intervention that allegedly occurred millennia ago. For example, there is much evidence that the ancient Sumerian civilization was sponsored by an extraterrestrial civilization known as the Anunnaki. [560] Sumer, known as the cradle of western civilization, was located in southern Iraq and was subjected to a number of archeological excavations supported by Saddam Hussein's regime.

There is growing evidence that the 1991 and 2003 U.S. led military interventions in Iraq were aimed at gaining access to some of the ancient archeological sites in Iraq in order to find any information or technology concerning the Anunnaki. [561] The fabrication of intelligence data concerning Iraq's Weapons of Mass Destruction (WMD) and alliance with terrorist organizations was a false flag operation intended to justify U.S. military intervention in 2003 in order to ensure Iraq's extraterrestrial assets could not be exploited by Hussein's regime or fall into the hands of strategic competitors such as Russia and China. Evidence for this fabrication came in the September 2006 Report by the Senate Select Committee on Intelligence that confirms that intelligence data used to justify the Iraq war was 'overstated'.[562]

The fourth exopolitical factor concerns the use of weather modification technologies that former Secretary of State William Cohen confirmed as existing in 1997.[563] False flag operations using weather modification technologies are used to shift blame onto 'unpredictable' environmental factors, when in fact such technologies are being used as an instrument of national policy. Such technologies can be used to create natural disasters or events that coerce nations into complying with the global secrecy system concerning extraterrestrial affairs. This global secrecy system ensures that scientific information, alternative energy technologies and information concerning extraterrestrials is not released to the global media. For example, the December 2004 Asian Tsunami affected a number of nations including the Indian sub-continent. At the time, India had been at the forefront of a growing number of disclosures concerning extraterrestrial visitation.[564] The disclosures were based on a number of sources within India's scientific military system who appeared to be covertly leaking information about extraterrestrial events in the Himalayas.[565]

If leaks were indeed emanating from India, it is then possible that the Asian Tsunami served as a signal to India that weather modification technologies could be used if India pursued its disclosure policies. Subsequently, the Bush administration signed in July 2005 an extraordinary agreement to help India develop its nuclear industry, and continued to allow U.S. industries to outsource jobs to India. This suggests that a mix of inducements and sanctions using weather modification technologies is used to gain the compliance of rising nations such as India that might otherwise challenge the global secrecy system.

The final exopolitical factor concerns the 'unofficial' black budget in the US. Official estimates of the black budget by the Federation of American Scientists (FAS) focus on CIA disclosures revealing the true size of the budget funding the activities of all U.S. intelligence agencies. Revealed by the CIA to be 26.7 billion dollars for fiscal year 1997, this money appears in single line items on the annual Pentagon budget, and has been estimated by the FAS to be 30.1 billion for fiscal year 2007. Conventional wisdom is that the 'black budget' is funded by the Pentagon which creates dummy projects and exaggerates the costs of actual defense expenditures (e.g., toilet seats), and channels all these funds into 'deep black' projects. However, the real size of the black budget was estimated in chapter three to be over one trillion dollars per calendar year which is more than double the whole Pentagon budget of $515 billion for Fiscal Year 2009.[566] This vast sum of money is accumulated by the CIA not for ensuring U.S. corporate profits nor for financial dominance, but to fund a secret network of deep black projects that constitute a second Manhattan Project.[567]

In his book, *The Dark Alliance*, Gary Webb revealed compelling evidence that the CIA was involved in the drug trade, and that local law enforcement agencies were deliberately undermined in their efforts to capture the major players in the drug trade due to CIA intervention. Evidence for this has been amassed by Michael Ruppert on his former "From the Wilderness" website and book, *Crossing the Rubicon.*[568] If the CIA is complicit in the funneling of drugs into the U.S. in order to generate an enormous pool of illicit funds, the main purpose of these funds is not to enrich 'drug barons' or corrupt politicians, but to fund the second Manhattan Project. Furthermore, profits generated from the armaments, oil and other industries, both legal and illicit, are accumulated by CIA front companies that are also funneled into deep black projects that escape Congressional scrutiny. These highly immoral funding activities are tolerated on the basis of the national security concern of hiding the true extent of the extraterrestrial related projects created in response to an extraterrestrial presence.

Conclusion: Incorporating the Exopolitical Perspective on 9-11 and False Flag Operations

False flag operations can lead to U.S. military intervention in areas that can help maintain the drug trade that the CIA uses to generate funding for black budget projects. False flag operations such as the Tonkin incident and the September 11 attack led to military intervention in areas vital for the drug trade: Indochina and Afghanistan. According to Zworkin and Jones, the Tonkin incident was orchestrated to ensure that the U.S. would enter the war in Vietnam to maintain U.S. global hegemony through military efforts to prevent communist expansion in Indochina, and provide armaments industries with new weapons orders. However, the Vietnam war fulfilled deeper exopolitical purposes for the U.S, one of which was to help the CIA to profit from lucrative drug running operations. This is something that Ruppert himself identifies but he opposes an exopolitical perspective due to his refusal to consider evidence substantiating UFOs.[569] Similarly, the U.S. intervention into Afghanistan was also motivated, according to Ruppert, by the desire to restore the drug trade that had been threatened by the policies of the fundamentalist Taliban regime that had all but eliminated the heroin production cycle.[570]

The 9-11 authors provide a cogent case that recent terrorist attacks in the US, Britain and other countries have the distinguishing features of false flag operations that have been used in the past by governments to target potential opponents, create contrived threats, and to erode civil liberties. The various books and videos dealing with 9-11 as a false flag operation are powerful warnings of the extent to which governments can go in order to augment their power. In explaining the ultimate goal of these false flag operations, the level of analysis of the most well known 9-11 authors, Jones, Zwicker, Ruppert and Griffin do not go deep enough into revealing the true agenda and beneficiaries.

According to Jones, Zwicker and many others, the ultimate beneficiaries of false flag operations are the corporate barons behind the oil and armaments industries, and the imperialistic designs of U.S. neoconservatives that dominated the Bush administration. This supposedly provides a persuasive explanation for who is ultimately behind the war on terrorism and why it is being pursued. Rather than corporate greed and imperialistic intentions driving the war on terrorism, there are deeper factors that concern covert policies involving deeply classified projects involving extraterrestrial technologies funded by illicit black budget sources that use front companies in the oil and armaments industries. This is where the explanations for 9-11 offered by Griffin, Jones, Ruppert and Zwicker do not go far enough in identifying the true parameters of the 'inside job' that led to 9-11. Corporate greed and neo-conservative imperialism are not the driving force behind the war against terrorism, but the vehicles used to generate funds for a second Manhattan project that trumps all other national security concerns in the U.S. and other major nations.

With the Internet and increased communications threatening to undermine the global secrecy system covering up evidence confirming an extraterrestrial presence, the war on terror provides a means of distracting the public, discrediting researchers seeking to expose this evidence. The war on terrorism also provides a useful cover for continuing to generate enormous sums of revenue for a second Manhattan project that escapes government oversight, and to increase the power of the secret government in control of the distribution of this revenue. The authors and researchers associated with the thesis that 9-11 was an 'inside job' have pointed us in the right direction in terms of government complicity. They deserve credit for helping open the eyes of the American public to what really transpired in 9-11 as evidenced in the recent Zogby and Scripps polls.

The main objection to the work of the 9-11 authors is that they not identify the different exopolitical factors that reveal the deeper agenda behind false flag operations. This is understandable given the way in which advocates of a 'Cosmic Watergate' concerning UFOs and extraterrestrial visitation have been ridiculed in the past. Invoking evidence pointing to a "Cosmic Watergate" could easily be perceived by some as a means of jeopardizing public consideration of objective studies of 9-11. Even worse, considering exopolitical factors may even lead to accusations of mis-information designed to throw 9-11 researchers off track. However, surveys such as the 2002 Roper Poll show that approximately 70% of the American public believes the government is not telling the truth about UFOs and extraterrestrial visitation.[571] This suggests that there is great benefit in connecting the 9-11 and UFO cover ups to better understand the key actors and institutions involved in false flag operations and possible exopolitical factors. It is only through a systematic understanding of the exopolitical perspective that the true motives underscoring the 'war on terror' and the nature of the 'secret government' can be fully gauged, and a durable solution found that prevents future false flag operations.

ENDNOTES CHAPTER TEN

[538] I am grateful to Hugh Matlock for his thoughtful ideas and suggestions for improving the substantive content and organization of this paper, and identifying a number of typographical errors.
[539] "Zogby Poll: 51% of Americans Want Congress to Probe Bush/Cheney Regarding 9/11 Attacks; Over 30% Seek Immediate Impeachment," available online at: http://www.zogby.com/news/ReadNews.dbm?ID=1354 . An earlier Zogby poll (May 2006) found that 42% of Americans believed that official explanations and the 9-11 Commission were covering up the truth. Go to: http://www.911truth.org/images/911TruthZogbyPollFinalReport.htm
[540] Go to: http://www.scrippsnews.com/911poll
[541] For Charlie Sheen's testimony go to: *http://www.prisonplanet.com/articles/march2006/200306charliesheen.htm*
[542] The original 911 Scholars for Truth website was split due to differing approaches by leading supporters. Its main offshoots include: http://911scholars.org and http://www.ae911truth.org .
[543] Cited from: http://en.wikipedia.org/wiki/False_flag .
[544] For an article discussing Griffin's views on Pearl Harbor and false flag operations go to: http://bohemian.com/bohemian/06.14.06/david-ray-griffin-0624.html .
[545] Available online at: http://www.gwu.edu/~nsarchiv/news/20010430/
[546] For information on the New American Century project, go to: http://www.newamericancentury.org
[547] Stanton Friedman, *Flying Saucers and Science: A Scientist Investigates the Mysteries of UFOs* (New Page Books, 2008) 103-28.
[548] For information on the Brookings Report go to the Wikipedia entry at: http://en.wikipedia.org/wiki/Brookings_Report .
[549] See Robert Salas and James Klotzhttp, *Faded Giant* (BookSurge Publishing 2005). Details available online at: www.ufopop.org/Special/FadedGiant.htm .
[550] See Michael E. Salla, *Exopolitics: Political Implications of the Extraterrestrial Presence* (Dandelion Books, 2004). Online articles are available at: http://www.exopolitics.org .
[551] http://www.disclosureproject.org .
[552] http://www.majesticdocuments.com .
[553] See Lewis Lapham, "Lights, Camera, Democracy, Harper Magazine, August 1996, excerpts available at: http://fdt.net/~aabbeama/PJB_from_left.html .
[554] For more information go to: http://presidentialufo.com .
[555] http://www.presidentialufo.com/part5.htm .
[556] http://www.exopolitics.org/Study-Paper-5.htm .
[557] See Jim Marrs, *Rule by Secrecy: The Hidden History That Connects the Trilateral Commission, the Freemasons, and the Great Pyramids* (Harper, 2001).
[558] http://www.majiceyesonly.com .

[559] For Gairy's account of what occurred, see Wesley Bateman, "Sir Eric Gairy, Prime Minister of Grenada: His UN UFO Meeting and his E.T. Secret," *UFO Digest* (March 12, 2008): http://www.ufodigest.com/news/0308/gairy.html
[560] See Zecharia Sitchin's *The Twelfth Planet* and other books from his Earth Chronicles series available at: http://www.sitchin.com .
[561] Go to: http://www.exopolitics.org/Study-Paper2.htm .
[562] See "Postwar Findings about Iraq's WMD Programs and Links to Terrorism and How they Compare with Prewar Assessments", available at: http://intelligence.senate.gov/phaseiiaccuracy.pdf.
[563] http://www.fas.org/news/usa/1997/04/bmd970429d.htm .
[564] For a number of stories concerning India's release of information on UFOs and extraterrestrials go to: http://www.indiadaily.com .
[565] "More evidence of Extra Terrestrial contacts with Indian Government and Military," available at: http://www.indiadaily.com/editorial/12-19c-04.asp.
[566] "Fiscal 2009 Department of Defense Budget is Released," *Defense Link*, February 04, 2008. Available online at: http://www.defenselink.mil/releases/release.aspx?releaseid=11663.
[567] See chapter three. An earlier version was published as Michael Salla, "The Black Budget Report," http://www.scoop.co.nz/stories/HL0401/S00151.htm .
[568] See Michael Ruppert, *Crossing the Rubicon: The Decline of the American Empire at the End of the Age of Oil* (New Society Publishers, 2004) and his former website: http://www.fromthewilderness.com.
[569] See "Michael Ruppert Responds to Victor Thorn's Ten Questions": http://www.fromthewilderness.com/10questions.shtml.
[570] See Michael Ruppert, http://www.fromthewilderness.com/free/ww3/10_10_01_heroin.html.
[571] See: http://www.scifi.com/ufo/roper.

Part D -
Overcoming the Challenge of Exopolitics

The primary challenge confronting exopolitics is to prepare the general public for the exposure of secret government policy concerning extraterrestrial life. This requires disclosure of evidence confirming the reality of extraterrestrial life so the public can participate in an informed way in future debates over appropriate government policy on extraterrestrial affairs. Much of this evidence and its public policy implications was disclosed in Part A. Another aspect of the challenge to exopolitics is to persuade policy makers that extraterrestrial disclosure is the most sensible policy to take despite the risks it poses in terms of a loss in public trust and confidence in government institutions. Part B focused on critiquing the policy responses that have been secretly implemented to deal with extraterrestrial life. The chapters in Part C began the educative process of preparing the public for exposure to the complex public policy issues concerning extraterrestrial life. Part D outlines the significance of public perception concerning extraterrestrial life, and how important public attitudes are in overcoming the challenge of exopolitics.

Chapter eleven provides a detailed critique of the debunking methods used by those critical of the whistleblower testimonies frequently used by exopolitics researchers. Being able to distinguish between objective criticism and common debunking methods provides an important conceptual tool against efforts to dismiss the testimonies of key whistleblowers. Whistleblower testimonies, such as Lt Col. Philip Corso, offer important insights into government policies on extraterrestrial life, and help mobilize the general public to take action.

Chapter twelve provides an idea of possible public reactions to the exposure of government policies on extraterrestrial life. The chapter is based on an online survey gauging public reactions to a series of public policy issues associated with government authorities covering up evidence of extraterrestrial life. The chapter provides a glimpse into the faultlines that will emerge as policy issues concerning extraterrestrial life and government responses become debated by the general public.

This book's final chapter describes the three ways in which publish opinion is being shaped for 'First Contact' with extraterrestrials. This chapter argues that the main issue is not whether disclosure of extraterrestrials will occur, but 'how' it will occur. Competing government agencies and military departments are trying to promote their own spin of the extraterrestrial presence to shape public perceptions. Influencing public perceptions will be critical to how much of the current management system, Manhattan Two, and the black budget that funds it, continue to operate at current levels. The goal is to encourage the development of an empowered and informed citizenry who can constructively deal with the problems raised by an undeclared extraterrestrial presence, and develop viable solutions.

Chapter Eleven

Crossing the Rubicon: Lt. Colonel Philip Corso and his Critics

In 1997, a retired Lt. Col., from the U.S. Army, Philip Corso, authored a book, *The Day After Roswell*, that quickly rose into the New York Time's best seller list with his revelations concerning his role in a classified program to seed extraterrestrial technologies into the private sector.[572] Corso had a distinguished career as a Military Intelligence officer, serving in senior positions during the Second World War, the Korean War, and under the Eisenhower administration. It was during his assignment as 'Special Assistant' to Lt General Arthur Trudeau, who headed Army Research and Development, that Corso became head of the newly established Foreign Technology Desk. During this assignment from 1961 to 1963, Corso claims to have regularly passed on to various corporations, key 'foreign technologies' that were in fact, extraterrestrial in origin. This led to breakthroughs in developing the integrated circuit, night vision technology, fiber optics, super tenacity fibers, lasers and other cutting edge technologies. Corso's book details a remarkable case; a former senior military official emerging as a whistleblower to reveal information about classified projects involving extraterrestrial vehicles (ETVs) or extraterrestrial biological entities (EBEs).

Since the publication of his book, there has been much controversy between those believing Col Corso was blowing the whistle on classified U.S. Army activities involving seeding extraterrestrial technologies into private industry, and those believing Corso distorted his distinguished military service in order to assume a historical role far beyond his actual achievements. Those most critical of Corso believe that he was prone to embellishing his service record. Most criticism has centered around a number of public statements Corso made that appear to be inconsistent with what can be verified in public documentation. Corso's case is important since he represents the kind of witness testimony that tells us most about secret government policies concerning extraterrestrial life.

In this book, I have introduced numerous testimonies by witnesses, including Corso, whose chief credibility comes from their backgrounds as military and/or corporate officials who served in places where they claimed to have witnessed classified events and documents. It is therefore important to familiarize oneself with the efforts by some to smear the credibility and dismiss the testimony of such witnesses. In my ongoing exopolitics research, I have found this to be the most difficult obstacle confronting researchers trying to understand and expose secret government policies on extraterrestrial life - continued efforts to smear and dismiss key witness testimonies. I have therefore chosen to analyze the chief arguments used to dismiss the testimony of one of the most reliable and credible witnesses to emerge confirming the existence of government and military policies on extraterrestrial life – Lt. Col. Philip Corso.

The most significant of Corso's claims that have been subjected to intense criticism are that: 1. he served as a staff member of President Eisenhower's National Security Council; 2. he was head of the Foreign Technology Desk at the Army Research and Development for two years; 3. he disseminated extraterrestrial technologies to private industry; and 4. he witnessed an extraterrestrial biological entity (EBE) being shipped overland from Roswell Army Air Force Base to Wright Patterson Air Force base. Further criticisms include Corso's claim to having been associated with a covert control group created to oversee the UFO phenomenon, MJ-12; to have served as a battalion commander at White Sands Missile range; to have concocted an alleged confrontation with the CIA's director of covert operations; and to have been promoted to full Colonel upon retirement.

I will discuss each of these criticisms in order to assess their: validity; damage to Corso's credibility as a whistleblower; discrepancies with available documentation; and impact on his central claim of having been part of a highly classified effort by the U.S. Army to seed civilian industries with extraterrestrial technologies. Corso's credibility as a distinguished military officer coming forward to reveal his role in such a classified program shortly before his death, is at the center of the debate of whether his claims are valid or not.

Corso's claims placed a number of veteran researchers of the UFO phenomenon in the uncomfortable position of dismissing the testimony of a highly decorated officer. Documentation does put him in places and positions where the events he claims to have witnessed could have occurred as he described. Nevertheless, there have been some inconsistencies found in what Corso claimed and what can be documented. This has lead to intense debate between those who consider these inconsistencies to be minor, and those believing the inconsistencies to be sufficiently significant to warrant dismissing Corso's credibility and testimony entirely.

Some of Corso's critics have gone as far as publicly dismissing Corso as a fraud and 'literary hoaxer'.[573] Corso's strongest critics include veteran UFO researchers such Stanton Friedman, Dr Kevin Randle and Brad Sparks who collectively have expressed their skepticism. Many of the criticisms made against Corso cross the Rubicon between objective criticism and outright debunking. This invites speculation of the motivations of Corso's critics who undertake such a concerted debunking effort against a highly decorated military whistleblower whose revelations do much to clarify the UFO phenomenon.

Files on Corso gained through FOIA include his service record and a declassified FBI report.[574] To assist my evaluation I use statements from an Italian version of Corso's original notes that were published in Italy as *L'Alba di una Nuova Era [Dawn of a New Age].*[575] These notes have not yet been published in English. They comprise Corso's raw beliefs on a number of UFO issues prior to his collaboration with co-writer William Birnes in *The Day After Roswell*. I examine each of the most significant criticisms raised against Corso's credibility as a whistleblower, and assess whether Corso's critics cross the line between objective criticism and debunking. First I will describe the difference between objective criticism and debunking to establish some guideline for determining when Corso's critics cross the Rubicon and become debunkers.

1. Objective Criticism versus Debunking

The UFO phenomenon has led to numerous claims by many individuals concerning various aspects of this complex phenomenon.

Analyzing these claims requires an objective approach to the evidence not overly influenced by the investigators own prior beliefs. I attempt to distinguish between critics committed to an objective investigation of the evidence, and critics who use their criticisms to promote their own established beliefs. Dr Bernard Haiasch defines skepticism, what I will consider here to be 'objective criticism', as:

> … one who practices the method of suspended judgment, engages in rational and dispassionate reasoning as exemplified by the scientific method, shows willingness to consider alternative explanations without prejudice based on prior beliefs, and who seeks out evidence and carefully scrutinizes its validity.[576]

This definition contrasts with 'debunking' which is driven by an investigator's prejudice based on prior beliefs, and disingenuous efforts to manipulate evidence to promote a particular conclusion. It is worth pointing out that debunking was officially sanctioned by the Robertson Panel as a means of discrediting a great number of claims concerning UFOs. In January 1953, a group of scientists chaired by Dr Howard P. Robertson and covertly funded by the CIA, recommended that UFO sightings be debunked due to the potential for manipulation of this information by 'foreign powers' in a way that would undermine U.S. national security. The panel recommended an "educational program" to deter the general public from taking interest and demanding serious investigation of UFO sightings: "The 'debunking' aim would result in reduction in public interest in 'flying saucers' which today evokes a strong psychological reaction."[577] Consequently, a CIA sanctioned policy of debunking UFO reports had begun. This needs to be considered when examining the critics of UFO related claims or witnesses.

Objective criticism can be most easily distinguished from debunking in three ways when it comes to whistleblower testimonies. First, the objective critic is willing "to consider alternative explanations" if any inconsistencies are found in what the whistleblower claims and what can be objectively verified. In contrast, a debunker will automatically reject alternative explanations and will dismiss UFO related claims if any inconsistencies are found. Second, the objective critic will scrutinize inconsistencies and seek to judge how significant these are in relation to the claims made by the whistleblower. In contrast, a debunker will highlight such inconsistencies, overplaying their significance in relation to the integrity and reliability of the whistleblower. Third, the objective critic will evaluate the pros and cons for a whistleblower's testimony and reach a balanced assessment. In contrast, a debunker will focus on the cons and argue for dismissing the testimony of the whistleblower, regardless of the pros.

2. Was Col. Corso a (staff) member of the National Security Council?

In the biographical description found in *The Day after Roswell*, Corso claimed that he served on "Dwight D. Eisenhower's National Security Council as a lieutenant colonel". Elsewhere in his book, Corso states that he was "on the NSC staff"[578]; and claims that in his fifth year he personally asked President Eisenhower to be released as a staff member of the National Security Council (NSC) so he could take up his own military command in New Mexico.[579] In his notes, he claims that from 1953-57 he was, "a member of the National Security Council Staff."[580] According to Corso, Lt General Trudeau had sent him to serve in the NSC under President Eisenhower. In his book he says that he "was working in some of the most secret areas of military intelligence, reviewing heavily classified information on behalf of General Trudeau."[581]

There have been two major criticisms of Corso's claims regarding his service with the NSC. One, by Stanton Friedman and Dr Randle criticize Corso for claiming to have served on the NSC itself, rather than as a liaison officer on an NSC committee. The second criticism by Brad Sparks claims that neither the Psychological Strategy Board (PSB) or the Operations Coordinating Board (OCB) both of which Corso served on, were part of the NSC. These critics all conclude that Corso embellished his precise role with the NSC and that his entire testimony therefore becomes unreliable. I deal with each of these criticisms in turn.

Corso's military record confirms that from 1953 to 1956, he was given intelligence staff assignments on both the Psychological

Strategy Board (PSB) and the Operations Coordinating Board (OCB). This is consistent with an FBI Report that states that Corso was "assigned to the Operations Coordinating Board (OCB), National Security Council."[582] It can therefore be confirmed that Corso was assigned as an intelligence staff member to at least two committees that performed important psychological warfare functions within the Eisenhower administration. Two of these committees, the PSB and OCB almost certainly dealt with managing the public response to UFO information. Friedman's criticism of Corso stems from a sworn affidavit made by Col Corso two months before his death in July 1998. In the affidavit Corso claimed that he "was a member of President Eisenhower's National Security Council."[583]

Friedman conducted research at the Eisenhower Library into Corso's claim of having being a 'member of the NSC'. Friedman says that the archivist never found any evidence that Corso served as a member of the NSC or attended any NSC meetings. This led him to dismiss Corso's claim of serving on the NSC. This is what Friedman wrote to me during an online debate over Corso's credibility:

> You want to believe that Corso was on the National Security Council. If you do any checking … you will find that the NSC's membership is determined by Statute. He had none of the positions that would have permitted him to be named a member. Do you have any reason to claim that the Eisenhower Library was lying when they said he was not a member and did not attend any meetings? A referral letter about him makes clear he was a liaison man... not a member.[584]

The problem in settling this issue is exactly what part of the NSC did Corso claim to be a member? Was it the cabinet level committee chaired by the President generally known as the NSC? Alternatively, was it one of the various interagency committees formally and/or functionally associated with the NSC. These interagency committees make up what is generally known as the NSC system. At the apex of the NSC are cabinet level officials and heads of various departments and agencies meeting regularly to discuss national security issues. During the Eisenhower administration, the NSC comprised the following:

> … five statutory members: the President, Vice President, Secretaries of State and Defense, and Director of the Office of Defense Mobilization. Depending on the subject under discussion, as many as a score of other senior Cabinet members and advisers, including the Secretary of the Treasury, the Chairman of the JCS, and the Director of Central Intelligence, attended and participated."[585]

Corso never claimed, in his book or notes, to have been a member of the NSC as described above, but that he had been on the NSC staff. This suggests that the Affidavit, signed only two months before his death at 83 years of age, containing the reference to him having been a member of the NSC, can be attributed to human error. The aged and ill Corso failed to insert the qualifying word 'staff' before the phrase "member of President Eisenhower's National Security Council."

Concerning what part of the NSC precisely Corso served on, we learn of the OCB association with the NSC in the following description of how the NSC discussed its agenda and implemented its decisions during Corso's service:

> President Eisenhower created the Operations Coordinating Board (OCB) to follow up on all NSC decisions. The OCB met regularly on Wednesday afternoons at the Department of State, and was composed of the Under Secretary of State for Political Affairs, Deputy Secretary of Defense, the Directors of CIA, USIA [US Information Agency]… and the Special Assistants to the President for National Security Affairs and Security Operations Coordination. The OCB was the coordinating and implementing arm of the NSC for all aspects of the implementation of national security policy. NSC action papers were assigned to a team from the OCB for follow-up. More than 40 interagency working groups were established with experts for various countries and subjects. This 24-person staff of the OCB supported these

> working groups in which officials from various agencies met each other for the first time.[586]

In addition to the 'Operations Coordinating Board' [OCB] being responsible for implementing NSC decisions it was also mandated to report to the NSC as stipulated in the executive order creating it. The role of the OCB is described in official history of the NSC which states of the OCB: "Established as an independent agency by EO 10483, September 2, 1953, to report to the NSC on the development, by appropriate Executive branch agencies, of operational plans for national security policies of international import."[587] While formally independent, the OCB and the PSB were functionally part of the NSC system, since it was required for them both to report to the NSC and implement NSC decisions.

Consequently, it can be concluded that Corso served in a support staff capacity to the NSC rather than having been a member of the NSC proper. NSC was the ultimate government entity to which the Operations Coordinating Board had to report and implement decisions received from. This view that the OCB was functionally part of the NSC was confirmed by the FBI report so it is true that Corso served on the staff of the NSC. The origin of Corso's sworn statement that he had been a member of the NSC related to his membership in one of the subordinate committees – the OCB and its predecessor the PSB.

Friedman has taken Corso quite literally to mean that he served on the NSC when it's clear from the context of his book, notes and interviews, Corso was only referring to his membership in the Operations Coordinating Board and other committees attached to the NSC. This has led to Friedman concluding that Corso was making misleading statements of serving both as a member of the NSC and attending NSC meetings involving the President and other Cabinet level officials. This explains why the Eisenhower Library archivist could find no evidence of Corso having been a member of the NSC or having attended NSC meetings, Friedman was looking at the wrong committee in terms of Corso's membership and attendance. Clearly, Corso attended meetings of the NSC Operations Coordinating Board (OCB) and Psychological Strategy Board (PSB), so Friedman's contention that he could not find records confirming Corso's attendance at NSC meetings is misleading. Corso clearly attended the PSB and OCB meetings during his four year assignment to the Eisenhower administration and the NSC.

A similar misunderstanding of Corso's role in the NSC is stated by Randle in the following discussion I had with him over Corso's credibility:

> ... the Eisenhower Library lacked the records to substantiate Corso's claim, not because those records were incomplete, but because they never existed in the first place. Here is another significant discrepancy that you choose to ignore by saying maybe, possibly, perhaps, but have no evidence to even begin a simple investigation, other than the word of a man who has been caught several times making false claims.[588]

Randle is also reaching a mistaken conclusion about Corso's veracity as a whistleblower based on his focus on a statement made in Corso's affidavit and taken out of context to infer something negative about Corso's background. Corso had earlier cleared such a possible confusion in his book and during subsequent interviews. Randle failed to examine the precise role Corso played in the NSC and the various committees he attended, and how the NSC is a multi-tiered institution. Corso was clearly assigned to the military staff of both the PSB and OCB that were part of the NSC system developed in the Eisenhower administration.

Another criticism is made by Brad Sparks who claims that the OCB did not become formally part of the NSC until 1957 as a result of Executive Order 10700 that incorporated the OCB into the NSC. Sparks claims that Corso was embellishing his military service by claiming that he had served in the more prestigious NSC as opposed to the less prestigious OCB. Sparks writes:

> Corso served as a staff member of an "independent agency," something called the OCB from Feb 24, 1954, to Oct. 20, 1956, according to his records, 'not' as a staff member of the NSC.... The OCB (Operations Coordinating Board and its predecessor the Psychological Strategy Board) was not a part of the NSC ...[589]

Sparks criticism is incorrect in a number of ways. First, the OCB was functionally part of the NSC from its inception due to its reporting to and implementing NSC decisions. The OCB's formal incorporation into the NSC in 1957 was done for organizational reasons, and did not change its chief function as an interagency committee that was part of the NSC system. Second, an FBI record refers to Corso having served on the OCB NSC, thereby confirming that it was widely understand that the OCB was part of the NSC from its inception. Third, Corso's sworn testimony to Congressional "Hearings Before The Select Committee On POW/MIA Affairs," in 1992, listed Corso as: "Lt. Col. Phillip [sic] Corso (USA, Retired) National Security Council Staff, Eisenhower administration." Fourth, Robert Cutler wrote an official history for the CIA about his experience while serving as Eisenhower's Special Assistant for National Security Affairs. Cutler served on the Psychological Strategy Board, the NSC Planning Board and the Operations Coordinating Board from the years 1951-58. Cutler described the role of the OCB in implementing policies approved by the NSC as follows:

> Finally, the President approves, modifies, or rejects the Council's recommendations, transmits those policies which he approves to the departments and agencies responsible for planning their execution, as a rule – where international affairs are concerned – [he] requests the NSC Operations Coordinating Board to assist these departments and agencies in coordinating their respective planning for action under the approved policies.[590]

A significant flaw in Sparks' argument is that he is not consistent in his criticisms. His more recent criticism against Corso is a reversal of his previous position that the PSB was part of the NSC and that Corso had been appointed to the NSC when serving in the Eisenhower administration. In his definitive 'expose' of Corso's book, written in August 1998, Sparks wrote: "The PSB was a division of the National Security Council (NSC), not the CIA, and it didn't exist in 1947. The PSB was created on April 4, 1951. Corso should have known this from his tour of duty at the NSC in the early 50's."[591]

The documentary and historical evidence supports Corso's contention that he served as a staff member of the NSC while assigned to the OCB and PSB. Furthermore, Sparks' criticisms of Corso fail to be consistent. Sparks has been the most dismissive of all Corso's critics when it comes to Corso's credentials and background. He has disparaged Corso regardless of the documentary evidence supporting Corso's claims. In the case of Friedman and Dr Randle, both also disparaged Corso by emphasizing his alleged claim in his Affidavit of having served on the NSC itself. They ignored Corso's repeated statements, made earlier, to having been a staffer assigned to the NSC. They put great emphasis on what is obviously an oversight on Corso's part that can be attributed to his deteriorating health. They ignore previous interviews and writing which consistently claim that Corso had served on the NSC staff. This suggests both Friedman and Randle disparaged the significance of Corso's testimony by over emphasizing inconsistencies in his testimony. The failure of Randle, Sparks and Friedman to consider alternative explanations for inconsistencies in Corso's testimony; their overblown emphasis on the significance of the inconsistencies; and their lack of effort to reach a balanced conclusion over the pros and cons of Corso's testimony, suggests they have crossed the Rubicon from objective criticism into debunking.

3. Did Col Corso officially work with Majestic-12?

According to Randle, Corso had made some public statements of having been officially associated with the secretive Majestic 12 (MJ-12) Group created to manage the UFO phenomenon.[592] Randle concludes that the absence of documentary support for such claims suggests that Corso was prone to embellishing his service background, therefore his testimony is unreliable. Randle dismissively writes: "I find the references to his personal involvement in MJ-12 to be the smoking gun about the credibility of the book."[593]

Documentary evidence for a possible official relationship between Corso and MJ-12 is found in his official military records. Corso's records point out that he served on the Psychological Strategy Board (PSB) in 1953; and also on its successor the

Operations Coordinating Board (OCB) from 1953-56. During Corso's service, these committees were both physically located at the Department of State, and headed by the Deputy Secretary of State. Corso describes his role in the PSB/OCB and the UFO information he had access to as follows:

> During my military career at one time or another, I counted nine clearances above "Top Secret," granted to me. These included cryptographic, satellite, code and intercept, special operational clearances and the "Eyes Only" category of special White House (NSC) matters. They made available to me all matters within the government which included "UFO" information. My colleagues of the NSC staff did not know of my special clearances. Only C.D. Jackson, my superior, and the President's special assistant and President Eisenhower knew of the clearances.[594]

Corso is here claiming that while serving as a staff member of Eisenhower's NSC, he was given access to 'UFO' information. Claims attributed to Corso by Randle that Corso served with Majestic-12 may be explained from the precise role played by the OCB. The OCB was the successor to the Psychological Strategy Board (PSB) that had been initially created by Gordon Gray, a former Secretary of the Army, in 1951. According to Stanton Friedman, Gray was a member of the original Majestic 12 Group mentioned in the Eisenhower Briefing Document.[595] Given the high level of security attached to all MJ-12 activities, it can be assumed that the PSB had been created to perform certain functions for the secretive MJ-12 Group. A still to be confirmed 'Majestic' document, allegedly leaked by government insiders, declares that the Psychological Strategy Board was created by MJ-12 to develop policies on the UFO phenomenon.[596]

The PSB was created "under the NSC to coordinate government-wide psychological warfare strategy."[597] Both the PSB and the OCB were based on developing psychological warfare strategies. Given the role recommended by the 1953 Robertson Panel to debunk UFO sightings and Gordon Gray's original role in setting up the PSB, it can be concluded that one of the functions of the OCB was to develop appropriate psychological warfare strategies to deal with the public response to the UFO phenomenon. Corso was most likely referring to his service on the PSB/OCB as the basis for his later claims to have been formally associated with MJ-12. Corso's background as a military intelligence officer would have equipped him well to serve on a committee (PSB/OCB) performing psychological warfare functions authorized by MJ-12 to manipulate the public response to the UFO phenomenon. The criticism against Corso that he embellished his service record in claiming to have been associated with MJ-12 is therefore not supported by the documentary evidence. The lack of effort of Randle to find a plausible explanation for Corso's claim regarding being professionally associated with MJ-12 suggests that once again he has crossed the Rubicon from objective criticism into debunking.

4. Did Col Corso head the Foreign Technology desk at Army Research & Development for two years?

Another criticism of Col Corso is Dr Randle's and Stanton Friedman's contention that Corso served only ninety days as head of Foreign Technology desk under Lt General Trudeau, and that he was embellishing his service record by claiming that he "for two incredible years" was "heading up the Foreign Technology desk in the Army Research and Development.[598] Col Corso's military record confirms that he served as Chief of the Foreign Technology Division from 18 April 1962 to 18 July 1962. Prior to this period he was assigned as a Staff Officer in the Plans Division from May 5 to June 25, 1961, and then as staff officer in the Foreign Technology Division from 26 June 1961 to April 1962. Furthermore, from 18 July, 1962 to his retirement on 1 March, 1963, he was once again assigned as a Staff Officer in the Plans Division of Army R & D. It is this entire period of serving in Army R & D that Corso describes as the "two incredible years" of heading the Foreign Technology Desk.

In Corso's notes, he declares that upon his return from Germany in 1960 where he was Inspector General for the U.S. Seventh Army, he became "Special Assistant to the Chief of Army Research and Development, Lt Gen. Arthur G. Trudeau".[599] He claimed that in "Army R& D, I had the title of Chief of Foreign Technology Division…. I was always the team chief and made all decisions."[600] Corso's claim is supported by his close relationship with Trudeau and his former senior positions as battalion commander at White Sands Missile Range and Inspector General of the 7th Army.

Independent corroboration that Corso served as head of the FTD, despite his military record confirming this only for a three month period, was established by Col. John Alexander in his own private research of Corso's background.[601] Alexander discovered in his research that Corso had another officer nominally above him in the organizational hierarchy, but Corso was known to be effectively in charge of the Foreign Technology desk created under General Trudeau. This was confirmed to Alexander by senior military officials aware of Corso's work with Trudeau. The FTD was a very small unit possibly comprising just Corso himself. Alexander discovered that the FTD was created when Corso started at Army Research and Development, and the office was abolished when he retired, along with Trudeau. This confirms Corso's claim that the FTD was created for him by Trudeau after his arrival at the Pentagon and required Corso's various security clearances.[602] This supports Corso's testimony that he was in charge of the Foreign Technology desk over a two year period 1961-63, and not solely the ninety days confirmed in his military record. The great emphasis placed in this discrepancy between what Corso claimed and what his record establishes, once again shows how Corso's critics fail to identify plausible explanations for this inconsistency. A number of plausible explanations exist for this discrepancy without undermining Corso's central claim of heading the FTD. Consequently, the overblown emphasis on this inconsistency between Corso's claims and his records, once again reveal that critics such as Randle and Friedman cross the Rubicon between objective criticism and debunking.

5. Did Col Corso Play a role in disseminating extraterrestrial technologies into private industry?

There has been much criticism of Corso's claims of seeding extraterrestrial technologies into civilian industries. The civilian technologies spawned by this covert seeding program include: Fiber Optics, Image Intensifiers, Super Tenacity Fibers, Lasers, Integrated

Circuits, and Irradiated Food. Critics such as Stanton Friedman argue that:

> Corso seems to be taking credit for the single handed introduction of a whole host of new technologies into American industry. All this is supposedly derived from the filing cabinet of Roswell wreckage over which he was given control by General Trudeau.... He is definitely NOT a scientist, but the implication is that in less than 3 years he could change the world's technology... Not very likely in my opinion.[603]

Similarly, Brad Sparks is very critical of Corso's claims regarding his seeding extraterrestrial technologies and concludes: "there really is no need to go into the rest of his confabulations about his heroic role in getting U.S. industry to "reverse engineer" microchips, fiber optics, lasers, Kevlar, etc., from his make-believe Roswell spacecraft."[604]

It needs to be pointed out that Corso consistently laid credit for the covert program to seed civilian industries with extraterrestrial technologies to his superior, Lt General Arthur Trudeau. Corso wrote that from the period 1947-58 that "military R & D was greatly disorganized" and that it was under his superior, General Trudeau, that the "Golden Age of R & D (1958-1963) blossomed.[605] Due to competing government agencies, Corso claimed that "R & D data, stemming from areas 'out of this world' had to be carefully hidden and the information kept among a select few."[606] As a former intelligence officer who served with Trudeau, former head of the Army's Military Intelligence (G-2), Corso was entrusted with extraterrestrial technologies to seed into civilian industries. He likely performed this covert function with the same single minded focus that exemplified his highly distinguished military career. Nevertheless, Corso consistently laid the chief credit for the covert extraterrestrial technology seeding program with Trudeau, and not himself. Nevertheless, he is assailed by critics for exemplifying hubris. For example, Brad Sparks claims in his 'expose': "Corso just can't resist putting himself at the center stage of great events of history, courted by the big names such as Robert Kennedy and his "old friend" J. Edgar Hoover (Corso's "other book" is called "I Walked With Giants"), and he is ever the powerful hero."[607]

Corso's critics have attempted to lay the charge of hubris on Corso without appreciating the implications of the unique circumstances that had placed in such a sensitive role. As the trusted personal assistant to the head of the Army R & D program, Corso was in the precise position to play his part in a covert program that could have had an enormous effect on human society. That is a statement of fact supported by documentation, rather than hubris which is based on the conjecture of critics. Consequently, the ad hominem attacks on Corso's reflections on the significance of his historical role in a secret Army program to seed civilian industries with extraterrestrial technologies are at best a distraction. At worst, such ad hominem attacks are more evidence of Corso's critics crossing the Rubicon between objective criticism and debunking .

6. Did Philip Corso Witness an EBE while Stationed at Fort Riley, Kansas?

Corso claimed that while on duty at Fort Riley Kansas, on July 6, 1947 he saw an Extraterrestrial Biological Entity (EBE) being shipped from Roswell, New Mexico to what is now Wright Patterson Air Force Base in Dayton, Ohio. In *The Day After Roswell* he described how he was informed about a mysterious shipment from Fort Bliss containing remains "from some accident out in New Mexico", Corso wrote:

> Whatever they'd crated this way, it *was* a coffin, but not like any coffin I'd seen before. The contents, enclosed in a thick glass container, were submerged in a thick light blue liquid … the object was floating, actually suspended, and not sitting on the bottom with a fluid over top, and it was soft and shiny as the underbelly of a fish. At first I thought it was a dead child they were shipping somewhere. But this was no child. It was a four-foot human-shaped figure with arms … thin legs and feet, and an oversized incandescent light bulb-shaped head that looked like it was floating over a balloon gondola for a chin.[608]

Corso's military records give credibility to his EBE story. He was stationed at Fort Riley Kansas from 21 April 1947 - 12 May 1950; with the rank of Major. Events he described as the alleged duty officer on the night the EBE body arrived at Fort Riley en route to Wright Patterson AFB; are corroborated, in part, by his military record.

Corso's story has been challenged by critics such as Stanton

Friedman. Friedman has questioned whether something as important as an EBE would have been shipped overland from Roswell Army Air Force Base to Dayton, Ohio. Friedman writes:

> I personally don't understand why the body would have been sent by truck (without a 24-hour guard) rather than plane, and why it came from Ft. Bliss which is Southwest of Roswell though it was HQ for the rocket scientists at White Sands Missile Range. Corso spoke of Rte. 40 being the only major EW highway in 1947. But Ft. Riley is West of Manhattan, Kansas, and well North of Highway 40, and not on the most direct route to Wright Field."[609]

Friedman is mistaken about Ft Riley's accessibility to Route 40, and misleading with his statement that Fort Riley is not the most direct route to Wright Patterson Air Field. As historic maps demonstrate (see Route 40 map), Route 40 was indeed the main thoroughfare for travel between the East and West coast – from Atlantic City to San

Francisco.[610] Second, Ft Riley is actually situated very close to Route 40 and is described as part of the historic Smokey Hill trail followed by U.S. Route 40: "From Fort Riley, Kansas to Denver, the Smoky Hill/Butterfield Trail was a route for both military and commercial efforts."[611] Fort Riley is situated close to Junction City, which is exactly where US Route 40 has historically passed.[612] For the majority of the State of Kansas (from Oakley Kansas, through Junction City and onward, to Kansas City, Route 40 coincides with Interstate 70; exactly where Fort Riley is situated.[613]

Consequently, Friedman's argument that Fort Riley lies "well North of Highway 40" is a gross error. Furthermore, Fort Riley was used as the key military staging post for maneuvers between the East and West coast, as corroborated by a report that President Eisenhower, when serving as a Captain in the pre-WWII era "found his command bogged down in spring mud near Ft. Riley, Kansas, while on a coast-to-coast maneuver."[614] So Fort Riley was indeed on the most direct route between the East and West coast, though not on the most direct route from Fort Bliss.

Friedman asks why the convoy came from Fort Bliss which is southwest of Roswell, rather than having proceeded directly north to Route 40 and onwards to Fort Riley and Wright Patterson AFB, the more direct route. While he acknowledges that Fort Bliss was the HQ of German scientists working at White Sands Missile base, he fails to identify the obvious answer for why the UFO artifacts were transported there. The German Scientists, experts in advanced aviation technologies and working on the stockpile of former Nazi V2 rockets at White Sands, were called upon to identify the artifacts from the New Mexico crashes at Roswell/Corona and 'Plains of St Augustine'. Their knowledge of advanced Nazi aviation systems would have been vital in determining the origins of the Roswell crash material. This is suggested in a leaked Majestic Document: "The inability of the German scientists from Fort Bliss and White Sands Proving Ground to make a positive identification of a secret German V weapon out of these discs."[615] Friedman is correct however that the more direct route from Fort Bliss could have included another route, at least part of the way, such as Route 66 which was at the time another major East-West corridor (see map below).

If the convoy did come from Fort Bliss as Corso suggests, why didn't it take the most direct route north to US 66, then East to St Louis Missouri, then on to US 40 for the remainder of the trip to the Wright Patterson? One answer might be that Fort Riley was a major military staging post for East-West travel as demonstrated by Eisenhower's pre-WWII military maneuvers. Another is that Route 66 may have not been suitable for such a sensitive military cargo. Fort Riley undoubtedly offered a number of benefits as a major military staging post and would have been a logical choice for the long road trip from Fort Bliss to Wright Patterson.

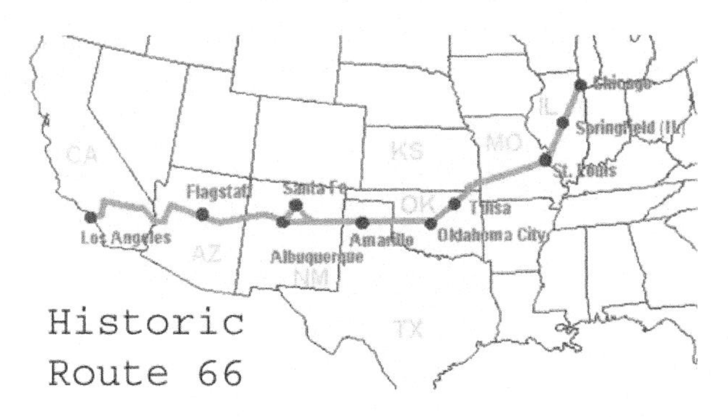

Friedman has also questioned Corso on the dates of the alleged incident Fort Riley and wrote:

> I asked how he knew the Kansas date was July 6 ... Was it notes, a diary? He was evasive... For me the simplest explanation is that the … background descriptions came from Crash at Corona .... The bodies from the Plains might have been picked up by July 6, but wouldn't they far more likely have gone to one of the nearby military bases, and either been studied there or flown out?

The date provided by Corso is consistent with what is known about the flying saucer crash that allegedly was scattered over two sites: Roswell/Corona and the Plains of St Augustine. According to various sources, both sites were independently discovered on July 3.[616] While only vehicle debris was found on the farm of Mac Brazel, four EBE bodies were allegedly found at the second crash site at St Augustine. This is partly confirmed by the Eisenhower

Briefing Document that refers to two crash sites and states that "four small human-like beings had apparently ejected from the craft at some point before it exploded."[617] Friedman posits that the bodies from the Plains of Augustin could have been picked up by July 6 as Corso claims, but suggests that it would have been more reasonable to have them studied at the nearby military base and/or flown out. As mentioned earlier, Fort Bliss was a logical choice given that it was the HQ for German scientists and others working on the White Sands rocket program. As for why the bodies weren't flown from Fort Bliss rather than trucked overland, safety concerns might have dictated that a land route was preferable to air travel. The crash of a truck would lead to minimal damage to an EBE in storage whereas an air crash may have led to the complete destruction of this valuable cargo. Indeed, it may have been decided to send the EBEs by both air and road since Corso claims to have seen only one body.

Overall, in his criticism of Corso's story concerning the dead EBE Friedman is mistaken and misleading in a number of ways. First, he makes a basic mistake concerning the proximity of Fort Riley to Route 40. Second, he is misleading in terms of Route 40 being the most direct route to Wright Patterson Air Field. Third, he overlooks a very plausible explanation for why retrieved artifacts from Roswell/Corona and Plains of St Augustine were taken to Fort Bliss. Finally, he overlooks why Fort Riley was a logical choice as stopping off point for a road convoy starting from Fort Bliss and traveling to Wright Patterson Air Field. Consequently, Friedman's claim that Corso "almost certainly" concocted the Fort Riley incident, has no merit. Friedman has again strayed from objective criticism into the debunking of Corso's claims.

7. Did Corso Confront the CIA while serving at the Foreign Technology Desk?

In his detailed 'expose' released on the internet in August 1998, Brad Sparks points to a number of inconsistencies in Corso's book and concludes that these "prove Corso to be a rank literary hoaxer."[618] One of the most important inconsistencies, in Spark's view, is Corso's description of an alleged confrontation with the former head of the CIA's covert operations Frank Wisner some time after Corso began working under General Trudeau at the Pentagon, in May 1961. In his book, Corso described the incident where he walked into Wisner's office and demanded that he put an end CIA agents following Corso. This had also, according to Corso, occurred earlier while he served in the Eisenhower administration:

> I told Wiesner [sic] to his face that yesterday was the last day I would walk around Washington without a handgun. And I put my .45 automatic on his desk. I said if I saw his tail on me tomorrow, they'd find him in the Potomac the next day with two bloody holes for eyes...Wiesner said, "You won't do that, Colonel." But I reminded him very pointedly that I knew where all his bodies were buried, the people he'd gotten killed through his own ineptitude ... I'd tell his story to everyone I knew in Congress. Wiesner backed down.[619]

Sparks writes:

> Problem is that Frank G. Wisner (not "Wiesner") had been hospitalized and replaced as top CIA covert operator nearly three years earlier in August 1958.... Worse still, Wisner's office was not even in the U.S. in 1961 but was in London. Wisner had been sent overseas to take the less demanding post of CIA Chief of Station in London on August 6, 1959, but was recalled from London in the spring of 1962 and resigned from the CIA entirely in August 1962.

It is very likely that in the communication between Corso and his co-writer, William Birnes, the precise date of the alleged confrontation encounter in Spring 1962, was mistakenly implied to be mid-1961 when Wisner was based in London. It is conceivable that it would have taken some time for Corso to realize he was being followed after taking up his new position at the Foreign Technology Desk, and to determine the person responsible for him being followed. Wisner knew Corso from the time of the latter's service in the Eisenhower administration, where they were antagonists. It is very likely either that Wisner played a role in what was occurring with Corso, or possible that Corso mistakenly assumed this to be the case. The important point is that Wisner was stationed in Washington DC at the same time as Corso was at the Foreign Technology desk. This makes it possible that the meeting actually occurred in Spring/Summer 1962, and not during mid 1961, as implied in the book.

Sparks also points out that Corso's claim that Wisner committed suicide in London in 1963, was incorrect and that Wisner actually took his own life at his family farm in Maryland in October, 1965. Spark's concludes: "these are not minor errors of abstract historical facts. These are stories of Corso's own alleged personal experiences involving supposed major episodes in his career and in world history."[620] The major problem with Spark's criticism is that the circumstances of Wisner's death were abstract facts that Corso was attempting to recall after more than 30 years. As for his alleged confrontation, Corso quite likely got the dates wrong, but that doesn't preclude the circumstances and dialogue at the confrontation that he described.

Sparks ignores the historical facts supporting Corso's testimony. Wisner was a former antagonist at the CIA who headed the CIA's covert programs, while Corso was simultaneously worked with Army Military Intelligence (G2) under Lt General Arthur Trudeau. This was the time of a major confrontation between Allen Dulles (CIA Director) and Trudeau where the latter was relieved from his command. The details of this conflict are still to be fully disclosed but there is no doubt that Trudeau still enjoyed the support of the US Army that 'promoted' him in 1958 to his new position as head of Army Research and Development. Corso subsequently served under Trudeau in a sensitive position with the Foreign Technology Desk, which the CIA would have had interest in monitoring. Finally, from Spring 1962 until August 1962, both Wisner and Corso were in Washington DC at the same time, a fact Sparks ignores.

In conclusion, Sparks' critique of Corso is mainly focused on historical details that the latter gets wrong in his book. This may be entirely due to the way in which Corso communicated with his co-writer, William Birnes, or insufficient details in his personal notes or his recollections. At the time of collaborating with Birnes in writing of *The Day After Roswell*, Corso was approximately 80 years of age and his health was deteriorating. He certainly would have been tested to get all the details right in his recollection and communications with Birnes, given the decades that had elapsed since his experiences. Sparks inclusion of the Wisner story as an example of Corso being a "rank literary hoaxer" is further evidence of Sparks unwillingness to consider alternative explanations for inconsistencies in Corso's claims. In not considering the alternative explanation that Corso got some dates and details wrong in his recollections due to poor health and/or sketchy notes, Sparks is once again crossing the Rubicon from objective criticism into debunking.

8. Was Corso Head of the White Sand's Missile Firing Range?

Corso has been accused by Dr Randle of embellishing his military record in a number of ways one of which concerns Corso's service at White Sands Missile Range. Randle says the following about Corso's testimony at a press conference in 1997:

> I watched him at the Roswell press conference where he claimed that he had been the Commander at the White Sands Missile Range. Not that he had been a Commander (of a Battalion) but the Commander. I have watched the tape dozens of times, and he clearly claims that he was "The Commander". The website of the White Sands Missile Range lists all the commanding officers and Corso is not among them. Again, this is not a mistake that can be blamed on Birnes.[621]

In his original notes Corso described himself as being "in command of the Army's Missile Firing Range at Red Canyon, New Mexico, part of the White Sands Proving Grounds."[622] In his book, he claims that he gained his command as a result of a promise made by President Eisenhower:

> Ike had once promised me a command of my own when I returned from Korea and was posted to the White House. And in 1957 the opportunity came up, a juicy assignment at a high-security base with the coveted green tabs and all the trappings: train and command an antiaircraft battalion to use the army's most secret new surface-to-air missile.[623]

In both his book and original notes Corso clearly is claiming that he was the commander of a battalion based at White Sands Missile Range. His military record confirms that in June 1957 he began a new position as Battalion Commander at White Sands Proving Ground. His military record supports the claims Corso made in his book and original notes.

In his criticism of Corso, Randle refers to the 1997 Roswell interview where Corso referred to himself as "the Commander" rather than "a Commander" at White Sands Missile Range. Randle goes on to conclude that Corso was deliberately embellishing his military record. Randle doesn't provide any transcript of what Corso precisely said and neither does he provide the full context for the latter's comments. While Randle claims to have repeatedly listened to the interview, he doesn't provide the context of Corso's discussion where he may have been referring to himself as "the Commander" of the missile battalion at White Sands, rather than "the Commander of White Sands". If the former, then Randle is at fault for not correctly identifying Corso's intention in making the comment and the correct context for Corso's comments. If Corso did refer to himself as "the Commander" at White Sands then he may have simply made a mistake in correctly identifying his former position, rather than trying to deliberately embellish his record. In 1997, Corso was 82 and his health was quickly deteriorating. His detailed recollection of events and positions would have been questionable in an interview. Yet in his book and original notes, there is no ambiguity here; Corso correctly identified himself as the Battalion Commander at White Sands, rather than the Commander of White Sands.

In making his claim that Corso was embellishing his military record, based on an interview, rather than the more precise original notes and book that described his position, Randle is going too far in his criticism. In the worst case scenario, Corso may have simply made a mistake in the interview and Randle is correct to point out the inconsistency. Yet this possible mistake is something Randle has not proved and merely asserted from his recollection. More importantly, Randle is claiming that Corso was deliberately embellishing his military record. Randle needs to come up with more instances where Corso is repeating such an error, rather than in one isolated interview. Consequently, Randle's claim that Corso deliberately embellished his military record is not an objective criticism, but a form of debunking.

9. Was Corso 'Unreliable' as claimed by the FBI?

An FBI report on Col Corso contained particularly ungenerous depictions of him as "shifty-eyed", a "rat", and "a parasite". These depictions stemmed from his involvement in rumors that Lee Harvey Oswald was a paid informant of the FBI, and for his earlier efforts in seeking to identify Fabian Socialists in various government agencies.[624] Even Corso's former boss, Lt General Trudeau who headed the Army's Military Intelligence (G-2) during the 1950's, received disparaging comments in the FBI Report for his and Corso's role in seeking to identify Fabian Socialists while at G-2 and at Army Research and Development. In 1955, Trudeau and Corso had compiled a list of alleged Fabian Socialists and passed this list on to different government agencies. This led to a serious confrontation between G-2 and the CIA that culminated in Trudeau's eventual replacement at G-2. Relevant passages from the FBI Report demonstrate the remarkable hostility towards both Corso and Trudeu on the part of both the FBI and the CIA in 1965:

> From your interview with Corso on 2-10-64, you got the definite impression that he was a rather shifty-eyed individual who fancied himself a great intelligence expert.... Trudeau has a fetish about security and intelligence work and cannot keep his fingers out of that area ... The Director [J. Edgar Hoover] noted: "Corso is a rat" ... [the] CIA characterized Corso as a parasite who has never produced any intelligence through his own efforts, but who has profited from information developed by hundreds of dedicated Government agents and investigators.[625]

Finally, in rejecting Corso's efforts in investigating the relationship between the FBI and Oswald, the FBI dismissively referred to the "tremendous amount of work his gossip had caused the FBI."[626]

The above criticisms are remarkable given Trudeau's military intelligence experience as the former chief of G-2, and Corso's role in some of the most sensitive committees in the

Eisenhower Administration involved in covert operations and counter-intelligence. Clearly, Corso and Trudeau had created powerful enemies in various government agencies for their efforts in identifying 'Fabian Socialists and 'communist sympathizers'. As part of a routine security check, the FBI passed on this damaging information to the Immigration and Nationalities sub-committee of the House of Representatives in 1965 that was considering employing Corso. The Report effectively stymied his application. Some parts of the classified report were even leaked by the FBI to a reporter who wrote a story on Corso being blackballed by the FBI.

The background of the FBI's damming report was due not only to Corso's work with Trudeau in forwarding a list of alleged Fabian Socialists in 1955, but also his accusation that Lee Harvey Oswald was a paid FBI informant. Corso had been told by a CIA informer, later identified as Frank Hand, that Oswald had FBI connections.[627] Corso refused to divulge his CIA source. This led to strained relations with the FBI who demanded to know who was spreading such rumors. The FBI was furious that Corso would not reveal his sources. On behalf of Senator Richard B. Russell, a senate member of the Warren Commission, Corso was investigating the effectiveness of the Warren Commission's own inquiry into the Kennedy assassination. Corso and Russell were seeking to discover evidence of a possible Cuban/Communist role in the assassination. The FBI strenuously denied any connection with Oswald and struggled to end rumors suggesting otherwise. Indeed, the final report of the Warren Commission explicitly discussed Oswald's being an FBI agent/informant but concluded insufficient evidence existed to support this.[628] The FBI was acutely aware of Corso's belief that the FBI had Oswald on its payroll. The FBI therefore had a direct interest in portraying Corso in a negative light, and to prevent his appointment to any Congressional committee.

The FBI assigned J. Edgar Hoover's aide, Cartha DeRoach, who performed special assignments for Hoover, to the Corso case. This was evidence that Corso was a significant player in the Warren Commission investigation and that the FBI took him very seriously. Consequently, the FBI report on Corso needs to be seen as the FBI's effort to tarnish an individual they believed directly threatened the reputation of the FBI. In seizing upon the FBI criticism of Corso as 'unreliable' Sparks, Randle and other critics suggest that this 'impartial' criticism casts doubt on his later UFO testimony and supports their view that Corso 'lied'. This ignores the context for the FBI's damning report on Corso, and ignores the direct interest the FBI had in discrediting Corso due to his investigation of the FBI-Oswald connection and his earlier work at G-2.

In a detailed response to accusations that Corso had lied and the FBI report was evidence of this, Alfred Lehmberg demonstrates that Corso certainly made mistakes in his testimony but this did not amount to lying.[629] In not revealing the FBI's interest in discrediting Corso, Corso's critics perpetuated the character assassination unleashed by the FBI. Corso had an impact on the Warren Commission investigation into the Kennedy Assassination and directly threatened the reputation of the FBI. Once again, in not considering the alternative explanation that the FBI report was slanted to discredit Corso, his critics have crossed the Rubicon from objective criticism into debunking.

10. Was Colonel Corso Promoted to Full Colonel Upon his retirement?

In *The Day After Roswell,* Corso claims that he "was a lieutenant colonel in the army heading up the Foreign Technology desk."[630] His military record verifies that he did have this rank while heading up the Foreign Technology desk, and that this was his final rank upon leaving active service. Corso was a US Army Reserve Officer who had been on active service for 21 years until his retirement in 1963. The Second World War had led to the greatest expansion of the US Army in history and many Reserve officers such as Corso continued to serve on extended active duty after the Second World War. There were differences in the promotion process for Reserve officers as compared to Regular Army officers, making it more difficult for the former to rise through the ranks. In an effort to assist Reserve officers, Congress had passed the Reserve Officer Promotion Act in 1954. According to Major David Cannon: "career Reserve officers on extended active duty did not receive equal consideration for promotion as regular officers. So to make amends, the Reserve Officer Promotion Act allowed these officers to receive a final promotion to the next rank on the day of their retirement."[631] Under the Promotion Act, Corso was eligible and apparently received a promotion upon his retirement, to redress the lack of promotion opportunities he enjoyed while on extended active service. Since this promotion was not part of Corso's active service as recorded on his DA 66, the record of the promotion is likely to have been documented elsewhere, according to Maj General David Bockel (ret.) who is currently the Deputy Executive Director of the Reserve Officers Association.[632]

The main critic of Col Corso's claim that he was promoted upon retirement is Dr Randle who is currently a Major in the Iowa National Guard. Given Randle's military background, his criticism has carried much weight. This is what he claims with regard to Corso's alleged promotion to full Colonel:

> First, when asked why the cover of his book said "Colonel" rather than "Lieutenant-Colonel", Corso replied that he had been promoted to Colonel in the Reserve so the title was appropriate. I won't mention here that publishers often make assumptions and the mistake could have been blamed on them. Instead, Corso chose to lie about it. His record clearly indicates that the highest rank he held was Lieutenant-Colonel. (And I won't even comment about how he was a Major in 1945 and retired in the early 1960s as only a lieutenant colonel).[633]

Now there are two points to be raised here. First, Randle claims that Corso lied since his DA 66 doesn't mention the promotion. Second, Randle makes a disparaging comment over the fact that while Corso had achieved the rank of Major in 1945 (the actual date was 1947), he retired in 1963 only one rank higher. On the surface, this appears to be a rather pedestrian military career and casts doubts on some of Corso's claims to have been in charge of very sensitive military projects. The problem with Randle's criticism is that he fails to mention the more difficult promotion opportunities for Reserve officers on extended active service. More to the point, he fails to mention the existence of the Reserve Officer Promotions Act. Under this Act, Corso would have been automatically promoted upon retirement, but this would not necessarily have been recorded on his DA 66.[634] Rather than the absence of any record of Corso's alleged promotion to full Colonel on his DA 66 conclusively showing that Corso lied; the absence instead shows how Randle fails to consider alternative explanations. Randle jumps to damming conclusions regarding Corso's claims that reflect Randle's own prejudices. So once again, the failure to consider alternative explanations is evidence that Randle has crossed the Rubicon from objective criticism into debunking.

11. Did Col Corso deceive Senator Strom Thurmond?

In the original hardcover version of *The Day After Roswell*, a preface by Strom Thurmond appeared. Subsequently, the preface was withdrawn allegedly due to the Senator Thurmond not having been aware that it would appear in a book about UFOs and Roswell. A number of Corso's critics have seized upon this incident as evidence that Corso is unethical. For example Randle argued back in May 2001:

> "Senator Thurmond was angry about the introduction because Corso had pulled the old bait and switch on him. Thurmond demanded the introduction be pulled because the book wasn't the one Corso had said that he was going to write. What does that say about the integrity of the man?[635]

Similarly, Stanton Friedman wrote in 1997: "Certainly there are some ethical questions about the use of an introduction by Senator Strom Thurmond, now in his 90s, written earlier for a memoirs book that had definitely been planned by Corso."[636]

Corso's critics have repeated this criticism that since Thurmond wasn't aware that Corso was going to use his preface for a book on Roswell and UFOs, that Corso lacked integrity. However this criticism was refuted by the reprinting of a release signed by Strom Thurmond in the October 2001 edition of *UFO Magazine*. Here is how French UFO researcher Gildas Bourdais declared the significance of the release and the earlier criticisms that Corso had deceived Thurmond:

> The UFO magazine article by Don Ecker shows the reproduction of the release signed by Senator Strom Thurmond, giving to Lieutenant Colonel Corso the

> "irrevocable right and permission to use and to publish the material described below, in any and all editions of the book presently entitled Roswell Book..." So, this authorization, dated 2-7-97, clearly referred to Roswell, although it was not the final title, 'The Day After Roswell'. He knew that Corso was writing on Roswell![637]

The fact that Thurmond had signed a release explicitly mentioning Corso's book on Roswell refutes the criticism that Corso "had pulled the old bait and switch" on Thurmond as Randle contends. Despite Thurmond's release having become public knowledge in October 2001, Randle nevertheless continued to claim that Corso had deceived Thurmond and therefore lacked integrity. For example, Randle wrote in December 2005, "Corso pulled a bait and switch on the foreword, which is not very ethical."[638] In the case of Friedman, he never replied to Bourdais' public notice of UFO Magazine's reprinting of Thurmond's signed release, and never retracted his criticism that Corso had "ethical questions" over the preface episode.

The above demonstrates Randle's own lack of ethics in continuing to essentially 'defame' Corso by repeating a criticism that had been conclusively shown to be baseless. Similarly, an ethical response from Friedman would have been to acknowledge his own error in raising "ethical questions" over Corso, but to date this has not occurred. So we have outstanding criticisms by Randle and Friedman against Corso on the basis of an allegation that was shown to be baseless. This demonstrates the unethical lengths to which veteran UFO researchers have gone in attempting to debunk Corso. This conclusively demonstrates the clear prejudices of Randle and Friedman when it comes to critiquing Corso, their lack of objectivity and efforts to ignore evidence that is contrary to their stated views that Corso willfully misled or lied in his testimony.

Conclusions

In bringing this chapter to an end it is worth recalling what I originally described as 'objective criticism' based on the work of Dr Haiash:

> … one who practices the method of suspended judgment, engages in rational and dispassionate reasoning as exemplified by the scientific method, shows willingness to consider alternative explanations without prejudice based on prior beliefs, and who seeks out evidence and carefully scrutinizes its validity.[639]

It is this willingness to "consider alternative explanations without prejudice" that helps identify the conceptual Rubicon between 'objective criticism' and 'debunking'. My analysis of Corso's critics shows that they routinely dismiss alternative explanations for a number of inconsistencies in Corso's claims, and for mistakes he made. In analyzing numerous claims made by Corso and subjecting these to detailed critique, they ignore the common sense view that mistakes and inconsistencies can easily be explained by the advanced age and deteriorating health of Corso in the twelve month period from the publication of his book in July 1997 to his death in July 1998, at the age of 83. While Corso predictably focused on communicating the substance of his experiences and information, the details would have become increasingly blurred as poor health set in. While it is desirable to have details correct when discussing the extraordinary events Corso disclosed, it's important to keep in mind that Corso was recalling events that occurred more than three decades earlier. It is very likely he made mistakes in recalling details when recounting incidents and positions in his book and interviews. This is especially the case given the level of sensitive classified information he was revealing and the obvious concern not to reveal anything that might negatively impact on U.S. national security.

In this analysis of Corso's critics what emerges is a pattern whereby they consistently focus on any inconsistence or mistakes made by Corso in his books and interviews, and suggest that these make Corso unreliable as a witness. In dismissing alternative explanations for why Corso may have made mistakes such as the correct position titles for his appointments as a 'staff member' and not a 'member' of the NSC system under Eisenhower; as a 'battalion commander' and not "the Commander" at the White Sands Missile Range; Corso's critics are not displaying objective criticism but are engaging in debunking. Furthermore, in making erroneous statements in discussing possible routes taken by an army convey traveling from New Mexico to Wright Patterson AFB, why Fort Bliss was a logical choice for the Roswell/Corona/St Augustine wreckage, and why overland travel was a sensible security precaution, critics such as Friedman display a lack of objectivity. Brad Sparks' overheated rhetoric over Corso's mistakes in recalling the correct details concerning his meeting and the demise of a former CIA antagonist in 1961-62, displays Sparks lack of objectivity. The references by Randle, Sparks and others to a critical FBI report of Corso, ignore Corso's role in investigating a link between the FBI and Lee Harvey Oswald on behalf of one of the Warren Commission's members, and how this directly threatened the FBI's reputation. The final episode concerning Corso's alleged deception of Thurmond has been shown to be baseless. Yet Randle continues to regurgitate this criticism as though it were valid, and Friedman has not publicly withdrawn his comments that the Thurmond issue raised 'ethical questions' about Corso.

In arguing that Major Kevin Randle, Stanton Friedman and Brad Sparks have routinely crossed the Rubicon from objective criticism into debunking in their criticisms of Corso, I have cited Dr Haiash's prescription that science works by assessing a range of alternative explanations for any phenomenon under scientific investigation. This is no less the case for social science phenomenon such as the extraordinary claims of whistleblower testimony, and possible inconsistencies and mistakes in these claims. In routinely ignoring alternative explanations for the inconsistencies and mistakes made by Corso; Randle, Friedman and Sparks have engaged in what appears to be the deliberate debunking of a very important whistleblower. In debunking Corso, each to varying degrees, have displayed a remarkable degree of prejudice concerning the usefulness of Corso's testimony. This prejudice has led to them concluding that Corso is a literary hoaxer, a liar and/or a fraud.

The above three critics of Lt Col Philip Corso have willfully hampered an objective examination of Corso's substantive views concerning his role in disseminating UFOs information by deliberately focusing on minor details, inconsistencies or mistakes in his testimony. Furthermore, these veteran UFO researchers with collectively over 100 years of UFO field work experience, have deliberately ignored evidence that supported Corso's claims as exemplified in the Thurmond preface issue. At the very least, each of these researchers deserves to be censored for their willful debunking of Philip Corso, and for the great harm they have done to his reputation, and to setting back UFO research for years by ignoring the important testimony offered by Corso. While seeking to cast doubt on Corso's integrity, what these critics have instead achieved is casting doubt on their own integrity as objective researchers of the UFO phenomenon.

I referred earlier to the debunking methods that had been recommended by the CIA sponsored Robertson Panel to diminish public interest in flying saucer reports. Since at least 1953, the CIA through its extensive network of agents, assets and informers has been actively debunking reports of extraterrestrial vehicles and life. In this effort, the CIA has been assisted by other intelligence agencies to diminish interest in extraterrestrial life in what I have called elsewhere, Galactic COINTELPRO.[640] The fact that veteran UFO researchers are using debunking methods against a prominent military whistleblower does raise the disturbing possibility that one or more may be associated with the CIA's historic debunking program. If so, that suggests that the CIA has infiltrated the UFO community and recruited assets to debunk important whistleblowers concerning extraterrestrial life or technology. Based on their willful debunking methods, I believe that one or more of Corso's critics indeed fall into this category.

Corso's credentials have been well documented. All UFO researchers would concede he is a vitally important whistleblower, without necessarily accepting all his claims. Nevertheless, given the available documentation substantiating many of Corso's claims in terms of his career positions and responsibilities, there is good reason to suppose that much of his testimony concerning extraterrestrial technology and EBEs is based on real events. His testimony clearly shows that the extent to which various government and military entities have formulated and implemented various policies regarding to extraterrestrial life. While there are certainly inconsistencies and mistakes in Corso's testimony, these largely concern details that have little to do with the substance of his claims that he was in charge of a covert Pentagon project to seed civilian industries with extraterrestrial technologies, and that he witnessed an EBE from the 1947 Roswell crash.

Corso's documented background inspires confidence in the credibility of his testimony. In attempting to debunk Corso in an effort to discredit his testimony, Corso's critics deserve to be admonished for distracting UFO researchers from the task of identifying the truth in Corso's remarkable testimony, and for other significant whistleblower testimonies. What remains to be done is a truly objective and impartial analysis of Corso's testimony, and its implications concerning a high level governmental cover up of UFO and EBE information. More importantly, by admitting past mistakes in evaluating the testimony of whistleblowers such as Col Corso, critics of many of the whistleblowers examined in this book, can play a more constructive role. This becomes especially important as government policies on extraterrestrial life are exposed due to the testimonies of individuals willing to stop forward and risk reputations, careers and finances in disclosing what they witnessed.

ENDNOTES: CHAPTER ELEVEN

[572] The book was written with the assistance of William Birnes. Philip Corso, *The Day After Roswell* (Simon and Schuster, 1997).
[573] See Stanton Friedman, http://www.virtuallystrange.net/ufo/updates/2005/may/m19-006.shtml; Dr Kevin Randle, http://www.virtuallystrange.net/ufo/updates/2005/may/m18-006.shtml ; and Brad Sparks; http://www.virtuallystrange.net/ufo/updates/2005/aug/m04-007.shtml [Note: In 2007 the previously free access to the UFO Updates Archive changed to a subscriber only service.]
[574] See http://www.cufon.org/cufon/corso_da66.htm. * I thank Paola Harris and Jan Aldrich for forwarding FOIA information available on Dr Phillip Corso which assisted me greatly in assessing the validity of Corso's testimony and criticisms made against him.
[575] Philip Corso, *L'Alba di una Nuova Era: I Segreti Alieni Nascosti dal Pentagono*, tr. Maurizio Baiata (Pendragon, 2003). I thank Paola Harris for generously giving me a copy of Maurizio Baiata's Italian version of Corso's original notes.
[576] Cited online at: http://www.ufoskeptic.org.
[577] Cited from online version of Robertson Panel at: http://www.cufon.org/cufon/robertdod.htm.
[578] *The Day After Roswell*, 62.
[579] *The Day After Roswell*, 38.
[580] *L'Alba Di Una Nuova Era,* 127.
[581] *The Day After Roswell*, 2.
[582] See: http://foia.fbi.gov/corso_philip_j/corso_philip_j_part01.pdf.
[583] See: http://www.ufocom.org/UfocomS/CorsoAffidavit.htm.
[584] The debate involved a series of posts on the UFO Updates forum during May 2005. See: http://www.virtuallystrange.net/ufo/updates/2005/may/m12-001.shtml.
[585] See: http://www.fas.org/irp/offdocs/NSChistory.htm#Eisenhower.
[586] Cited online at: http://www.fas.org/irp/offdocs/NSChistory.htm#Eisenhower.
[587] Cited online at: http://www.archives.gov/research/guide-fed-records/groups/273.html.
[588] Discussion occurred on UFO Updates in May 2005 and is recorded online at: http://www.virtuallystrange.net/ufo/updates/2005/may/m16-001.shtml.
[589] Cited online at: http://groups.yahoo.com/group/exopolitics/message/220.
[590] Cited online at: http://www.cia.gov/csi/kent_csi/docs/v03i4a05p_0003.htm.
[591] Cited online at: http://www.virtuallystrange.net/ufo/updates/1998/aug/m11-001.shtml.
[592] See: http://www.virtuallystrange.net/ufo/updates/1997/jan/m17-016.shtml & http://www.virtuallystrange.net/ufo/updates/1997/feb/m25-007.shtml.
[593] See: http://www.virtuallystrange.net/ufo/updates/1997/jan/m17-016.shtml.

[594] *L'Alba Di Una Nuova Era,* 31.
[595] See Stanton Friedman, *Top Secret/Majic* (2005) 56-85.
[596] "Majestic Twelve Project: 1st Annual Report," The Majestic Documents, ed., Robert Woods, 110
[597] Cited in *Foreign Relations of the United States*, 1964-1968, vol. XII, Western Europe, pp. XXXI-XXXV, April 16, 2001. Available online at: http://www.fas.org/sgp/advisory/statc/covert.html.
[598] *The Day After Roswell*, 1. For Randle's criticism go to: http://www.virtuallystrange.net/ufo/updates/2005/dec/m13-004.shtml. For Friedman's criticism go to: http://www.geocities.com/Area51/Lair/7676/stanlog.htm
[599] *L'Alba Di Una Nuova Era,* 29.
[600] *L'Alba Di Una Nuova Era,* 31.
[601] Private email from Col Alexander on May 20, 2005.
[602] *L'Alba Di Una Nuova Era,* 44.
[603] Cited online at: http://www.v-j-enterprises.com/sfcorso.html.
[604] Cited online at: http://www.virtuallystrange.net/ufo/updates/1998/aug/m11-001.shtml.
[605] *L'Alba Di Una Nuova Era,* 15.
[606] *L'Alba Di Una Nuova Era,* 16.
[607] Cited online at: http://www.virtuallystrange.net/ufo/updates/1998/aug/m11-001.shtml .
[608] Corso, *The Day After Roswell*, 34
[609] Stanton Friedman, "A Review of Col. Philip J. Corso's Book: "The Day After Roswell" (1997): http://www.v-j-enterprises.com/sfcorso.html .
[610] http://www.route40.net/index.shtml .
[611] Cited online at: http://www.route40.net/history/index.shtml .
[612] See http://www.route40.net/history/40n-40s.shtml .
[613] US 40 joins I-70 across Kansas as described depicted here: http://www.cityofatchison.com/nationalhighwaysystem9d.jpg .
[614] Cited online at: http://www.route66.com/66History.html .
[615] "Air Accident Report on "Flying Disc" aircraft near the White Sands Proving Ground, New Mexico," *The Majestic Documents*, ed., Robert and Ryan Wood, 25. Available online at: http://209.132.68.98/pdf/airaccidentreport.pdf .
[616] Kevin Randle & Donald Schmidt, *UFO Crash at Roswell* (Avon Books, 1991) 28-32.
[617] "Eisenhower Briefing Document," *The Majestic Documents*, ed., Robert and Ryan Wood, 129. Available online at: http://209.132.68.98/pdf/eisenhower_briefing.pdf .
[618] Sparks, "Colonel Philip Corso and William Birnes' Bestselling Book Exposed as a Hoax!" http://www.virtuallystrange.net/ufo/updates/1998/aug/m11-001.shtml.
[619] *The Day After Roswell,* 94.
[620] Cited online at: http://www.virtuallystrange.net/ufo/updates/1998/aug/m11-001.shtml .
[621] http://www.virtuallystrange.net/ufo/updates/2001/may/m14-024.shtml .

[622] *L'Alba di una Nuova Era,* 39.
[623] *The Day After Roswell*, 38.
[624] FBI records on Col Philip Corso, http://foia.fbi.gov/foiaindex/pjcorso.htm .
[625] See M.A. Jones memo to Mr DeLoach, November 2, 1965, http://foia.fbi.gov/foiaindex/pjcorso.htm .
[626] See M.A. Jones memo to Mr DeLoach, November 2, 1965, http://foia.fbi.gov/foiaindex/pjcorso.htm .
[627] For discussion about Frank Hand and the FBI files on Corso see: http://www.virtuallystrange.net/ufo/updates/2001/may/m06-018.shtml .
[628] See Warren Commission Report available at: http://www.archives.gov/research/jfk/warren-commission-report/appendix-12.html#usgov
[629] See Alfred Lehmberg, "Corso's FBI Files Revisited" http://www.virtuallystrange.net/ufo/updates/2001/may/m06-018.shtml .
[630] Corso, *Day After Roswell*, 1
[631] Originally posted at: http://www.dcmilitary.com/airforce/beam/6_09/commentary/5388-1.html . A copy exists here: http://tinyurl.com/4a523h .
[632] Initially described in a phone conversation with the author on December 13, 2005, and confirmed in a private email on March 31, 2005. Gen Bockel can be reached at: dbockel@roa.org ; ph: (202) 646-7705.
[633] http://www.virtuallystrange.net/ufo/updates/2001/may/m14-024.shtml
[634] This was confirmed to me in private correspondence with Major General Bockel from the U.S. Army Reserve from March-April 2006.
[635] http://www.virtuallystrange.net/ufo/updates/2001/may/m19-024.shtml .
[636] "My Take on Corso," http://www.v-j-enterprises.com/sfcorso.html .
[637] http://www.virtuallystrange.net/ufo/updates/2001/oct/m31-002.shtml .
[638] http://www.virtuallystrange.net/ufo/updates/2005/dec/m24-010.shtml
[639] Cited online at: http://www.ufoskeptic.org .
[640] See Michael Salla, "Galactic COINTELPRO: Exposing the Covert Counter-Intelligence Program against Extraterrestrial Contactees," *Exopolitics Journal* 2:3 (2008): 167-89.

Chapter Twelve

Public Response to Exposure of Government Policies on Extraterrestrial Life

Introduction[641]

So far, I have presented evidence and analyses showing how a range of official policies have been secretly implemented to cover up the existence of extraterrestrial life. I have shown how these policies extend from secret agreements with extraterrestrial life, creation of joint extraterrestrial government bases, black budget funding of extraterrestrial projects, and implementation of many covert activities to maintain secrecy. A select group of public officials have participated in the development and implementation of these policies. As official policies concerning extraterrestrial life are exposed, a number of obvious questions arise over how the public will respond, and what happens to officials that participated in such policies. To answer these questions, an online survey was conducted over a twelve month period from March 17, 2006 to March 19, 2007 concerning extraterrestrial visitation to Earth.

1099 individuals participated in the survey which featured questions ranging from belief in extraterrestrials visiting Earth, to responses on possible government policies. The survey is very helpful in developing an idea of public responses to some of the public policy issues that have been secretly implemented by governmental entities with regard to extraterrestrial life. As government policies on extraterrestrial life are exposed, the survey offers an independent means of gauging how the public might respond. Most importantly, the survey helps exopolitics researchers and activists develop the optimal strategy for ensuring that the exposure of government policies continues in a transparent and accountable way, while minimizing potential societal disruption.

Key results of the survey are the following:

1. 85% of respondents believe that extraterrestrial civilizations are visiting the Earth;
2. 86% believe that the U.S. and other national governments are "covering up information about extraterrestrial visitors;"

3. 73% of respondents would be "excited and hopeful" if national governments announced the existence of extraterrestrial visitors;
4. 57% of respondents said they "would understand" an official policy of covering up extraterrestrial visitation on national security grounds;"
5. 48% of respondents would be "very angry and call for the punishment of responsible officials" if agreements with extraterrestrials were outside of constitutional processes;
6. Almost 62% did not support the use of space weapons against extraterrestrial visitors;
7. And, over 85% wished for extraterrestrials to "show up" and "indisputably prove their existence to the world".

Survey Goal

The "Online Survey on Extraterrestrial Visitation" was conducted to assess public attitudes on a number of issues relating to the "extraterrestrial hypothesis" - that UFOs are interplanetary in origin - and that various government authorities have been suppressing this information for over five decades. The survey used as its sample population Internet users familiar with some of the literature on UFOs and extraterrestrials in order to gain informed feedback on key issues concerning the way information on extraterrestrial visitation has been historically managed. The survey also provided feedback on the suitability of questions for later surveys intended to be conducted offline with the general public who are largely unaware of UFO/exopolitical literature available on the Internet. The main goal of the survey is to gain information on the general public's opinions on important issues concerning extraterrestrial visitation which include the cover up of such life, and the implementation of secret policies by various public officials. These issues are likely to rapidly emerge in mainstream public debates as government policies on extraterrestrial life are increasingly exposed.

Survey Method

Survey questions were drafted after review of questions used by two earlier public surveys. The Roper Poll surveying 1021 adults was conducted in 2002 on the topic "UFOs and Extraterrestrial Life:

Americans' Beliefs and Personal Experiences."[642] The National Geographic Poll surveying 1000 adults was conducted in 2006 by The Center for Survey Research and Analysis and focused on the topic of extraterrestrial life in the universe.[643] The draft survey was then distributed on March 13, 2006 to members of the Exopolitics Institute for feedback and assessment. Based on feedback, a final set of questions was developed and presented through a professional Internet polling company, QuestionPro Web Services.[644] This provided an independent tabulation of survey responses. QuestionPro allowed poll respondents to directly enter their responses online and to view final results online. QuestionPro used a format that encouraged users to respond but once, and discouraged repeated responses. This policy discourages duplication and possible skewing of results. The survey is ongoing, thereby allowing a wider sampling of Internet users familiar with information on extraterrestrials.

The survey was publicly launched on March 17, 2006 and was promoted through the websites and forums associated with the Exopolitics Institute and Exopolitics.Org, as well as popular UFO forums. Website visitors would click on a live link that invited them to take an online survey.[645] Upon completion they would be able to view the cumulative results.[646]

As of March 19, 2007, the survey had a total of 1099 individuals complete it online. A total of 1312 individuals began the survey with 213 dropping out at various stages or not completing all questions. The survey completion rate was 83.77%. The average survey completion time was 6 minutes. Respondents were also able to provide comments at the end of the survey that provided some insights into the appropriateness of questions and of possible revisions.

Survey Analysis

The online survey contained ten questions that tested public views on a range of issues associated with extraterrestrial visitation. In order to better evaluate the survey results, I used earlier surveys by the Roper Poll and National Geographic as comparative sources. The main difference between the polls was that the Roper Poll and the National Geographic polls used random samples drawn from the USA. In contrast, the Exopolitics Institute survey was based on

Internet respondents drawn from an international audience and was based on self-selection by interested online respondents. What follows are the raw results of the online survey followed by commentary contrasting results with the Roper and National Geographic polls.[647]

Q. 1. Do you believe that advanced extraterrestrial life is currently visiting the Earth in UFOs?

	Answer	Count	Percent
1.	**Yes**	**1021**	**85.44%**
2.	No	64	5.36%
3.	Don't know	110	9.21%
	Total	**1195**	**100%**

Analysis.

The affirmative result is significantly higher than comparable questions in the two other sample polls. The Roper Poll asked respondents if they believed UFOs were real and have visited the earth in some form. Almost 48% of respondents answered yes. The most similar question in the National Geographic poll asked whether there is life on other planets besides earth, 59.5% answered yes. The statistically higher result in the Exopolitics Institute survey can be attributed to the target population being conversant with literature on extraterrestrial civilizations and having had direct personal experiences validating the extraterrestrial hypothesis.

2. Do you believe that your national government is covering up information about extraterrestrial visitors and/or UFOs?

	Answer	Count	Percent
1.	**Yes**	**1026**	**86.31%**
2.	No	68	5.71%
3.	Don't know	95	7.98%
	Total	**1191**	**100%**

Analysis

A similar question appeared in the Roper poll which asked respondents if they believe the "Government does not tell everything it knows about UFOs and extraterrestrial life." The result was that 72% and 68% respectively said the government is covering up information about UFOs and extraterrestrial life. The higher percentage in the Exopolitics Institute survey (86.31%) might be attributed to the following factors. One, there is growing public awareness of government cover ups of information. Two, online users interested in UFOs and extraterrestrial issues are more disposed to believing in a government cover-up of extraterrestrial information. And three, an international audience is more likely to believe in a government cover up of UFO/extraterrestrial information.

3. How would you react if your government announced that it had just learned that extraterrestrials are visiting the Earth?

	Answer	Count	Percent
1.	**Excited and hopeful**	**857**	**73.31%**
2.	Afraid and nervous	83	7.10%
3.	Don't know	229	19.59%
	Total	**1100**	**100%**

Analysis

A similar question appeared in the National Geographic Survey requesting reactions to any announcement of life on other planets. The results for the National Geographic survey were 72.1% respondents replied they would be "excited and hopeful"; 19.6% replied they would be afraid and nervous, while 7.9% replied don't know. The similar result with the Exopolitics Institute survey of 73.31% replying they would be excited and hopeful at the announcement of extraterrestrial life/visitation suggests that there are strong positive views associated with such an event. This suggests that public attitudes towards extraterrestrial visitation and/or life anticipates many positive societal and technological changes associated with such an announcement. In contrast, the relatively low percentage of 7.10% saying they would be afraid and nervous was significantly less than the random population recorded in the National Geographic survey of 19.6%. This suggests that as individuals become more informed about extraterrestrial visitation, that they are less likely to be afraid and nervous at any public disclosure. Importantly, the result also suggests that any future government announcement 'spinning' the extraterrestrial presence in ways that manipulate residual fear among the population, would not be believed by a significant proportion of the population.

4. How would you feel if extraterrestrial visitors showed up in large numbers over major cities?

	Answer	Count	Percent
1.	**Excited and hopeful**	**589**	**50.69%**
2.	Afraid and nervous	313	26.94%
3.	Don't know	260	22.38%
	Total	**1162**	**100%**

Analysis

This question is a follow up to question three and gives more of an idea of the impact of extraterrestrial visitation becoming an incontrovertible fact. The result suggests that direct physical evidence of extraterrestrial visitation leads to appreciably greater public concern than the announcement of extraterrestrial life. Nevertheless, half the respondents (50.69%) believe that extraterrestrials showing up would lead to many positive societal and technological changes. A very significant minority (26.94%) would be nervous and afraid. This may be explained in two ways. One, there is public awareness of what has historically occurred with colonialism when one society with superior technical capacities appears on the shores of another. Two, media portrayals of extraterrestrial invasions have deeply influenced a segment of the population. This segment could be easily manipulated by individuals and groups desiring to exploit fears of extraterrestrial colonialism and/or invasion.

5. How would you react if your government announced that it has for several decades covered up the truth about extraterrestrial visitors for national security reasons?

	Answer	Count	Percent
1.	I would be very angry and call for the punishment of responsible officials	333	28.81%
2.	**I would understand this policy and ask for information on why it was adopted**	**664**	**57.44%**
3.	I would not want to know the true reasons for why this policy was adopted	83	7.18%
4.	Don't know	76	6.57%
	Total	**1156**	**100%**

Analysis.

This question is the first of three that addresses issues arising from an alleged cover up of information of extraterrestrial visitors identified by the Roper Poll and Exopolitics Institute survey question #2 concerning an official government cover up. It raises the issue of national security as a plausible justification for covering up such information. The response suggests that a clear majority (57.44%) would seek to understand the national security reasons for such a cover up. A significant minority (28.81%) would seek to have officials punished regardless of the national security reasons they might offer. A smaller number (7.18%) would defer to responsible public officials in managing the extraterrestrial phenomenon without public revelations.

6. How would you respond to an official announcement by the United States that former government officials have entered into agreements with extraterrestrial visitors outside of the processes described by the US Constitution?

	Answer	Count	Percent
1.	**I would be very angry and call for the punishment of responsible officials**	**549**	**48.28%**
2.	I would understand this policy and ask for information on why it was adopted	425	37.36%
3.	Don't know	163	14.34%
	Total	**1137**	**100%**

Analysis

This question is the second of three that addresses issues arising from an alleged cover up of information of extraterrestrial visitors identified by the Roper Poll and question #2 of the Exopolitics Institute survey. It raises the specific issue of alleged agreements between US governmental authorities and extraterrestrial visitors reached outside of US constitutional processes. The response suggests that respondents are more willing to accept a cover up due to national security reasons than for agreements outside of constitutional process. Most respondents (48.28%) would act to have responsible officials punished for violating constitutional processes. A significant minority (37.36%) would seek to better understand the reasons for such a departure from constitutional processes.

7. What should be done if it were discovered that officials were complicit in unconstitutional activities in dealing with extraterrestrial visitors and keeping this secret?

	Answer	Count	Percent
1.	Officials should be forced to resign and charged in a court of law	440	39.22%
2.	**Officials should be given amnesty in exchange for telling the truth**	**437**	**38.95%**
3.	Officials should not be forced to resign or charged if they performed actions that were for legitimate national security purposes	169	15.06%
4.	Don't know	76	6.77%
	Total	**1122**	**100%**

Analysis

This question is the last of three that addresses issues arising from an alleged cover up of information of extraterrestrial visitors identified by the Roper Poll and question #2. It raises the specific issue of unconstitutional or illegal activities by public officials in maintaining secrecy concerning the cover up of extraterrestrial visitation. The responses are divided between respondents not accepting national security justification for performing such actions and those accepting national security justifications. A clear majority of those rejecting national security reasons for such activities are almost equally divided between those wanting to punish such officials and those desiring an amnesty in exchange for full disclosure of their activities. A relatively small minority (15.06%) of respondents would accept such activities for legitimate national security justifications. This suggests that justifications for unconstitutional actions based on national security will not be widely accepted by the vast majority of the general public.

8. Do you agree that advanced space weapons are necessary for defending the Earth against extraterrestrial visitors?

	Answer	Count	Percent
1.	Agree	155	13.08%
2.	**Disagree**	**694**	**61.80%**
3.	Don't know	274	24.40%
	Total	**1123**	**100%**

Analysis

This question addresses the issue of using space weapons against extraterrestrial visitors. A clear majority (61.80%) reject the need for and use of such weaponry. A relatively small minority (13.08%) support such weapons presumably on the basis of extraterrestrial visitors posing a credible national security threat. A relatively large minority (24.40%) remain undecided presumably due to conflicting information on the motivation and activities of alleged extraterrestrial visitors.

9. Do you think a United Nations supervised "Decade of Contact" is desirable for preparing the global population for the truth about visiting extraterrestrial civilizations?

	Answer	Count	Percent
1.	**Yes**	**569**	**51.17%**
2.	No	323	29.05%
3.	Don't know	220	19.78%
	Total	**1112**	**100%**

Analysis:

A simple majority of respondents (51.17%) are supportive of multilateral organizations such as United Nations playing a supervisory role in educating the global public about extraterrestrial visitors. A significant minority (29.05%) are opposed and presumably would desire either national organizations and/or non-governmental organizations to play this role. This suggests that there is significant opposition to centralizing any educative processes to prepare the global population for extraterrestrial visitation. A relatively large proportion of respondents (19.78%) remain undecided as to the best means of educating the global population of extraterrestrial visitation.

10. Do you wish for extraterrestrials to "show up" and indisputably prove their existence to the world?

	Answer	Count	Percent
1.	Yes	954	85.29%
2.	No	63	5.69%
3.	Don't know	100	9.03%
	Total	1108	100%

Analysis

This question addresses the possibility that extraterrestrial visitors might take the initiative in showing up. In contrast to question four that addressed individuals feelings if extraterrestrial visitors showed up, this question seeks to identify levels of public approval for such an initiative taken by extraterrestrials. An overwhelming majority (85.29%) would be comfortable in giving their permission for extraterrestrials to show. Only 5.69% would be opposed to extraterrestrials showing up. Recalling from question four that 26.94% would be "nervous and afraid" if ETs showed up en masse over major cities, this result suggests that individual anxiety over extraterrestrial visitation would not preclude such individuals from giving permission for extraterrestrials showing up. The large affirmative answer is likely based on three factors: 1 the high level of dissatisfaction with the government cover up of extraterrestrial information; 2. participants being willing to approve extraterrestrials showing up; 3. individuals desiring incontrovertible action in ending the government cover up.

Conclusions

Based on the number of respondents, the high completion rate and participant feedback, the survey achieved its primary goal of providing feedback on public responses to exposure of government policies concerning extraterrestrial life. It's important to point out that survey participants were self-selecting; finding a link to the poll on websites or discussion forums dealing with UFOs/extraterrestrials. Survey respondents therefore represent individuals familiar with some of the information available on the internet concerning possible extraterrestrial visitation. The survey outcome therefore reflects a relatively well informed sample population concerning national governments covering up information related to extraterrestrial visitation.

Survey participants display an eagerness to respond to issues concerning a possible government cover up of extraterrestrial visitation. For many participants, this was an important opportunity to possibly influence the policy making process concerning extraterrestrial visitation and was a valuable exercise. The high completion rate suggests that many participants found the survey a valuable means of expressing their opinions of government policy concerning possible extraterrestrial visitation, an area that is still not addressed in the public arena. This observation is reflected in policy questions two, five and seven, each of which had less than 8% of respondents answering “Don’t know”. A number of respondent comments confirmed the self-empowering nature of the survey. This suggests that it is a valuable exercise to survey individuals on a variety of issues concerning possible extraterrestrial visitation and resulting government policy.

There were also a number of suggestions for improving the survey. First, participants are interested in a more nuanced set of responses for dealing with government complicity in covering up information or for government officials violating constitutional processes. A number of respondents raised the idea of a “Truth Commission” for extracting information from complicit government officials. Second, a more nuanced set of emotional responses for extraterrestrials showing up were requested. This is reflected in the relatively high percentage of “Don’t know” responses for questions three (19.59%) and four (22.38%). And third, a number of respondents were interested more nuanced questions in terms of possible extraterrestrial motivations and activities. This is confirmed by the relatively high number of “Don’t know” responses to question eight (24.40%) and also partly for question ten (9.03 %).

In conclusion, the survey indicates a high degree of intellectual and emotional maturity of respondents in dealing with a range of very complex public policy issues concerning possible extraterrestrial visitation and government cover-up of evidence. Individuals are eager to have governments disclose the truth about extraterrestrial visitation, and to deal with the policy implications of the cover up in a manner that respects national security concerns. Significantly, over 85% of respondents desire for extraterrestrials to indisputably demonstrate their presence. This suggests widespread public opposition to any government cover-up of extraterrestrial information, and a desire for greater transparency concerning extraterrestrial visitation. In general, the survey demonstrates that the general public is ready to play a more active role in ensuring greater transparency and accountability regarding government policy on extraterrestrial life.

ENDNOTES – CHAPTER TWELVE

[641] I wish to thank members from the Exopolitics Institute for their suggestions in formulating questions. I especially thank Hugh Matlock for his assistance in helping analyse the results of this survey, and identifying typographical errors. I finally thank Jack Davis for proof reading an earlier version of this chapter that was published in the *Exopolitics Journal* 2:1 (April 2007): 50-62.
[642] Roper Poll, "UFOs & Extraterrestrial Life: Americans' Beliefs and Personal Experiences," Roper Number: C205-008232. http://www.roper.com
[643] Conducted on behalf of National Geographic by the Center for Survey Research and Analysis, http://www.csra.uconn.edu/
[644] Company website is: www.QuestionPro.com .
[645] Survey Url is: http://www.questionpro.com/akira/TakeSurvey?id=391646 .
[646] Url for for March 19, 2007 survey results is: http://www.exopoliticsinstitute.org/Survey-Results-March-19-07.htm . Nov 25, 2006 survey results is: http://www.exopoliticsinstitute.org/Survey-Results-Nov-25-06.htm .
[647] For the original table generated by Questionpro on November 25, 2007 go to "Survey on Extraterrestrial Visitation - Public Feedback & Analysis," *Exopolitics Journal* 2:1 (April 2007): 50-62.

CHAPTER THIRTEEN

Political Spin and Shaping Public Opinion for 'First Contact'

Introduction[648]

There has been a worldwide suppression of a secret extraterrestrial presence on Earth for at least 60 years from the general public and most elected public officials. The official public disclosure of extraterrestrial life has long been speculated to be imminent. In an alleged 1954 meeting between President Eisenhower and an extraterrestrial delegation, for example, it was reported that disclosure of the extraterrestrial presence was imminent.[649] The repeated delays have led to much uncertainty over when the secret extraterrestrial presence will eventually be disclosed. Some whistleblowers persuasively argue that once international terrorism fails to be a credible justification for the vast weapons expenditures by the U.S. military, then military-intelligence agencies will turn to the extraterrestrial presence to justify such expenditure.[650] However, rather than 'when' being the critical issue to be decided, it appears that the more difficult issue is 'how' the extraterrestrial presence will be disclosed or 'politically spun'. There appears to be a secret effort to shape public opinion of extraterrestrial life in a way that prepares the public to accept a particular 'first contact' scenario.

It appears that what has yet to be decided is when public disclosure of extraterrestrial life occurs and how it will be 'spun' to facilitate continued control by small clandestine groups of public officials not governed by usual democratic rules over accountability and transparency. The different scenarios of a first contact that have emerged into the public arena by various UFO researchers/whistleblowers point to a competition between and within government agencies for how 'First Contact' will be 'spun' for world-wide consumption. It appears that there are strong factional rivalries within clandestine organizations that respectively have their own favored contact scenario. It is these rivalries that best explain the long delay in public disclosure of the extraterrestrial presence.

Preparing for 'First Contact' is a means of understanding the full extent of the extraterrestrial presence, the accompanying secrecy that has accompanied this, and being ready for a 'First Contact' event that firmly transforms human life on Earth. There are, however, a number of contact scenarios that put a particular 'spin' on the extraterrestrial presence that would allow clandestine national security agencies to continue to control extraterrestrial affairs in a secret and undemocratic manner. Significant changes in public opinion of extraterrestrials can be attributed not just to alleged extraterrestrial behavior and spontaneous changes in public attitudes, but to a secret competition between different factions of the 'shadow government' promoting perceptions that support a particular First Contact scenario that best permits their continued influence and power. Beginning in the months of October/November 2003, an alternative scenario began circulating on the World Wide Web that has led to the emergence of a new actor in how public opinion is being shaped for a 'First Contact' event. This new actor is outside of the mass media system that is largely controlled by a small number of elites associated with management groups of extraterrestrial affairs, and appears to be solely a result of a spontaneous global response to 'when' and 'how' First Contact should occur.

The new actor comprises a number of rapidly emerging 'contact groups' that believe global humanity has been recently contacted by extraterrestrial races that want to know if ordinary citizens want extraterrestrials to simply 'show up' and end public secrecy over the extraterrestrial presence. The rapid emergence of these 'contact groups', their impact on global public opinion on extraterrestrials, and repression of key spokespersons of these contact groups, suggests a secret struggle exists between multiple players over 'when' and 'how' First Contact will occur. In what follows, I examine three First Contact scenarios that have varying degrees of support and can be considered most likely to occur. Finally, I examine how public opinion is being shaped in ways that promote particular First Contact scenarios, and the respective roles of extraterrestrials, national security agencies, UFO/exopolitics researchers, and the general public.

Political Spin and Extraterrestrial Life

William Safire defines 'political spin' as "a deliberate shading of news perception; attempted control of political reaction."[651] The terms 'political spin' and 'spin doctors' first came to be used in U.S. Presidential campaigns.[652] The following editorial by the New York Times referred to how 'political spin' was professionally handled by President Reagan's senior advisors shortly before the 1984 elections:

> A dozen men in good suits and women in silk dresses will circulate smoothly among the reporters, spouting confident opinions. They won't be just press agents trying to impart a favorable spin to a routine release. They'll be Spin Doctors, senior advisors to the candidates, and they'll be playing for very high stakes. How well they do their work could be as important as how well the candidates do theirs.[653]

Rather than something that pertains solely to the conventional political process, 'political spin' has been used in managing the extraterrestrial phenomenon from the 1940's due to the covert work of military intelligence agencies whose task it has been to cover up the extraterrestrial presence to the general public. Official documents leaked to the general public show that a secrecy policy was initiated as early as 1947 under the Truman administration.[654] Walter Haut was the Public Information Officer at Roswell Army Air Field who on July 8, 1947 distributed the initial news release about the flying saucer crash at Roswell. He authorized the release of an affidavit after his death where he revealed that the Roswell crash involved extraterrestrial entities, and the Pentagon had decided to keep this secret.[655]

The following passage from an 'alleged official document' leaked to UFO researchers, describes in stark detail the official secrecy policy as it had evolved by April 1954:

> Any encounter with entities known to be of extraterrestrial origin is to be considered to be a matter of national security and therefore classified TOP SECRET. Under no circumstances is the general public or the public press to learn of the existence of these entities. The official

> government policy is that such creatures do not exist, and that no agency of the federal government is now engaged in any study of extraterrestrials or their artifacts. Any deviation from this stated policy is absolutely forbidden.[656]

The officially sanctioned secrecy policy was supported by military intelligence agencies whose task it has been to deflect public attention away from the extraterrestrial presence. Arguably the single most important achievement in deflecting public attention was in developing the term 'UFO', which was supposedly coined by Captain Edward Ruppelt in 1951 to replace the less scientifically precise term 'flying saucer'. Ruppelt claimed that "UFO is the official term that I created to replace the words 'flying saucers'."[657] Yet as Dr Steven Greer discovered in his consultations with a range of military-government insiders, the term UFO was not widely used at all by insiders: "They're actually ETV, extraterrestrial vehicle, related. No one uses the word UFO, by the way. UFO was coined after they knew they weren't unidentified."[658] The term UFO therefore provided a useful cover for the extraterrestrial vehicles that were known rather than unidentified. This piece of word sophistry proved to be invaluable in the succeeding decades for senior officials who might have to occasionally go on the public record. So rather than outright lying, senior government and military officials who knew about the extraterrestrial presence were strictly telling the truth when they could say, for example, 'that they had seen no evidence supporting the existence of UFOs.'

Such denials of the existence of UFO's or evidence supporting them was simply military intelligence 'spin' based on secret military knowledge of extraterrestrial piloted craft that were 'identified', rather than 'unidentified'. According to John Maynard, a former Defense Intelligence Agency analyst who helped in covering up the extraterrestrial presence this was done through what he described as 'disinformation' which has a similar dynamic to political spin:

> Disinformation or misinformation: The art of providing information in a form that has a certain amount of truth in the statement to make it a plausible answer to a question or a possible solution to the topic at hand. Yet, if employed

> correctly will lead the person to believe the opposite of what is correct, in other words, come to the wrong conclusions... [For example] A simple program, say changing the shape of an object, such as flying saucers. State the real fact of what was stated, but add that you 'thought it was saucer-shaped', and suggest that the person who was looking at it from a different angle, saw something like this: "You said it was cigar-shaped, I thought it was more of a saucer shape myself, probably the angle made the difference." If you keep repeating this eventually they will believe it was saucer-shaped. The truth: the person saw a cigar-shaped object. You changed their minds, and that is what will be reported.[659]

Along with disinformation, 'political spin' made it possible for senior officials to cover up for decades what they knew, and to allow the general public to remain in the dark about visiting extraterrestrial races. Rather than a new development, 'political spin', along with other military intelligence strategies such as disinformation, has been used since the very beginning of the UFO phenomenon to shape public perceptions about the reality of visiting extraterrestrial races and their vehicles. I now examine two 'officially sanctioned' scenarios that are likely to be 'spun' to prepare the general public for 'first contact' with extraterrestrial races in a way that will assist the long term agenda of national security agencies.

Contact Scenario 1: 'War of the Worlds' – The Hostile Extraterrestrial

In 1938, Orson Welles produced a radio adaptation of H.G. Wells, 'War of the Worlds'.[660] In the famous broadcast, listeners believed they were hearing genuine news reports of an attack by Martians on Earth, and the destruction of the United States. While Welles' production shocked listeners, it gave a classic example of how mass communication could very easily shape public opinion of extraterrestrial races. Moving to the present era, Dr Steven Greer, director of the 'Disclosure Project', has interviewed over 450 whistleblowers who are former or current employees in the U.S. military-intelligence community, corporations working on military projects, or the aviation industry.[661] In his interviews he has learned of a secret plan that involved producing another fictitious 'War of the Worlds' as a 'First Contact' event whereby the global population would officially learn of the hitherto secret extraterrestrial presence in terms of a contrived extraterrestrial invasion:

> To justify eventually spending trillions of dollars on space weapons, the world would be deceived about a threat from outer space, thus uniting the world in fear, in militarism and in war. Since 1992 I have seen this script unveiled to me by at least a dozen well-placed insiders. Of course, initially I laughed, thinking this just too absurd and far-fetched. Dr. Rosin gave her testimony to the Disclosure Project before 9/11. And yet others told me explicitly that things that looked like UFOs but that are built and under the control of deeply secretive 'black' projects, were being used to simulate - hoax - ET-appearing events, including some abductions and cattle mutilations, to sow the early seeds of cultural fear regarding life in outer space. And that at some point after global terrorism, events would unfold that would utilize the now-revealed Alien Reproduction Vehicles (ARVs, or reversed-engineered UFOs made by humans by studying actual ET craft - see the book 'Disclosure' by the same author) to hoax an attack on Earth. Like the movie Independence Day, an attempt to unite the world through militarism would unfold using ET as the new cosmic scapegoat (think Jews during the Third Reich).[662]

The fake extraterrestrial invasion would presumably happen at a time and place that suits the interests of clandestine organizations that have secretly managed extraterrestrial affairs since the Second World War era.[663]

A significant development that supports such a possibility was the release of a modern version of 'War of the Worlds'. Directed by Steven Spielberg, staring Tom Cruise and produced with a budget of $130 million, the remake was released in June 2005. The movie would, like the "Independence Day" movie (1999), popularize in the U.S. and global mindset the idea of an extraterrestrial invasion, and the need for a coordinated global defense. Such a need was something that former U.S. President

Ronald Reagan fervently believed was necessary based on his secret knowledge of the extraterrestrial presence:

> In our obsession with antagonisms of the moment, we often forget how much unites all the members of humanity. Perhaps we need some outside, universal threat to make us recognize this common bond. I occasionally think, how quickly our differences worldwide would vanish if we were facing an alien threat from outside this world. And yet, I ask is not an alien force ALREADY among us?" "There are only a handful of people who know the truth about this.[664]

The association of Spielberg with the new 'War of the Worlds' is quite significant since there have been rumors that his earlier movie, "Close Encounters of the Third Kind" was secretly an effort to prime the general public for disclosure of the extraterrestrial presence.[665]

A contrived 'War of the Worlds' would allow military-intelligence organizations in the U.S. and elsewhere to continue their vast network of secret projects that are funded by 'black' budgets that in the case of the US, go as high as $1.7 trillion dollars annually.[666] The 'fake invasion' would allow the passage of strict national security laws that would benefit those factions within the national and global extraterrestrial management groups that desire to maintain full control of all aspects of the extraterrestrial presence without being scrutinized by open and transparent democratic processes. The strongest supporters of a fake extraterrestrial invasion have been described by former government and/or corporate insiders. Daniel Salter, Dr Carol Rosin and (Dr) Michael Wolf, refer to a mysterious military 'Cabal' within the 'shadow government' running extraterrestrial affairs, that has in the past approved policies targeting and shooting down visiting extraterrestrial space craft. A "renegade force called the Cabal," according to Salter, "is responsible for attacking and retrieving extraterrestrial entities and craft." [667] He goes on to say this "may be the group that is aggressively disturbing the potential of contact between the ETs and humankind."

According to Greer and another UFO researcher, Dr Richard Boylan, many of the recent reports of extraterrestrial abuses are related to military abductions (MILABs). They cite the work of Dr

Helmut Lammer who has provided extensive analysis of the role of military-intelligence agencies in the abduction experience.[668] Lammer's work suggests that these MILABs have a genuine extraterrestrial component in them implying either cooperation or connection with extraterrestrial abductions. For example, if an extraterrestrial abduction occurs, this is monitored and the same 'victim' is abducted and examined by military-intelligence forces using invasive medical and psychological techniques. Reflecting on the relationship between extraterrestrial abductions and MILABs, Lammer writes: "If one speculates that a core of the alien abduction phenomenon is indeed real, the same people who are behind these [secret military] projects would have an interest in alien biology/genetics and mind control procedures."[669]

Prominent UFO 'abduction' researchers such as Dr David Jacobs, Budd Hopkins and the late Dr Karla Turner have provided detailed case studies of the abusive aspects of UFO 'abductions'.[670] These researchers found disturbing evidence of abusive treatment of individuals taken into UFO craft, of women being involuntarily subjected to a genetic program aimed at producing human-extraterrestrial hybrids, and of adult hybrids performing humiliating sexual activities on female abductees. Jacobs elaborates on the possible goal of the extraterrestrial abduction program as follows:

> With the use of superior technology, both physical and biological, they are engaging in the systematic and clandestine physiological exploitation, and perhaps alteration, of human beings for the purposes of passing on their genetic capabilities to progeny who will integrate into the human society and, without doubt, control it.... In the end it is possible that it will be of some benefit to us but if we survive as a species, the price for this charity will be relinquishment of the freedom to dictate our own destiny and, most likely, our personal freedom as well.[671]

Elaborating on recent reports of abusive human extraterrestrial encounters, the well-known UFO writer, Whitley Strieber suggested that a 'dark chapter' has started as far as the extraterrestrial presence is concerned for those experiencing the abduction phenomenon.[672] More disturbingly, he cites reports of human mutilations as worrying testimony of this disturbing new phase. A detailed study of one human mutilation was evidence that the perpetrators had no concern about the life of the victim and of leaving the evidence behind.[673] In addition to the human mutilation phenomenon, are reports of underground bases where extraterrestrials perform a variety of experiments on abducted humans who are held indefinitely and appear to be little more than laboratory specimens. Most disturbing is evidence that national security agencies are aware of such abuses and even complicit in their occurrence.[674]

The increasing evidence of hostile extraterrestrial behavior has contributed to shifts in public opinion of extraterrestrials. The friendly 'space brothers' of early UFO experiencers such as George Adamski, has been replaced by the 'hostile visitors' that need to be closely monitored and even militarily opposed by national security agencies.[675] This increase in reports of abusive extraterrestrial behavior may have different explanations. The first is that there has been an increase in extraterrestrials performing abductions and/or humans remembering and reporting these negative encounters as Jacobs and Strieber contend. The second is that there has been an upsurge in military-intelligence abductions which have thrown a distortive layer into the more benign human-extraterrestrial encounter as Greer and Boylan contend. It is likely that both explanations are valid which accounts for the wide range of perspectives found by those studying the abduction phenomenon.[676]

Consequently, the evidence in terms of increased reports of abuses related to the abduction phenomenon points to the conclusion that there has been a distinct shift in the way an extraterrestrial presence is being managed and being 'leaked' to the general public. It is very likely that the military-intelligence community is playing a prominent role in leaking information that extraterrestrials visiting Earth are hostile and regularly violate human abductees. This 'spinning' of the extraterrestrial data would make possible a First Contact scenario where an extraterrestrial invasion is faked either entirely by military-intelligence units, staged with cooperative factions of extraterrestrials, or represent a limited military confrontation with extraterrestrial races performing unauthorized abductions.

As Greer suggests, the contrived war on terrorism and invasion of Iraq are stepping-stones to the ultimate 'war of the worlds'.[677] The 'Cabal' was very influential within the Bush administration as evidenced by the preemptive war in Iraq, and viewed its long term interests as best served with continuation of a strict national security system.[678] The 2008 election of Barack Obama has brought in a new Presidential administration yet there will almost certainly be elements in his administration sympathetic to maintaining a strong national security response to any future contingency, especially those involving extraterrestrial life. A contrived extraterrestrial invasion would allow 'Cabal' elements of the new Obama administration to release sufficient information about the historic extraterrestrial presence to support past U.S. military intelligence polices regarding the cover-up of the extraterrestrial presence. This would ensure that former officials involved in secretly managing extraterrestrial affairs would not be made accountable for past actions, and would be protected from legal prosecution. While there appears to be support from within the U.S. military-intelligence community for a 'contrived invasion', there has also been significant opposition that has led to factional splits in the 'shadow government' responsible for managing extraterrestrial affairs.[679]

Furthermore, there appears to be only weak support from global institutions for a contrived 'war of the worlds'. Many nations are influenced by moderate extraterrestrial control management groups associated with international institutions such as the Bilderberg Group and the Trilateral Commission. According to one researcher:

> The "progressives" within Bilderberg and within the National Security apparatus of the U.S. have as their objective that the world's conflicts be ended, and that thus, there be no temptation to weaponize ET technology, before ET high-tech such as zero-point energy devices are allowed to go into public circulation.[680]

This is reflected in major global opposition to the former Bush administration's policies in Iraq which was a cover for a more aggressive extraterrestrial management role by the Cabal embedded within the U.S. national security system.[681] It appears that there is a genuine factional struggle between a hard-line control group apparently wanting to have or to create the impression of a need for a war with extraterrestrial races, and another faction seeking cooperation and a more genuine form of disclosure. The 2008 election of Barack Obama indicates a more cooperative faction of global elites has moved into positions of power. Consequently, while a contrived "War of the Worlds' remains a possible extraterrestrial contact scenario that would be spun for general public consumption, it has diminishing support in the secret management groups that run extraterrestrial affairs.

Contact Scenario 2: Close Encounters of the Third Kind - The 'Friendly Enigmatic ET'

This contact scenario would use a variation of scripts popularized by Steven Spielberg's *Close Encounters of the Third Kind,* and the more recent television mini-series he produced *Taken.*[682] Here the extraterrestrials would be depicted in a more friendly though enigmatic light as a technologically advanced race that has entered into some loose agreements with the U.S. and possibly other national governments. In these agreements, the extraterrestrials exchanged their advanced technology for the U.S. government acquiescing to the extraterrestrials using human genetic material for the biological enhancement of their race. The agreements portray the relationship and motivations of both the extraterrestrials and clandestine government authorities as benign, but that these agreements suffered hiccups due to the willful activities of a renegade group of military-intelligence officials - the 'Cabal'.

The secrecy surrounding extraterrestrial-government agreements, extraterrestrial abuses of civilians, shooting down of extraterrestrial ships would presumably be attributed to the willful activities and disinformation stemming from the 'Cabal', and/or the possible assistance of 'rogue' extraterrestrial groups.[683] Military-intelligence officials associated with the 'Cabal' would be identified and made accountable for their activities, and/or 'rogue extraterrestrials' would be forced to leave. The script for this scenario would then involve the world celebrating the open appearance of 'friendly' extraterrestrials. They would then assist humanity to acquire advanced technology, purge the 'Cabal' from the military intelligence community, and/or force the departure of 'rogue' extraterrestrials. Remaining extraterrestrials would subsequently be depicted in a more positive light as friendly though enigmatic entities who can assist in the development of human civilization.

Supporters of Spielberg's Close Encounters 'contact scenario' within the military intelligence community have long leaked information of the benign intentions of extraterrestrial visitors. This 'leaked' information comes from 'whistleblowers' or those embedded with national security organizations that may be part of a covert campaign to shape public opinion for a forthcoming public disclosure. Researchers such as Steven Greer and Richard Boylan enthusiastically support the view that extraterrestrials are friendly and that all stories of abusive extraterrestrial behavior is due to disinformation stemming from the 'Cabal'.[684] Greer in particular cites an impressive array of military whistleblowers he has interviewed who testify to the benign nature of the extraterrestrials. For example, Clifford Stone who served for twenty years in covert retrievals of extraterrestrial craft, stated the following in an interview with Greer:

> We have contact with aliens not originating from some foreign country but from some other solar system. And I have been a party to that. I've worked it. I've been there. And I know some of the things we do is really, really, really, really terrible. They are not hostile toward us. We are the enemy in this instance – but we are the enemy, I like to think, for the good reasons."[685]

Another whistleblower Greer interviewed, Daniel Salter, also attests to the benign nature of extraterrestrials: "[Werner] von Braun knew that from 1947 through 1951, we had shot down, captured and arrested extraterrestrials with their vehicles so we could study them. Yet the ETs have never committed an aggressive act towards humans; humans have always shot first."[686] Boylan relies on interviews with (Dr) Michael Wolf to assert the benign intentions of extraterrestrials.[687]

Despite these clear references to benign extraterrestrials, there are references by some of these same whistleblowers to 'rogue extraterrestrials' in other interviews not cited by Greer or Boylan.[688]

For instance in another interview, Clifford Stone distinguishes between 'good' and 'bad' extraterrestrials, and clearly refers to one group, 'the Grays', as committing egregious abductions and that the U.S. government is unsure how to disclose this to the general public:

> "The good guys [ETs] are, well, I like to refer to them as being nomadic. What you're talking about, about the non-intervention with other intelligent life forms is a universal law. The nomadics go along with that. The grays violated the universal law…. I think there is the effort for the good guys to make contact with the people within our government, but I think now what is happening is that the U.S. government learned in 1983 or thereabout that they are NOT dealing with the good guys, but really don't know what to do about it.[689]

Michael Wolf also elaborated on the motivations of extraterrestrial races in an interview where he stated:

> Most are benevolent. Occasionally some get through the alien barrier, but they don't generally come back. They don't come back here once they are spotted and identified. Once they have hidden agendas, once they are identified, they are barred from coming here…. But those are out of a myriad of races, and they are few and far between.[690]

The idea that most extraterrestrials are benign, but that a few are rogue who form a troublesome minority in the galactic community has been supported by the remote viewer, Dr Courtney Brown who has conducted numerous remote viewing sessions of visiting extraterrestrials.[691] He argues, for example, that the "reptilians are involved with weapons manufacture... I suggest that these prototypes are designed to shoot down ships aligned with the Galactic Federation, particularly Grey ships."[692]

The most intriguing whistleblower information concerning different extraterrestrial factions come from a microbiologist, (Dr) Dan Burisch, who allegedly worked closely with a 'Gray' extraterrestrial known as J-Rod.[693] According to Burisch he actually took biological samples from the extraterrestrial that was from Zeta Reticulum: "I was briefed that J-Rod was an alien, specifically from the (Zeta) Reticuli 1 and 2 (binary) system, specifically from Reticulum 4 (fourth planet from one of the suns)."[694] Using the knowledge and material gained from his interaction with J-Rod, Burisch allegedly worked on a highly classified project called 'Lotus' which focused on acquiring knowledge of a mysterious 'Ganesh Particle' that could lead to cell regeneration and the creation of life.[695] The case involving Burisch has led to the release of information of his classified work with J-Rod, his work on Project Lotus, and his communications with select shadow government committees.

A very significant fact about Burisch is that a number of independent researchers conducted face to face interviews concerning his activities and information he was distributing when he claimed he was still employed in classified projects. These include well known researchers such as Linda Moulton Howe, Bill Hamilton and Paola Harris.[696] I was in 2004 able to have a limited email communication with Burisch that discussed aspects of the classified projects he was engaged in before personally meeting him.[697] I personally met him in 2007 where he responded to my and others questions about his extraterrestrial experiences.[698] Most researchers who have met him have detected something of great significance occurring in the Burisch case.

The unprecedented public access to Burisch who claimed to be actively engaged in a classified project suggested that the disclosures made by Burisch had insider support.[699] Prominent individuals within one of the key shadow government committees, apparently the 'Committee of the Majority', were facilitating access, and enabling the distribution of the Burisch material.[700] According to Burisch's supporters, this is because Burisch is insisting on the information he possessed being distributed to the public, otherwise he wouldn't cooperate in Project Lotus. Burisch was claimed to be essential to the project since he was the only microbiologist with the requisite knowledge to understand the Ganesh particle.[701]

Another significant aspect of the Burisch saga is that there is apparently a policy schism within the secret committee system that runs extraterrestrial affairs. While Burisch has had access to the general public and has been able to release classified information, there has also, allegedly been efforts to intimidate and silence him. Insider factions opposed to the disclosure process he was participating in were behind such efforts. Apparently, Burisch was physically attacked, had his memories removed, was taken to remote locations, and was held incommunicado for extensive periods.[702]

Some of the major exopolitical themes coming through the Burisch saga are that there are two factions of J-Rod extraterrestrials. One faction apparently helped Burisch in his research, is benign, wants the knowledge concerning the 'Ganesh particle' disseminated in a way that helps humanity, and assists the Grays/J-Rods themselves in repairing their own damaged DNA. The other faction of J-Rods/Grays is somehow causing problems that leads to 'reactionary' or ultra-nationalistic national security officials (i.e., 'the Cabal') implementing xenophobic policies towards extraterrestrials. Evidently, the Cabal wants to gain control of the Ganesh Particle so it can be used for the usual range of self-serving reasons of power, greed and exploitation.

Burisch's information and public interviews is evidence of a factional struggle between different control groups within the extraterrestrial management system over how to present the first contact scenario.[703] 'Progressive controllers' are allegedly in an intense struggle against 'reactionary' controllers ('the cabal') in setting up policy on extraterrestrials and how to respond to Dan Burisch. There is also a split between friendly J-Rods/Grays and rogue J-Rods/Grays in terms of extraterrestrial motivations and activities towards humanity. Individuals following the Burisch saga believe that the very fate of humanity is being decided through this clandestine struggle, and the general public is being urged to support Burisch in releasing the information and appearing before the U.S. Congress.[704] This implies supporting the progressives within the management system in their 'difficult struggle' against the reactionaries and rogue 'J-Rods'. Such a struggle is alluded to by Boylan in his discussion of progressive and reactionary management factions in U.S. and global institutions, and his support for 'progressive' factions.[705]

What can be concluded from the Burisch material is that it has been largely developed to present a credible contact scenario sought by military-intelligence organizations managing extraterrestrial affairs. The unprecedented public access to Burisch and his ability to disclose classified information indicates he is 'unknowingly' part of a covert campaign to influence public opinion about the extraterrestrial presence and classified projects. Burisch's work with J-Rod/Grays and his involvement with 'Ganesh particle' indicates a joint government/ extraterrestrial effort to give a more morally positive image to the extraterrestrial presence, and to create the perception that their biological work has beneficial applications for both humanity and the Gray extraterrestrial race. At the same time, the existence of 'rogue extraterrestrials' and a reactionary 'Cabal' provides the basis for explaining the more negative aspects of the extraterrestrial presence found in numerous abduction reports and whistleblower testimonies.[706]

Another variation of the 'friendly though enigmatic' extraterrestrial contact scenario emerges from the recent publication of a whistleblower's experiences with a race described as 'Tall Whites'.[707] Charles Hall was stationed at Nellis Air force base from 1965-68 where his duty was to use weather balloons for the Air Force from the Indian Springs location on the base. He describes his interactions with 'Tall Whites' beginning in 1965 and how he and other servicemen coped with their disturbing presence. Hall described a catalogue of incidents where the 'Tall Whites' terrorized other military servicemen who didn't understand them, surprised them or threatened them in some way. The 'Tall Whites' are described in enigmatic terms as a race that physically intimidated some servicemen, yet were capable of displaying sincere friendship and appreciation to Hall since he had apparently saved the life of a 'Tall White'.[708] This is where the Tall Whites display more positive qualities such as friendship and superior knowledge that they shared with Hall and with the U.S. Air Force.

Significantly, the 'Tall Whites' began to be seen in the Mojave desert area in 1954 indicating that they were associated with the agreement(s) reached between the 'Tall Grays' and the Eisenhower administration in 1954. [709] Hall further describes regularly seeing them in the presence of Air Force generals and other senior officials who recognized the ambassadorial status of the Tall White leader.[710] This indicates that a disclosure announcement will likely be made that spins information in a way justifying the shadow government's agreements with the 'Tall Whites', and casts them as 'friendly though enigmatic' extraterrestrials.

Yet another version of the friendly though enigmatic extraterrestrial concerns an alien exchange program known as the

Serpo Project wherein 12 military personnel were taken to the planet Serpo in the constellation, Zeta Reticulum. The Project allegedly lasted from 1965 to 1978, when some of the original group returned. Given the similarities with final scenes in *Close Encounters of the Third Kind* and Ronald Reagan's comments about the truth of Spielberg's movie, many quickly accepted the Serpo story as having some truth in it.[711] After its emergence in Fall of 2005, a number of former military intelligence officials have come forward to support the factual basis of Project Serpo. These include Richard Doty, Gene Lakes and Paul McGovern who all worked with military intelligence agencies.[712] Doty, in particular was prominent in military deception programs associated with Paul Bennewitz and whose recent public disclosures lead to suspicion that he is again involved in promoting deception programs. Perhaps the Serpo Project is one of these.[713]

In conclusion, the contact scenario that is being spun for public consumption is based on success by one faction of an extraterrestrial control management group (the 'progressives') over a more reactionary faction (the Cabal). The public disclosure process and the subsequent purging of the Cabal would be 'spun' in a way that legitimizes the policies and approach of the 'progressive' faction of the management groups responsible for extraterrestrial affairs. This First Contact scenario would be more peaceful than the 'War of the Worlds' scenario and would lead to a more genuine account of the extraterrestrial presence. However, it would still be 'spun' in a way that disguises the full extent of extraterrestrial abuses, government complicity, and the presence of more 'ethical' extraterrestrial races that have not been permitted to operate openly in human affairs.[714] This First Contact scenario would be based on cooperation between 'progressives' and extraterrestrials participating in secret agreements, to hide the full extent of the extraterrestrial presence on the planet, and abusive activities that have occurred.[715] The shaping of public perceptions for a 'First Contact' scenario with 'friendly though enigmatic' extraterrestrials is well advanced as evidenced by public interest in the Burisch saga, the extraterrestrial abduction phenomenon, the popularity of the mini-series *Taken,* the recent publication of Charles Hall's memoirs and the Serpo Project revelations.

Scenario 3: Star Trek – The Galactic Federation Shows Up!

Another First Contact scenario could very easily have come from the pen of famous Star Trek producer Gene Rodenberry. It involves a number of telepathic messages allegedly from extraterrestrial races in contact with private citizens. These messages are addressed to ordinary citizens and operate under a principle very similar to the 'Prime Directive' which Rodenberry attributes to the Galactic Federation of his Star Trek series. Under the Prime Directive, extraterrestrials seek to get permission to "Show Up" and assist humanity in the global challenges that lie ahead. Such extraterrestrials appear to be conducting a global education program wherein they identify their concerns about the future of humanity and the irresponsible policies of global elites. An increasing number of such individuals have been coming forward to divulge such messages that are increasingly circulating through the Internet.

In 1974, a Peruvian teenager, Sixto Paz Wells began receiving telepathic messages from extraterrestrials. These communications were followed by multiple sightings of UFOs, film and photographic evidence.[716] Wells claims that the extraterrestrial gave him and a small group spiritual teachings aimed at raising their consciousness, preparing for Earth changes, and revealing to the world the presence of benign extraterrestrials genuinely wishing to assist:

> Mission Humanity is an awakening of consciousness, a wake up call and a warning message from sidereal civilizations … Mission Humanity symbolizes the hope and solace that we are brothers and children in a Universe which is the home of many…. Mission Humanity reassures us that we have been adopted by kind beings, our Elder Brothers, because they believe in us and know that there is more good than bad in humanity.[717]

J.J. Benitez, a prominent Spanish journalist investigated Wells claims and found them credible. Benitez newspaper stories on Wells contact experiences made Wells widely known throughout the Spanish speaking world.[718] Wells then established an organization, Mission Rama, which quickly spread around the globe and continues in various forms to the present.[719] Wells and his organization's mission was to prepare humanity for extraterrestrial contact. In 2006, Paz Wells recently released a video titled the *Cosmic Plan*, describing how extraterrestrials have been gradually preparing humanity through spiritual teachings for earth changes and open contact. Wells and others involved in Mission Rama claim that sightings of extraterrestrial vehicles will become more prominent around the globe, and will result in open contact. The extraterrestrials have offered to show up in an indisputable way and thereby end the secrecy system.

Another individual circulating messages of impending extraterrestrial contact is James Gilliland who has documented an extensive number of UFOs visiting the Mt Adams area of Washington State. Gilliland claims to have experienced telepathic communications with the extraterrestrials and to have had physical contact with them. He has circulated a number of messages from the extraterrestrials describing the situation confronting humanity. For example, he writes as follows about the nature of the extraterrestrial visitors and their concern:

> Rather than being called aliens, it is more appropriate to call them members of the greater family of man/woman. They are not here to be worshiped. They are not here to conquer Earth and it's inhabitants. They are not here to take our natural resources. The simple fact that they have not done so by now shows that this is not their agenda. They are here to inspire each individual to make their own personal God connection and live by the Universal Principles necessary for a healthy society and environment. They are here to assist Humanity in a birthing process into the Fifth World, or the 'Golden Age of God' spoken of in ancient prophecies in most every culture on Earth. It is a turbulent, rocky road with many personal and collective challenges. They are here to alleviate the severity of some of the events in the days to come. Some in the past have referred to them as Gods. Others as angels.

Gilliland has hosted numerous scientists and researchers to investigate the sightings and contacts occurring at Mt Adams, and organized a series of international conferences at his Mt Adams ranch wherein participants could experience the situation first hand. [720] An extensive report on Gilliland and his evidence confirming numerous UFO sightings has concluded that these are genuine, thereby supporting Gilliland's claims that extraterrestrial visitation is regularly occurring at Mt Adams.[721] I traveled in August 2006 to Gilliland's Mt Adam's ranch and was able to personally confirm the UFO sightings regularly occurring there.[722] Gilliland believes that the extraterrestrials are increasing their flyovers and are preparing for a mass showing that would be catalyst for public disclosure.

Another prominent individual claiming to have had telepathic communications with extraterrestrials wanting to show up is former French aviation expert, Jean Ederman who circulated the popular internet message, "Change the World"; this gained worldwide attention.[723] The alleged extraterrestrial sponsors of the message transmitted through Ederman wanted to ask "individuals without distinction" the question "Do You Wish That We Show Up?" The extraterrestrials described how they had earlier attempted to reach agreement with government representatives on establishing First Contact but were rejected:

> There are two ways to establish a cosmic contact with another civilization: via its standing representatives or directly with individuals without distinction. The first way entails fights of interests, the second way brings awareness. The first way was chosen by a group of races motivated by keeping mankind in slavery, thereby controlling Earth resources, the gene pool and human emotional energy. The second way was chosen by a group of races allied with the cause of the Spirit of service. We have, at our end, subscribed to this disinterested cause and introduced ourselves a few years ago to representatives of the human power who refused our outstretched hand on the pretext of incompatible interests with their strategic vision.[724]

The reference to abusive extraterrestrial races that had signed secret agreements with human representatives is an accurate description of what has historically occurred. This presented a dilemma for more 'ethical' extraterrestrials civilizations that wanted to assist global humanity but were limited to something similar to Rodenberry's

Prime Directive.[725] In explaining how they would establish contact by raising 'awareness' the extraterrestrials wrote about how a positive response to the question over them showing up would be the catalyst for the First Contact scenario they had in mind. A simple answer could be monitored and tabulated in some way as part of a ballot of global humanity:

> "The truth of soul can be read by telepathy. You only need to clearly ask yourself this question [Do You Wish That We Show Up?] and give your answer as clearly, on your own or in a group, as you wish. ... YES or NO, IMMEDIATELY AFTER ASKING THE QUESTION!"[726]

In November 2003 I closely examined Ederman's message and concluded that he was very likely a genuine communication from extraterrestrial civilizations.[727] To date of writing, nearly six thousand individuals had signed a petition approving for the extraterrestrials in Ederman's message to show up.[728]

Another possible telepathic communication occurred in April 2006 with Angelika Whitecliff, who co-organized a series of conferences in Hawaii on themes related to extraterrestrial civilizations, world peace and earth transformation.[729] Her message, "We Need Your Consent" described how extraterrestrials were keenly aware of the dire nature of global situation confronting humanity and the urgency for individuals to voluntarily seek extraterrestrial assistance:

> Who are we? We are you, your family from the stars, beings of God, of love and of the highest integrity. We are those who watch over you in your hours of need and whisper to you that all will be well. We inspire and assist your creations from the realms of the unseen and yet we are as real as you, in every way we are you. We are just a little more spiritually advanced, technologically and socially superior because we have already traveled this road you now walk upon. We offer you our most sincere assistance in this latest hour, this time when your Earth Changes can and by necessity will tear certain constructs apart.... The time of a new balance, a restored balance is close at hand. World leaders will change

> in their actions or be plunged from their offices in most exceptional ways. Why? Because the great change is upon you, upon the entire planet.[730]

The above messages and others are consistent with contactee reports of extraterrestrials visiting and physically interacting with humanity.

Ever since George Adamski co-wrote, *Flying Saucers have Landed,* in 1954, there has been a succession of private citizens who have claimed to have been contacted by extraterrestrial races and had extensive communications and interactions with them.[731] Along with Adamski, some of these initial contactees include Howard Menger, Orfeo Angelucci, Paul Villa and George Van Tassel.[732] These communications and interactions with extraterrestrials varied considerably depending on the contactee. Essentially all the contactees revealed that extraterrestrials were contacting private individuals to disseminate information about the existence of extraterrestrial civilizations, and the benevolent intentions of extraterrestrials who were making contact.

Over the years, the list of 'contactees' has grown considerably. The more well known in the recent era include Billy Meier, Carlos Diaz, Alex Collier, Enrique Castillo, and Phillip Krapf.[733] These 'contactees' have given public lectures, written books, formed support groups, and communicated with key elites, all with the purpose of conveying the information given by extraterrestrials and convincing a skeptical public of the friendly nature of these extraterrestrials. The messages distributed by Paz Wells, Gilliland, Ederman and Whitecliff are very consistent with the information distributed by most of these contactees. They commonly describe secret agreements involving national governments, deception by 'rogue' or 'manipulative' extraterrestrials, use of extraterrestrial technologies for military purposes, and widespread global environment damage caused by existing government policies.

The above messages describing extraterrestrial offers to assist humanity and to 'show up' relate to a very different First Contact scenario to the first two described in this chapter. These different spins on the extraterrestrial presence are created by the shadow government responsible for extraterrestrial affairs. The extraterrestrial showing up messages provide offers of tangible assistance to a global political problem we have - world wide suppression of evidence confirming the extraterrestrial presence and secret agreements that exist. By going directly to the general population, extraterrestrials behind these messages have sparked a very different process for shaping public opinion concerning First Contact. At the time of this writing, there continues to be an increased number of UFO sightings over major cities and remote locations. Most prominent have been sightings of fleets of UFO over parts of Mexico, including Mexico City. These have astounded observers studying the hundreds of UFOs flying high over one of the world's major cities since June 2004.[734] Similarly, Gilliland's Mt Adams retreat has witnessed a spectacular increase in UFO traffic since 2006, which are being documented.[735]

The spread of messages describing extraterrestrials 'showing up' and the enthusiasm they generate for an alternative contact scenario has had a surprising effect on public opinion of the extraterrestrial presence. Contact groups are emerging around the planet united by enthusiasm for the prospect of First Contact and promise to be a significant new actor in how extraterrestrial life is understood and managed.[736] The emergence of these contact groups and the impact on public opinion they generate may well have been the primary purpose of the message – preparing humanity to openly interact with extraterrestrial races.

Conclusion: Political Spin and Extraterrestrial Disclosure

In startling testimony for the Disclosure Project, Dr Carol Rosin testified how she had been present in confidential corporate discussions wherein disclosure of the extraterrestrial presence would occur, after international terrorism failed to be a credible justification for vast military expenditures by the U.S. military.[737] These expenditures are vital to major U.S. corporations that have played a vital role in secretly servicing the vast network of projects directed towards the extraterrestrial presence. In an interview, Dr Rosin revealed how Dr Werner Von Braun who had intimate knowledge of the vast covert projects that dealt with extraterrestrials, catalogued the list of future 'threats' used to justify military expenditures.

> He [Von Braun] would say that starting where I entered the industry with the supposed Russian threat, but never actually existed the Russians were made to be the enemy. Then there would be terrorists, Third World country threats, there would be an asteroid threat. They might even say to us to try to influence the public into believing that there are many reasons for why we should put weapons in space. There might be a reason to protect our assets in space. But, the real one that he was always holding off on and would say again with tears filling his eyes every time he said this to me repeatedly was that the last card they are holding is the 'alien card,' the extraterrestrial card and none of them are hostile.[738]

The eventual exhaustion of conventional threats that justify growing military expenditures related to extraterrestrial projects is certain to result in eventual disclosure of an extraterrestrial presence. Furthermore, the growing amount of extraterrestrial related information released on to the internet points to a critical stage being reached making disclosure unavoidable. Consequently, it can be asserted with some confidence that public disclosure of extraterrestrial life is inevitable. What remains to be decided is how this will happen. The role of public perception is the key to understanding 'how' First Contact will occur and how political spin will be used in this process. There is evidence that powerful factions within the control groups managing extraterrestrial affairs are competing to secretly shape the public's perceptions of extraterrestrial life in a way making possible a contact scenario suiting the long terms agendas of these factions.[739]

One of these factions, described as the 'Cabal', represents a very nationalistic and militaristic approach to extraterrestrial affairs based on distrust over extraterrestrial motivations and activities. Another faction, the 'progressives', represents a more internationalist approach to extraterrestrial affairs depicting extraterrestrials that have cooperated with covert agencies as 'friendly though enigmatic'. It is expected that different factions in the extraterrestrial management groups would attempt to shape public opinion due to their long history of non-disclosure and complicity in this secrecy and use of 'political spin'. The rapid spread of messages claiming extraterrestrials are about to "show up", however, have come as a major surprise.

Around the world, groups of individuals are emerging convinced that they have a role to play in managing the extraterrestrial presence, and how First Contact emerges. Unifying principles of 'transparency', 'openness' and 'participatory democracy' will guide how extraterrestrial affairs are managed. As these groups communicate and network amongst themselves, they have the potential to become a global mass movement. This movement will become a major player in the way in which extraterrestrial life is managed at the national and global levels. Already, one popular Yahoo discussion group with over 1800 members by September 2008, 'prepare4contact', has drafted and voted on a document that outlines the aspirations and expectations of private citizens in how extraterrestrials need to conduct themselves when visiting Earth. [740] In addition, international conferences organized in Kona, Hawaii in 2006 and 2007, released consensus documents catalyzing global awareness of the need to work with extraterrestrials to promote global peace.[741] Finally, a consortium of citizen organizations launched an initiative to declare all secret agreements concerning extraterrestrial life null and void. The Galactic Freedom Day Declaration has to date been signed by over 1800 individuals giving their assent to the abrogation of all secret agreements.[742]

There is consequently a competition occurring between two factions of the clandestine groups that manage the extraterrestrial presence around the planet. They are the 'progressives' and an ultra nationalistic 'Cabal' ostensibly representing the 'light' and 'dark' sides of how extraterrestrial life will be disclosed and 'spun' to the general public. A third actor in the form of an emerging global mass movement has been sparked into action by an unknown group of extraterrestrials responsible for initiating a series of global ballots on whether extraterrestrials should show up and assist humanity in the dire challenges that lie ahead. These contact groups represent a genuine revolution in management of extraterrestrial affairs, going far beyond the limited reforms promised by 'progressive' global insiders. The progressives desire to remove the 'Cabal' from dominating the management of extraterrestrial affairs, while still maintaining a high degree of secrecy over the true extent and history of extraterrestrial life.

The effort to shape public opinion is likely to enter unchartered waters as the two rival factions in the extraterrestrial global management system find that the rise of a broad based global movement of contact groups represents a new dynamic in 'when' and 'how' First Contact will occur. The contact scenarios supported by opposing factions of the shadow government are variations of two dominant themes. Both involve extraterrestrials that have been parties to various agreements with the shadow government. The first presents 'hostile extraterrestrials' and a 'War of the Worlds' promoted by 'reactionary insiders', or the 'Cabal'. The second is the emergence of 'friendly though enigmatic extraterrestrials' that are given a cautious welcome by 'progressive' elements of the shadow government. These two insider supported contact scenarios have been joined by a third scenario – a plausible 'Star Trek' - like contact event involving extraterrestrials who have not previously entered into agreements with military intelligence organizations. The emergence of this group of extraterrestrials with no track record of secret agreements or intrusive interactions with the global population is gradually capturing the hearts and minds of many familiar with evidence of extraterrestrial life.

The political spin surrounding First Contact is already well underway, and it is up to every individual to learn as much as possible in the remaining time. This needs to happen before disclosure of extraterrestrial life is made or extraterrestrials emerge into the public consciousness in some unanticipated way. Understanding and learning about extraterrestrial life and First Contact is the best way in which private citizens can influence 'when' and 'how' First Contact will occur. This will help limit the political spin that will be used to shape public perceptions about extraterrestrial life.

Exposing the hitherto secret policies of various government agencies will help prepare many citizens for the rich complexities of extraterrestrial intentions and activities. Dealing with these complexities in a responsible manner is essential to transforming our planet into a mature galactic society where open contact with extraterrestrial life occurs. A transformed world awaits us all with disclosure of an extraterrestrial presence. Now is the time to contribute to how that transformed world will be shaped by our expectations and aspirations concerning extraterrestrial life.

ENDNOTES: CHAPTER THIRTEEN

648 I sincerely thank Angelika Whitecliff for her enthusiastic support and encouragement in the revision and completion of this chapter.
649 See chapter one.
650 "Testimony of Dr. Carol Rosin," available online at: http://www.davidicke.net/mysteries/reports/rosinreport.html .
651 William Safire, *Safire's New Political Dictionary*, Revised edition (Random House Reference;, 1993).
652 For an discussion on the development of political spin, see Ira Basen, 'The Spin Cycle "Spin": A primer for voters,' CBS News, May 23rd, 2004. Available online at: http://www.cbc.ca/canadavotes/analysiscommentary/columns/spincycle230504.html .
653 New York Times editorial on Oct. 21, 1984. Cited in Basen, 'The Spin Cycle "Spin": A primer for voters,' Basen, 'The Spin Cycle "Spin": A primer for voters,'
654 For establishment of a secret committee to run extraterrestrial affairs, see "President Truman to Secretary of Defense James Forrestal" (24 September 1947), Majesticdocuments.com. Available online at: http://209.132.68.98/pdf/truman_forrestal.pdf . For further Presidential correspondence supporting the start of a secrecy campaign, see "Secretary of State Marshall to President Truman" (25 September 1947), Majesticdocuments.com, http://209.132.68.98/pdf/marshall-truman-25sept47.pdf .
655 Haut's testimony was published in Thomas Carey and Donald Schmidt, *Witness to Roswell: Unmasking the 60-Year Cover Up* (New Page Books, 2007) 209-218.
656 Majestic 12 Group, "Special Operations Manual, SOM1-01 - Extraterrestrial Entities and Technology, Recovery and Disposal," April 1954 Part 2 http://209.132.68.98/pdf/som101_part2.pdf .
657 Ruppelt, *Report on Unidentified Flying Objects* (Doubleday, 1956) 6.
658 Richard M. Dolan, "Aliens, Coverups, and Free Energy - an interview with Dr. Steven Greer," Phenomena Magazine, Issue #4 (September 10, 2004). Available online at: http://disclosureproject.com/PhenomenaMagazineSGInterviewSept102004.htm
659 John Maynard, "From Disinformation to Disclosure," *Surfing the Apocalypse,* http://www.surfingtheapocalypse.com/maynard.html
660 Herbert George Wells, *War of the Worlds* (1898). For online information go to: http://www.war-ofthe-worlds.co.uk .
661 Steven Greer, ed., *Disclosure: Military and Government Witnesses Reveal the Greatest Secrets in Modern History* (Crossing Point Inc., 2001). See Disclosure Project website: http://www.disclosureproject.com .

[662] Steven M. Greer, "Al Qaeda to ET's - The Search For Bogeymen," *Global Village News and Resources* Issue 74 (November 17, 2003). Available online at: http://www.gvnr.com/74/editorial.htm .
[663] See Michael Salla, *Exopolitics: Political Implications of the Extraterrestrial Presence* (Dandelion Books, 2004), ch 2. Early version available online at: http://www.exopolitics.org/Study-Paper-5.htm .
[664] Reagan's speech to the Forty-second General Assembly of the United Nations, September 21, 1987.
[665] For discussion of how major films have been released that reflect the kind of images of extraterrestrials favored by the shadow government running extraterrestrial affairs, see http://www.weirdload.com/disclosure.html .
[666] See chapter three.
[667] Daniel Salter, *Life With a Cosmos Clearance* (Light Technology Publishing, 2003) 128. See also Richard Boylan interview of Michael Wolf, "Official Within MJ-12 UFO-Secrecy Management Group Reveals Insider Secrets," cited online at: http://www.drboylan.com/wolfdoc2.html .
[668] See Helmut Lammer, *Milabs: Military Mind Control & Alien Abductions* (Illuminet Press, 1999). For online article, see Helmut Lammer, "Further findings of Project MILAB: Looking behind the alien/military abduction agenda," http://members.aol.com/nymush/correcte.txt .
[669] Helmut Lammer, "Further findings of Project MILAB: Looking behind the alien/military abduction agenda," http://members.aol.com/nymush/correcte.txt .
[670] See David Jacobs, *The Threat* (Simon and Schuster, 1998); Budd Hopkins, *Intruders* (Ballantine Books, 1987); & Karla Turner, *Taken: Inside the Alien-Human Abduction Agenda* (Kelt Works, 1994).
[671] Jacobs, *The Threat*, 257.
[672] Whitley Strieber, "Whitley's Journal: Shedding Light on the Dark Side," (03-Dec-2003) available online at: http://www.unknowncountry.com/news/?id=3366 .
[673] See G. Cope Schellhorn, "UFO-Related Homicide in Brazil: The Complete Story;" & Don Ecker, "The Human Mutilation Factor," & Tim Schwartz, "Are UFOs responsible for mysterious human mutilations?" http://www.think-aboutit.com/mutilations/Human_Mutilations.htm .
[674] See chapter two.
[675] George Adamski's, *Inside the Flying Saucers*, is available online at: http://www.universe-people.com/adamsk_e.htm .
[676] For a range of perspectives on extraterrestrial abductions, see C.D.B. Bryan, *Close Encounters of the Fourth Kind: Alien Abduction, UFOs, and the Conference at M.I.T* (Alfred Knopf, 1995).
[677] Steven M. Greer, "Al Qaeda to ET's - The Search For Bogeymen," *Global Village News and Resources* Issue 74 (November 17, 2003). Available online at: http://www.gvnr.com/74/editorial.htm .
[678] For discussion of the preemptive war in Iraq and the role of the 'Cabal', see Salla, *Exopolitics*, chs. 5 & 6. An early version of this idea is available online at: http://www.exopolitics.org/Study-Paper3.htm .

[679] See Richard Boylan, "Birds of a Feather No Longer: Policy Split Divides "Aviary" UFO-Secrecy Group. Available online at: http://drboylan.com/aviary2.html .
[680] Richard Boylan, "Bilderbergs, ETS and World Peace," http://drboylan.com/bldrbg2.html .
[681] For European opposition to the Bush administration's preemptive war in Iraq and the extraterrestrial dimension, see Salla, *Exopolitics,* 227-60. An early version of this idea is available online at: http://www.exopolitics.org/Study-Paper3.htm .
[682] For online information on these two Spielberg productions, see http://www.spielbergfilms.com .
[683] For discussion of rogue extraterrestrial races responsible for problems on Earth, see Courtney Brown, *Cosmic Explorers: Scientific Remote Viewing, Extraterrestrials, and a Message for Mankind* (Signet, 2000).
[684] I have had intense debates with Greer and Boylan that can be respectively read online at: http://exopolitics.org/Exo-Comment-44.htm & http://exopolitics.org/Exo-Comment-22.htm .
[685] "Testimony of Clifford Stone," *Disclosure: Military and Government Witnesses Reveal the Greatest Secrets in Modern History,* ed., Greer, 330.
[686] Salter, *Life With a Cosmos Clearance*, 16.
[687] See Richard Boylan interview of Michael Wolf, "Official Within MJ-12 UFO-Secrecy Management Group Reveals Insider Secrets," cited online at: http://www.drboylan.com/wolfdoc2.html .
[688] See Michael Salla, "Exopolitics versus Exospin: A Response to Dr Steven Greer," *Exopolitical Comment* # 44 (May 5, 2006). Available at: http://exopolitics.org/Exo-Comment-44.htm .
[689] Robert W. Boyajian, "Exclusive Interview with Sergeant Clifford Stone, on assignment at Roswell, New Mexico," UFO UNIVERSE (Spring of 1989) available online at: http://www.eboards4all.com/866799/messages/23.html .
[690] Paola Leopizzi Harris, *Connecting the Dots ... Making Sense of the UFO Phenomenon* (Wild Flower Press, 2003) 98.
[691] Brown, *Cosmic Explorers*, 211-21.
[692] Brown, *Cosmic Explorers*, 129.
[693] "Whistleblower Microbiologist Speaks Out About Alleged "Alien" Named J-Rod," *Earthfiles* 09/15/2003. See also Linda Moulton Howe, "Update About Microbiologist Dan Burisch, Ph.D." 04/26/2004. Both articles available online at: www.earthfiles.com . For more background information, see Bill Hamilton, "Mystery Of Dr. Dan Burisch - Beginning To End," *Rense.com* (10/1/03) http://www.rense.com/general42/mssy.htm .
[694] Linda Moulton Howe, "Whistleblower Microbiologist Dan Burisch Interview," *Earthfiles.com* (June 7, 2003) available at: http://earthfiles.com/news/news.cfm?ID=715&category=Real+X-Files
[695] For more information see BJ Wolf, "Burisch's Ganesh Particle Acknowledged By Caltech," http://www.rense.com/general33/searcasdh.htm .
[696] Recently, Burisch has come forward to give a number of radio interviews including popular alternative media such as Rense and the Jerry Pippin Show. See

http://www.rense.com/general72/danb.htm and
http://www.jerrypippin.com/UFO_Files_b-files.htm .
[697] See "Correspondence Between Dr Dan Burisch & Dr Michael Salla," *Exopolitical Comment* #13 (April 13, 2004), http://www.exopolitics.org/Exo-Comment-13.htm; and "Dr Dan Burisch Responds to April 13 Communication, and Dr Salla's Response," *Exopolitical Comment* #14 (April 20, 2004), http://www.exopolitics.org/Exo-Comment-14.htm .
[698] I thank Paola Harris who helped arrange for Burisch to meet with me and others at the 2007 International UFO Congress in Laughlin, Nevada.
[699] The most detailed attempt to document and substantiate the Burisch case is by Bill Hamilton in *Project Aquarius*. A book review of *Project Aquarius* is available online at: http://exopoliticsjournal.com/Journal-vol-1-3-Rev-Salla-Aquarius.pdf .
[700] For Burisch's discussion of this Committee and its role, see "Whistleblower Microbiologist Dan Burisch Interview," *Earthfiles.com* (June 7, 2003) available at: http://earthfiles.com/news/news.cfm?ID=715&category=Real+X-Files
[701] See Bill Hamilton, "Mystery Of Dr. Dan Burisch - Beginning To End," *Rense.com* (10/1/03) http://www.rense.com/general42/mssy.htm .
[702] See Bill Hamilton, "Mystery Of Dr. Dan Burisch - Beginning To End," *Rense.com* (10/1/03) http://www.rense.com/general42/mssy.htm .
[703] See Michael Salla, "Exopolitical Comment #12 - Dr Dan Burisch, Project Lotus and Disclosure of the Extraterrestrial Presence,"
http://www.exopolitics.org/Exo-Comment-12.htm .
[704] Sterling Allen, "Establishment Fighting Disclosure of Extraterrestrial Presence," *Greater Things News Service*, April 27, 2004. Available online at: http://www.prweb.com/releases/2004/4/prweb121437.php
[705] Richard Boylan, "Bilderbergs, ETS and World Peace,"
http://drboylan.com/bldrbg2.html .
[706] For discussion of rogue extraterrestrials as Reptilians see Brown, *Cosmic Explorers,* 211-21.
[707] See chapter six for earlier discussion of the Tall Whites. See also Charles Hall, *Millennial Hospitality* (Firstpublisher, 2002).
[708] See Hall, *Millennial Hospitality,* vol 1., 451-54.
[709] See chapter two for Eisenhower-Extraterrestrial agreement. For information on when the Tall Whites were first seen, see Hall, *Millennial Hospitality,* vol 1., 236.
[710] Hall, *Millennial Hospitality,* vol 1., 440-54.
[711] Online articles on Project Serpo include, Mark Pilkington, *Fortean Times,* May 2006, at: http://serpo.org/article5.asp . Project Serpo was featured in the February/March edition of UFO Magazine, at www.ufomag.com . Finally, a popular online website is: www.serpo.org .
[712] For description of these three individuals in relation to Project Serpo, see Robert Collins, *Exempt from Disclosure*, 2nd ed., (Peregrine Communications, 2006): 185-86.
[713] See Michael Salla, "Richard Doty and Project Serpo: Public Acclimation or Deception Program" February 18, 2006 at: http://www.exopolitics.org/Exo-Comment-41.htm .

[714] For description of different extraterrestrial races and their motivations, see chapters two and three. An earlier version appeared as "A Report on the Motivations and Activities of Extraterrestrial Races," Exopolitics.org (July 26, 2004). Available online at: http://www.exopolitics.org/Report-ET-Motivations.htm.

[715] See chapter two.

[716] For full description of these events, see Sixto Paz Wells, *The Invitation* (1st World Library, 1997).

[717] Sixto Paz Wells, *The Invitation*, 206.

[718] Benitez immediately wrote a book upon his return to Spain of his investigation of the Peruvian sightings, *OVNIS, S.O.S. A La Humanidad* (Plaza and Janes, 1976).

[719] Paz Wells officially ended his organization in 1991, but a new one soon emerged in Peru with the name Mission Rahma. Official website is: http://www.misionrahma.com/ingles/ingles.htm .

[720] I was present at the first conference and had personal sightings of anomalous phenomena. My report, "Skywatching at Sattva Sanctuary, the 2006 ECETI Conference & Galactic Peace Sanctuaries," *Exopolitics Journal* 1:4 (2006) is available online at: http://exopoliticsjournal.com/Journal-vol-1-4-Exp-Salla.htm .

[721] Steve Moreno, "James Gilliland/Mt Adams Investigation," available online at: http://psi-app.com/gillrep.html

[722] See Michael Salla, "Skywatching at Sattva Sanctuary, the 2006 ECETI Conference & Galactic Peace Sanctuaries," *Exopolitics Journal* 1:4 (October 2006): pp. 319-30). Available online at: http://exopoliticsjournal.com/Journal-vol-1-4.htm .

[723] "Change the World By the Lever Effect,", is available online at: http://www.geocities.com/changetheworld_now/Changetheworld1.htm .

[724] "Change the World By the Lever Effect," is available online at: http://www.geocities.com/changetheworld_now/Changetheworld1.htm .

[725] For description of different extraterrestrial races and how these have historical interacted with humanity, see chapter six, "A Report on the Motivations and Activities of Extraterrestrial Races."

[726] "Change the World By the Lever Effect," available online at: http://www.geocities.com/changetheworld_now/Changetheworld1.htm .

[727] Michael E. Salla, "Message to Humanity: A Genuine Communication from an Extraterrestrial Race - Exopolitical Comment #7," *Exopolitics.Org*. Available online at: http://www.exopolitics.org/Exo-Comment-7.htm . Ederman's claims were given support by the publication of his book describing the scientific principles learned from the extraterrestrials, see Eric Julien (aka Jean Ederman), The Science of Extraterrestrials (Allies Books, 2006).

[728] See "We Are Ready to Change the World", http://www.petitiononline.com/readynow/petition.html .

[729] Conference websites are: www.earthtransformation.com and www.etworldpeace.com .

[730] Angelika Whitecliff, We Need Your Consent, available online at: http://www.petitiononline.com/ethelp/petition.html .
[731] George Adamski's, *Inside the Flying Saucers*, is available online at: http://www.universe people.com/adamsk_e.htm .
[732] For discussion of experiences of an extensive number of contactees, see Timothy Good, *Alien Base: The Evidence for Extraterrestrial Colonization on Earth.*
[733] See Gary Kinder, *Light Years: An Investigation into the Extraterrestrial Experiences of Eduard Meier* (Publisher Group West, 1987); Phillip Krapf, "The Challenge of Contact: a mainstream journalist's report on interplanetary diplomacy," (Origin Press, 2001). An online article on Carlos Diaz is available at: http://www.ufoevidence.org/documents/doc1180.htm; A book by Alex Collier, Defending Sacred Ground is available online at: http://www.exopolitics.org/collier-dsg1.pdf. Finally, see Enrique Castillo Rincon, *UFOs: A Great New Dawn for Humanity* (Blue Dolphin Publishing, 1997).
[734] Santiago Yturria, "Update - Amazing UFO Fleets Over Mexico, available online at: http://www.rense.com/general66/uupd.htm .
[735] James Gilliland, "UFOs and the Days to Come," http://groups.yahoo.com/group/eceti/message/2429
[736] One internet discussion group created in response to the 'Change the World' message was formed on November 3, 2004, and by August 2006 had over 1300 members. Go to: http://groups.yahoo.com/group/prepare4contact/ .
[737] "Testimony of Dr. Carol Rosin," available online at: http://www.davidicke.net/mysteries/reports/rosinreport.html .
[738] Linda Moulton Howe, "German Scientist Werner von Braun Anticipated Terrorists, Asteroids and ETs on American 'Enemy's List'," *Earthfiles.Com* (June 18, 2004).
[739] For discussion of these factions and their relationship to the 2004 Presidential election, see Michael Salla, "The U.S. Presidential Election and Extraterrestrial Disclosure," *Exopolitics.Org* (November 2, 2004) http://www.exopolitics.org/Exo-Comment-19.htm .
[740] Distributed December 9, 2003 on the discussion forum http://groups.yahoo.com/group/prepare4contact/ . http://groups.yahoo.com/group/prepare4contact/message/1063 .
[741] See, "Hawaii Declaration on Peaceful Relations with Extraterrestrial Civilizations" at: http://etworldpeace.earthtransformation.com/Hawaii-Declaration.html , and the "Earth Transformation Declaration" at: http://earthtransformation.com/declaration.htm .
[742] For more information visit the Galactic Freedom Day website at: http://www.galacticfreedomday.com .

INDEX

A

B

C

D

E

I

J

K

L

M

N

O

P

R

S

T

U

V

W

Z

Biography

Dr. Michael Salla is an internationally recognized scholar in international politics, conflict resolution and U.S. foreign policy. He has held academic appointments in the School of International Service & the Center for Global Peace, American University, Washington DC (1996-2004); the Department of Political Science, Australian National University, Canberra, Australia (1994-96); and the Elliott School of International Affairs, George Washington University, Washington D.C., (2002). He has a Ph.D in Government from the University of Queensland, Australia. During his academic career he was author/editor of four books including *The Hero's Journey Toward a Second American Century* (Greenwood Press, 2001); *Essays on Peace* (Central Queensland University Press, 1995); *Why the Cold War Ended* (Greenwood Press, 1995); *Islamic Radicalism, Muslim Nations and the West* (1993) . He has conducted research and fieldwork in ethnic conflicts involving East Timor, Kosovo, Macedonia, and Sri Lanka. He has been awarded significant financial grants from the United States Institute of Peace and the Ford Foundation for peacemaking initiatives involving mid-to-high level participants from the East Timor conflict.

Dr. Salla is more popularly known as a pioneer in the development of 'Exopolitics', the study of the main actors, institutions and political processes associated with extraterrestrial life. His groundbreaking *Exopolitics: Political Implications of the Extraterrestrial Presence* (Dandelion Books, 2004) presented the first scholarly framework for understanding the political implications of an undisclosed extraterrestrial presence. In addition to *Exposing US Government Policies on Extraterrestrial Life*, he has another book scheduled for release in 2009 that reveals his most recent exopolitics research and its relationship with international politics: *Galactic Diplomacy*. He is Founder of the *Exopolitics Institute*, and the *Exopolitics Journal*, and Co-Organizer of the *Earth Transformation* series of conferences in Hawaii. His main website is: www.exopolitics.org

About the Exopolitics Institute

The *Exopolitics Institute* is a 501 (c) (3) non-profit educational organization dedicated to studying the key actors, institutions and political processes associated with extraterrestrial life. The Institute supports the study and dissemination of information and technologies from 'whistleblowers' or 'private citizens' who claim to have physically interacted with extraterrestrials, or had access to covert military-corporate programs involving extraterrestrial technologies.

The Exopolitics Institute has sponsored a number of exopolitical inititiatives such as the peer reviewed *Exopolitics Journal;* sponsored several exopolitical conferences and seminars in Hawaii and Italy from 2006-2008; provides a popular online webpage with the latest exopolitical news and events; and created an Exopolitics Certification Program whereby students can complete online courses of study to gain exopolitics certificates..

The Exopolitics Institute was created to simultaneously provide support for scholars engaged in exopolitical research, whistleblowers disclosing information about covert projects allegedly involving extraterrestrials or their technology, and/or individuals claiming to have experienced extraterrestrial contact.

The Exopolitics Institute Advisory Board and Board of Directors comprises over 50 international scholars, activists, journalists and 'experiencers' who are leading exponents of exopolitics. The Exopolitics Institute was incorporated as a non-profit educational organisation in the State of Hawaii, U.S.A., on April 7, 2005; and succesfully gained 501(c)(3) tax exempt status with the Internal Revenue Service on March 6, 2007.

If you wish to support the work of the Exopolitics Institute by participating in events; purchasing products; making a tax exempt donation; or seek more information, please visit us at: www.ExopoliticsInstitute.org ; or write to us at: PO Box 2199, Kealakekua, HI 96750 USA.

Made in the USA
Coppell, TX
03 February 2021